FV_

Communication in the Age of Virtual Reality

LEA'S COMMUNICATION SERIES
Jennings Bryant/Dolf Zillmann, General Editors

Selected titles include:

For a complete list of other titles in LEA's Communication Series, please contact Lawrence Erlbaum Associates, Publishers.

Communication in the Age of Virtual Reality

edited by

Frank Biocca
University of North Carolina

Mark R. Levy
University of Maryland

LEA LAWRENCE ERLBAUM ASSOCIATES, PUBLISHERS
1995 Hillsdale, New Jersey   Hove, UK

Lawrence Erlbaum Associates, Inc., Publishers
365 Broadway
Hillsdale, New Jersey 07642

Cover design by McKevin Shaughnessy

Library of Congress Cataloging-in-Publication Data

Communication in the age of virtual reality / edited by Frank Biocca,
    Mark R. Levy.
        p.   cm.
    Includes bibliographical references and index.
    ISBN 0-8058-1549-X (c : alk. paper). — ISBN 0-8058-1550-3 (p :
alk. paper)
    1. Human–computer interaction.   2. Virtual reality.   I. Biocca,
Frank.   II. Levy, Mark R.
    QA76.9.H85C655   1995
    302.23 — dc20   94-20994
                                                              CIP

Books published by Lawrence Erlbaum Associates are printed
on acid-free paper, and their bindings are chosen for strength
and durability.

Contents

PART III THE SOCIAL REALITY
OF VIRTUAL REALITY

Preface

This book is about virtual reality (VR), a tantalizing communication medium whose essence challenges our most deeply held notions of what communication is or can be. Part computer simulation, part "consensual hallucination," virtual reality offers us the opportunity to surf through information-rich cyberspace; to "be" in worlds that exist only in our imaginations, more so than we have with other media, and to manipulate (for better or worse) virtual environments, ranging from the smallest chemical compound to the entire surface of a distant planet. Communication becomes simulation. Inspired by William Gibson's science fiction novel *Neuromancer* and underwritten by the Pentagon and Sega, the age of VR has begun. The communication process — and, possibly, the human condition — may never be the same again.

Yet despite the historic changes that are occurring, most communication scholars have only vague ideas about virtual reality. Virtual reality, we believe, may become too important, too wondrous, and too powerful a medium to permit disciplinary ignorance and passivity toward what may become the next dominant medium.

In part I of this volume, Virtual Reality as a Communication Medium, we introduce the medium of virtual reality, some of the major concepts that it embodies, and the wires, silicon chips, and displays that make it all work. In part II, Designing Virtual Environments, we explore the emerging issues in the creation of communication applications and experiences. Finally, in part III, the Social Reality of Virtual Reality, we take a step back and examine social and cultural issues impelled by the age of virtual reality.

Some of the ideas for this book started to take shape when Frank Biocca was on leave at the University of California and at Stanford. It was a chance to return to questions that had gotten him interested in communication, the kinds of questions he used to hear at Marshall McLuhan's lectures while he was an undergraduate in Canada. Although he was aware that the University of North Cartolina had a long-standing research program in virtual environments, in California he could see that VR was beginning its journey from the lab into the home. It was becoming not a mass medium, but a medium for the masses, a "personal reality engine," with all the social implications and meaning that these words now imply. Although many were heralding the emergence of a new communication medium, he could not find a single communication researcher truly exploring it. So he decided to explore it himself and to encourage other communication researchers to do the same.

ACKNOWLEDGMENTS

The VR community of researchers is an interesting and open group. We would like to acknowledge some of the many who were ready to sit down and talk about the communications implications of the new medium. At NASA Stephen Ellis, Mike McGreevy, and Bob Welch eagerly discussed their work; at SRI Tom Piantanida and Duane Bowman warmly received Frank and allowed him to test drive their new VR system that was "fresh out of the box." Jaron Lanier sat down for a long interview on the communication implications of VR, while Howard Rheingold enthusiastically discussed the social implications of VR and gave us a sneak peek at his manuscript for *Virtual Reality*. At conferences, VR diva Sandra Helsel introduced Frank to some of the other early members of the VR tribe, pioneers like Myron Krueger and new visionary designers and entrepreneurs eagerly creating the public reality of virtual reality. In the heart of Silicon Valley, he met fellow communicators like cyberjournalist Ben Delaney, who had just launched the *CyberEdge* journal. Together with Kenny Meyer, VR journalist, entrepreneur, dramatist, and all round "great guy," they argued and speculated about VR over cups of Italian coffee in San Francisco's cafes.

Back on the east coast, Mark Levy was tapping into the early buzz about VR on the nets. When Frank called him to discuss an unorthodox journal article (an interview with Jaron Lanier), he seized on the importance of the new medium and asked not just for an article, but for a whole journal issue. At that moment, this book began to take shape. Some of the chapters took their initial form as a special issue of the *Journal of Communication*. As the first VR wave swept the nation, this book was created to add the voices of other communication researchers and to bring these ideas to new readers. This book, our collective attempt to probe some of the implications of VR, is only the beginning of the exploration of communication in the age of VR. We hope some of our readers will join us in helping shape, define, and understand this new medium.

Frank Biocca
Mark R. Levy

VIRTUAL REALITY AS COMMUNICATION MEDIUM

1 The Vision of Virtual Reality

Frank Biocca
Taeyong Kim
University of North Carolina at Chapel Hill

Mark R. Levy
University of Maryland

> When anything new comes along, everyone, like a child discovering the world, thinks that they've invented it, but you scratch a little and you find a caveman scratching on a wall is creating virtual reality in a sense. What is new here is that more sophisticated instruments give you the power to do it more easily. Virtual reality is dreams.
>
> —Morton Heilig[1]

The year is 1941. Engineers and industrialists are introducing a new medium to the country. Few can predict the significant influence of this new "gadget" with the odd name, tele-vision—vision at a distance. It is not just a novelty in a research lab or an amusement at a World's Fair. Although a technological reality, it is not yet a psychological and cultural reality. In the early 1940's there are less than 5,000 sets in the United States. But soon, the light from the TV screen will flicker in every home and mind in the country.

Change the channel. The year is 1988.[2] Engineers and industrialists are

---

[1]Quoted in Hamit (1993, p. 57).

[2]Unlike television, dating the "public introduction" of virtual reality is more than a bit difficult. The full-scale introduction of television required legislation allocating parts of the electromagnetic spectrum to broadcasters. Historians date public introduction of TV as the emergence of the first permanent broadcasts using those frequencies. VR, on the other hand, is a heterogeneous cluster of simulator technologies that has been slowly diffusing for decades. There is, strictly speaking, no starting point, and, as this chapter suggests, VR is part of the grand evolution of media technology toward the reproduction of the "essential copy" and the achievement of "physical transcendence." We use the year 1988 because it marks a milestone

3

introducing another new medium to the country. Like television, virtual reality (VR) is not just a novelty in a research lab or an amusement at a World's Fair. More than 50 years after the introduction of television, VR technology presents us with devices such as the head-mounted display, a television set that wraps itself around our heads both literally and meta-phorically.

This book is an attempt to explore the vision of communication in the age of virtual reality. VR dangles in front of our eyes a vision of the media's future, changes in the ways we communicate, and the way we think about communication. The medium that tantalizes us so has gone by a number of names: computer simulation, artificial reality, virtual environments, aug-mented reality, cyberspace, and so on. More terms are likely to be invented as the technology's future unfolds. But the enigmatic term *virtual reality* has dominated the discourse. It has defined the technology's future by giving it a goal — the creation of virtual reality. Virtual reality is not a technology; it is a destination. In this book we look toward this destination and collectively ask ourselves a deceptively simple, but profoundly nuanced question: What is communication in the age of virtual reality?

Virtual reality? It is a quirky phrase, but it seems inspired. Attributed to the quodlibetic mind of Jaron Lanier, the phrase united the many voices of it rivals — virtual environments, virtual worlds, virtual space, artificial reality — into a single chant seeming to emanate from a distant future. Not everyone likes it. The scientific community at places like MIT, University of North Carolina, and at military research centers were uncomfortable from the start with this upstart, pop culture term. On the net and in scientific journals like *Presence,* researchers insisted that their work would be better described by terms like *virtual environments* or *simulation.*

But Lanier's VR cyberslogan and its uncertain vision was spread at warp speed by a technophilic press. For TV, magazine, and newspaper journalists virtual reality was a "sexy" term for computer experiences. Many of the smitten reporters were children of the 1960s (e.g., Rheingold, 1991). To these and other observers the more pedantic term, *simulation,* suggested something more akin to silicon implants than a slogan for info-revolution. In article after article the vision of VR was dangled in front of a public entranced by the curious pleasures of interactive technology. In a field that was dominated by military applications, the childlike, dreadlocked Lanier sounded more like a poet or new age prophet than a "computer geek." In a typical early interview in 1989, the pied piper of VR played his song:

> Virtual reality will use your body's movements to control whatever body you choose to have in Virtual Reality, which might be human or be something

---

in the general public's awareness of the technology and the beginning of a significant rise in public discourse about the vision of virtual reality (see Figs. 1.1 & 1.2).

different. You might very well be a mountain range or a galaxy or a pebble on the floor. Or a piano . . . I've considered being a piano. . . . You could become a comet in the sky one moment and then gradually unfold into a spider that's bigger than the planet that looks down at all your friends from high above. (Kelly, 1989, p. 34).

This was a very different vision of the computer, something more in tune with science fiction or fantasy play. Some researchers in areas like scientific visualization and flight simulation were uncomfortable with what this vision promised. "We can't really do that," some objected. "Hype!" others protested. But word of the vision of virtual reality ricocheted around the interiors of the public imagination and resonated with some primal desire for a dream machine. Lanier and his supporters in the press provided an outlet for that ancient desire.

The meteoric trajectory of the phrase *virtual reality* is a metaphor for the rise of virtual reality technology as a whole. The first phase of the diffusion of a technology is the knowledge phase (see Valente & Biardini, this volume). Figures 1.1 and 1.2[3] plot the different trajectories of the phrase *virtual reality* and a competing term for the same technology, *simulation*, in newspapers and magazines in the early 1990s. As the graphs reveal, usage of the term *simulation* declined and phrases like *virtual environment* barely registered a blip on the public radar screen. Usage of the phrase *virtual reality* rose rapidly, especially in newspapers where it surpassed usage of the more general term *simulation*.

Along with the term *cyberspace,* the phrase *virtual reality* has come to

---

[3]Method: The diffusion of the terms *virtual reality* and *simulation* was measured by counting the number of articles that mentioned the term *virtual reality* and/or *simulation* once or more in their titles or in the body of the texts.

The terms were searched in a large sample of articles in 96 newspapers and 173 magazines published in the United States in the period from January 1, 1988 to December 31, 1993. These publications were searched on NEXIS, a popular on-line data service providing full-text articles in newspapers, magazines, journals, and other mass publications.

Only publications that were part of the database for the whole period of 1988–1993 were used. Among the newspapers and magazines available in NEXIS, 96 papers (approximately 58% of the available newspapers) and 173 magazines (55% of the available magazines) turned out to have been present throughout the research period.

The two terms, *virtual reality* and *simulation,* were searched throughout the titles and main texts of the articles of the selected publications in the database. Because the term *simulation* may have been used for other meanings (e.g., children's simulations of adults), only the articles that contain the words "simulation" and "computer" were counted.

First, the number of newspaper articles containing the term *virtual reality* and/or *simulation* were counted for every 6-month period starting January 1, 1988. The same search was again conducted in magazines. Second, the number of newspaper articles that mentioned the term *simulation* with *computer* were counted and the magazine articles were also examined in the same manner. Finally, to measure the overlap between the two searches, the number of newspaper and magazine articles containing both terms, *virtual reality* and *simulation* (with *computer*), were counted.

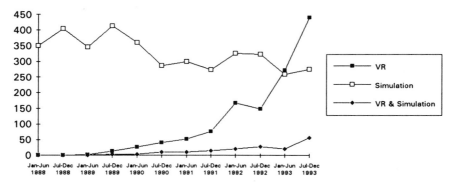

FIG. 1.1.   Graph shows the frequency that the terms *virtual reality* and *simulation* were used in 96 daily newspapers from Jan. 1988 to Dec. 1993 (see footnote 3).

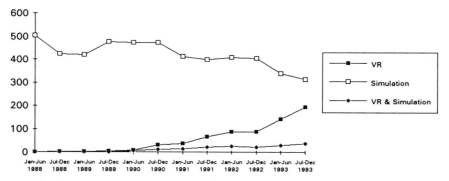

FIG. 1.2.   Graph shows the frequency that the terms *virtual reality* and *simulation* were used in 176 news and business magazines from Jan. 1988 to Dec. 1993 (see footnote 1).

symbolize both our enthusiasm and ambivalence about social and cultural transformation through technology. For some, virtual reality is the first step in a grand adventure into the landscape of the imagination. Virtual reality promises a kind of transcendence of the limits of physical reality. Others are more cynical or uncomfortable about the whole idea of virtual reality. They feel the phrase is an oxymoron; it promises the impossible. Like an Escher drawing of impossible staircases, it offers a vivid vision of something that can never be. But reality has never been the concern for some virtual reality enthusiasts; they want a computer-generated world where an Escher staircase can be experienced rather than imagined. As respected VR computer scientist Fred Brooks put it, the technology allows one to experience "worlds that never were and can never be" (Brooks, 1988). If the reader finds that Brooks' words seem vaguely familiar, perhaps you hear the echo of a very ancient promise of *all* media technologies.

THE 2,000-YEAR SEARCH FOR THE ULTIMATE DISPLAY

Is virtual reality technology the first step toward the ultimate display or the ultimate communication medium? Some of the pioneers of virtual reality have heralded it as the "ultimate form of the interaction between humans and machines" (Krueger, 1991, p. vii) and "the first medium that does not narrow the human spirit" (Jaron Lanier, quoted in Rheingold, 1991, p. 156). Although some of this rhetoric is clearly overblown, VR embodies a number of conceptual breaks with existing media as it tries to reach out to some vision of the ultimate medium.

A powerful and unusual vision of the ultimate medium surely gripped the work of one of the most revered pioneers in computer graphics and VR, Ivan Sutherland (1965): "A display connected to a digital computer gives us a chance to gain familiarity with concepts not realizable in the physical world. It is a looking glass into a mathematical wonderland. . . . There is no reason why the objects displayed by a computer have to follow the ordinary rules of physical reality. . . . The ultimate display would, of course, be a room within which the computer can control the existence of matter" (pp. 506, 508).

At first, the idea of the "ultimate display" seems rather startling. Many see Sutherland's paper as particularly inspired and novel; it is often quoted. Sutherland was clearly a visionary, but his dream is an ancient one. The dream of the "ultimate display" accompanies the creation of almost every iconic communication medium ever invented. There are two aspects to this dream, and VR shares these with older iconic media like painting, photography, film, and television. The drive powering the creation of many of these media has included (a) the search for the *essential copy* (Bryson, 1983), and (b) the ancient desire for *physical transcendence,* escape from the confines of the physical world. Seeking the *essential copy* is to search for a means to fool the senses — a display that provides a perfect illusory deception. Seeking *physical transcendence* is nothing less than the desire to free the mind from the "prison" of the body.

Almost 2,000 years before Sutherland's musings about the ultimate display, we can see the stirrings of the search for the essential copy in a story recounted by the Roman naturalist, Pliny. It is an anecdote from ancient Greece, but imagine it, if you will, as a modern competition between two VR programmers to see who can produce the best perceptual illusion:

> The contemporaries and rival of Zeuxis were Timanthes, Androcydes, Eupompus, and Parrhasius. This last, it is recorded, entered into a competition with Zeuxis. Zeuxis produced a picture of grapes so dexterously represented that birds began to fly down to eat from the painted vine. Whereupon Parrhasius designed so lifelike a picture of a curtain that Zeuxis,

proud of the verdict of the birds, requested that the curtain should now be drawn back and the picture displayed. When he realized his mistake, with a modesty that did him honour, he yielded up the palm, saying what whereas he had managed to deceive only birds, Parrhasius had deceived an artist. (Pliny, 1938, pp. 64–65)

In later years, painters expressed the desire for the essential copy as a desire for a canvas that would become a magic window or mirror on the virtual world created with brush strokes. This vision of the ultimate "windowed" display finds expression in the world of the painter, architect, and theorist of linear perspective Leone Battista Alberti (1462/1966). He espoused the technology of perspective to produce a painting so perfect that it would dissolve into a window — an ultimate display of the virtual scene.

The search for the ultimate display sometimes involved a celebration of the ability to use the senses for communication. Today, communication through sensory-intensive means like "visualization" is sometimes opposed to communication through more abstract means such as words or numbers (Mitchell, 1986). In the past, this desire for displays that "spoke" to the senses sometimes expressed itself as a critique of other forms of representation like words, narratives, and texts. For example, the painter Francastel was so moved by the power of the perspective realism of Masscio's Renaissance masterpiece, Tribute Money, that he declared; "Henceforth man will be defined not by the rules of narrative, but by an immediate physical apprehension. The goal of representation will be appearance, and no longer meaning" (Francastel, quoted in Bryson, 1983, p. 3). In this prediction of the future, it is interesting that the sensory realism of the essential copy is seen as opposed to the text and narrative — the icon would eventually overcome the linguistic sign.[4]

By 1760, prior to the arrival of photography, de la Roche was predicting the emergence of a medium that would lead users to question reality:

You know the rays of light that reflect off bodies are like an image that paints these bodies on polished surfaces, the retina of the eye, and for example, on water, and on mirrors. The elemental spirits have sought to fix these passing images. They have composed a material . . . so that a painting is created in the blink of an eye . . . and . . . trace on canvases images that are imposing to the eye and make one doubt one's reason, so much so that what we call reality may be nothing more than phantoms that press upon our vision,

---

[4]But even today where visual culture seems in ascendance there are still many who argue for the superiority of text and narrative over the image: "My suspicion is that, in general, words are much more powerful than images, and that images have relatively little effect unless they are verbalized by the addition of narrative fantasy" (Mitchell, 1986, p. 89).

hearing, touch, and all our senses at once. (Authors' translation of quote in Fournier, 1859, pp. 18, 20; see Biocca, 1987)

With the arrival of photography, the dream of the essential copy became even more intense. Far more stunning and prescient than Sutherland's vision is that of Oliver Wendell Holmes Sr. In 1857 Oliver Wendell Holmes, father of the famous jurist, saw a glimpse of the future of VR when he lifted a stereoscope to his eyes for the first time. After the initial strain, as the lenses forced his eyes to fuse the different images only inches away, Holmes saw a vision. Holmes prophesied the creation of a giant universal database that would house essential copies of all things, something on the scale of Ted Nelson's hypermedia Xanadu. Holmes, of course, saw the essential copy through the eyes of the 19th century. Globe-trotting adventurer-scientists would stock a curio cabinet of essential samples of reality, a collection so large that it would be housed in an immense stereographic library or museum. Essential copies of all things would be gathered from around the world and kept for 3-D examination in the vast, cyberspatial museum of forms (see Biocca, 1987). After peering through his stereoscope, Holmes took up his pen and wrote the following in the prophetic voice that seems to accompany much writing at the birth of a new medium:

Form is henceforth divorced from matter. In fact, matter as visible object is of no great use any longer, except as the mold on which form is shaped. . . . Matter will always be fixed and dear; form is cheap and transportable. . . . The consequence of [photography] will soon be such an enormous collection of forms that they will have to be classified and arranged in vast libraries. . . . The time will come when a man who wishes to see any object, natural or artificial, will go to the . . . stereographic library and call for its skin or form. . . .

We do now distinctly propose the creation of a comprehensive and systematic stereographic library, where all men can find the special forms they particularly desire to see as artists, or as scholars, or as mechanics, or in any other capacity. . . . This is a mere hint of what is coming before long. (Holmes, 1859, pp. 251–253)

Holmes' library of 3-D forms is slowly being constructed polygon-by-polygon in a worldwide, broad-band network of computers. Holmes' magnifying glass has been melted down and reshaped into a fiber optic cable.

With the arrival of radio and television, it became clear to the searchers for the ultimate display that the essential copy needed to take in more senses, and that this was possible! The baton was passed to other visionaries like the Italian Futurists. Dizzy with the technopower of radio and early television in the 1930s, they looked forward and trumpeted the inevitable arrival of virtual reality: "We now possess a television of fifty thousand points for every large image on a large screen. As we await the invention of teletouch telesmell and teletaste we Futurists are perfecting radio broadcasting . . ." (Marinetti & Masata, 1922/1992, p. 265). To this vision of telepresence, the Futurists added, "In its second National Congress Futurism decided that the following have been overcome. . . . Overcome the machine 'with an identification of man with the very machine destined to free him from muscular labor and immensify his spirit . . .' " (Marinetti & Masata, 1922/1992, p. 265).

In this second quote we see an early 20th-century example of the second goal driving the search for the ultimate medium, the desire for physical transcendence, a desire that permeates most visions of future technologies, be they concrete models or science fiction.

The search for the essential copy and the desire for physical transcendence find expression at the birth of the computer revolution as well. Just at the end of World War II, Vannevar Bush wrote an influential article that claimed that "there are signs of a change as new and powerful instrumentalities come into use" (Bush, 1945, p. 101). The vision in this article would later influence key engineers at the Advanced Research Projects Agency (ARPA), the Stanford Research Institute (SRI) XEROX Park, and many others (see Englebart, 1962, 1988). Echoing Holmes' fascination with stereoscopic photography he argued that, "Certainly progress in photography is not going to stop" and that "improvements in stereoscopic technique are just around the corner" (Bush, 1945, pp. 102–103).

But the adumbration of the arrival of VR lies not just in Bush's musings about 3-D images but also in his desire to have a machine that would assist in the "manipulation of ideas." This was his famous proposal for a machine he called *Memex,* a hypermedia computer. Unlike Holmes' naturalistic library of forms, Bush's Memex was to be a personal library of thought, but one that would eventually expand into a cyberspatial associative network of various forms of information: text, images, audio clips, and so forth.

With Memex, the notion of the essential copy takes an important step — the essential copy becomes an *all-encompassing virtual environment* of information. It is an environment in which the mind lives and works. In his seminal article the desire for physical transcendence also displays an important VR theme. The desire for physical transcendence is cast as not just some general desire to overcome the limitations imposed upon humans by the physical environment, but to *overcome the limitations of the senses, to augment the senses* through electrical means. Bush (1945) wrote:

All our steps in creating or absorbing material . . . proceed through one of the senses. . . . Is it not possible that some day the path may be established more directly? . . . In the outside world, all forms of intelligence, whether of sound or sight, have been reduced to the form of varying currents in an electric circuit in order that they may be transmitted. Inside the human frame exactly the same sort of process occurs. Must we always transform to mechanical movement in order to proceed from one electrical phenomenon to another? (pp. 107–108).

Here we see the expression for a communication medium on par with a VR interface connected to highly networked cyberspace. Bush presented us with a modern form of the vision of the ultimate display.

This modern vision of the ultimate display coalesces into sensory experience in the work of Morton Heilig (1955/1992). Heilig's work on his vision of the ultimate display has been recently rediscovered and embraced by the virtual reality community (e.g., Heilig, 1955/1992; Rheingold, 1991). Studying filmmaking in Rome on the GI Bill and a Fulbright, the young Heilig was intrigued by U.S. press reports about Cinerama and 3-D films in the early 1950s. His experience of Cinerama in a Broadway theater was, according to Heilig, "a really pivotal experience in my life" (Hamit, 1993, p. 54). That experience awakened Heilig, and he inherited the ancient vision of a destination called virtual reality. We can see all the elements of the ancient vision in an article he published in a Spanish/English publication called *Espacios* in 1955. In Heilig's article we hear the modern echo of the age-old call for a technology that will create essential copies of sensory reality:

> Man's nervous system — sensory nerves, brain, and motor nerves — is the seat of his consciousness. . . . In time all of the above elements will be recorded, mixed, and projected electronically — a reel of the cinema of the future being a roll of magnetic tape with a separate track for each sense material. With these problems solved it is easy to imagine the cinema of the future. Open your eyes, listen, smell, and feel — sense the world in all its magnificent colors, depth, sounds, odors, and textures — this is the cinema of the future! . . . For without the active participation of the spectator there can be no transfer of consciousness, nor art. Thus art is never "too" realistic. (Heilig, 1955/1992, pp. 281–282, 285)

The way Heilig's vision is articulated would seem familiar to the modern communication researcher. He writes of the inadequacy of language; of "more direct forms of communication — painting, sculpture. . . ."; and of media as "extensions" of the senses (see Fig. 1.3). Heilig would later be embraced by VR engineers because he successfully embodied his vision of an "experience theater" in a multisensory entertainment simulator called Sensorama, patented in 1962 (Rheingold, 1991). Heilig's arcade ride was only a small realization of a much grander plan for a mass medium that would beam multisensory experiences to a nation eager to "feel physically

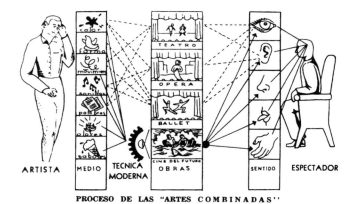

PROCESO DE LAS "ARTES COMBINADAS"

FIG. 1.3.   Graphic model of mediated, multisensory communication between an artist and a spectator. From Heilig (1955/1993). Reprinted by permission of MIT Press.

and mentally transported into a new world" (Heilig, 1955/1992, p. 284) (see Fig. 1.4).

Today, as it has for over 2,000 years, the vision of ultimate display continues to race ahead of VR technology. Ivan Sutherland and all his progenitors are the latest prophets in a long chain of VR prophecy. The vision that is expressed in this prophetic search for the ultimate display is more than just "hype"; it is desire. As with the Futurist manifestos, we often read and hear a technohubris fed by an age-old desire for physical

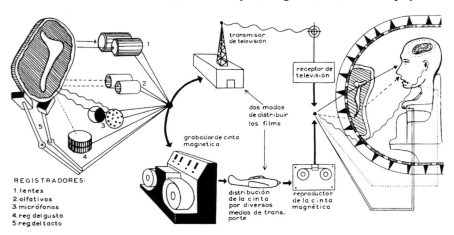

FIG. 1.4.   Heilig's (1955) vision of a multisensory mass medium of the future. On the left electronic sensors probe some real-world object. The sensation of that object is transmitted via broadcast or magnetic tape to a spectator who experiences it in a multisensory experience theater. From Heilig (1955/1993). Reprinted by permission of MIT Press.

transcendence. This desire is one of the most powerful forces driving the history of communication. Looking back at the history of communication technologies, Daniel Czitrom observed, "The dream of transcendence through machines is an ancient one, and the urge to annihilate space and time found particularly intense expression through new communication media. . . . The accelerated evolution of media hardware and software has been fueled by the persistence of utopian urges in the population at large" (1982, pp. 187, 194).

IS IMMERSIVE VIRTUAL REALITY
THE ULTIMATE MEDIUM?

We see that the vision behind the creation of VR is consonant with the vision behind the creation of many of our communication media. But this leaves open an important question: Does this mean that VR represents the early stages of the arrival of the ultimate medium? Or, as in the past, are we just projecting this longstanding desire for the essential copy and for physical transcendence — for a dream machine — onto yet another promising but inadequate technology? It is too early to tell, but this book asks the question (see Steuer, this volume).

The promise of VR has yet to be proven — it's still mostly a vision. At the time of this writing, most virtual reality technology still has the look and feel of a prototype, a jumble of wires, LCDs and artful technical compromises (Brooks, 1988), just a portal looking out on a more mature technology to come. These improvised introductory systems remind us of the very early television set, a low-resolution array of black and white lines barely sketching a snow-spotted image. Just as with the early television sets, the image of a new, radically different communication technology is visible.

It is fitting that VR appears at the end of the millennium. One suspects that the ultimate display wears a messianic crown of thorns; it is a techno-Godot, long awaited but yet to arrive. It may even be an expression of our desire to assume a Godlike control of reality. The ultimate display will never arrive. It is a moving target. Like addicts for sensory stimulation, we will always crave more convincing and exhilarating "essential copies," more overwhelming sensations, more physical transcendence.

REFERENCES

Biocca, F. (1987). Sampling in the museum of forms: Photography and visual thinking in the rise of modern statistics. In M. McLaughlin (Ed.), *Communication yearbook 10* (pp. 684–708). Hillsdale, NJ: Lawrence Erlbaum Associates.

Brooks, F. (1988). *Grasping reality through illusion: Interactive graphics serving science* (Tech. Rep. No. TR88-007). Chapel Hill: University of North Carolina at Chapel Hill, Dept. of Computer Science.

Bryson, N. (1983). *Vision and painting: The logic of the gaze.* New Haven: Yale University Press.

Bush, V. (1945, July). As we may think. *The Atlantic Monthly,* pp. 101–108.

Czitrom, D. (1982). *Media and the American mind: From Morse to McLuhan.* Chapel Hill: University of North Carolina Press.

Englebart, D. (1962, October). *Augmenting human intellect: A conceptual framework* (Summary report, contract AF 49(638)-1024). Stanford: Stanford Research Institute.

Englebart, D. (1988). The augmented knowledge workshop. In A. Goldberg (Ed.), *A history of personal workstations* (pp. 187–232). New York: ACM Press.

Fournier, E. (1859). *Le vieux-neuf, histoire ancienne des inventions et dicouvertes modernes* [The old–new, history of ancient inventions and modern discoveries] (Vol. 1). Paris: Dentu.

Hamit, F. (1993). *Virtual reality and the exploration of cyberspace.* Carmel, IN: SAMS Publishing.

Heilig, M. (1992). El cine de futro: The cinema of the future. *Presence, 1* (3), 279–294. (Original work published 1955)

Holmes, O. W. (1859). The stereoscope and the stereograph. *Atlantic Monthly, 3*(25), 249–262.

Krueger, M. (1991). *Artificial reality.* Reading, MA: Addison-Wesley.

Marnietti, F.T., & Masata, P. (1992). La radia. In D. Kahn & G. Whitehead (Eds.), *Wireless imagaination: Sound, radio, and the avant-garde* (pp. 265–268). Cambridge, MA: MIT Press.

Mitchell, W. J. T., (1986). *Iconology: Image, text, ideology.* Chicago: University of Chicago Press.

Pliny (1938). *Natural history.* Cambridge, MA: Harvard University Press.

Rheingold, H. (1991). *Virtual reality.* New York: Summit.

Sutherland, I. (1965). The ultimate display. *Proceedings of the International Federation of Information Processing Congress, 2,* 506–508.

2 Virtual Reality as a Communication System

Frank Biocca
University of North Carolina at Chapel Hill

Mark R. Levy
University of Maryland

The "MEDIA"? You often read or hear reference to this mammoth, wired, humming beast. But this popular usage of the word "media" can be misleading. The phrase is sometimes used to mean not just the technological tool used to communicate (e.g., clay or video tape) but also the content of the medium (e.g., nightly news, "violent" drama) and organizations supporting the medium (e.g., the networks, cable companies, or "the press"). The term *media* even encompasses the whole social and cultural system built around transmission channels or interfaces like television. The problem: the term conflates too many elements.

The term *virtual reality* (VR) has similar problems. People frequently jump between different levels of the technology, as they discuss its prospects. Some are talking about a piece of the interface hardware (e.g., head-mounted displays), an application (e.g., medical imaging), a VR industry (e.g., the VR entertainment industry), or the cultural environment emerging around the use of VR technologies (e.g., cyberfiction, cyberspace, cyberpunks, etc.). The phrase, virtual reality, increasingly refers not to a piece of technology but to an emerging communication system.

What is a communication system? Fig. 2.1 helps illustrate the basic elements of such a system. A communication system is composed of a communication interface, transmission channels, and organizational infrastructures. Each component is actually a subsystem with its own dynamics and actors. We can use Fig. 2.1 to discuss some of the issues facing the emergence of VR as a communication system, and to give an overview of

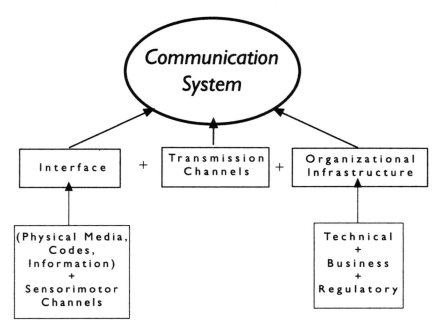

FIG. 2.1.   A communication system can be defined as the combined functions of a dominant interface, transmission channel(s), and organizational infrastructures.

how the chapters in this book attempt to shine light on various facets of the VR communication system.

THE VR INTERFACE

A communication interface can be defined as:

> Communication Interface = (physical media, codes, information) + sensorimotor channels.

McLuhan (1964, 1966, 1988) made it clear that the body is the primordial communication interface and the physical world is its content. For McLuhan all media are "extensions of the senses" (or more precisely, sensorimotor channels). Many feel that VR embodies radical and exciting approaches to interface design—it focuses on the extension of the senses. But VR is the just the forward edge of general evolution of present communication interfaces like television, computers, and the telephone toward the emergence of a metamedium (Kay, 1984; Kay & Goldberg, 1977). The VR form of this emerging metamedium is like a diving suit with which one can plunge into and explore the electronic ocean. What makes VR different is that it explicitly embodies a destination for the evolution of the metamedium. As chapter 1 pointed out, VR is not a technology; it's a destination. The ultimate goal of VR interface design is nothing less than the *full immersion of the human sensorimotor channels* into a vivid computer-generated experience. In the ideal system, the body is wrapped in communication and pulsates with information. Media have always been environments — both radio and television dominate the rooms in which they are used and the minds that use them. But the VR environment surrounds the senses. The optimist would say VR embraces the senses; the pessimist would say it kidnaps them.

Any discussion of VR interfaces always returns to questions about how the primordial communication medium, the body and its sensorimotor channels, are extended. How do the sensorimotor channels interact with the physical media, codes, and information of the technology? Chapter 4 by Biocca and Delaney examines the physical media of virtual reality, the input and output devices that make immersive VR possible, devices such as head-mounted displays, spatial audio, position sensors, and so on. The chapter tries to answer the basic question that should inform all other communication discussions of VR: How does VR technology work? Looking into the future it also asks: How might VR technology evolve? The chapter holds true to the previously discussed definition of interfaces. The discussion focuses on the sensory information and how each component strives to perfectly match the information needs of the sensorimotor channels. The chapter discusses how VR output devices attempt to fool the senses and how input devices help further insert the body of the user into the virtual world. Trends in the development of the technology are spotlighted with a focus on the psychoperceptual design challenges that must be met.

But what about the codes of this new interface? There is more here than random sensory "stimuli." The physical media are tapping out a kind of Morse code of the senses, sending and receiving patterns that contain information: perspective cues on HMDs, spatial cues beeping and hissing information to our ears, textured forces pushing the hand, "intelligent" forms floating inside the virtual environment. Clearly, there is much more to the creation of virtual worlds than a bunch of wires, LCD panels, and computer chips. The famous broadcast journalist, Edward R. Murrow, used to say that without the "software" created by his colleagues, television would be nothing more than "colored lights in a box." The colored lights must emit a pattern — the codes of the senses and the codes of our culture.

Head-mounted displays, data gloves, and force feedback are only a part of the defining experience of virtual reality. The magazine pictures of VR mislead by showing us mostly the hardware. In the 1950s we would not have understood television by only examining the walnut cabinets that surrounded cathode ray guns, vacuum tubes, and wires. But in this early stage—just as in the early stages of the development of television—it is the hardware that is the focus of public attention. It deserves to be. But as the communication systems of VR mature, the codes and information in the interface must receive more and more attention. Communication researchers will have to better understand the psychosemiotics of VR to meet the human factors design challenges of the technology.

In his chapter on presence, Steuer explores the variables that give us the sense of telepresence—how elaborate codes and techniques structure the information of a virtual world to give it meaning. The experience of VR is made up of blue-skied worlds, mythic adventures, human and robotic agents, room-size molecules, and bar graphs the size of city blocks. It is a wraparound mirror reflecting the mind's contents and the world's information.

The philosopher of science, Karl Popper, suggested that we think of three worlds when we consider the spheres of human action: "First, there is the physical world—the universe of physical objects . . . this I will call 'World 1.' Second, there is the world of mental states; this I will call 'World 2.' But there is also a *third* such world, the world of the contents of thought, and, indeed of the products of the human mind; this I will call 'World 3' " . . . (Popper & Eccles, 1977, p. 38).

With VR, Popper's World 3 enters a new stage of growth. It starts to edge out World 1. Why? For millennia the communication medium of the body has been an interface between World 1, physical nature, and World 2, mental states. In fact the body evolved to be a good conduit for that communication; it assisted the mind to model space, to act with movement, and so forth (Gibson, 1979; Ornstein, 1991). With VR the growing environment of World 3 wraps around a body designed for World 1. In Ivan Sutherland's ultimate VR display (Sutherland, 1965) the body is fully immersed in World 3, an electronic "mathematical wonderland." The natural World 1 is muffled, the senses immersed in the creations of our minds. A feedback loop is set up between the changing mental states of World 2 and the sensory experience of World 3. This feedback loop between the mind's objectification and the subsequent sensory experience of that objectification has always existed. But now the loop may take on all the insistence and vividness of the physical world. How will this feedback affect the mental states of World 2, our mental states? Will it make us "smarter" by making it easier for us to learn the contents of the culture's objectified thoughts, as some VR designers suggested (Furness, 1993; Krueger, 1991)? Or will this feedback loop, as McLuhan saw it, immerse us in a Narcissistic trance where the forms (codes) of the medium (World 3) and the operations of our mental states (World 2) unite in some distorted, psychic isomorphism. We cannot yet know.

This suggests the following question: How can we communicate most effectively using VR interfaces? The best answer is: We're not sure, but we'll soon find out. Communication through VR is not yet well understood. Of course, the VR interface will use existing human codes of communication (Eco, 1976; Ekman, 1974) and it will draw on techniques devised for other media. For example, in chapter 10, Palmer looks at the ancient interpersonal codes of communication and discusses the challenges of mapping and extending those codes in virtual environments. But clearly, something new has been added with the arrival of VR, and the process of meaning construction and meaning reception will be subtly altered. For example, the narrative film was not just a form of filmed theater — although some early directors filmed that way. Film generated new ways of experiencing stories and narrative space.

Perhaps then, it will be in entertainment that VR's most varied use of communication codes will be seen, defined, and, hopefully, extended. A number of chapters in this book explore how communication might be designed for VR entertainment interfaces. In chapter 6 Hawkins discusses the maturing location-based VR industry and its design plans for various genres of VR experience. For chapter 7 Heeter reports on early users of VR and discusses how users of the location-based entertainment systems have responded to VR experiences using violent or military-based genres. In chapter 8 Meyer takes a closer look at the art of storytelling and suggests ways to adapt the ancient techniques of dramatic narrative to virtual environments. Listening to the sound of VR, Kramer in chapter 9 hones in on codes of hearing to discuss how VR can be used to orchestrate a rich symphony of information. Taken together these four chapters confront some of the critical design issues that will shape how users experience VR.

Indeed VR calls out for new communication designs — new ways to communicate with others and with the pattern of information and practices that make up our culture. The static virtual environments in most early VR demos are hauntingly empty. They are like ghost towns waiting to be populated by stories about determined settlers, wild saloons, cyberoutlaws, and crusading journalists. Such "characters" are but quotations from old genres that will be recycled, reformed, and transcended in the semiotic dust storm that will likely whirl inside virtual reality. The voyeur will become actor; faces will be replaced by virtual masks.

As virtual reality takes shape, an attempt is underway to insert *real* communication into the artifice of technology. There is a big gap in real communication between a sterile lab demo and a virtual world pulsating with the messages, forms, and the wired bodies of millions of people. *Real* communication has always been about our collective creation and mastery of *artifice,* the building of Popper's World 3. The exploration of communication codes will be the key to the exploration of communication expression and experience in VR, and to building the continents and metropolises of objectified thought, the virtual worlds of World 3.

TRANSMISSION CHANNELS

Communication in the age of virtual reality is in some ways about transportation. Tele-presence replaces tele-vision. The body's sensorimotor channels are conveyed to distant real and virtual worlds. Experience is transmitted. Transmission and transportation share more than a common root word. In the 19th century, telegraph wires and train tracks raced side-by-side across the fields and forests of America's western frontier. These two transmission channels, the train and the telegraph, competed to "transport" information. Trains, planes, and trucks still transport information carried on physical media like paper and ink: mail, newspapers, and magazines — consider, for example, the postal system. Although the telegraph had far less information-carrying capacity than the train, it easily outraced the physical transportation channel. The telegraph's thin flow of information was more valuable than the train's car loads of slow information. The flow of communication is now sent across space and time through various transmission channels: copper wires, fiber optic cables, the electromagnetic spectrum, and so forth. Millions of miles of wires criss-cross the planet and wrap it like a giant ball of string. Surrounding this giant ball, the electromagnetic spectrum thrums with the chant of millions of messages. The transmission of information surrounds us.

Communication in the age of virtual reality occurs at a time when there is phenomenal competition among transmission channels. Where once there was the telegraph's slim reed of information flow, giant pipes now gush information. The capacity limits of the older communication systems are being effectively removed. In the next century, the descendants of the telegraph — fiber optic channels, for example — may eventually carry hundreds of train loads of information. A 40-strand fiber optic wire can carry 1.3 million phone conversations or 1,920 TV channels. Compare this to the twisted-copper wire that in the past could carry little more than 1,000 simultaneous telephone conversations and not a single TV channel. With information capacity greatly expanded, the physical transportation of information goods using channels represented by those old train tracks are likely to become a less and less attractive means of moving information. Human exchange is migrating from physical space into cyberspace.

VR Gateways to Cyberspace

The electric transportation system did not just collapse space in Innis–McLuhan-like fashion, it expanded into a new parallel universe — cyberspace.

Cyberspace is a particularly plastic form of Popper's World 3. The growth of cyberspace is entering a decisive phase—the opening of a new electronic frontier. Scouts in this new frontier (e.g., Lucky, 1991) consistently report the following:

"The rivers are wide."–There is an increase in overall capacity for each transmission channel (aided by information compression).

"There is a lot of space."–There is an expansion in the communication system's global capacity for information.

"Leave your wagons and ride the wide rivers."–There is a shift in communication traffic towards new transmission channels like fiber optics.

"We'll need different routes through the mountains."–There will be communication specialization and niche building for each transmission channel.

And there are corporate prospectors on the electronic frontier, rubbing their hands at the trillion-dollar, digital gold mine expected by the year 2000. Take, for example, Ray Smith, the CEO of Bell Atlantic who in 1993 led an attempted merger with the largest cable company, TCI. With a prospector's twinkle he pronounced the modern equivalent of "there's gold in them there hills":[1] "It won't be just 500 channels; it will be everything, everywhere" (Schniedawind, 1993, p. B1). Thus, the dream of physical transcendence, of being everything or going everywhere, takes on another form.

Others are staking out a slightly different claim. Robert Lucky, former head of Bell Labs and research head at Bellcore peers into the vast expanding cyberspace and sees not just open plains, but a giant black hole. To an audience of computer graphics programmers at the 1992 meeting of SIGGRAPH,[2] he puzzled on what might fill this void. He doubted that it could be filled. Only intensive "interactive, graphics traffic" could fill the void—the kinds of digital traffic that only a networked virtual reality system could create. Cyberspace is a vast frontier and only VR can fill it.

VR as the Great Conduit of Thought

As we look out at the growth of the so-called "information superhighway," virtual reality interfaces become part of the vehicles to transport consciousness through the thin fiber optic highways of cyberspace. The transporta-

---

[1]Dan Duncan, known in some circles as the "poet laureate" of virtual reality, used this phrase to capture the gold rush fever at one of the early meetings of the San Francisco Virtual Reality conference, a business-oriented gathering sponsored by the publisher, Meckler.

[2]Special Interest Group for Graphics, part of the Association for Computing Machinery (ACM).

tion metaphor contained in a phrase like the "information superhighway" is a root metaphor in communication (Carey, 1988). It can be traced at least as far back as Locke's definition of communication as the "Great Conduit," a vehicle for the transportation of thoughts — telementation.[3]

The transportation of information — be it thought or encapsulated experiences — is degraded by the impoverished interfaces and overly ambiguous codes like the printed word, the image, and even the film clip. Information is lost. Noise, ambiguity, and mental effort appear to fill the void presented by the vague smoke signals of traditional codes and media. We have been forced to transmit less information via more abstract codes because that is all our transmission channels could carry. We have made noises with our voices, scribbled in the sand, made vague black marks on pieces of paper.

Does VR finally solve this ambiguity and give us a pure way to transport information from one mind to another? Circulating in cyberspace is the notion that with VR interfaces and bigger transmission pipes, information can be purer, more realistic, especially if it "realistically" addresses more senses. Communication can be clearer with less noise. Somehow, with virtual reality our abstract codes and symbols can be overcome. Jaron Lanier suggests that we have entered a period of "postsymbolic communication" (Lanier & Biocca, 1992). What is postsymbolic communication? According to Lanier, it is an age wherein the thing itself, say for example a vivid 3-D house, can be displayed to the receiver/audience instead of some impoverished symbol, like the word, "house." Lanier feels that this will transform communication; the symbol will be replaced with something closer to thing symbolized, the thing-in-itself. It is an intriguing notion.

But in the "sensory realism" of virtual reality the problems of communication abstraction do not go away as some cyberpioneers may hope. Rather, the problem is simply refracted through new codes. If Locke were to walk up to us today in cyberspace, he would no doubt point out that a 3-D model of a house can be as ambiguous a sign as the word "house." The semiotic philosopher, Charles Sanders Peirce (Peirce, 1991) might add that, yes, in VR the icon may dominate over the symbol, but postsymbolic never means postsemiotic, as Lanier's notion seems to suggest. Does a 3-D model of a house mean anything more clearly than the word "house"? Although *more information* can be transported in the 3-D model of a house, it is not certain that the *meaning* of the house — which is never transported or transport-

---

[3]"The Comfort, and Advantage, of Society not being to be had without Communication of Thoughts it was necessary that Man should find out some external sensible Signs. . . . To make words serviceable to the ends of Communication, it is necessary . . . that they excite, in the Hearer, exactly the same *Idea,* they stand for in the Mind of the Speaker. . . . For Language being the great Conduit, whereby Men convey their Discoveries, Reasonings, and Knowledge, from one to another . . ." (Locke, 1959, pp. 54–55).

able — is clearer (see Eco for discussion of iconcism and absolute icons; Eco 1976, 1979).

A VR communication system is not really transporting things or even experiences but *ideas* from one mind to another. A 3-D house in VR is just an objectified idea, a simulation of the mental model of the experience of that house. This may be a *better way of coding* that information. But we doubt that there is a "pure" or "natural" code for transmitting ideas or experience. Nonetheless, Lanier is right in sensing that we want to be transported to a simulation of a house rather than read the word "house" and provide most of the simulation in our heads. We want codes and an interface that can capture all the dynamism and nuances of our mental models — codes with maximum bandwidth.

Transporting the Senses

The distant transmission of information — especially sensory information — is a driving desire pushing the envelop of virtual reality. In his greeting at the first IEEE Virtual Reality Annual Symposium (VRAIS), Tom Furness (1993), Air Force VR pioneer and leading engineering researcher, proclaimed that "advanced interfaces will provide an incredible new mobility for the human race. We are building transportation systems for the senses . . . the remarkable promise that we can be in another place or space without moving our bodies into that space" (p. i).

Again we hear echoes from the early days of modern communication. The shouts that "space will be annihilated" were first clearly audible with the arrival the telegraph (Carey, 1988; Czitrom, 1982). The gentle tapping of a finger on a telegraph key collapsed miles. Now the rest of the body is being attached to the descendants of the telegraph wire. In telepresence, virtual reality joins other media in the task of transporting experience.

At the distant frontiers of VR's transportation mission lies an agency whose sole mission is the collapse of space. NASA is developing virtual reality as a means of transmitting the experience of being telepresent on distant planets (McGreevy, 1993). The human on earth controls a proxy robot kicking up dust on the craggy wastelands of our solar system. Why risk transporting people to distant planets when we can extend their senses into space! This is ambition for telepresence on a cosmic scale. But this is communication evolution, not revolution. Media theorist Harold Innis (1951) would recognize it as the age-old attempt to use communications to control space, but now with a grasp that reaches out to grab distant planets.

At the other end of the spatial scale are VR systems squeezing the human senses down into the space that surrounds atoms. Work at the University of North Carolina (Robinette & Williams, 1991) ties the virtual reality interface to the end of a scanning-tunneling microscope. Atoms become mounds on what looks like a beach of pink sand. Atoms can be "touched" and even moved; the pink sand reshapes itself and new mounds appear. Media's relentless collapse of space extends into the microworlds of World 1, the physical world.

Solving the Information Crisis in Cyberspace

Cyberspace is vast. This vastness may be the source of a crisis in cyberspace. The expansion of the capacity of our transmission channels and the interconnection of the world's computers into systems like Internet create not just opportunities but problems as well. The problems of *information navigation and information filtering* rise up like fog over the vast oceans of information. VR is being offered as a possible solution.

Consider this analogy. Have you ever been in a large library and not quite known where you were? The long rows of books seemed so similar, the numbers on the shelves provided so little guide as to where you were—is this ancient Egypt or brain chemistry? Now imagine an immense library—perhaps even as large as Borges' famous library of all the books ever written. Imagine a place where all of the world's books are stored along with millions of newspaper and magazine articles, countless pictures, posters, film clips and television programs. The aisles of this library stretch for miles, longer than the miles of corridors in the Library of Congress, larger than all the national libraries of the world assembled under one roof. As you wander dazed and confused in the cavernous halls of this immense library, where are you? Where is the information you are looking for? You are lost, adrift in cyberspace.

It is apparent to some that the information stacks building up inside the anarchic structures of cyberspace present significant navigation problems. The intrepid infonauts who today try to find their way around Internet must still call on scouts—reference books, programs, agents, and the colleague in the office next door—to find their way around. Cyberspace is out of control; it's like a city where there are no zoning laws and skyscrapers and shanties rise in no apparent order.

Order is related in powerful ways to communication. Modern communication systems emerged out of a crisis of control in the industrial system. According to James Beniger, "Just as the Commercial Revolution depended on capital and labor freed by advanced agriculture, for example, the Industrial Revolution presupposed a commercial system for capital allocations and the distribution of goods, the most recent technological revolution developed in response to problems arising out of advanced industrialization—an ever-mounting crisis in control" (p. 15). This crisis was brought on by the increasing volume and speed of the processing of matter, energy, and information. Later in this century, the very networks that constitute cyberspace were proposed as a means of dealing with a crisis in the control of information. For example, in 1945 Vannevar Bush complained that: "There is a growing mountain of research . . . [and] there is increased evidence that we are being bogged down . . . human experience is being expanded at a prodigious rate, and the means we use for threading through the consequent maze to the momentarily important item is the same as it was in the days of square-rigged ships" (Bush, 1945, p. 101–103).

Bush warned of "catastrophes" where important information would be lost for years. He proposed various solutions such as information compression, new sensory interfaces, and a hypermedia system to organize and navigate through information (Bush, 1945). All have been implemented. But the very success of the computers and the networks envisioned by people like Bush has brought us to a new level of the problem of the control of information.

The present expansion of cyberspace further increases the volume and speed of the processing of information. With the improvement of our transmission channels we possibly face another kind of crisis of control. VR scientists respond to this crisis with the following question: What if cyberspace took on the properties of physical space? What if all information, including abstract information, were increasingly spatial and sensory? Evolution has designed us to navigate around a physical world of three-dimensional space, sounds, textures, smells, and motions. Finding information, even abstract information, might be easier if you could walk to where you last encountered it, listen to see if you could hone in on it, or even pick up its scent. Information is transformed from noumena into phenomena. Information, the environment of the mind, becomes an environment for the body.

How to structure and control the information environment? Old information control metaphors like museums and libraries creep into some proposals. VR architects like Benedikt suggest schemes for the "built environment" of cyberspace (Benedikt, 1992). Other spatial and physical scenarios offer solutions to the information management crisis with models of endless spiral walkways along museum walls of information (e.g., Benedikt, 1991), giant file drawers you can enter, walls filled with Post-it™ notes (e.g., Xerox Parc's Perspective Wall Visualization), trees of knowledge connecting branches of information (e.g., Xerox Parc's Cone Trees). Elsewhere, "fly over" metaphors born of flight simulators suggest other ways to transport us across terrains of information (e.g., Silicon Graphic's Navigator) (see e.g., Bylinsky, 1993; Fairchild, 1993).

Many proposals are emerging to control the information tidal waves sloshing around on the oceans of cyberspace. Most assume that making information more physical — giving it more sensory properties — will help us navigate the giant information seas of cyberspace. From a bird's eye view above the oceans we might perceive patterns rippling on the information waves below. In some VR scenarios, the information navigation problem is solved by the apparent freedom and ease of flight. The user would dive into the sea for a piece of information as pelicans dive for fish. But as any pilot knows, it is easy to get lost when your only points of reference are the indistinct wave patterns of the oceans.

VR and Transmission Channels.   The growth of virtual reality interfaces are linked in a number of ways to changes in transmission channels of the emerging communication systems; developments are interrelated. To summarize the connections that relate to VR:

1. As changes in transmission channels expand cyberspace, there will likely be a phenomenal demand for information goods to transport. The shortage will not just be of "content" such as old mass media products like films and shows, but of other new forms of information, experiences and ideas. The information contained in shared virtual environments may help fill this information void.

2. As cyberspace expands, the sheer volume and speed of information may create crises in cyberspace. These information crises have four components: the first is related to information organization, the second to information navigation, the third to the problem of information filtering, and the fourth, pattern detection. These are modern developments in the crisis that Beniger (1986) identified with the rise of control technologies.

In a number of technological and government circles, one can hear the suggestion that 3-D interfaces like VR technology may provide tools to help organize, travel, and find information in the vast data oceans of cyberspace.[4] Many are working on a VR *cyberspace interface.* We turn now to this governmental, technical, and business infrastructure in this next section.

THE EMERGING INFRASTRUCTURES

As virtual reality emerges as the interface for a new communication system, interest in this medium ties together a network of research, regulatory, financial, production, and support organizations. VR hardware would be useless without these organizations.

The organizational needs of specialized institutions like NASA, the U.S.

---

[4]For example, this theme was apparent in the remarks of government officials in charge of grant funding gathered at the VRAIS conference in Seattle in September 1993.

Air Force, Bell Labs, and others helped fuel early developments (see Hamit, 1993; Kalawsky, 1993; Rheingold, 1991; Rolfe & Staples, 1986, for brief histories of R&D development). Three institutional needs related to military and space applications provided the rational for the early development of some of the advanced interfaces:

1. *Flight training* in the military, civilian, and space aviation industry benefited from and demanded increasingly sophisticated and realistic flight simulators.

2. As cockpits became increasingly complicated, *flight cockpit design* drew on flight simulator technology to develop new ways of displaying and managing the complex human–computer information exchanges required in advanced flight equipment.

3. Early attempts at *telerobotics* (the control of robots at a distance in military, nuclear, and oceanographic applications) led to the development of some early interface prototypes in the telepresence area.

Academic centers such as the University of North Carolina extended this work into other areas such as scientific, architectural, and medical visualization (see the review in Holloway, Fuchs, & Robinett, 1991).

Around this pioneering core group of institutions, the number of supporting technical and business organizations has grown rapidly to support the emergence of other VR applications and eventually a VR-based communication system. Some are in key related industries such as computer graphics (e.g., Silicon Graphics) or in location-based entertainment (e.g., Disney). The publicity and excitement regarding the promise of virtual reality has apparently mobilized the resources of a number of institutions, including some communication companies with few ties to the early development of VR interfaces (e.g., U.S. West, NYNEX, Seaga). Many companies are suiting up for entry into cyberspace.

The 1990s are witnessing a significant expansion of VR research centers worldwide in academic, governmental, and business institutions. Each institution has some, or large, institutional commitment to an aspect of VR technology, design, or support. At the beginning of the decade only a few organizations could be identified as virtual reality centers—even with the most generous definition. In 1993 directories listed over 400 academic research labs, governmental centers, and companies actively engaged in the creation and expansion of virtual reality (e.g., Panos, 1993). Most of the directories were quickly dated—small companies enter the field, large military, communication, or consumer electronics companies suddenly take on a "VR flavor." The retooling of some defense companies has sometimes involved movement toward some communication application of VR: telecommunications, information visualization, and control.

The first wave of VR entrepreneurs has been composed mostly of a host of Lilliputian companies. Concentrated on the west coast, many of these companies had hoped to rise up and surf a giant wave in the VR market. Many hungered for injections of financial steroids, or dreamed of an alliance with a corporate giant. VPL, the leading start-up and number one VR media star, went down in flames in 1993. Consumer electronic giants like Matsushita had brief flings with companies such as VPL, but most have kept much of their gold in their pockets as they too wait for a bustling VR market to emerge.

Not surprisingly, the increase in VR-related activities in all business, technical, and governmental infrastructures has created a phenomenal thirst for information about VR. An army of entrepreneurs, technocrats, and cyberpirates reaches out for a spyglass to survey the rough seas ahead. This search for information has been met by an armada of industry newsletters (e.g., the various editions of *CyberEdge Journal; Virtual Reality Report, VR News,* etc.), research journals (e.g., *Presence*), and annual conferences (e.g., Virtual Reality, VRAIS, Cyberthon, etc.).

The buzz of all this activity is the sound of institutions and society coming to grips with a new communication technology. It is the sound of the organizational infrastructures of an emerging communication system. Nowhere is this sound more audible than in the sheer volume of public discussion about VR. The figures on VR articles in chapter 1 are one example. They are one social indicator picking up only a few of the millions of voices that are simultaneously discussing the new technology.

More is going on here than the sheer need of organizations for informational fodder for internal reports. It suggests that we are well on our way in the first stages of diffusion discussed in chapter 11 by Valente and Bardini. We estimate that awareness of this technology has penetrated over 90% of the institutional elites in the communication, computer, and information processing communities, and over 50% of the general public. Both are key to the building of a VR communication system.

Government's Gloved Hand

In the 18th century the government and law eventually followed the rush of settlers into the new frontier. As we rush into the 21st century, the pattern is repeated. The gloved hand of government has entered cyberspace. Government's hand has been both open and nurturing and fisted and regulative. While the hand of the 18th-century lawman reached for the gun, the hand of modern government reaches for a handle on the rusted control panel of our regulative machinery. The media elites, especially those in control of the transmission channels, complain that the regulatory system must be overhauled: "The current regulatory framework is built on the concept of scarcity, that there was only a limited amount of capacity that must be carefully regulated. . . . But the whole country and the wholeworld are moving towards abundance." (Daniel G. Burton, president of the Council on Competitiveness in Andrews, 1994, p. C3).

Government money helped develop VR technology. Government funding agencies like the National Science Foundation supported much work at university research centers such as the University of North Carolina and MIT. Other agencies like the U.S. Air Force, the Navy, and NASA were instrumental in building early versions of many components. Government officials and agencies are quick to claim credit. Referring to the vast range of computer networking technologies, Vice-President Al Gore pointed out that, "Virtually all of the leading-edge discoveries in this field have come with government support, and government will continue to stimulate investments in the cutting-edge technologies that are beyond the investment horizons of the private sector" ("Conversation," 1993, p. 62).

In the short term, government agencies will be called upon to pursue industrial management or regulatory legislation as the technology leaves the lab and enters the home. As VR becomes an interface to cyberspace, the regulatory demands are likely to focus on standards, equity of access, and consumer safety areas. According to Vice-President Al Gore, "Government will play a catalyzing role and will set the standards and protocols to ensure interconnection and compatibility and universal access" ("Conversation," 1993, p. 62). Health and safety problems such as those related to simulation sickness (Biocca, 1992) may lead to regulations related to product safety and design. More nettlesome, perhaps, are issues related to virtual property. Who owns a virtual table, a virtual sea breeze, or the 3-D face of the Mona Lisa? In chapter 14 Harvey outlines some of the legal and regulatory challenges in growth of multisensory experiences and experiential "property" inside cyberspace.

THE AGE OF VIRTUAL REALITY?

The elements of a new dominant medium are in place: a paradigmatically different communication interface design, new channels of sensory information, and new modes of mediated communication (see chapter 4, Biocca & Delaney). Simultaneously there are significant changes in the transmission channels: new channels, increased capacity, increased competition and instability across channels. Is this a new communication system emerging? We believe that the answer is most likely yes. Will it be called virtual reality or cyberspace? Maybe. The name is not important. But it is clear that radically different communication capabilities are being designed for an emerging communication system and VR interfaces are an example of these new capabilities.

There are many possible responses to these new capabilities. Some plan designs to best use the capabilities of VR (see the chapters by Heeter; Kramer; Meyer; Palmer). Some look back in time to look forward towards the possible psychological, social, and cultural effects of VR. For example, Shapiro and McDonald in chapter 12 look at previous confusions about the "reality" of cyberspace. Some challenge the designers of this technology to consider and discuss the social construction of this communication system (e.g., Harvey, this volume; Lanier & Biocca, 1992). In chapter 13 Balsamo shows us some of the emerging features of cyberspace culture.

Many believe that any radical change in communication systems and practices is likely to change the way we think about communication. The study of communication has often been transformed by changes in communication technology. This is part of a more general belief in some form of technological determinism. Notions of technological determinism are so common in our society that they pervade the thinking of many elites right up to the country's leaders. "In a real sense, the printing press made possible the modern nation-state and representative democracy" said Vice-President Gore. "If the printing press did that, then how much richer in spirit can our country be if our people are empowered with the knowledge capacity that these high-capacity computer networks can distribute" ("Conversation," 1993, p. 62). The classic U.S. belief in the transforming and liberating power of information, education, and technology remains very strong.

All assumptions about VR and communication need to be stated and submitted to inquiry. This book is part of a general inquiry into the implications of new technologies like VR. Elsewhere, we have suggested that the shifting structures of communication systems present historic opportunities and challenges for communication researchers (Biocca, 1992) and that these require multidisciplinary approaches to communication research (Biocca, 1993). Virtual reality may become the ship that helps us sail the vast oceans of cyberspace. Rough seas lie ahead. This book is our attempt to construct a paper telescope to scan the horizon for signs of communication (and life) in the age of virtual reality.

REFERENCES

Andrews, E. (1993, Nov. 10). A wireless upstart gets bigger. *New York Times,* pp. C1, C5.

Benedikt, M. (Ed.). (1991). *Cyberspace: First steps.* Cambridge, MA: MIT Press.

Beniger, J. (1986). *The control revolution: Technological and economic origins of the information society.* Cambridge, MA: Harvard University Press.

Biocca, F. (1992). Communication within virtual reality: Creating a space for research. *Journal of Communication, 42*(3), 5–20.

Biocca, F. (1993). Communication research in the design of communication interfaces and systems. *Journal of Communication, 43*(4), 59–68.

Bush, V. (1945, July). As we may think. *The Atlantic Monthly,* pp. 101–108.

Bylinsky, G. (1993). The payoff from 3-D computing. *Fortune, 128* (7), pp. 32–40.

Carey, J. (1988). *Communication and culture.* Cambridge: Unwin Hyman.

Conversation with Al Gore, White House Vision. (1993). *U.S. News & World Report, 115* (22), p. 62.

Czitrom, D. (1982). *Media and the American mind: From Morse to McLuhan.* Chapel Hill: University of North Carolina Press.

Eco, U. (1976). *A theory of semiotics.* Bloomington: Indiana University Press.

Eco, U. (1979). *The role of the reader.* Bloomington: Indiana University Press.

Ekman, P. (1974). *Unmasking the face.* Englewood Cliffs, NJ: Prentice-Hall.

Fairchild, K. M. (1993). Information management using virtual reality-based visualizations. In A. Wexelblat (Ed.), *Virtual reality applications and explorations* (pp. 45–74). Boston: Academic Press Professional.

Furness, T. (1993). Greetings from the general chairman. In *IEEE Virtual Reality Annual International Symposium* (pp. i–ii). Piscataway, NJ: IEEE.

Gibson, J. J. (1979). *The ecological approach to visual perception.* Boston: Houghton Mifflin.

Hamit, F. (1993). *Virtual reality and the exploration of cybserspace.* Carmel, IN: SAMS Publishing.

Holloway, R., Fuchs, H., & Robinett, W. (1991, November). Virtual-worlds research at the University of North Carolina at Chapel Hill. In *Proceedings of Computer Graphics '91.* London.

Innis, H. (1951). *The bias of communication.* Toronto: University of Toronto Press.

Kalawsky, R. S. (1993). *The science of virtual reality and virtual environments.* Reading, MA: Addison-Wesley.

Kay, A. (1984, September). Computer software. *Scientific American, 251* (3), pp. 52–59.

Kay, A., & Goldberg, A. (1977, March). Personal dynamic media. *Computers & Operations Research, 10,* 31–41.

Krueger, M. (1991). *Artificial reality.* Reading, MA: Addison-Wesley.

Lanier, J., & Biocca, F . (1992). An insider's view of the future of virtual reality. *Journal of Communication, 42*(4), 150–172.

Locke, J. (1959). *An essay concerning human understanding.* New York: Dover.

McGreevy, M. (1993). Virtual reality and planetary exploration. In A. Wexelblat (Ed.), *Virtual reality applications and explorations* (pp. 163–198). New York: Academic Press.

McLuhan, M. (1964). *The Gutenberg galaxy.* New York: Signet.

McLuhan, M. (1966). *Understanding media.* New York: Signet.

McLuhan, M., & McLuhan, E. (1988). *Laws of media, the new science.* Toronto: University of Toronto Press.

Ornstein, R. (1991). *The evolution of consciousness.* New York: Simon & Schuster.

Panos, G. (Ed.). (1993). *Virtual reality sourcebook.* Lakewood, CA: SophisTech Research.

Peirce, C. S. (1991). *Peirce on signs: Writings on semiotics* (1839–1914). Chapel Hill, NC: University of North Carolina Press.

Popper, K., & Eccles, J. C. (1977). *The self and its brain: An argument for interactionism.* Boston: Routledge & Kegan Paul.

Rheingold, H. (1991). *Virtual reality.* New York: Summit.

Robinett, W., & Williams, R. S. (1991). *Touching atoms: Micro-teleoperation at atomic scale* (Grant proposal National Science Foundation). Chapel Hill: University of North Carolina.

Rolfe, J., & Staples, K. (1986). *Flight simulation.* Cambridge: Cambridge University Press.

Schniedawind, J. (1993, April 22). Bell's brash CEO bets big on TV dream. *USA Today,* pp. 1B–2B.

Sutherland, I. (1965). The ultimate display. *Proceedings of the International Federation of Information Processing Congress, 2,* 506–508.

3 Defining Virtual Reality: Dimensions Determining Telepresence

Jonathan Steuer
Stanford University

Virtual reality (VR) has typically been portrayed as a medium, like telephone or television. This new medium is typically defined in terms of a particular collection of technological hardware, including computers, head-mounted displays, headphones, and motion-sensing gloves. The focus of virtual reality is thus technological, rather than experiential; the locus of virtual reality is a collection of machines.[1] Such a concept is useful to producers of VR-related hardware. However, for communication researchers, policymakers, software developers, or media consumers, a device-driven definition of virtual reality is unacceptable: It fails to provide any insight into the processes or effects of using these systems, fails to provide a conceptual framework from which to make regulatory decisions, fails to provide an aesthetic from which to create media products, and fails to provide a method for consumers to rely on their experiences with other media in understanding the nature of virtual reality.

Theoretically, these inadequacies are manifest in three ways. First, a technology-based view suggests that the most salient feature in recognizing a "VR system" is the presence or absence of the requisite hardware.[2] In

---

[1]This chapter presumes broad definitions of technology and media, such as those given by Beniger (1986, p. 9), who defined *technology* as "any intentional extension of a natural process, that is, processing of matter, energy, and information that characterizes all living systems," and McLuhan (1964, p. 21), who defined a *medium* as any "extension of man."

[2]See Nass and Mason (1990) for an in-depth discussion of the practical and theoretical limitations of object-centered views of technology, and of the importance of variable-based strategies in overcoming these limitations.

other words, a given system is arbitrarily classified as "VR" or "not-VR," depending on whether it includes a minimal corpus of particular machines. Second, such a definition provides no clear conceptual unit of analysis for virtual reality. If VR consists of a hardware system, where do we look to identify a single "virtual reality"? Examining the technological apparatus alone does not seem adequate for this purpose. A third and related problem is the lack of theoretical dimensions across which virtual reality can vary. All systems meeting the basic hardware requirements "are VR," and all others are "not-VR." However, once this initial classification has been made, such a dichotomous definition offers no suggestion of how systems classified as "not-VR" may resemble those that "are VR," nor how different virtual reality systems can be compared. In the absence of a clear theoretical unit or any relevant dimensions for study, it is difficult to perform social science research that addresses the similarities and differences among various virtual reality systems, or that examines VR in relation to other media.

Probably the most effective solution to the problems with the current usage of "virtual reality" would be to abandon it entirely (at least for research purposes), in favor of a more theoretically grounded term. However, the term has stuck in academic as well as popular usage. It is therefore expedient to form a theoretically useful concept out of virtual reality. This chapter is an effort to fill this need, addressing the aforementioned faults by defining virtual reality as a particular type of experience, rather than as a collection of hardware. Defining virtual reality in this way provides (a) a concrete unit of analysis for VR, (b) a set of dimensions over which VR can vary, and, perhaps most importantly, (c) a means for examining VR in relation to other types of mediated experience.

DEFINING VIRTUAL REALITY

Most popular definitions of virtual reality make reference to a particular technological system. This system usually includes a computer capable of real-time animation, controlled by a set of wired gloves and a position tracker, and using a head-mounted stereoscopic display for visual output.[3] The following are three examples of such definitions:

> Virtual Reality is electronic simulations of environments experienced via head mounted eye goggles and wired clothing enabling the end user to interact in realistic three-dimensional situations. (Coates, 1992)

---

[3]See Biocca (this volume) for a thorough description of the hardware involved in such systems, ans for a brief review of the perceptual processes involved in the creation of such hardware.

Virtual Reality is an alternate world filled with computer-generated images that respond to human movements. These simulated environments are usually visited with the aid of an expensive data suit which features stereophonic video goggles and fiber-optic data gloves. (Greenbaum, 1992, p. 58)

The terms *virtual worlds, virtual cockpits,* and *virtual workstations* were used to describe specific projects. . . . In 1989, Jaron Lanier, CEO of VPL, coined the term *virtual reality* to bring all of the virtual projects under a single rubric. The term therefore typically refers to three-dimensional realities implemented with stereo viewing goggles and reality gloves. (Krueger, 1991, p. xiii)

Although these three definitions vary somewhat, all include the notions of both electronically simulated environments, and of "goggles 'n' gloves" systems as the means to access these environments. The application of these definitions (and any other definition that is similarly based on a particular hardware instantiation) is thereby limited to these technologies; their units of analysis and potential for variance are left unspecified. However, it is possible to define virtual reality without reference to particular hardware.

Presence and Telepresence

The key to defining virtual reality in terms of human experience rather than technological hardware is the concept of presence. Presence can be thought of as the experience of one's physical environment; it refers not to one's surroundings as they exist in the physical world, but to the perception of those surroundings as mediated by both automatic and controlled mental processes (Gibson, 1979). *Presence* is defined as the sense of being in an environment.[4]

Many perceptual factors contribute to generating this sense, including input from some or all sensory channels, as well as more mindful attentional, perceptual, and other mental processes that assimilate incoming sensory data with current concerns and past experiences (Gibson, 1966). Presence is closely related to the phenomenon of distal attribution or externalization, which refer to the referencing our perceptions to an external space beyond the limits of the sensory organs themselves (Loomis, 1992).

In unmediated perception, presence is taken for granted—what could one experience other than one's immediate physical surroundings? However, when perception is mediated by a communication technology, one is forced

---

[4]*Presence,* as used here, refers to the experience of natural surroundings; that is, surroundings in which sensoiry input impinges directly upon the organs of sense. The term is also sometimes used to describe the mediated experience of a physical environment; this is further discussed later in this chapter.

to perceive two separate environments simultaneously: the physical environment in which one is actually present, and the environment presented via the medium.[5] The term *telepresence* can be used to describe the precedence of the latter experience in favor of the former; that is, telepresence is the extent to which one feels present in the mediated environment, rather than in the immediate physical environment. *Telepresence* is defined as the experience of presence in an environment by means of a communication medium.

In other words, *presence* refers to the natural perception of an environment, and *telepresence* refers to the mediated perception of an environment. This environment can be either a temporally or spatially distant "real" environment (for instance, a distant space viewed through a video camera), or an animated but nonexistent virtual world synthesized by a computer (e.g., the animated "world" created in a video game).

Reeves (1991), in a discussion of responses to television, described this experience as a sense of "being there." He claimed that a combination of automatic perceptual processes, mindful direction of attention, and conscious processes such as narratization all contribute toward our perceiving mediated experiences as if they are real.[6] Others have also constructed taxonomies for examining mediated experience. Shapiro and McDonald (this volume) differentiate between reconstructed reality, which is created in individuals based on accumulated data from mediated presentations or memories of events, and constructed reality, which focuses on how individuals accept mediated presentations of events as real. Heeter (1992) described three distinct types of presence that contribute to the experience of "being there": subjective personal presence, social presence, and personal presence. Robinett (1992) drew a similar distinction between real (unmedia-

---

[5]For the purposes of this chapter, a *communication technology* can be defined as any means of representing information across space or across time. *Mediated communication* and *mediated experience* are therefore considered to be essentially equivalent. Again, this is a very broad definition that differs from many typical views.

[6]This is not to say that people are "fooled" into believing that TV or other mediated experiences are "real." However, two distinct research programs currently underway at Stanford under the general rubric Social Responses to Communication Technologies have demonstrated that in certain contexts, people respond to mediated stimuli in ways similar to their real-life counterparts. The research on "being there," led by Byron Reeves, includes a study that suggests that images of faces presented on a television screen evoke similar rules of interpersonal space as do actual faces (Reeves, Lombard, & Melwani, 1992), as well as a study to determine the effects of representing auditory and visual fidelty and spatial characteristics in engendering "real-world"-like responses from televised messages (see Reeves, Detenber, & Steuer, 1993). The Computer as Social Actor project, led by Clifford Nass, has shown that computers can evoke social responses similar to those evoked by other humans, even in situations where there is no logical explanation for such behavior (see Nass & Steuer, 1993; Nass, Steuer, Henriksen, & Dryer, 1994).

ted) and synthetic (mediated) experience in the context of discussing presence.

The use of "telepresence" to refer to any medium-induced sense of presence is similar to some, but not all, previous uses of the term. The term was coined by Marvin Minsky (1980) in reference to teleoperation systems for remote manipulation of physical objects. Sheridan and Furness (1992) continued this tradition by adopting the name Presence (rather than Telepresence) for a journal dedicated to the study of both teleoperator and virtual environment systems. In the first issue of the journal, an entire section is devoted to the concept telepresence. Sheridan (1992) used the term *presence* to refer to the generic perception of being in an artificial or remote environment, reserving *telepresence* only for cases involving teleoperation. However, in the same section of the journal, Held and Durlach (1992) used *telepresence* to refer to the experience common to both teleoperation and the experience of virtual environments. The broader term is used here in order to highlight the similarities between teleoperation and virtual environments.

By employing the concept telepresence, *virtual reality* can now be defined without reference to any particular hardware system. A *virtual reality* is defined as a real or simulated environment in which a perceiver experiences telepresence.[7]

Admittedly, this definition does not mesh precisely with typical uses of the term. Indeed, given the broad definitions of the concepts involved, this definition of virtual reality includes virtually all mediated experience. In so doing, it suggests an alternative view of mediated communication in general. Traditionally, the process of communication is described in terms of the transmission of information, as a process linking sender and receiver.[8] Media are therefore important only as a conduit, as a means of connecting sender and receiver, and are only interesting to the extent that they contribute to or otherwise interfere with transmission of message from sender to receiver. In contrast, the telepresence view focuses attention on the relationship between an individual who is both a sender and a receiver, and on the mediated environment with which he or she interacts. Information is not transmitted from sender to receiver; rather, mediated environments are created and then experienced (see Sheridan, 1992). A graphical contrast between these two views of mediated communication is shown in Fig. 3.1.

---

[7]I first encountered a similar definition of VR in a posting to the WELL computer conferencing system by Howard Rheingold, dated May 23, 1990. Rheingold's book *Virtual Reality* (1991) is an excellent survey of the history of VR.

[8]Examples of models meeting this general description can be found in DeFleur and Ball-Rokeach (1989), Schramm (1974), Shannon and Weaver (1962), or in virtually any introductory communication text.

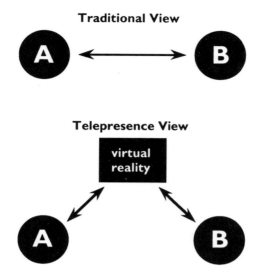

FIG. 3.1.   Two models of mediated communication (after Krueger, 1991, p. 37).

Virtual Realities and Media

Machines mentioned in previous definitions of virtual reality (computers, position sensors, head-mounted displays, etc.) are all relatively recent developments. However, the definition of VR as telepresence can be applied to past, present, and future media technologies. Consider, for example, the telephone. Most users take for granted the possibility of talking to someone who is not physically present as if they were standing in the same room.[9] But imagine this scene (adapted from the film *Being There*; Ashby & Kosinski, 1979):

> You receive your first-ever telephone call. You are handed the telephone and lift it to your ear. You hear nothing, and exclaim, "No one is there." A friend standing nearby takes the receiver, speaks into it, and hands it back to you. "Oh yes, he's there," your friend replies. You look at your friend quizzically, then point to the telephone, point to your immediate surroundings, and inquire, "Where is he? There or here?"

How can one explain the seemingly bizarre ability to speak to someone who is not present by means of talking into a piece of plastic? Of course, as

---

[9]Obviously, telephone-mediated communication is not exactly the same as face-to-face communication: Only auditory cues are provided over the telephone, and even these are very limited in terms of dynamic range and frequency spectrum. However, there is stil a sense in which the experiences are quite similar.

mentioned earlier, this process can be conceived in terms of senders, receivers, and messages. However, such an explanation fails to account for the odd experience of speaking to someone who is not actually there. Where does such a conversation take place? The most plausible conceptual model is that both parties, by means of the telephone, are electronically present in the same virtual reality created by the telephone system. A few additional examples illustrate this difference with respect to a number of different media:

- Reading a letter from a distant friend or colleague can evoke a sense of presence in the environment in which the letter was written, or can make the distant party seem locally present. This feeling can occur even when one is unfamiliar with the remote physical surroundings.
- When people telephone an airline using a toll-free number to make reservations for a flight, they often ask the operator where he or she "really is." They do this because they are uncomfortable interacting in a virtual reality that has no other contextual clues, and I therefore wish to create a background into which to place the operator's character.[10]
- Users of multiple online systems (such as bulletin boards, conferencing systems, etc.) report that each system provides a distinct "sense of place."
- Listening to live recordings of music (recordings made during a performance) gives the listener a sense of presence in the room (e.g., concert hall) in which the recording was made. However, recordings made in a studio can also evoke such feelings, even though there was no single "performance" at which a listener could have been present.
- Nuclear power plant operators observe the inside of the reactor by means of a remotely mounted moveable camera, and handle radioactive chemicals by means of remotely controlled mechanical "hands."
- Video game players describe the experience of moving an animated car on the screen as "driving."

Each of these situations evokes, in some sense, a feeling of telepresence. A similar sense can be experienced via virtually any technology used in mediated communication. Newspapers, letters, and magazines place the

---

[10]For a discussion of the importance of "grounding" communication in this way, see Clark and Brennan (1992).

reader in a space in which the writer is telling a story; television places the viewer in a virtual space in which both viewer and on-screen objects are present; and video games create virtual spaces in which the game-player is an actor.

Thus, the definition of virtual reality in terms of telepresence provides a conceptual framework in which such newly developed technologies can be examined in relation to other media technologies. Furthermore, defining virtual reality in terms of telepresence alleviates the three difficulties enumerated above. First, VR refers to an experience, rather than to a machine. The definition thereby shifts the locus of VR from a particular hardware package to the perceptions of an individual. Second, this definition specifies the unit of analysis of VR—the individual—because it consists of an individual experience of presence. Thus dependent measures of VR must all be measures of individual experience, providing an obvious means of applying knowledge about perceptual processes and individual differences in determining the nature of VR. Finally, because this definition is not technology-based, it permits variation across technologies along a number of dimensions. The remainder of this chapter is dedicated to explicating virtual reality in relation to two such dimensions—vividness and interactivity.

VARIABLES PREDICTING VIRTUAL REALITY

First-person experiences of the real world represent a standard to which all mediated experiences are compared, either mindfully or otherwise: Face-to-face interaction with other humans is used as a model for all interactive communication (Durlach, 1987). The human perceptual system has been tuned through the process of evolution for the perception of real-world environments. The experience of virtual realities can be enhanced by appealing to these same perceptual mechanisms (see Reeves, 1991). However, because it is defined in terms of an individual experience of a particular kind, it is difficult to arrive at operational measures of telepresence (see Held & Durlach, 1992). Because telepresence is necessarily experienced by means of a medium of some kind, properties of the medium will also affect the perception of virtual reality. Factors influencing whether a particular mediated situation will induce a sense of telepresence include the following: the combination of sensory stimuli employed in the environment, the ways in which participants are able to interact with the environment, and the characteristics of the individual experiencing the environment. Thus, telepresence is a function of both technology and perceiver.

Variation Across Technologies

Sheridan (1992) identified five variables that contribute to inducing a sense of telepresence. Three of them are technological: the extent of sensory information, control of sensors relative to environment, and the ability to modify the physical environment (see Biocca, this volume, for a graphical depiction). The other two are task-, or context-based: task difficulty, and degree of automation. Zeltzer (1992) provided a similar matrix of variables that describe the capabilities of graphic simulation systems, which he terms autonomy (human control), interaction (real-time control), and presence (bandwidth of sensation). Naimark (1992) employed a six-category taxonomy for visually representing and reproducing experience. Robinett (1992) presented a more technically driven nine-category taxonomy to describe environments presented by head-mounted displays: causality, model source, time, space, superposition, display, sensor, action measure, and actuator.

Two major dimensions across which communication technologies vary are discussed here as determinants of telepresence. The first, *vividness,* refers to the ability of a technology to produce a sensorially rich mediated environment.[11] The second, *interactivity,* refers to the degree to which users of a medium can influence the form or content of the mediated environment. Media artist Michael Naimark (1990) referred to these same properties as *realness* and *interactivity.* Others, including Laurel (1991) and Rheingold (1991) made similar distinctions. See Fig. 3.2 for a graphical depiction of these two dimensions, and for some of the variables that contribute to each.

When considering these dimensions, one should remember that virtual realities reside in an individual's consciousness; therefore, the relative contribution of each of these dimensions to creating a sense of environmental presence will vary across individuals. Similarly, differences in the content of the mediated environment, that is, in the kinds of entities represented and in the interactions among them, will also affect the perception of presence. However, the variables vividness and interactivity refer only to the representational powers of the technology, rather than to the individual; that is, they determine properties of the stimulus that will have similar but not identical ramifications across a range of perceivers. The remainder of this section considers these two dimensions in some detail.

---

[11]Note that this definition does not make reference to resembling objects in the real world, and thereby avoids problems in describing the experience of artificial situations. For instance, how does one determine whether a unicorn in virtual reality looks like a "real-world unicorn?" By referring only to sensory richness, this definition avoids such concerns.

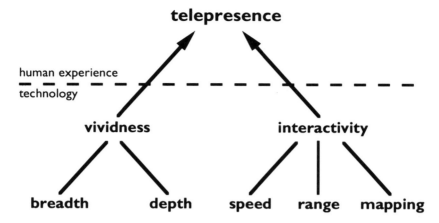

FIG. 3.2.   Technological variables influencing telepresence.

Vividness

One variable property of media technologies that influences their ability to induce a sense of presence is vividness. *Vividness* means the representational richness of a mediated environment as defined by its formal features; that is, the way in which an environment presents information to the senses.

Vividness is stimulus-driven, depending entirely on technical characteristics of a medium. Rafaeli (1985) referred to this property as "transparency" (p. 9). A highly vivid medium can be considered "hot" in the McLuhanesque (1964) sense, as it "extends one [or many] sense[s] in 'high definition.'" (p. 36). Many factors contribute to vividness. Two generalized but important variables are discussed here: sensory breadth, which refers to the number of sensory dimensions simultaneously presented, and sensory depth, which refers to the resolution within each of these perceptual channels.

Breadth is a function of the ability of a communication medium to present information across the senses. Gibson (1966) defined five distinct perceptual systems: the basic orienting system (which is responsible for maintaining body equilibrium), the auditory system, the haptic (touch) system, the taste–smell system, and the visual system. Inputs to several of these systems from a single source can be considered informationally equivalent (Gibson, 1966). However, the redundancy resulting from simultaneous activation of a number of perceptual systems reduces the number of alternative situations that could induce such a combination of perceptions, and therefore strengthens the perception of a particular environment.

This concept is best illustrated by an example. Imagine standing on a street corner in a rainstorm. Which sense is responsible for generating a sense of presence in that environment? The haptic system is activated by raindrops hitting the body—but a similar sensation could result from being sprayed by a nearby sprinkler. Similarly, the smell of a soggy dog standing nearby could result from other situations. But when these perceptions occur simultaneously with the image of raindrops falling on the streets and the buildings, the sound of the raindrops hitting the ground and the cars driving across wet pavement, and the taste of wet diesel exhaust from passing buses, a sense of being on a street corner in the rain is clearly generated. The vividness of the street corner scene is not generated by any single sensory input alone, but by the simultaneous juxtaposition of all sensory input. Often, redundant information is presented simultaneously: One hears an explosion, sees the flash, and smells the smoke simultaneously. This redundancy serves to further enhance vividness.

Traditional media such as print, telephone, television, and film are relatively low in breadth, relying primarily on the visual and auditory channels. However, some artists have attempted to expand these boundaries. Films such as Earthquake (Robson, 1974) and The Tingler (Castle, 1959) included vibrating devices attached to theater seats in order to add haptic sensation; the film Polyester (Waters, 1981) was originally presented in "Odorama"—on entering the theater, theatergoers were presented with a "scratch-and-sniff" card and were instructed to smell certain scents at appropriate points during the film. One notable early example of an attempt to provide great sensory breadth in a mediated presentation is the Sensorama device, developed by Mort Heilig (see Krueger, 1991, and Rheingold, 1991 for more detailed descriptions). This arcade game-style simulator utilizes four of the five senses to simulate a motorcycle ride: Users see the Manhattan streets go by, hear the roar of the motorcycle and the sounds of the street, smell the exhaust of other cars and pizza cooking in roadside restaurants, and feel the vibration of the handlebars. Similarly, many theme park attractions, particularly those at Walt Disney World and Disneyland, use a high degree of breadth in order to simulate a sense of presence. The addition of changes in orientation, haptic sensations, smells, and tastes, in combination with auditory and visual sensation, are particularly effective in this regard. For example, the Star Tours and Body Wars simulators combine a motion platform with multichannel sound and film to simulate space travel and a tour through the human body, respectively. Other attractions use similar means to enhance the sense of presence induced by scenes employing animated three-dimensional figures: In the Pirates of the Caribbean attraction, the smell of gunpowder is used to enhance the illusion of being in the midst of a battle; the Universe of Energy in the EPCOT Center employs heat lamps and humidifiers to simulate the experience of being among the dinosaurs; and the Spaceship Earth utilizes chemical smoke to enhance the perceived realism of sending smoke signals with a simulated campfire.

Newer media technologies have made similar efforts to augment the breadth of mediated experience (see Biocca, 1992). For instance, sound has become increasingly important in computer interface design, and new tactile-feedback controllers have been developed for use in computer-based interactive systems. Given the great attention such technologies have achieved in recent years, it seems safe to assume that substantial advances will be made in this direction in the near future.

The vividness of a particular mediated representation also depends on the depth of the sensory information available in each perceptual channel. This concept can be described in terms of "quality": an image with greater depth is generally perceived as being of higher quality than one of lesser depth; the same is true for auditory representation. Informationally, depth depends directly on the amount of data encoded and the data bandwidth of the transmission channel. In real-world perception, depth is taken for granted, as our sensory mechanisms almost always operate at full bandwidth. However, the same is not true of mediated perception. In designing media systems, sacrifices in bandwidth must always be made: No currently available auditory or visual recording systems match the capabilities of the human auditory and visual system.

For instance, in the case of the auditory system, our ability to recognize the particular sounds, such as those of different musical instruments or different voices, results from the simultaneous perception of a complex combination of amplitude and frequency cues, as well as differences in arrival time and intensity between the signals from the two ears (see Wenzel, 1992). In order to represent a sound precisely by means of a medium, all of these characteristics must be precisely recreated. However, depending on the intended purpose of a medium, this is not always necessary: The telephone system has been optimized for the transmission of comprehensible speech in the minimum possible bandwidth, and therefore utilizes only the minimum level of sound quality required for comprehensibly transmitting speech signals. Because speech perception is a direct symbolic process (Gibson, 1966), a lower bandwidth representation is sufficient for conveying content. In contrast, compact discs (CDs) have been optimized for distribution of recorded music, and thereby must be capable of representing a far wider auditory bandwidth. They therefore encode a substantially greater quantity of data, and can provide much greater depth. But neither of these systems is capable of encoding the full range of ambient and spatial information that is essential in presenting a realistic auditory representation of a space; however, both "surround-sound" systems that use loudspeakers to create an illusion of space (Dressler, 1988; Mead, 1987), and immersive, headphone-based auditory displays that present acoustic environments keyed to the motion of the wearer (Durlach et al., 1992; Wenzel, 1992) promise to extend the ability of media systems to recreate the spatial detail that is so important in inducing a sense of presence (see Blauert, 1983).

A similar tradeoff is evident in the case of television transmission. Most commercial films are shot using 35 mm film, which has a high visual resolution, in terms of both number of picture elements (pixels) per unit area, and the range of different colors that can be represented by any given pixel. Film therefore exemplifies great sensory depth. In contrast, television is technologically limited to only 525 lines of resolution (for the NTSC video standard used in the United States) regardless of screen size, and can capture a much narrower range of colors with each pixel. Television is therefore considerably lower in depth than film. The desire to bring greater sensory depth to the television image is the motivating force behind the Advanced Television (ATV) systems currently under study; however, these advantages come at great cost in terms of bandwidth requirements.[12] Various nonimmersive "three-dimensional" visual systems, including the ViewMaster, "three-dimensional" films, and holograms attempt to accurately portray a sense of depth across part of the visual field, whereas immersive visual displays such as stereoscopic head-mounted displays create a sense of presence by presenting a visual environment that moves with the viewer.

The relative contributions of breadth and depth to vividness are not constant. For example, a silent film has considerably greater image detail than does a video presentation with sound; it is therefore greater in depth but lesser in breadth. Similarly, a compact disc recording of an opera has much wider frequency bandwidth and greater dynamic range in the auditory domain than does a standard videotape of the same performance, but the videotape includes image. The simultaneous engagement of multiple perceptual systems is an extremely effective means of engendering a sense of presence, even if some stimuli are quite low in depth (as is the case in the aforementioned Disney attractions). It is likely that breadth and depth are multiplicatively related in generating a sense of presence, with each dimension serving to enhance the other; the exact nature of this interaction clearly warrants further study.

New technologies promise to expand both the sensory breadth and depth of mediated experience (see Biocca, 1992, for a review). As media technologies become more and more vivid, it is possible that we will some day have systems capable of passing a "perceptual Turing test." The ramifications of media systems whose representations are perceptually indistinguishable

---

[12]Indeed, the development of algorithms capable of compressing the huge amount of data required for the transmission of high-resolution moving pictures into a manageable bandwidth has been the primary obstacle in the development of ATV systems.

from their real-world counterparts is both exciting and terrifying — exciting because of the possibilities afforded by such systems to experience distant and nonexistent worlds, yet terrifying because of the blurring of distinction between representation and reality.

Interactivity

Communication media can also be classified in terms of interactivity. *Interactivity* is the extent to which users can participate in modifying the form and content of a mediated environment in real time.

Interactivity in this sense is distinct from engagement or involvement as these terms are frequently used by communication researchers (see Rafaeli, 1986, 1988); for the purposes of this chapter, interactivity (like vividness) is a stimulus-driven variable, and is determined by the technological structure of the medium. This definition of interactivity differs substantially from that used by most communication researchers. Consider Rafaeli's (1988) definition: "Interactivity is a variable characteristic of communication settings. Formally stated, interactivity is an expression of the extent that in a given series of communication exchanges, any third (or later) transmission (or message) is related to the degree to which previous exchanges referred to even earlier transmissions" (p. 111). The difference between Rafaeli's definition and the one offered previously is not surprising, because his definition, like others in the communication literature (see Durlak, 1987; Rafaeli, 1988), is based on the traditional view of mediated communication discussed earlier. In contrast, the definition given here is based on a telepresence view of mediated communication, and thereby focuses on properties of the mediated environment and the relationship of individuals to that environment.

Interactivity is a variable of great concern to researchers in human–computer interaction (see Heckel, 1991; Laurel, 1986, 1990, 1991; Norman, 1986, 1988; Schneiderman, 1992; Turkle, 1984). As discussed earlier, both Sheridan (1992) and Zeltzer (1992) included variables that resemble the definition of interactivity given here as part of their discussions of presence. Indeed, the definition of interactivity used here may be viewed as collapsing two of the three dimensions in each of their models — control of sensors and ability to modify environment in Sheridan's model; autonomy and interaction in Zeltzer's model — into the single dimension that includes all aspects of the perceiver's control of his or her relationship to the environment.

A limitation of defining interactivity in terms of the malleability of a medium's form and content is that such a definition does not include control over how the medium can be experienced. Thus, a book, which cannot be changed easily in real time without cutting it apart, is not considered interactive, though one can certainly read a book interactively, jumping at will from page to page and from chapter to chapter. Conversely, a laserdisc system that includes programming that enables a user to control the order in which its content is presented in real time is considered somewhat interactive, because the medium itself can change, and both a position-sensing head-mounted display controlling a computer-generated graphical environment in real time and a text-based multiuser dungeon (MUDs, see Bruckman, 1992; Rheingold, 1993) that allows physically distant participants to interact with each other are considered quite interactive. Most traditional media systems are not particularly interactive in this sense: Interaction with a newspaper is possible only by writing letters to the editor or by writing stories for inclusion; call-in shows and request lines provide the only means of interaction with radio; most paintings are not interactive at all.

Three factors that contribute to interactivity are examined here (although many others are also important): *speed,* which refers to the rate at which input can be assimilated into the mediated environment; *range,* which refers to the number of possibilities for action at any given time; and *mapping,* which refers to the ability of a system to map its controls to changes in the mediated environment in a natural and predictable manner.

Speed of interaction, or response time, is one important characteristic of an interactive media system. Real-time interaction clearly represents the highest possible value for this variable: The actions of a user instantaneously alter the mediated environment. Many new media attempt to reach this level of interactivity, thereby enabling mediated experience to substitute for or amplify perception of the world in real time. This immediacy of response is one of the properties that makes even low-resolution video games seem highly vivid. Computerized virtual-world systems using "goggles 'n' gloves" also seem highly interactive, as they attempt to map user actions to actions in the virtual environment in real time (though some delay is still common). The telephone permits such real-time interaction between two parties (three or more in the case of a conference call); teleconferencing systems and groupware computer applications similarly extend real-time interactivity to multiple users and multiple modalities. Other media systems permit less immediate interaction: Films, like books, allow no interaction at all (a long time!); an answering machine allows messages to be left and retrieved at a later time, but offers no indication of how long the intervening interval may be; and computer conferencing systems permit nearly instantaneous interaction, requiring users only to finish typing a message before sending it. Both MUDs and online "chat" systems (such as Internet Relay Chat and the "chat rooms" on commercial online services) expand this level of interactivity to include 30 or more simultaneous users.

The range of interactivity is determined by the number of attributes of the mediated environment that can be manipulated, and the amount of variation possible within each attribute. In other words, range refers to the amount of change that can be effected on the mediated environment. The specific dimensions that can be modified depend on the characteristics of the particular medium, but include temporal ordering (discussed later), spatial organization (where objects appear), intensity (loudness of sounds, brightness of images, intensity of smells), and various frequency characteristics (timbre, color). The greater the number of parameters that can be modified, the greater the range of interactivity of a given medium. Video-based systems, listed here by increasing range, provide a good set of examples along which a subdimension of range, temporal ordering, can vary:[13] A television broadcast permits a very small number of possible actions at a given instant, because a particular program is either on or off (continuous play). A program recorded on videotape can be paused at any time (start–stop), and portions may be skipped or repeated at the whim of the viewer (search). An interactive laserdisc augments these capabilities by allowing random-access jumps to any portion of the program in a matter of seconds. A computer-based animation system actually can permit interaction with objects in the mediated environment (rather than with the environment as a whole) in real time.

Mapping refers to the way in which human actions are connected to actions within a mediated environment (see Norman, 1986, 1988). At one extreme, these mappings can be completely arbitrary and unrelated to the function performed. For instance, wiggling one's left toe might increase the loudness of sound from the television speaker, or typing arbitrary commands into a computer might shift the perspective of the image in a head-mounted display. At the other end of the spectrum, mapping may be completely natural: Turning a steering wheel on an arcade video game might make the "virtual car" on the screen move accordingly, or mimicking the action of throwing a ball while wearing a glove controller might initiate the throwing of a "virtual ball." Mapping is thus a function of both the types of controllers used to interact with a mediated environment, and the ways in which the actions of these controllers are connected to actions within that environment. In situations in which action in a mediated environment has a direct real-world counterpart, such as with the aforementioned automobile and baseball examples, the appropriate mapping strategy should match the natural action as closely as possible. In other cases, appropriate use of metaphor can help match controller and controlled: For example, the Apple Macintosh computer uses a "desktop metaphor" for organizing its file system (see Erickson, 1990); the "jog-

---

[13]Of course, each of these media also has a range of interactivity across many other dimensions, such as image brightness, contrast, color, hue, and so forth. However, the technologies listed do not differ in this regard.

shuttle" motion—control wheel found on many VCRs uses a directional metaphor for mapping hand controls to tape motion—twisting one way moves forward, the other backward, and the amount of twist determines the shuttle speed. In some cases, a completely arbitrary system must be learned, such as is the case with the QWERTY layout of most typewriter and computer keyboards. However, even an arbitrary but standardized mapping system is better than no system at all, because such a system need be learned only once.

Because our perceptual systems are optimized for interactions with the "real world," mapping is generally increased by adapting controllers to the human body. Many such controllers are now under development (see Biocca, 1992); speech-recognition systems and gloves epitomize such designs. As these and other technologies become more advanced, the mapping of controller actions to actions in mediated environments is likely to become increasingly natural.

Variation Across Individuals

If virtual reality is defined in terms of telepresence, then its locus is the perceiver. Under this definition, virtual reality refers only to those perceptions of telepresence induced by a communication medium. Therefore, virtual reality can be distinguished from both purely psychic phenomena (such as dreams or hallucinations), because these experiences require no perceptual input at all, and from the "real" reality as experienced via our unaided perceptual hardware, because virtual realities (unlike real realities) can be experienced only through a medium.

The number of actors present in a virtual world can also affect the perception of telepresence. Because humans are well accustomed to interacting with other humans in the real world, the apparent presence of others in virtual worlds should enhance the experience of telepresence. Although virtual reality refers to individual experience, multiple individuals can experience similar virtual realities by sharing the same virtual space, either electronically or through other technological means. This process occurs over a wide range of technologies: in electronic bulletin board systems (BBSs), conferencing systems, and MUDs, by means of text, in teleconferencing systems by means of video, and in movie theaters, by simultaneously bringing everyone in the theater into the same projected world.

Both immediate situational factors and ongoing personal concerns (referred to as background by Winograd & Flores, 1986) are important in determining the extent of telepresence. These factors also interact with the vividness and interactivity of the medium itself: The relative importance of each input modality varies from situation to situation. Consider the earlier example involving standing on a street corner in the rain: Which sensory input is most important in generating the impression of being present on the street corner? The answer depends on the particular individual. If a friend is waving from across the street, then sight is most important; however, if he or she is yelling rather than waving, then hearing is most important. An asthmatic might rely on smell to identify situations in which breathing problems might arise, whereas touch is most important to the Wicked Witch, who must seek shelter or melt in the rain. Situational characteristics are also important: A low-flying jet aircraft renders the auditory channel temporarily useless for attracting attention, a city bus similarly blocks vision, and an oxygen mask or raincoat could help the asthmatic or the witch.

Laurel (1986, 1990, 1991) emphasized the experiential nature of our interaction with media technologies.[14] Laurel described media use in terms of mimesis (a form of artistic imitation typically applied in dramatic contexts), likened the relationship between user and technology to action in a play, and emphasized the importance of encouraging the user of a technology to develop a first-person, rather than third-person, relationship with his or her mediated environment. Engagement, which Laurel (1991) described as a primarily emotional state with cognitive components, serves as a critical factor in engendering a feeling of first-personness (p. 113). Engagement was likened to what poet Samuel Taylor Coleridge called the "willing suspension of disbelief":

> Coleridge believed that any idiot could see that a play on stage was not real life. (Plato would have disagreed with him, as do those in whom fear is induced by any new representational medium, but that is another story.) Coleridge noticed that, in order to enjoy a play, we must temporarily suspend (or attenuate) our knowledge that it is "pretend." We do this "willingly" in order to experience other emotional responses as a result of viewing the action. . . . The phenomenon that Coleridge described can be seen to occur almost identically in computer games, where we feel for and with the characters (including ourselves as characters) in very similar ways. (Laurel, 1991, p. 113)

This willingness to interpret mediated experiences as if they are veridical results from a complex interaction among factors including both the conscious desire to "let oneself go," and less mindful processes entailed by the formal characteristics of the medium itself (see Reeves, 1991) and by the social content of that environment (see Nass & Steuer, 1993; Nass, Steuer,

---

[14]Although Laurel explicitly discussed human–computer interface design, most of her points are equally applicable to other media as well. Indeed, what makes her writing fascinating is the extent to which her concepts apply across media.

Henriksen, & Dryer, 1994). This process is of great interest in the context of all kinds of mediated experience; however, further discussion is beyond the scope of this chapter.

DIMENSIONS AND MEDIA

Media systems that are both highly vivid and highly interactive are not yet widely available. Indeed, video games are the closest most people have come to such systems. So too, media systems that allow individuals to interact with each other in natural ways within virtual environments are not yet common, nor are systems that can represent the seemingly infinite range of sensory raw materials present in the real world. However, systems that rate high on both dimensions are quite common in science fiction: The Holodeck on "Star Trek: The Next Generation" provides real-time interactive multisensory simulations, as does the nursery in Bradbury's short story *The Veldt* (1951). Cyberspace, an electronic realm conceived by science fiction author William Gibson (1984), provides a somewhat different vision of an interactive multisensory environment. Cyberspace encompasses both real and synthesized realities as a unified matrix of data, and is experienced by jacking in one's nervous system directly to the mediated world by means of special hardware. Thus, unlike traditional mediated experience, cyberspace bypasses the sense organs completely, presenting its stimuli directly to the perceptual systems in the brain, thereby presumably maximizing both sensory breadth and depth. Gibson delineated the experience of cyberspace from another, noninteractive medium called simstim, which is also experienced via direct neural interface, but permits only passive experience (much like television).

Figure 3.3 classifies a wide range of media technologies, both real and fictional, in terms of vividness and interactivity.[15] In considering this chart, it is interesting to note both the areas that are covered by technologies that are currently present, and the areas that remain blank, for which the appropriate technologies have not yet been developed.

Because the dimensions discussed here depend on a wide variety of independent variables, the exact relationship between these properties and the experience of telepresence (a dependent variable) is a matter for empirical study (although many hypotheses can be generated). It seems that vividness and interactivity are both positively related to telepresence; that is,

---

[15]Because interactivity and vividness are such rich concepts, some of the placements are somewhat arbitrary, as they result from differences between media across many different dimensions.

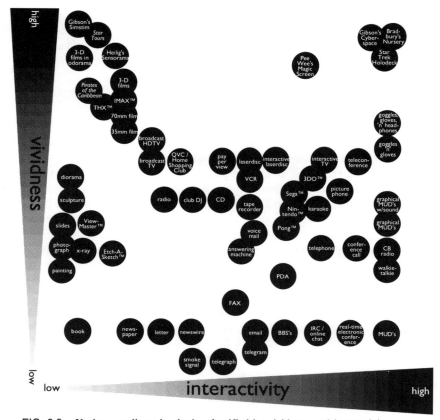

FIG. 3.3.   Various media technologies classified by vividness and interactivity.

the more vivid and the more interactive a particular environment is, the greater the sense of presence evoked by that environment. However, these predictions may not always hold, and may be dependent on other mitigating factors. For example, as McLuhan (1964) predicted, an extremely "hot" medium (one designed to maximize vividness) may actually decrease the ability of subjects to mindfully interact with it in real time. This may be a result of limitations on cognitive processing power available in the perceiver: Rapid-fire, high bandwidth, multisensory stimulation might engage such a great portion of the brain's cognitive capacity that none is left for more mindful processes (see Lang, 1992; Reeves, Detenber, & Steuer, 1993).

COMMUNICATION RESEARCH AND VIRTUAL REALITY

Many studies regarding media content and individual factors contributing to mediated perception have been performed in the field of communication.

6owever, few studies explicitly address interactivity, vividness, or similar variables. Quite a bit of research on interactivity has been done in the field of human–computer interaction, but as noted by Rafaeli (1985, 1988), interactivity research has been sorely neglected by communication researchers. Similarly, most of the research on vividness has been technology-oriented, in order to determine whether the cost of implementing a particular technological improvement is warranted by users' increased "liking" (see McFarlane, 1991, and Neuman, Crigler, Schneider, O'Donnel, & Reynolds, 1987, for examples of such studies; see Reeves, Detenber, & Steuer, 1993, for one counterexample). Thus, the precise ramifications of these variables and others like them are largely unknown.

Progressively more advanced media technologies will enhance the sense of telepresence in a wide variety of virtual realities. Rapid advances in both multimedia computer technologies and in high-speed data networks hasten the development of a truly global village, in which our ability to interact with friends, family, and others who share interests similiar to our own will no longer be limited by physical proximity. Such "virtual communities" represent one of the most exciting aspects of these developing new media, as they offer individuals a method for participation in, rather than mere observation of, the mediated worlds that surround them. The Internet, commercial online services, and BBSs have already begun to offer the interactive capabilities required for such communities to form on a large scale.[16] The development of increasingly vivid media is likely to further expand these possibilities, although the exact nature of the effects of these changes on the characteristics of interpersonal interactions in these virtual realities remains an open (and fascinating) empirical question.

New media may greatly expand the ability to experience telepresence in virtual realities; however, these new developments are also certain to enhance the possibilities for using the media to manipulate and control beliefs and opinions. Furthermore, as an increasing proportion of most individuals' experiences come via mediated rather than direct sources, the potentially detrimental effects of such manipulation increase exponentially. Regardless of the particular medium used, be it telephone, electronic mail, online chat system, computer-video conferencing, or immersive virtual reality, all mediated interactions fall within the domain of communication research. Indeed, communication researchers are uniquely suited to address the perceptual, technological, and social issues surrounding new media technologies before they become problematic by building upon the lessons learned through the study of earlier media. Rather than relying on engineers in laboratories to design the media systems of the future and then waiting

---

[16]See Rheingold (1993), for a ground-breaking in-depth discussion of virtual communities and the factors underlying their formation.

for media behemoths to implement and distribute these new media, communication researchers have a responsibility to respond proactively by using what they have learned about people and media to study the concepts related to these developments, to make predictions about their possible effects, and to become involved in the design and implementation of new media systems before they are institutionalized. Rather than waiting for media industries to develop new offerings to be studied post hoc, researchers should be prepared to address general variables and to look across media while their work can still have significant impact on design and development of new media. It is hoped that the definitions and dimensions described here will facilitate the study of virtual realities in this way.

ACKNOWLEDGMENTS

This chapter was originally published under the same title in *Journal of Communication, 42*(4), 73–93. Copyright 1992, International Communication Association, Oxford University Press. Used with permission.

The author wishes to express his gratitude to Clifford Nass for his invaluable assistance with this chapter. Thanks also to Henry Breitrose, Jennifer Cool, Benjamin Detenber, Gens Johnson, Shari Levine, Matthew Lombard, Geetu Melwani, Dave Voelker, and many others who have read and commented on various drafts for their insightful and thought-provoking comments, and to Lisa Seaman for her design assistance with Fig. 3.3. Finally, thanks to Byron Reeves, whose interest in the idea of "being there" helped to motivate this discussion.

REFERENCES

Ashby, H. (Director), & Kosinski, J. (Screenwriter). (1979). *Being there* [Film]. Los Angeles: Northstar International Pictures.

Beniger, J. R. (1986). *The control revolution.* Cambridge, MA: Harvard University Press.

Biocca, F. (1992). Virtual reality technology: A tutorial. *Journal of Communication, 42*(4), 23–72.

Blauert, J. (1983). *Spatial hearing: The psychophysics of human sound localization.* Cambridge, MA: MIT Press.

Bradbury, R. (1951). The veldt. In *The illustrated man.* Garden City, NY: Doubleday.

Bruckman, A. S. (1992). *Identity workshop: Emergent social and psychological phenomena in text-based virtual reality.* Cambridge, MA: MIT Media Laboratory.

Castle, W. (Director). (1959). *The tingler* [Film]. Duluth, GA: Colombia Pictures.

Clark, H. H., & Brennan, S. E. (1991). Grounding in communication. In L. B. Resnick, J. M. Levine, & S. D. Teasley (Eds.). *Perspectives on socially shared cognition* (pp. 127–149). Washington, DC: APA Books.

Coates, G. (1992, March). *Program from Invisible Site—a virtual sho.* A multimedia performance work presented by George Coates Performance Works, San Francisco, CA.

DeFleur, M., & Ball-Rokeach, S. (1989). *Theories of mass communication* (5th ed.). New York: Longman.

Dressler, R. (1988). *Dolby pro logic surround decoder: Principles of operation.* San Francisco, CA: Dolby Laboratories.

Durlak, J. T. (1987). A typology for interactive media. In M. L. McLaughlin (Ed.), *Communication yearbook 10.* Newbury Park, CA: Sage.

Durlach, N. I., Rigopolus, A., Pang, X. D., Woods, W. S., Kulkarni, A., Colburn, H. S., & Wenzel, W. E. (1992). On the externalization of auditory images. *Presence: Teleoperators and Virtual Environments, 1*(2), 251–257.

Erickson, T. D. (1990). Working with interface metaphors. In B. Laurel (Ed.), *The art of human-computer interface design* (pp. 65–74). Reading, MA: Addison-Wesley.

Gibson, J. J. (1966). *The senses considered as perceptual systems.* Boston: Houghton Mifflin.

Gibson, J. J. (1979). *The ecological approach to visual perception.* Boston: Houghton Mifflin.

Gibson, W. (1984). *Neuromancer.* New York: Ace Books.

Greenbaum, P. (1992). The lawnmower man. *Film and Video, 9*(3), 58–62.

Heckel, P. (1991). *The elements of friendly software design.* Alameda, CA: SYBEX.

Heeter, C. (1992). Being there: The subjective experience of presence. *Presence: Teleoperators and Virtual Environments, 1*(2), 262–271.

Held, R. M., & Durlach, N. I. (1992). Telepresence. *Presence: Teleoperators and Virtual Environments, 1*(1), 102–112.

Krueger, M. W. (1991). *Artificial reality* (2nd ed.). Reading, MA: Addison-Wesley.

Krueger, M. W. (1990). VIDEOPLACE and the interface of the future. In B. Laurel (Ed.), *The art of human-computer interface design* (pp. 417–422). Reading, MA: Addison-Wesley.

Lang, A. (1992, May). *A limited capacity theory of television viewing.* Paper presented at the conference of the International Communication Association, Miami, FL, May.

Laurel, B. (1986). Interface as mimesis. In D. N. Norman & S. W. Draper (Eds.), *User-centered system design* (pp. 67–86). Hillsdale, NJ: Lawrence Erlbaum Associates.

Laurel, B. (Ed.) (1990). *The art of human-computer interface design.* Reading, MA: Addison-Wesley.

Laurel, B. (1991). *Computers as theatre.* Reading, MA: Addison-Wesley.

Loomis, J. M. (1992). Distal attribution and presence. *Presence: Teleoperators and Virtual Environments, 1*(1), 113–119.

Mead, W. (1987). *Multi-dimensional audio for stereo television.* San Francisco, CA: Dolby Laboratories.

McFarlane, C. (1991). *Should the CBC be going into MTS stereo: The results of a research project testing reactions to mono, synthetic stereo, and stereo television.* Unpublished manuscript, CBC Research, Ottawa, Canada.

McLuhan, M. (1964). *Understanding media: The extensions of man.* New York: Penguin.

Minsky, M. (1980, June). Telepresence. *Omni,* pp. 45–51.

Naimark, M. (1990). Realness and interactivity. In B. Laurel (Ed.), The art of human-computer interface design (pp. 455–459). Reading, MA: Addison-Wesley.

Naimark, M. (1992). *Elements of realspace imaging* (Apple Multimedia Lab Tech. Rep.). Cupertino, CA: Apple Computer.

Nass, C., & Mason, L. (1990). On the study of technology and task: A variable-based approach. In J. Fulk & C. Steinfeld (Eds.), *Organizations and communication technology* (pp. 46–67). Newbury Park, CA: Sage.

Nass, C., & Steuer, J. (1993). Computers, voices, and sources of evaluation. *Human Communication Research, 19*(4), 504–527.

Nass, C., Steuer, J., Henriksen, L., & Dryer, D. C. (1994). Machines, social attributions, and ethopoeia: Performance assessments of computers subsequent to "self-" or "other-" evaluations. *International Journal of Human-Computer Studies, 40,* 543–559.

Neuman, W. R., Crigler, A., Schneider, S. M., O'Donnel, S., & Reynolds, M. (1987). *The television sound study.* Unpublished manuscript, Massachusetts Institute of Technology, Media Laboratory, Advanced Television Research Program, Audience Research Facility, Cambridge, MA.

Norman, D. N. (1986). Cognitive engineering. In D. N. Norman & S. W. Draper (Eds.), *User-centered system design* (pp. 31–61). Hillsdale, NJ: Lawrence Erlbaum Associates.

Norman, D. N. (1988). *The design of everyday things.* New York: Doubleday.

Rafaeli, S. (1985, May). *If the computer is the medium, what is the message?: Exploring interactivity.* Paper presented at the conference of the International Communication Association, Honolulu, HI.

Rafaeli, S. (1986). *Interactivity: Do computers do it differently?* Unpublished manuscript, Stanford University, Institute for Communication Research, Stanford, CA.

Rafaeli, S. (1988). Interactivity: From new media to communication. In R. P. Hawkins, J. M. Wieman, & S. Pingree (Eds.), *Advancing communication science: Merging mass and interpersonal processes* (pp. 110–134). Newbury Park, CA: Sage.

Reeves, B. R. (1991). *"Being there:" Television as symbolic versus natural experience.* Unpublished manuscript, Stanford University, Institute for Communication Research, Stanford, CA.

Reeves, B. R., Detenber, B., & Steuer, J. (1993, May). *New televisions: The effects of big pictures and big sound on viewer responses to the screen.* Paper presented at the conference of the International Communication Association, Washington, DC.

Reeves, B. R., Lombard, M. L., & Melwani, G. (1992, May). *Faces on the screen: Pictures or natural experience?* Paper presented at the conference of the International Communication Association, Miami, FL.

Rheingold, H. R. (1991). *Virtual reality.* New York: Summit Books.

Rheingold, H. R. (1993). *The virtual community: Homesteading on the electronic frontier.* New York: Addison-Wesley.

Robinett, W. (1992). Synthetic experience: A proposed taxonomy. *Presence: Teleoperators and Virtual Environments, 1*(2), 229–247.

Robson, M. (Director). (1974). *Earthquake* [Film].

Schramm, W. (1974). The nature of communication between humans. In W. Schramm & D. F. Roberts (Eds.). *The process and effects of mass communication* (3rd ed., pp. 3–53). Urbana, IL: University of Illinois Press.

Shannon, C., & Weaver, W. (1962). *The mathematical theory of communication.* Urbana, IL: University of Illinois Press.

Sheridan, T. B. (1992). Musings on telepresence and virtual presence. *Presence: Teleoperators and Virtual Environments, 1*(1), 120–126.

Sheridan, T. B., & Furness, T. A. (Eds.). (1992). *Presence: Teleoperators and virtual environments.* Cambridge, MA: MIT Press.

Shneiderman, B. (1992). *Designing the user interface: Strategies for effective human-computer interaction* (2nd ed.). Reading, MA: Addison-Wesley.

Turkle, S. (1984). *The second self: Computers and the human spirit.* New York: Simon & Schuster.

Waters, J. (Director). (1981). *Polyester* [Film]. Los Angeles: New Line Cinema.

Wenzel, E. M. (1992). Localization in virtual acoustic displays. *Presence: Teleoperators and Virtual Environments, 1*(1), 80–107.

Winograd, T., & Flores, C. (1986). *Understanding computers and cognition: A new foundation for design.* Reading, MA: Addison-Wesley.

Zeltzer, D. (1992). autonomy, interaction, and presence. *Presence: Teleoperators and Virtual Environments, 1*(1), 127–132.

4 Immersive Virtual Reality Technology

Frank Biocca
University of North Carolina

Ben Delaney
CyberEdge Journal

This chapter steps inside virtual reality (VR) to examine the technology that makes this novel interface possible. In chapter 1 of this volume, Biocca and Levy defined communication interfaces as:

Communication Interface = (physical media, communication codes, information) + sensorimotor channels (see Fig. 4.1.).

In this chapter we pick up each component of the "physical media," examine it, describe how it works, and suggest how it might evolve. The emphasis is on trends in the development of VR's physical media.

VR technology takes many forms. Like the computer itself, it is a protean technology. There will be no single type of VR system and no paradigmatic virtual environment. We are more likely to see tailored combinations of components and applications, each capable of producing various levels of sensory experience. Table 4.1 lists the more common types of virtual environments. This chapter focuses on the last and most sensory-immersive type of virtual environment technology.

Figure 4.2 shows a classic system first built for NASA and presents an array of components characteristic of highly *immersive*[1] systems. These highly immersive systems tend to envelop the senses with computer-generated stimuli. The components are discussed later, but for now we should describe virtual reality technology as a whole.

---

[1] *Immersive* is a term that refers to the degree to which a virtual environment submerges the perceptual system of the user in computer-generated stimuli. The more the system capivates the senses and blocks out stimuli from the physical world, the more the system is considered immersive.

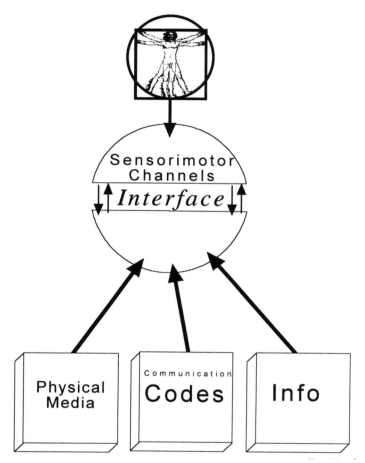

FIG. 4.1. Communications interfaces can be defined as interaction of the physical media, codes, and information with the sensorimotor channels of the user. In an interactive interface like virtual realityd, information/sensation is exchanged (input and output) across the boundaries of the interface.

PSYCHOLOGY IS THE PHYSICS OF VIRTUAL REALITY

William Bricken captured the essence of VR when he pithily pronounced: "Psychology is the physics of virtual reality" (quoted in Wooley, 1992, p. 21). Virtual worlds are constructed by the senses and only really exist in the minds of users.

VR is a medium for the extension of body and mind. McLuhan (1966; McLuhan & McLuhan, 1988) would surely smile upon such a definition. The technology is designed to serve the needs of the users' sensorimotor channels: our eyes, ears, hands, and so forth. Each sensory channel "expects" informatiom in a certain way. The needs and demands of our

TABLE 4.1
A Classification of Virtual Reality Systems[1]

Types	Description[2]
Window systems	A computer screen provides a window or portal onto an interactive, 3-D virtual world. Desktop computers are often used and users sometimes wear 3-D glasses for stereoscopic effects.
Mirror systems	The users look at a projection screen and see an image of themselves moving in a virtual world. Video equipment is used to record the user's body. A computer superimposes a cut-out image on a computer graphic background. The cut-out images of themselves on the screen mirrors their movements, hence the name *mirror systems*.
Vehicle-based systems	The users enter what appears to be vehicle (e.g., tank, plane, car, space ship, etc.) and operate controls that simulate movement in the virtual world. The world is most often projected on screens. The vehicles may include motion platforms to simulate physical movement.
Cave systems	Users enter a room or enclosure where they are surrounded by large screens that project a nearly continuous virtual scene. 3-D glasses are sometimes used to enhance the sense of space.
Immersive virtual reality systems	Users wear displays that fully immerse a number of the senses in computer generated stimuli. The stereoscopic head-mounted displays (HMD) are a distinctive feature of such systems.
Augmented reality systems	Users wear a visual display (e.g., transmissive HMD) that superimposes 3-D virtual objects on real-world scenes.

[1]Adapted from a classification used by Louis Brill at Virtual Reality '93, San Francisco.
[2]All true virtual reality displays are normally responsive to user action, especially physical movement.

"expects" information in a certain way. The needs and demands of our senses play a major role in determining the value, quality, and utility of a component. Therefore, each physical component is judged on how well it matches the properties of the sensorimotor channel it serves. The technology's effect on human perception and cognition defines the value of VR. Even when our attention turns to a discussion of the "nuts and bolts" of each component, intriguing psychological and epistemological questions inevitably emerge (e.g., Loomis, 1992). As we see here, the design of virtual reality hardware and software is inevitably an exploration of how we see, hear, move, touch, smell, and—most of all—think.

For some researchers active in the development of this medium, the ultimate goals of the technology are nothing short of the amplification of human perception, cognition, and even intelligence (e.g., Brooks, 1977, 1988; Furness, 1988, 1989; Krueger, 1991; Lanier & Biocca, 1992; Rheingold, 1991). Although similar goals can be found in the development of the computer (Englebart, 1962) and of much older media (e.g., Biocca, 1987, 1988b; Czitrom, 1982), no medium in history has been so self-consciously designed as an extension of our senses. According to Warren

FIG. 4.2.   A picture of a classic virtual reality system produced for NASA. Providing rich multisensory environments, versions of this technology are emerging as the platform for a general-purpose communication medium. Visible components include a head-mounted display (output), data gloves (input), "Convolvotron" 3-D audio system (output, headphones only), and magnetic position trackers (input, sensors only). Courtesy of NASA Ames Research Center.

Robinette, a key designer who worked on NASA's and the University of North Carolina's VR systems, "The electronic expansion of human perception has, as its manifest destiny, to cover the entire human sensorium" (Robinett, 1991, p. 19).

But the promise is not yet proven. At the time of this writing, virtual reality technology still has the look and feel of a prototype, a jumble of wires, LCDs and artful technical compromises (Brooks, 1988), just a portal looking out on a more mature technology to come. These improvised introductory systems remind us of the very early television set, a low-resolution array of black and white lines barely sketching a snow-spotted image. Just as with the early television sets, the image of a new, radically different communication technology is visible. Inside the low-resolution head-mounted displays we can barely see the outlines of a new way to produce and experience mediated information. When fully implemented and diffused, the medium could be the catalyst for a revolutionary change in the way we communicate. At least, this is the vision.

THE DEVELOPMENTAL LOGIC OF THE VR INTERFACES

Considered as a system, the technology can be said to possess a *developmental logic* that circumscribes the various versions of virtual reality. This logic is a set of goals for the future of the technology. Looking at the limitations of video monitors back in 1965, an inventive computer scientist named Ivan Sutherland (1965), an often cited pioneer of virtual reality technology, issued this challenge: "The screen is a window through which one sees a virtual world. The challenge is to make that world look real, act real, sound real, feel real" (p. 507).

His challenge has since become the research agenda for a rapidly growing community of researchers and industries. The long-term developmental goal of the technology is nothing short of an attempt to have our perceptual systems accept the reality of a computer-generated illusion, "to fool eye and mind into seeing . . . worlds that are not and never can be" (Brooks, 1988, p. 1). According to Nat Durlach of MIT, the development of the technology involves solving "questions about how you can map human perception onto virtual worlds" (quoted in Rheingold, 1991, p. 389).

The mapping of mediated information to the needs of our perceptual systems is psychologically complex. NASA VR scientist Stephen Ellis reminded us that the sense of physical reality is "a consequence of internal processing rather than being something that is developed only from the immediate sensory information we receive" (Ellis, 1991, p. 323). Therefore, the successful creation of perceptually engaging virtual environments "depends on the extent to which all of these constructive processes are triggered" (Ellis, 1991, p. 323). The medium provides the cues to trigger the psychological constructive processes of the user. An array of light on a visual display becomes a lush landscape in the mind of the viewer.

The Search for Presence

The strong perceptual illusion sought is often referred to as an engaging sense of *presence*. The word *presence* immediately suggests that the user will have sensations of being present in an environment, and will perceive objects found there as equally present. The process of creating a strong sense of presence begins by coupling the sensory organs of the user to the output devices of the computer. The output devices are orchestrated by one or more computers to generate a convincing simulation of the look, feel, and sound of another environment: a virtual reality. The eyes, ears, hands, and proprioceptive senses receive electromechanical stimuli that attempt to simulate a world pressing upon the senses. Some of the perceptual illusions used are as old as perspective drawing, some are as new as an electrotactile illusion of virtual sandpaper.

It is fitting that the word *presence* proposes not a goal but a destination, a psychological place, a virtual location. *Presence* has been enshrined as the name of a new journal devoted to virtual environments. Although some skeptics doubt that the medium can achieve anything more than a schematized "virtual surreality" (Dennett, 1991, p. 6), it is likely that a strong illusory presence is only the last stop on a long trip to come. Presence is a construct, a variable with various levels and dimensions. Few are under the illusion that the technology can ever pass some Turing test of reality. But even the imperfect illusions of presence might appear so convincing in their perceptual realism that they may influence the reactions and behaviors of users (Shapiro & MacDonald, this volume).

In an attempt to define the illusive destination of virtual reality technology, MIT's Sheridan (1992) placed the concept of presence on a continuum (see Fig. 4.3), a matrix defined by three axes: (a) the extent of sensory information, (b) the control of sensors, and (c) the ability to modify the environment. On a vertex of this matrix, Sutherland's vision becomes a point called "perfect presence," a phrase that curiously suggests a religious state rather than a technical goal. It is perhaps telling of the state of the art that in Sheridan's diagram the arrows extend beyond the limits of the matrix, suggesting that the technical search for "perfect presence" will

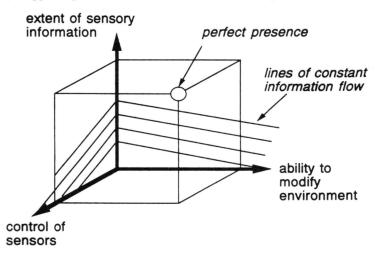

FIG. 4.3.   The principle components of the sense of presence. From Sheridan (1992). Reprinted by permission.

always be outside the grasp of the technology, although the sense of presence may steadily increase.

Immersing the Sensorimotor Channels

"In 1969 I reasoned that the ultimate computer interface would be to the human body and its senses," said Myron Krueger, VR pioneer (1993, p. 363). Another defining goal in the developmental logic of virtual environments is the attempt to turn the whole body of the user into an input device (Krueger, 1991). As Sheridan (1992) suggested, the user's control of the sensors and ability to modify the environment are essential to a strong sense of presence. Body movements, eye movements, facial expressions, and even unconscious physiological processes may be attached to the sensors of the computer.

In virtual environments the computer makes use of the natural way we interact with the physical world. Intuitive movements and actions become computer commands. All kinds of conscious and unconscious bodily movements or changes of state, such as heartbeat or diastolic blood pressure, are potential computer input. The intent of all this input is to sensitize the computer to the user, to turn every movement into a creative tool and a means of communication. Some propose to use neural impulses themselves (microelectrical) to drive the computer.[2] Like a foot on an accelerator pedal, small physical movements can be linked to large movements or effects. The goal is a computer interface that is fully responsive to actions of the user.

The current virtual reality systems may have already crossed a threshold. It is a psychological threshold, a point at which our perceptual systems are so immersed in the simulation that the user already begins to feel some of the sense of "being there,"[3] the early flushes of a powerful presence. Virtual reality technology can be defined as the sum of the hardware and software systems that seek to perfect an all-inclusive, immersive, sensory illusion of being present in another environment, another reality; a virtual reality.

Viewing older technologies through McLuhan's (1966) "rear-view mirror," virtual environments are the latest development in the evolution of media technology and techniques toward greater perceptual verisimilitude. Past media have sought to refine the perceptual illusions within each

---

[2]BioControl Systems (Palo Alto, CA) has released commercial products that use the electrical signals from the nerves that move the eyes to provide input for computerized devices. Other systems they have developed combine these signals with the myoelectrical signals generated by muscle movement, even movement too slight to actually cause visible motion.

[3]I am grateful to Byron Reeves' discussion of his concept of "being there" and the evolution of media technologies.

sensory channel. For example, we can trace the evolution of illusions in visual media from perspective painting, to photography, to dioramas, to moving pictures, to wide-screen cinema, to earlier experiments with "head-sight television" (Comeau & Bryan, 1961).

We can also discern the tendency to include more senses into media illusions. The coordination of aural and visual illusions in film and television is a good example. Predating the present technology are the pioneering multisensory systems of Morton Heilig, such as his famous 1960s VR prototypes, "Sensorama" and the prescient "Telesphere mask" (see Rheingold, 1991, pp. 49–67). Because media are often seen as tools for thinking, there is the underlying assumption that "we can build yet more powerful tools by using more senses" (Brooks, 1977). Even in 1965 Sutherland argued that the computer "should serve as many senses as possible" (p. 507). This goal is still chased in mainstream entertainment, as characterized by the movie director John Waters' (1981) "Odorama", in which he provided each audience member with a strip-of-scratch and sniff aromas, keyed to various episodes in his film.

Through McLuhan's rear-view mirror, all past media can be character-ized as our previous attempts to provide engaging simulations of not only perceptual sensations of an environment separated from us by space (e.g., the telephone) or time (e.g., the photograph), but simulations of another human's perceptions, thought processes, or fantasies. Virtual environments may become *the* communication crucible, a challenge for communicators and designers ready to employ the tools of this medium. We now turn to a discussion of those tools.

THE PHYSICAL MEDIA

Unlike most developments of television hardware, changes in the hardware of virtual environments have direct bearing for communication, informa-tion design, and the social impact of the technology. Communication designers and researchers will not want to ignore the technical dimensions of this medium. Technical decisions are decisions about communication; they are decisions about how we communicate with the computer and with each other in this medium.

Virtual reality technology can be considered as an array of possible input and output devices, each device serving a sensorimotor channel and linked to the user's body movements and responses (see Fig. 4.4). This section discusses the perceptual and communication ramifications of technical options and trends.

Both input and output hardware are essential to an immersive illusion of presence, of being inside a simulated world. We begin with a discussion of

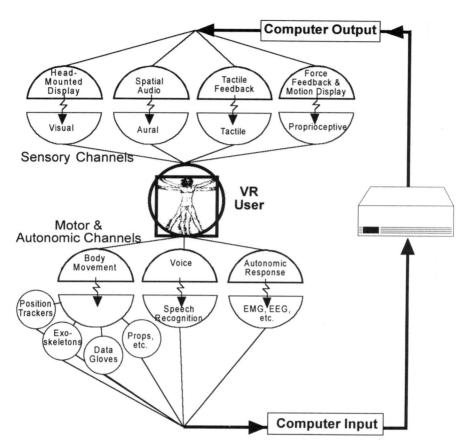

FIG. 4.4.   Virtual reality technology can be thought of an array of possible input and output devices coupled to the user's sensorimotor channels. Each output device serves a sensory channel. Each input device is linked to a user's motor or autonomic channels.

the output[4] devices because they more closely resemble other mass media technology and may be more instrumental to creating the illusion of presence or "being there."

Output Devices

If the output devices try to couple the computer to the human senses, we should consider each device in relation to the characteristics of the sensorimotor channels (see Fig. 4.4). In an attempt to realize the overall

---

[4]*Output* here refers to the output of the computer, which is input to the human being.

goal of presence, each device is being refined so that it comes closer and closer to optimally matching the parameters needed for powerful perceptual illusions in each sensory channel. In this continuous process of design the engineer looks for interface devices that are so innocuous as to become "second nature" and in the long run invisible.

Visual Displays

We live in a visual culture; our eyes are an important gateway for information. It has been estimated that normally sighted people receive 80% of their information input through the eyes. A great percentage of our brain is dedicated to processing the information we absorb through our eyes. When we want information, we "look into it": we glance around us, read, gaze at pictures, watch television, view graphs, and so forth. It is not surprising that a significant part of virtual reality development has tried to create better illusions for our eyes.

Head-Mounted displays.   The head-mounted display is the latest technical twist to a centuries-long dream of creating an image that is perceptually convincing (Gombrich, 1961). When, in 1965, Ivan Sutherland wanted to make the virtual world behind the video screen look, act, sound, and feel real, his first step was to work on the video image. His goal was no different from that of the 15th-century painter, Alberti, who thought he could simulate a scene so perfectly that his painting would appear to dissolve and become a window on another world (Alberti, 1458/1966). Although separated by 500 years, Alberti's and Sutherland's goals were to successfully simulate the codes present in the visual array[5] (Gibson, 1966, 1979) of light that a viewer would see if he or she looked at a real scene. Alberti's answer to the millennial search for presence was a treatise on the physical media and codes of perspective painting. Sutherland's answer was a design for the physical media of head-mounted displays and some computer codes for painting perspective illusions with stereoscopic images.[6]

The head-mounted display builds on the ability of earlier visual media to give the viewer a slight sense of presence (see Ellis, Kaiser, & Grunwald, 1991). Each development in visual media has added greater perceptual cues

---

[5]The phrase *visual array* refers to the pattern of light rays that reach the eye when a viewer looks on a scene. Pictures and film record the pattern of light. Information contained in the recorded visual array is reconstituted as a perceptual experience when light is shown on a printed picture or passed through a celluloid film. A somewhat distorted simulation of the visual array of the original scene (Hochberg, 1986) is etched on the retina and is experienced as an information-rich representation of the original scene.

[6]For a history of HMD development see Rheingold (1991) and Sutherland (1968). For a review of the technology see Aviles et al. (1992) and Robinette and Rolland (1992).

TABLE 4.2
Spatial and Motion Cues Added by Each Innovation in Visual Media

Medium	Date Developed	Spatial Cues[1]
Perspective paintings and photography	Middle ages	Linear perspective Interposition (object overlap) Texture density gradients Aerial perspective
Stereoscope	18th century	Static binocular disparity
Film and video	Late 19th century	Camera centered motion parallax Optical flow patterns Image shear
Cinerama and omnimax	Mid 20th century	Peripheral visual stimulation (vection effects)
3D movies and 3D flat panel displays	Mid 20th century	Dynamic binocular disparity (binocular parallax)
Head-mounted stereographic displays	Late 20th century	Head centered motion parallax
Some visual spatial cues not well integrated into most head-mounted displays		Accommodation (focus of eye lens) Vergence (horizontal rotation of eyes)

[1]Each display incorporates cues developed in earlier systems.

to produce more convincing illusions of presence. This progression of cues is summarized in Table 4.2.

In pictures and paintings, the still image simulates the cues in the array of light in a "real" visual scene with such three-dimensional codes as linear perspective; for example, trees get smaller in the distance (Sedgwick, 1980). Other cues of depth in the virtual space of a picture come from interposition, the overlap of pictorial objects (e.g., objects close to the viewer obscure (occlude) objects further away as when a glass in a still life painting overlaps a bottle); changes in color and texture at points in the image that are farther away (i.e., aerial perspective, texture density gradients); as well by other 2-D depth cues (see Gibson, 1966, 1979; Hagen, 1980; Nagata, 1992).

Film and television add another level to our sense of presence in simulated visual space. Motion and motion-related depth cues, especially passive, motion parallax cues (Gibson, Olum, & Rosenblatt, 1955) give us a sense of the depth of a scene. When the camera moves, stationary objects slide across the screen at a speed directly proportional to their distance from the camera.[7] Distant objects seem to move more slowly than near ones. The

---

[7]If the concept of motion parallax is not clear, a classic simple demonstration will make the idea more intuitive. Stretch your arm in front of you with your thumb as if you were sighting something in the distance. Now move your head slightly from side to side. Notice how your thumb appears to sway back and forth more rapidly than objects slightly further away, and

perceptual system has evolved to use these cues, and we now use them to separate the distances of objects in the video scene (Hochberg, 1986).

But the video and film image fails to provide all the cues necessary for a truly convincing perceptual illusion. The perceptual system immediately detects the perceptual impostor. For example, each eye sees the same scene, instead of the slightly different perspective on the scene projected on each eye when viewing a physical scene (i.e., "stereoscopic vision," binocular parallax). Second, the viewer can't really get a different perspective on the virtual video scene by moving. When we move our heads in the physical world, our viewpoint changes. The relation between the objects in a scene before us changes (i.e., motion parallax cues derived from the motion and occlusion of the projected object surfaces on the retina; Gibson, 1979). But in film and video, these motion parallax cues are connected to the viewpoint of the camera rather than the viewpoint of the viewer. Only camera movements and cuts change the spatial characteristics of the image, and these are not in the control of the viewer. We are not inside the space of the video image, only the camera is. We are spectators, not actors.

That is why the many immersive virtual displays are head-mounted. A head-mounted display (HMD) adds greater verisimilitude to the image by incorporating two additional perceptual cues to the standard video image, (a) binocular (stereographic) disparity, and (b) head-centered motion parallax cues. With a HMD the viewer ceases to be a voyeur and comes closer to being an actor in the visual world.

HMDs use an old stereo imaging trick that goes back to the 19th-century Brewster stereoscope used to view stereo photographs. The head-mounted display puts a slightly different video image in front of each eye. Because our eyes are set apart (interpupilary distance), each sees a slightly different view of any scene (binocular disparity).

Most HMDs simulate the different viewpoints of each eye by placing a slightly different view of the same image in front of each eye. The images may be generated by a variety of imaging technologies such as two small cathode ray tubes (CRTs), small liquid crystal displays (LCDs), fiber optic pipes, or other devices. Table 4.3 lists the types of imaging technologies commonly used in most HMDs. The tiny monitors and lenses may be mounted into the front or side of head gear that looks like a scuba mask[8]

---

these more rapidly than objects far on the horizon. As we evolved to walk, run, and hunt, our visual system evolved to make use of motion parallax cues to determine the distances between us and the objects around us and to generate three-dimensional models of the world around us inside our brains.

[8]In the spring of 1994 there were numerous HMD optical systems available, for example: two LCDs in front with LEEP-type optics (VPL, W Industries, Virtual Research, VRontier); one LCD in front (Liquid Image, LEEP); LCDs with new, proprietary optics (Kaiser); CRTs at the temples (CAE, VRG, Kaiser); CRTs in front (Virtual Research, Fake Space); fiber optic pipes to mirrors in front of the eyes (Pollhemus); LCDs at the temple (Kopin/Sarnoff).

TABLE 4.3
Typology[1] of Head-Mounted Displays by Type of Imaging System

Type[2]	Typical Resolution[3]	Notes	Sample Systems
LCD (single panel)	~79 × 234 ~300 × 200	Most common. Inexpensive. Game systems tend to have lower resolution and FOV than stated values.	Leep Systems, *Cyberface 2 & 3;* VPL *Eyephone;* Virtual Research *Flight Helmet;* Virtuality *Visette;* Sega, *Virtua VR*
LCD (multi-panel)	~640 × 220	Proprietary technology	Kaiser Electro/Optics, *VIM*
CRT (color wheel/filter)	~1280 × 960	More popular in higher end systems	Fake Space Labs *Boom 3C;* n-Vision *Datavisor 9c;* Virtual Research *EyeGen 3*
CRT (with fiber optic light pipe)	~1280 × 1024	Expensive. More common in military and high end research systems.	CAE *FOHMD;* Polhemus Labs *Looking Glass*

[1]Represents common systems as of fall 1993.
[2]This table assumes color displays, although earlier systems tended to be monochrome.
[3]Resolution quoted for mid-to-higher quality systems.

whereas others are mounted onto a helmet (see Figs. 4.5, 4.6, 4.7, & 4.8; CAE, 1986; Chung et al., 1989; Fisher, McGreevy, Humphries, & Robinette, 1986).

The images on the small monitors are usually too small to adequately cover the user's visual field and too close to the eyes for the users to easily focus on the image. A set of lenses is placed between the monitor and the user's eyes to solve this problem. The lenses expand the image to fill more of the user's visual field and to make it easier to focus (accommodate) by placing the focal point of the image at infinity (Robinett & Rolland, 1992).[9]

Graphic software calculates the geometrical difference corresponding to the views the user would receive in each eye if he or she were standing in front of the physical scene. The different images are displayed on the tiny screens of the HMD.[10] Each eye sees a different image but fuses a complete scene inside the brain. The computer-generated world is suddenly three-dimensional. This computer graphic world appears to recede in all directions onto a distant virtual horizon.

---

[9]To compensate for distortions caused by the lens, the image may sometimes be systematically distorted (anamorphic projection) to assure the right proportions when the magnifying lenses stretch the image.

[10]It should be noted that on many of the early systems, the interpupillary distance (IPD) assumed by the optics and the image projection system do not match the user's (Robinette & Rolland, 1992). Most newer systems provide for easy adjustment of IPD. Also, the binocular disparity of the image pair may sometimes be exaggerated to produce desirable perceptual depth effects.

FIG. 4.5.   The EyeGen 3 head-mounted display employs twin, monochrome CRTs and color wheels to provide medium resolution (439 × 250) at the cost of a narrow field of view (~48° horz). Courtesy of Virtual Presence.

Most head-mounted displays add the second critical visual cue to create the illusion of a physical scene: head-centered motion parallax. When the viewer moves his or her head, the stereographic image changes just as it would if the viewer were looking at a physical scene. This is accomplished by computer computations triggered by head movement information provided by the head-tracking input devices (discussed later). Sophisticated graphic software rapidly changes the images to mimic the spatial relations of objects in the physical world. The result is the illusion that one is looking at a stable, 3-D world. With a stereographic display and head-centered motion parallax cues the user is an actor in the virtual world. The user is immersed in a visual environment and can look around and visually explore the computer graphic world that surrounds the user.

Although HMDs provide a strong sense of presence, the illusion is far

FIG. 4.6.   The *VIM Personal Viewer* is designed tor use in public systems such as those in location-based entertainment. It is a two-part design, with the optic module detaching from the headband, facilitating easy cleaning. More notable is the innovative folded-optic image path, which provides light weight and a wide field of view (30°V × 210°H). Courtesy Kaiser Electro Optics.

from optimal at this time (Robinett & Rolland, 1992). There are a number of visual perceptual cues and parameters (ocular convergence, accommodation, user adjusted interpupilary distance, and visual lag)[11] that are not adequately simulated. Although not all visual cues are equally important to the perception of depth and presence (Kilpatrick, 1976), more would

---

[11]If head-mounted displays are to be truly coupled with human vision, there are other design issues that must be perfected. Displays involving images suspended in front of the eyes can conflict with other cues used by our vision to construct a three-dimensional scene. For example, our eyes rotate in their sockets. The visual system uses information from the efferent muscle receptors of the eye as a spatial depth cue (binocular convergence). The eyes converge closer together when looking at close objects and diverge to point straight ahead when looking at objects on the horizon (infinity). The location of represented objects on the two screens in head-mounted displays need to be placed correctly so that the vergence of the eyes is either closer together or further apart to match their represented location (close or far) in space. But this is rarely the case (Robinett & Roland, 1992). Muscles, which focus the eye, also provide incorrect spatial cues because the eye is focused to clearly resolve the image on a screen only a few centimeters from the eye. If truly viewing a physical scene rather than a virtual scene, the eye's accomodation would vary depending on the depth of the focused object. In addition,

FIG. 4.7.   Using only one LCD panel, the *MRG2* head-mounted display provides a medium resolution (720 × 240), monoscopic image. The innovative helmet design uses flexible plastics to create a head-gripping system that is easy to don and doff, but stays securely in place. Courtesy of Liquid Image.

because all images are displayed as if they were located at optical infinity (about 3 meters from the eye), there is no focus blurring of distant objects when looking at closer objects.

Other cues that need to be optimized to minimize subtle distortions in the stereoscopic image include software adjustments and HMD displays that account for interpupilary distance, correct geometry for the field of view, as well as other changes in HMD and computer optics (see Hochberg, 1986, for a discussion of the perception of visual displays, and Robinett & Roland, 1992, for a discussion of these issues as they pertain to the design of HMDs.).

There are other problems that are experienced with head-mounted displays but have their sources in other points in the system. There is a noticeable visual lag between user movements and the image. This may give the users a feeling that they are moving through a liquidlike environment. The images may also jump and jitter. Both problems, as well as some of the others mentioned earlier, may contribute to reports of simulation sickness (Biocca, 1992). It is believed that inefficiences and lags in position tracking and computing are the sources of some of these problems.

Like the ubiquitous television screen, the present family of head-mounted displays are not yet optimized to our visual perception. They come closer to making the image "look real" but still have some ways to go. But like the television set, the imperfections in the displays may be acceptable for many uses while refinements in display technology bring visual displays closer and closer to Sutherland's long-dreamed of "ultimate display."

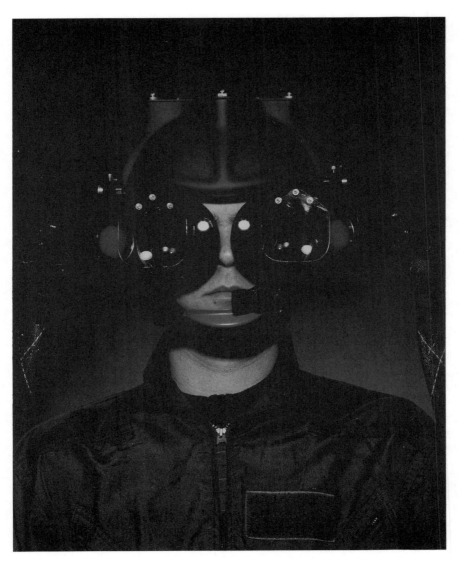

FIG. 4.8. The system supporting the CAE head-mounted display begins with a pair of stereoscopic images from high-resolution video projectors. The images are condensed and "piped" through thick fiber optic bundles (at back) where they are reflected to the eyes through a reflector and lens system. Though the result is a high-resolution virtual image, the current cost of this head-mounted display is very high. Courtesy of CAE Electronics.

probably have to be coordinated before HMDs get closer to making a virtual scene look as perceptually real as a physical scene.

Where is the development of HMDs going? Below we note some existing trends in attempts to overcome the limitations of the current HMD.

Alternative display techniques.   Although LCDs and CRTs provide the images in most head-mounted displays, there are other potentially promising technologies for virtual reality visualization. Consider the following: What if instead of assembling the image line-by-line on the picture surface, you were to assemble the image line-by-line on the retina itself? This is the basic principle behind one family of visual display technologies variably known as virtual image displays, retinal scanners, or direct retinal write (DRW) displays (Holmgren, 1992). The term "retinal write" can be misleading, because in the optical sense all images that we see are "written" on the retina. The systems differ from CRTs and LCDs in that the scanners do not use an intermediate display surface like a screen. The pin-point light that constructs the image is directed at the eye. The pin-point of light is quickly and systematically moved (scanned) to create a virtual image that is suspended in space. Anyone who has quickly twirled a light source like a sparkler to create a circle has created a "virtual" image of a circle from a single point of light.

Laser-driven Displays.   Lasers can be used to paint an image on the retina. A University of Washington research team headed by Tom Furness is working on the development of a laser-based, retinal scanning system. Laser light can be narrowed into a very fine beam. Luminance levels can be well within safe ranges. Various ways of scanning the laser light (e.g., a spinning multifaceted mirror, vibrating acoustic films) can be used to build the image on the retina, turning the retina into the ultimate screen. A bench prototype of such a system has been demonstrated at the Human Interface Technology Laboratory (HIT LAB) at the University of Washington in Seattle, Washington.[12] A monochrome image is built using a low-powered laser.

A number of potential properties recommend this technology. Laser retinal scanners offer the possibility of achieving resolution levels commensurate with the resolving power of the eye itself. The laser and mirror mechanism could be made very light and tiny; it can lessen the weight and bulk of head-mounted displays. Laser diodes are not very expensive. Unobtrusive scanners might be a means of developing a virtual overlay system, a system that overlays virtual images on top of natural scenes.

But a successful HMD-using laser imaging must overcome a number of

---

[12]*CyberEdge Journal,* November/December 1992.

daunting technical challenges. A significant drawback with this sort of display is the need to track where the user is looking, so that the image can be properly directed through the retina. This involves not simply tracking the direction in which the head is pointed, as is done with contemporary HMDs, but very rapidly and accurately tracking where the eyes are looking, a more difficult problem.

Informed skeptics have other doubts about this route to the ultimate visual display (Holmgren, 1992). Some doubt that the higher resolution levels can be achieved, or that lasers are the best way to proceed. Others have doubts about the various ways a laser beam could be deflected to produce high-resolution scan lines. There are also a number of technical problems in creating a laser-based, color imaging system.

LED-Driven Displays.   Much simpler than laser imaging is a family of systems that construct virtual images line-by-line using mirrors (see Fig. 4.9; Wells, 1992). In a system called *Megapixel,* the image begins as a single, magnified line of 1,120 tiny light-emitting diodes (LEDs). In continuous

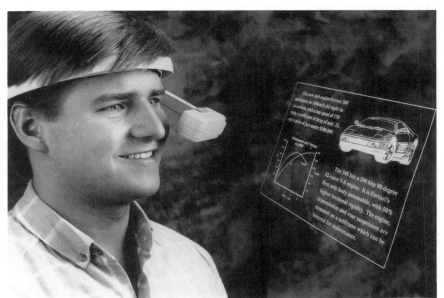

FIG. 4.9.   Example of a virtual image display. These displays assemble the image line-by-line on the retina. In this system, an image begins as a single column of 280 tiny light-emitting diodes (LEDs). In continuous motion, a mirror swivels horizontally (50Hz) to reflect the light pattern of the LEDs. As the LED line changes, the mirror projects the new column. Doing so for each column, the mirror rapidly assembles the image without using an intermediate display surface like a screen. The image, which is assembled on the retina, appears to float in space about 2 feet in front of the user. Courtesy of Reflection Technologies.

motion, a mirror swivels (50Hz) to reflect the light pattern of a line of LEDs. As the LED line changes, the mirror projects the new line lower down on the retina. Doing so for each line, the mirror rapidly assembles the image on the retina without the use of an intermediate display surface. The image appears to float in space about two feet in front of the user's eyes. The system's limitations include a narrow viewing angle (approximately 30°) and monochrome monocular displays. But resolution levels can be good (up to $1,120 \times 900$) and the HMDs are light (2.25–10.8 oz.)

Trend Toward Higher Resolution.   Displays are composed of picture elements (pixels), little squares or dots that make up the image. The width of the field of view also affects resolution (assuming a fixed pixel density).

The ideal visual display would match the highest resolving power of the eye (~ 30 seconds of arc). One can see a trend toward the development of higher resolution systems to achieve the goal of higher verisimilitude.

The common LCD systems have low resolution, especially when placed close to the eye (see Table 4.3).[13] They are very popular because of their light weight and cost.

CRTs can achieve higher resolutions but at a higher cost and weight (Aviles, Durlach, Held, Pang, & Spain, 1992). Because standard color CRTs use multiple scanning guns and tight pixel arrays, it is physically difficult to squeeze this technology into tiny, high-resolution monitors. To get CRT resolution levels in full color, some HMD designs use small monochrome CRTs in front of which sits a color wheel (red–green–blue). The color wheel spins rapidly in phase with the changing images on the monochrome monitor (phase sequential color). The end result? The eye sees a full-color image.

There are other ways to squeeze CRT resolution and color into a head-mounted display. Some high-resolution systems get around the size limitations of standard CRTs by using fiber optic light pipes (CAE, 1986; see Fig. 4.8 & Table 4.3). The large image from the CRT is reduced in size and pumped to the eye via a fiber optic light pipe. A bright high-quality display is the result.

The Trend Toward Displays That Fill More of the Visual Field.   When we look at a physical scene, our eyes can give us a field of view (FOV) that measures approximately 200° horizontally X 120° vertically. Figure 4.10 shows the irregular shape of the human visual field.

---

[13]Reports of resolution on LCDs can sometimes be misleading. Picture elements (pixels) are sometimes reported as the total number of color elements (red, blue, yellow) as opposed to each picture element that the three colors comprise. In such cases, the resolution numbers have to be divided by three before they can be compared to other technologies like CRT (Gary Bishop, personal communication, University of North Carolina).

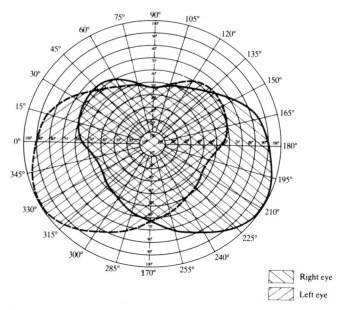

FIG. 4.10.   A polar chart of the shape of the normal human visual field. Assuming that a human observer is looking straight on, the chart shows the area of human vision in degrees of visual angle (the width in degrees is calculated from the focal center of each eye). From Kalawsky (1993). Reprinted by permission.

Verisimilitude calls for displays that come closer to matching the width and height of our full field of view. Previous media technologies like Cinerama and existing display systems such as those in the large-screen, IMAX theaters obtain powerful perceptual effects by filling much of the users' visual field with a vivid moving image. When the image filling the visual field is in motion, viewers may have the illusion of self-motion, called vection (Dichgans & Brandt, 1978). Feelings of vection can greatly increase our sense of presence. For example, the reader may have experienced that tug at one's stomach when a plane turns or dives in an IMAX film.

Apart from generating a feeling of presence, there are other reasons for wanting to fill the visual field. Our peripheral vision (i.e., ambient as opposed to focal processing) is sensitive to certain types of information (Held, 1970). Peripheral vision is particularly tuned to detect motion such as an animal running in the bushes or a waving hand in the corner of our eye. Peripheral vision is also sensitive to luminance changes such as a blinking light or a mirror flashing in the distance. To put it in a nutshell, our peripheral vision is great at signaling sudden changes in the world around us. This can be as useful in a virtual world as it was for our ancestors on the savanna.

A small visual field has drawbacks. When the visual angle presented by a head-mounted display is small, users may feel as if they are looking on the world through a portal or scuba mask. This may lessen the user's sense of presence. But a smaller visual field may also lead to distortions in depth perception. Generally, objects on the horizon may seem further away and surfaces immediately below the user may seem higher.

Although a wide viewing angle may seem valuable, head-mounted displays vary greatly as to how much of the visual field they cover (Aviles et al., 1992). Popular head-mounted displays may typically cover a field of view of approximately 110° × 75°. This is far less than our 200° × 120° capability. Some expensive head-mounted displays report fields of view as high as 160° × 80° (e.g., CAE's Phase V HMD — see Fig. 4.8).

Why not just fill the visual field with a big image? There's a technological roadblock. Designers are faced with a trade off between visual angle and resolution. Most systems have a limited pixel density (discussed earlier). As lenses stretch this image to fill more of the visual field, the resolution of the image drops. A vicious trade-off is created between higher resolution on the one hand, and higher FOV on the other. Which is more important? Researchers have begun asking questions as to what is more important under what circumstances (e.g., Aviles et al., 1992). But it remains an open question — as it was for Cinerama — whether the greater field of view is worth the additional cost to obtain it.

Trend Toward Lighter and Smaller Head-Mounted Displays.   Back in the 60s, Sutherland's original head-mounted display was so heavy it had to be suspended from the ceiling. The display was nicknamed the "Sword of Damocles." Like the legendary sword, the mechanical system attached to the display hung precariously above the user and might kill him if it fell. Users of the early head-mounted displays at NASA and the University of North Carolina reported fatigue in their necks and shoulder muscles from the weight of the display (Chung et al., 1989).

Commercially available head-mounted displays have gotten lighter since their introduction. Lighter materials in the helmets and lenses have helped. Some of the electronic parts that were part of the early displays have been removed from the display and placed elsewhere in the system so as to lighten the load. Better balancing of the weight can make head-mounted displays feel lighter. Some of the HMDs used in game systems (e.g., Sega) weigh less than 8 oz., although their optics and performance is less than optimal.

Extrapolating this trend into the future, one can foresee the development of head-mounted displays that may be as small and as light as a pair of glasses. The VIM system shown in Fig. 4.6 shows some evolution in this direction.

Trend Toward See-Through Displays. Complete immersion into a virtual world appears to call for total immersion of the visual sense. But in many settings, like the office, the car, or even the home, it may not be practical to have one's vision of the real world completely occluded. For example, an office worker immersed in a virtual environment might want to look up when someone comes in the door. But the first few generations have been cumbersome to put on and take off. For this reason some advocated boom-mounted HMDs that were held up to the face by the user's hands (see Fig. 4.11) or nonimmersive, 3-D displays (windowed VR; see Fig. 4.12).

But what if the virtual visual display were transparent? Transparent displays are sometimes referred to as "augmented reality" (Feiner, MacIntyre, & Seligmann, 1993). With transparent displays the user might choose to see either a full virtual image or a superimposition of virtual images upon physical scenes (see Lanier & Biocca, 1992). From the beginning the superimposition of virtual objects on real world scenes has

FIG. 4.11.   An immersive, boom-mounted, head-coupled display. Unlike the present generation of head-mounted displays, this display allows user to easily peer into the virtual world and just as easily look away. Note that this freedom comes at a cost; movement occupies the hands of the user. Courtesy of NASA Ames and Fake space, Inc., 4085 Campbell Avenue, Menlo Park, CA 94025.

FIG. 4.12.   Example of nonimmersive, windowed VR system suitable for office use. The glasses on the right provide a modest view of a 3-D image bounded by the window of the monitor. A position tracker above the monitor coordinates the image with user's head movements. The system can be linked to a camera for telepresence applications. Courtesy of Stereographics.

been the goal of a number of research groups (e.g., the University of North Carolina). Information about an object can be superimposed on the object itself. This can range from something like a virtual Post-it™ note on objects in someone's office (e.g., Fitzmaurice, 1993) to a doctor superimposing X-ray images of internal tissue on the actual body of a patient. Researchers have experimented with half-silvered mirrors and the video mixing of images from head mounted cameras with computer-generated virtual images. The perceptual alignment of virtual and real objects presents a number of difficult design challenges. At the time of this writing, these were only beginning to be solved.

The Ideal Head-Mounted Display?   Reviewing the development trends above, we can see that the ideal, practical head-mounted display would probably:

1. Weigh as little as a pair of glasses.
2. Fill the visual field.
3. Match the resolving power of the eye.
4. Properly coordinate all the visual spatial cues.
5. Allow for both the transparent intermingling of virtual and real objects or full visual immersion into the virtual world.

Such a display appears to be the destination. At the time of this writing, we are still a number of technological generations away from such a display. But a number of existing systems suggest that the ideal HMD may be attainable.

Aural Displays

Fully experiencing a virtual environment means hearing it as a space (Aviles et al., 1992; Wenzel, 1992). Hearing is three-dimensional; it is one of the ways you model the space around you (Blauert, 1983). Think of how you rely on your hearing to track the sound of a mosquito buzzing around your head. The aural realism of virtual spaces requires replicating the spatial characteristics of sounds like the changing intensity of a race car engine as it approaches a listener and screeches past (Doppler effect); or the tapping of footsteps as they echo in a dark, empty corridor; or the chatter of a conversation off in the corner of a room (cocktail party effect).

Our minds extract the spatial characteristics of sound from differences in sound patterns reaching our ears. One spatial cue is the difference in the sound intensity from ear to ear and the slightly different delay between the time a sound reaches one ear and then the other (duplex theory). But a more discriminating set of cues comes from the way our outer ears (pinnae) generate different spectral distributions of frequencies when sounds differ in location, be it differences in azimuth (left–right, front–back) or elevation (up–down) (Shaw, 1974). If spatially distinct, audio "objects" are to be part of the illusion of presence in virtual reality, they should ideally:

1. Be stereophonically matched to the acoustic properties of our two ears including the spectral mix of frequencies, delays, and distortions.

2. Change in relation to the acoustics of a space such as the size of the
   space, its shape, and the sound absorption properties of its
   surfaces.
3. Smoothly change in relation to the virtual location and position of
   the user's ears in the space.

Like the changing geometry of VR graphics when the user is in motion,
an aural virtual space has to mathematically model the changing properties
of the acoustic space as the users walk about and swivel their heads to and
from virtual voices, musical instruments, clanging metal objects, and
roaring virtual engines.

Audio systems, like the one developed for NASA (Foster, 1988; Wenzel,
1992), attempt to mathematically map the time and frequency properties of
a sound source as its virtual position from the user's two ears varies. Sound
sources are mathematically modified using a set of calculations called a
head-related transfer function (HRTF) to make the sound appear as if it
comes from a specific location relative to the user.

The mathematical formulae at the basis of the virtual acoustic display are
based on research using tiny microphones inside the ears of a sample of
subjects. The research team mapped the changing acoustics as the ears were
bombarded by various sound frequencies from 144 differently positioned
speakers in a soundproof, dome-shaped, anechoic chamber (Wenzel,
Wrightman, & Foster, 1988). The results have been translated into a
software and hardware package called the Convolvotron (Foster, 1988) that
can give spatial properties to a limited number of sound sources in a virtual
space.

The Convolvotron system can also model the echoic properties of a small
volume such as a room. Similar commercial systems exist for the Macintosh
(Focal Point System), and other systems are under development.

The cheapest and most flexible way to couple acoustic systems to our
sense of hearing remains the ubiquitous pair of headphones. Headphones
are head-mounted audio devices well suited to combination with the
head-mounted visual displays. High-quality headphones used in VR help
shut out sounds from the physical space and replace them with the
high-resolution sounds from the virtual space. Insert earphones (ear plugs)
also have desirable sound qualities and can be lighter and less noticeable
(skin pressure) than more bulky headphones.

The key difference between the aural experience on a standard set of
headphones and the aural experience produced in a virtual system is the
element of user motion. When a user listens to a standard stereo recording,
the user's movement does not change the properties of the sound. The
properties of the audio space are fixed and determined at the time of the
recording and mixing. But in a head-centered virtual audio space, the sound

is dynamic and interactive; it changes as the user's head swivels away or toward the virtual sound source. Move your head closer to the virtual drum and the sound changes.

There is little doubt that audio imaging is an essential part of generating the full illusion of presence, of being there. Fully coordinated with other perceptual illusions, spatial audio can enhance the verisimilitude of visual and tactile illusions. Powerful audio imaging also can provide valuable spatial information about objects. Spatial audio can alert a user to objects and virtual beings that are visually occluded.

Trends in the Development of Aural VR Displays. Audio illusions are quite advanced in their development because of a history of experimentation in audio engineering (see Blauert, 1983; Wenzel, 1992). But the optimization of the aural imaging systems must face a number of design challenges to optimize the verisimilitude of the illusion.

Each one of us hears slightly differently and our individual differences can affect the success of the illusion. Each pair of human ears has slightly different acoustic properties, but an acoustic imaging system needs to be designed for an "average" set of ears.[14] In some cases, audiospatial illusions are subject to distortions such as perspective reversals — the user perceives that a sound source is behind him or her when the intention is to create the illusion of a sound source in front of the user. Users also may sometimes misperceive the elevation of the sound source. The use of headphones and anechoic sound models sometimes leads users to perceive the sound as localized "inside" their heads, rather than outside. But those perceptual distortions are rare and are more common when the user has no visual cue to match the aural location of a sound source. Distortions are also less likely if the user's head is in motion. Dynamic cues help resolve spatial ambiguities in both visual and aural perception as well as environmental audio cues such as echoes and reverberations in a simulated, asymmetric room (see Wenzel, 1992).

The calculations necessary to tailor various sound sources to the location of the user's head in space take time. Users report the perception of lag as the sound "catches up" to their current locations (Rheingold, 1991). Lags can be as long as 90 msec on current systems (Wenzel, 1992). Whether the lag is perceptible varies from user to user. Higher head and body velocities (e.g., dancing) make the lag more perceptible. One can only imagine that the computational demands will continue to increase as virtual reality

---

[14]It may be possible to calibrate systems in the future to adapt them to individual users. Our perceptual systems are also highly adaptable and this may help smooth over imperfections in the audioimaging systems. It is possible that users will adapt and adjust for spatial mismatches in the audio system by adjusting the mental program that calculates the location of a sound source in space.

systems must accommodate whole groups of moving, bobbing, and swiveling heads in multiuser spaces and as the number of sound sources that must be modeled in a space increases. Luckily, one can also assume that computing power will increase at the geometric rates that have occurred since the 1970s, soon to provide lag-free sound processing.

Haptic (Tactile) Output

A number of existing communication media provide stimuli for the visual and aural sensory channels. For example, you can experience the look and sound of a violin. Few media attempt to represent the feel of an object such as feeling the weight of the violin, the resistance of the bow on the strings, or the vibration in the body of a violin when a note is played (see Rheingold, 1991, pp. 325ff). The presence of the object in one's hands is communicated to the user by the surface skin sensations and pressures such as the smoothness of the varnished surface of the violin. Signals from muscle proprioceptors communicate the pull of gravity when the violin is picked up and the resistance of pushing the violin against the chin.

It is part of the ambition of the virtual reality technologies to direct information to the tactile and proprioceptive sensors. A virtual environment that truly "feels real" should be able to simulate the sensation of surface textures like sandpaper or velvet, the resistance of surfaces like rocks or pillows, and the sensation of physical resistance like moving an oar or stick through water, mud, oil, or rocks. Systems that attempt to produce these illusions are sometimes called haptic interfaces and are of significant interest to VR researchers (Salisbury & Srinivasan, 1992; Shimoga, 1993a, 1993b). The term *haptic,* which contains the Greek root meaning to "fasten," suggests the interactive nature of the sensations. Part of the body is "fastened" to part of the world, and feedback results from the active exploration of a surface or object by the limbs, hands, and skin of the user. For example, we make full use of our haptic sensorimotor channel when our hand searches for a set of keys in a bag or pocket.

Why the need for haptic and tactile imagery in a communication interface? In an age when most information is fed to us through visual and aural media, we can easily forget the importance of touch in exploring our physical world. Haptic imagery could greatly enhance our exploration and use of virtual worlds as well. For example, a number of studies show that haptic feedback can reduce the time it takes to complete manual tasks by as much as 10%–75% (see review by Shimoga, 1993a, 1993b).

If all information—even abstract information—could be something we physically touch and manipulate, our ease of understanding and our sense of presence could be significantly increased. To "put your hands" on something is to truly feel that the thing is present; it is so real "you can feel it." That kind of language suggests the essence of the concept of presence.

Tactile images can be used to communicate very subtle information in telepresence applications and can even provide for new insights in more abstract displays such as 3-D, tactile graphs. For example, a team at the University of North Carolina has demonstrated that the incorporation of haptic information in computer models of physical systems such as molecules can significantly enhance the problem-solving ability of chemists who use the system (Brooks, Ouh-Young, Batter, & Kilpatrick, 1990; Minsky, Ouh-Young, Steele, Brooks, & Behensky, 1990). If an engineer designing a motor could not only see and move the parts, but also feel how well they fit together, his or her insights during the design stage could be greatly enhanced. There is no doubt that tactile or haptic displays venture into new ground in the evolution of communication media and present significant new challenges and opportunities.

Tactile Displays.   If the goal is to create tactile illusions, then a good place to start is with that part of our body we use to explore the world of surfaces and textures, the skin and pressure sensing organs on our hand — especially the fingertips. Figure 4.13 shows the skin surfaces that provide us

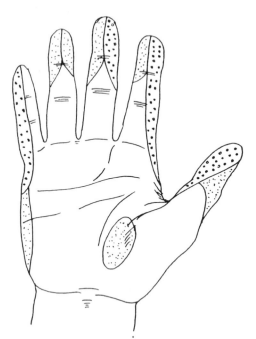

FIG. 4.13.   Shows the skin surfaces that provide us the greatest amount of information when we are engaged in grasping and manipulation tasks like moving a pencil, manipulating a pin, or handling a tennis ball. The area with larger dots indicate more active regions than those with smaller dots. From Shimoga (1993). Reprinted by permission.

the greatest amount of information when we are engaged in tasks like moving a pencil, manipulating a pin, or handling a tennis ball.

The fingers are only a small percentage of our skin surface, but a significant part of our brain is dedicated to them. To successfully communicate tactile information to the brain, we must find ways to stimulate the tactile receptors that lie just below the surface of the skin. Over 17 million of these lie waiting in the skin of our hands for information about the shape of the outside world. They are called *mechano-receptors,* and they give the brain information about the shape, texture, and temperature of surfaces pressing on the skin.

The arrays of receptors on our fingertips are particularly sensitive and discriminating. For example, if you press the skin with two small prods, the mechano-receptors in the skin on our backs can only discriminate between the two pressure points to a resolution of no more than 70 mm. But those on our fingertips can discriminate to resolutions of 2 mm or less! That's one reason why we use our fingers to sense subtle textures like sandpaper and velvet.

Four types of mechano-receptors feed this subtle information to our brains. Table 4.4 lays out the properties of these oddly named sensors.

When users of a virtual reality system bend down to pick up a computer graphic cube, the illusion (and information!) would be greatly enhanced if they could rub the smooth surface of the cube, or feel the edge of the cube pressing on their fingertips. Various shape-changing devices have been used against the skin to simulate textures and the slight pressures of surfaces.

Tactile displays could also be used to communicate (translate) visual or auditory information into tactile sensations for the blind or hearing impaired (Bach-y-Rita, 1982; Reed, Durlach, Delhorne, Rabinowitz, & Grant, 1989) or for enhancing "pressing" information (Bliss, King, Ko-

TABLE 4.4
Properties of the Four Cutaneous Mechanoreceptors in the Human Hand

Property	Meissner Corpuscles	Pacinian Corpuscles	Merkel's Disks	Ruffini Corpuscles
Location in the skin	Shallow (Superficial Dermis)	Deep (Dermis & Subcutaneous)	Shallow (Basal Epidermis)	Deep (Dermis & Subcutaneous)
% in the skin	43%	13%	25%	19%
Spatial resolution	poor	very poor	good	fair
Mean receptive area	13 mm^2	101 mm^2	11 mm^2	59 mm^2
Frequency range of response	10–200 Hz.	70–1000 Hz.	1–200 Hz.(?)	1–200 Hz.(?)
Rate of adaptation	Rapid	Rapid	Slow	Slow

Note. From Shimoga (1993a, 1993b). Adapted by permission.

tovsky, & Crane, 1963) in situations where the user's attention may be engaged or other sensory channels may be overloaded with information.

Four different approaches are commonly identified: pneumatic, vibro-tactile, electrotactile, and neuromuscular stimulation (e.g., Shimoga, 1993a, 1993b). In what follows, we describe these technological approaches briefly.

Pneumatic Stimulation.   Air can exert pressure against our skin. That pressure can be rapidly increased and decreased to gently squeeze or prod the skin. Simulated pressure can be directed at the skin of the user's fingers by air jets, air pockets, or pneumatic rings (see Fig. 4.14). A similar pneumatic device, the "g-seat" even simulates the pressure of gravitational

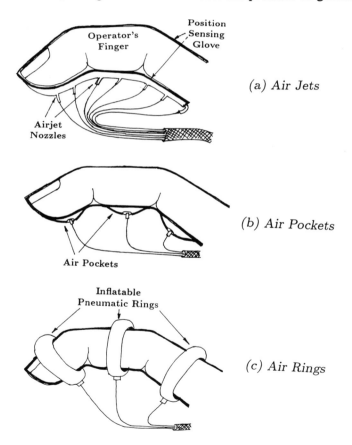

FIG. 4.14.   Example of three pneumatic methods for applying tactile sensation to the fingers: (a) air-jets, (b) air-pockets, (c) air-rings. When the air is pressurized it provides a slight sensation of resistance on the skin. From Shimoga, 1993. Reprinted by permission.

forces (g-forces) on a pilot's buttocks by inflating air cells in the pilot's seat (Mathews & Martin, 1978; Rolfe & Staples, 1986)!

Vibrotactile Stimulation. Vibrotactile devices (Kaczmarek, Webster, Bach-y-Rita, & Tompkins, 1991) attempt to produce surface illusions on a user's fingertips by stimulating the skin's mechano-receptors with tiny vibrating mechanical prods, voice coils, or piezoelectric crystals (see Fig. 4.15; Shimoga, 1993b). The concept behind these devices is a simple one. If visual images on a video screen are composed of the varying illumination of a matrix of tiny dots, then tactile images might be created by a matrix of tiny pin-like rods ("piezoelectric vibrotactile actuators,") or other microme-chanical systems (see Salisbury & Srinivasan, 1992; Shimoga, 1993a, 1993b). Each fingertip can be covered by one of these matrices. Simulations might be created of edges and bumps, or surface textures like sandpaper by varying the height of these rods. The rods are normally vibrated to maintain an illusion and prevent our natural tendency to habituate to the pressure.

Electrotactile Stimulation. Electrotactile stimulation makes use of tiny electrodes attached to the skin (see Fig. 4.16). Electrical pulses provide a slight tingling sensation. This tingling may be interpreted by a user as a signal that his or her hand has touched some virtual object.

Functional Neuromuscular Stimulation. Neuromuscular stimulation is still in its infancy. This approach bypasses the skin and attempts to provide neurological stimulation directly to the nervous system. In some cases, electrodes must pierce the skin and be attached to muscles. Such systems are obviously not yet practical.

Issues in the Development of Tactile Feedback Systems. Think of passing your finger over the wood of a hammer, sandpaper, or velvet. The

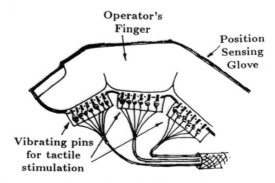

FIG. 4.15. Example of vibrotactile method for applying tactile sensation to the fingers. Small arrays of blunt metal prods are vibrated against the skin for a slight sensation of pressure and texture. From Shimoga, 1993a. Reprinted by permission.

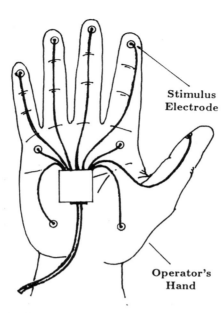

FIG. 4.16.   Example of an electrotactile method for applying tactile sensation to the hand. Small arrays of electrodes apply a small voltage to the muscles. This produces a painless tingling sensation that signals contact with a virtual surface. From Shimoga, 1993a. Reprinted by permission.

movement of your finger across the surface produces a distinctive signature of pressure and vibration of the mechano-receptors. We have only a limited understanding of the psychology of haptic perception. The knowledge does not appear well enough advanced to provide clear guidelines for the engineering of tactile simulations.

Engineers need to know answers to a number of design questions before they can simulate the wide range of textures we experience in the world. For example, what is the amplitude of pressure at each point on the skin that must be exerted for various sensations? What are the rates (in Hz.) at which the stimulation should be applied to the skin to prevent habituation and reproduce patterns like rubbing a finger across the teeth of a comb? What are the larger patterns of stimulation across the effector arrays attached to the skin that constitute the signatures for surfaces like velvet, sandpaper, wood grain, etc.? Engineers are asking these questions (e.g, Shimoga, 1993b). But it is only recently that there has been a greater urgency to find answers.

Force Feedback Devices

Although tactile surface images are one way of simulating the look and feel of things, it is clear that to get to a point that satisfies Sutherland's quest for a world that "feels real" (Sutherland, 1965) would require more than tactile illusions on the surface of one's fingertips. When you reach out and touch the virtual world, the full illusion of presence requires a world that "pushes back at you."[15] For example, when you press down on a bed mattress to feel its firmness, receptors in large groups of muscles in the arms and back tell the brain the level of force resistance your muscles are encountering. The hands only provide a small part of that information. Back in the early 1970s, tactile & force feedback pioneer, Michael Noll (1972), urged researchers " . . . to explore the potential of new sensory modalities as new communication channels between man and machine in applications where graphical communication would not be sufficient or appropriate." (p. 8).

When we slide an object like a cube across a surface or pick up a rock, part of the information of the physical sensation of the object comes not just from the surface of the skin but from various other sensors attached to our muscles and joints. These are part of the proprioceptive systems that tell us about the location and movement of our limbs in space, the pull of gravity, and resistance of surfaces.

Some force feedback devices use some mediating object to transmit the "feel" of hitting a hard surface, moving through a liquid, or swizzling a stick in a bucket of ice. Just as a blind man may use a cane to feel surfaces and objects he cannot see, a user may grasp a mediating object like a joystick (Minsky et al., 1990; Noll, 1972; Rheingold, 1991), a steering wheel (Hard Drivin', see Rheingold, 1991), or a mechanical hand grip (Brooks et al., 1990) to "probe" the virtual world. Mathematical models run by the computer are used to apply forces to the joystick or another object to create haptic illusions described by such words as springiness, bumpiness, hardness, or viscosity. For example, the user might see a stick in a virtual bucket of ice, grab it, and feel the sensation of stirring the ice in the bucket, feeling the stick press and slide past virtual ice cubes. Illusions of the feel of a virtual world can be very startling and engaging. "Haptic illusions like the ones Margaret Minsky demonstrated," reported Howard Rheingold (1991), "shook my reality sense far more than the cartoon like visual worlds I had explored. . . . I'll always remember that as a particularly weird moment in my personal history of reality" (p. 313).

Another way of obtaining haptic illusions is to encase the hand or, more radically, most of the body in an external brace-like device known as an exoskeleton (see Fig. 4.17). As the name suggests, an exoskeleton is like an

---

[15]This is a kind of phrasing that Brenda Laurel (1990) used to describe criteria for a satisfactory world (see also Rheingold, 1991, p. 298). In Laurel's case, the meaning extends beyond satisfactory tactile illusions and metaphorically suggests the kind of interactive realism that will ultimately characterize the more engaging and satisfying virtual worlds.

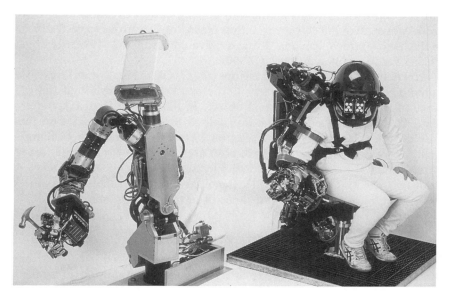

FIG. 4.17.   This force-reflecting exoskeleton is used to give the operator the sensation of being present in some distant location (telepresence). The unit on the right controls the actions of the robot on the left. The user sees the 3-D world of the robot and experiences some of the sensations of touching the objects the robot touches. This particular system is used to control and experience the actions of a robot in remote-sensing underwater applications. A version of the unit on the left can also be used to see and touch purely virtual objects created by a computer. Courtesy of Naval Ocean Systems Center.

external skeleton with joints at the same locations as joints in the hands, arm, or other points of movement. When fully anchored and connected to motors controlled by a computer, an exoskeleton can apply forces to the arm that simulate sensations like grasping and using a hammer, pushing a large rock across a table, or picking up a heavy object from the ground.

The development of exoskeletons for force feedback has been fueled by telepresence applications. Examples are the remote manipulation of robot arms in dangerous environments such as nuclear plants or remote areas such as deep sea or space. Because an exoskeleton can also monitor the motion of the body it can also be used as an input device (see section on kinematic input).

Some of most sophisticated force feedback systems, such as one developed at the Naval Ocean Systems Center (see Fig. 4.17), incorporate the so-called Utah/MIT arm and hand ("Dexterous teleoperator system master," Jacobsen, Iversen, Knutti, Johnson, & Biggers, 1986). This device can register and apply forces to a number of the joints with up to seven degrees of freedom and with high levels of sensitivity ("high bandwidth"). Although this is a top-shelf system suitable only for big budget organizations, there are less expensive but lower resolution means of delivering force feedback to the hand (Burdea, Zhuang, Roskos, Silver, & Langrana, 1992; Shimoga, 1993a; Venkataraman & Iberall, 1990).

Experience with early exoskeletons (e.g., GE's Handyman) revealed potential dangers to the operator if the exoskeleton transmitted the full force of the push of some virtual object. In most force feedback systems (e.g., UNC's Grope system) the transmitted forces are attenuated so that they do not accidentally injure the user by overly straining or bending a limb. Force feedback systems have been used to create the delicate feel of virtual musical instruments (Cadoz, Florens, & Luciani, 1984; Cadoz & Ramstein, 1988; Rheingold, 1991), the electric field of surrounding atoms (Brooks et al., 1990), or the resistance of moving massive objects.

Whole Body Movement Displays

Some virtual environments attempt to simulate the feeling of the user's body moving through a large space. This can be the illusion of actively walking around a space or being passively transported in a vehicle such as a car or plane. But most virtual equipment is confined to a small space like a room or to the even smaller space covered by the position tracker (discussed later). It is usually not possible for the individual to actually walk around the physical space to simulate walking around the virtual space. Treadmills may sometimes provide the solution (see Fig. 4.18, see also DiZio & Lackner, 1986), and bicycles and stair-stepping equipment have also been used (Faxon, 1993; Walser, 1990b). One manufacturer puts the user in the middle of a set of gimbals that passively respond to the user's motion and give the illusion of free movement in space (see Fig. 4.19).

Some simulations require that the user have the illusion of significant motion through the virtual space, illusions like acceleration, deceleration, or the rocking motion of a ship, and so forth. Morton Hellig's now famous 1960s arcade ride, Sensorama (Rheingold, 1991), included a vibrating seat and handlebars to simulate the "feel" of a motorcycle. The most widely experienced examples of such illusions are the well known fantasy rides at Disney World and Universal Studios. These are large-scale simulations that require that the user have the vivid illusion of acceleration, deceleration, and other motion and inertial forces.

Some of the most advanced simulations of strong gravitational and inertial forces are found in flight simulators, a form of virtual environment (Flexman & Stark, 1987; Haber, 1986; Rolfe & Staples, 1986). These strong, visceral physical illusions are produced by *motion platforms* (Fig. 4.20; see also Figs. 6.1, 6.2, 6.3, & 6.7 in chapter 6, by Hawkins). The user is usually seated, though he or she may, in some cases, lie or stand on the platform.

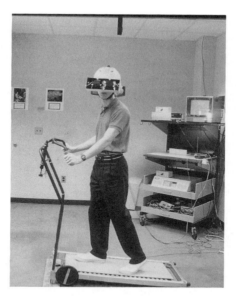

FIG. 4.18. Example of an early input device for an architectural "walk-through" application. The user walked on a treadmill that helped generate the illusion of strolling through the virtual building seen on the head-mounted display. The treadmill recorded the direction (using handlebars) and extent of the user's walking. Distance walked in the virtual world was matched to distance walked on the treadmill. Courtesy of the Computer Science Dept., University of North Carolina at Chapel Hill.

Carefully calibrated movements, vibrations, and jolts are applied to the platform by hydraulic or pneumatic cylinders as well as motor-driven mechanical devices. By carefully applying the inertial forces in conjunction with visual and audio illusions, the user may have the illusion of having moved far greater distances than the actual short movements of the platform. There are many applications in the areas of entertainment and training where the forces of motion may be major components of the sense of presence.

The use of such platforms for training raises some difficult questions regarding the relationship of the forces exerted in the simulation and the actual physical forces modeled (Flexman & Stark, 1987; Lackner & DeZio, 1992). For example, the sensations generated by gravitational and inertial forces are used by pilots to make judgments about their position in space or the correctness of a maneuver (e.g., "flying by the seat of your pants"). There is a question as to whether the user's physical learning, which involves the subtle calibration of muscles, will transfer positively to the actual world where the environmental forces are different.

The motion platforms used in the military and major amusement parks are large, expensive, and relatively inflexible (i.e., they tend to be dedicated

FIG. 4.19. The *CyberTron* provides motion cues at relatively low cost, being powered by the user's movements. Courtesy of Straylight Corporation, Warren, NJ.

to a limited class of illusions). One can foresee a cheaper class of small, single-user motion platforms intended for a wide range of VR entertainment applications. These single-user platforms are under development for the location-based entertainment industry. (But at least one consumer electronics manufacturer has tested and abandoned the development of motion platforms because users appeared to adapt to them too quickly.)[16] At some stage, safe and programmable motion platforms might find their way into the home.

Trends in the Development of Motion Platforms.   In the development of motion platforms we can already see two very distinct levels of

---

[16]Mark Johnson Williams, Sega, personal communication, December 1993.

FIG. 4.20. Motion platforms are used to simulate gravitational and inertial forces. They can give the user strong, visceral illusions of motion. This very large motion platform is used in simulation studies at NASA. Courtesy of the NASA Ames Research Center.

development. A split occurs over the level of attention to (a) the sensory fidelity of the motion display, and (b) the coordination of the motion display with other perceptual cues in the environment.

The location-based entertainment industry will likely spearhead the development of most common motion platforms. Like the 25¢ pony ride outside grocery stores, the verisimilitude of the proprioceptive illusion may have a very low criterion for acceptability. The motion platforms used in the location-based entertainment industry (see Hawkins, this volume) involved manually "scripted" movements that are roughly coordinated with the visual and auditory displays. The large jerky movements mask the imprecision of the motion. The sensory fidelity of the display is clearly not a very critical issue. It is not clear that sensory fidelity will become a critical issue in such markets unless the miscoordination of motion-sensory cues is a large contributor to high incidences of simulation sickness (see Biocca, 1993).

Some training applications, on the other hand, may require the development of much higher levels of sensory fidelity and sensory cue coordination. For example, flight and battle training as well as remote exploration and other telepresence applications require that the user develop an accurate proprioceptive model of the physical forces. This internalized model of the proprioceptive cues is key to preparing the mind and body for the actual experience of those forces in battle, space exploration, or telepresence. In such situations, failures in the fidelity may lead to "negative training." It can be hoped that higher end developments that emerge in this sector will be diffused to lower end communication applications.

Nasal Displays

Compared to the other sensory channels, the nasal and oral[17] senses are rarely engaged or participating in virtual environments. There are, obviously, clear reasons for this. Both senses are chemical interfaces with the physical world. Chemicals must be applied to the senses to obtain the sensation. It is easier to have computer control over light, sound, and motion than over odors and flavors.

But nasal sensory illusions have been part of past simulations and media. A precursor to present virtual reality systems, Morton Hellig's 1960s Sensorama simulated the smell of exhaust, pizza, and flowers by releasing puffs of artificial aromas into the nasal passages of the user at the appropriate points in the ride (Heilig, 1993; see also Rheingold, 1991). Some of the amusement simulations found at Disney's Epcot Center use aromas to increase the illusion of displays such as an orange grove, a smoke-filled prehistoric scene, and a humid underwater simulation.

It is clear that the stimulation of the nasal sense blurs the distinction between real and virtual stimuli. Real physical scents must be used to simulate the smell of the real environment. Sometimes those chemicals are derivatives of the actual object being simulated (e.g., perfumes for flowers, orange distillations for the smell of oranges, etc.). Illusions for these senses are still clumsy to control and deliver. For example, once released into the air, aromas linger in the air and in nasal passages, so it is hard to quickly change from one nasal illusion to another.

---

[17]In the case of oral displays, it could be argued that junk food is already a "simulation" of real food; nothing could be more artificial. The author is not aware of any simulation of the oral sense that does not involve the ingestion of some form of food.

Although the addition of this sensory input can add to the sense of presence in certain environments, there has been limited interest in pursuing the development of VR illusions in this sensory channel.[18] Although arguing for the inclusion of more senses, Ivan Sutherland (1965) dismissed the nasal and oral senses: "So far as I know, no one seriously proposes computer displays of smell, or taste" (p. 507). This was the case in 1965, and appears to be the case today, with a few minor exceptions. For example, VR pioneer, Myron Krueger, reported in mid 1994 that ARPA had funded his effort to include realistic sensations of smell for telepresence surgery and battle simulations (Myron Krueger, personal communication, April 1994). His work was to include the simulation of diverse aromas including the smell of blood! The history of perfumes suggests that as a species we have long been interested in simulating pleasant aromas (Ackerman, 1990). Nasal sensations may play an important role in developing a feeling of presence in certain simulated environments (i.e., a rain forest). Although nasal displays may increase presence or provide some hedonistic value, the lack of interest in this perceptual channel may be due to the fact that the sense is rarely used by humans to encode the higher level symbolic information often found in the visual, aural, and tactile sensory channels.

Input Devices

To create a powerful virtual illusion, the computer must be able to sense the location and actions of the user's body in space. This is necessary to (a) accurately represent the user's body in the virtual space, and (b) turn specific body movements and actions into commands for the computer.

The input devices of highly immersive virtual environments try to conform to the way we interact with the physical world by making use of things such as the movement of our limbs, head, eyes, and other motions in physical space. The difference is best illustrated by an example. Say you want to move a computer graphic representation of a cube. In a nongraphic system you might type: Move cube, Location $x = 10$, $y = 55$, $z = 42$. In virtual reality you simply bend down and pick up the computer graphic cube with your hand and place it on a computer graphic table. The floor, the cube, the table, and the graphic representation of your hand are all data entities in a program, as is the computer's representation of your movement. To you it appears as a naturalistic perceptual event.

Virtual reality technology tries to make greater use of the natural skills we have acquired from our interaction with the physical world, evolutionary

---

[18]A meeting of VR experts convened by the National Science Foundation focused little attention on developments in this channel. A major VR training proposal (Durlach, 1992) covering various forms of input and output makes no mention of nasal displays.

skills that are coded in the operation of our perceptual and motor systems. It is clear that a wider range of input devices used in virtual reality systems change what we think of as computer input, and especially the associated concept of "data entry." When the computer monitors the movement of the user's head, hand, and body, the user is inputting information into the computer, and, in a general way, "entering data." But this is, of course, unconscious, unwilled, and, in most cases, passive. The computer responds to both these passive data entry methods and active entry methods such as the use of a coded hand gesture. For example, in some VR programs a set of pointing gestures is used to signal to the computer the user's desire to fly in a specific direction.[19]

But it is still easy to overwhelm the computer's current capacity to process information. As Krueger (1991) pointed out; "The design of a perceptual system (the sensors that comprise the input for the computer) requires a trade-off between the need for the computer to know as much as possible about a participant's behavior and its commitment to respond in real time" (p. 103).

The intuitive simplicity of input devices that conform to everyday actions has clear and revolutionary implications for the training, communication, and data manipulation applications that will be discussed later.

Let us consider some of the input devices sometimes found within virtual reality systems.

Kinematic Input Devices

Movement is an inherent factor in communications. Our body language, a fleeting glance, fidgeting, shifting from side to side, standing motionless, all provide valuable cues to our mental state. This nonverbal communication, so valuable in interpersonal communications, can be used to let a computer know how we fit into a virtual world, and what we want to happen there. Table 4.5 lists areas of human motion and activity that are used in interpersonal communication.

Kinematic input devices turn the movement of some body part into computer input. There is a large family of such devices. Each concentrates on a limited class of movements or uses different means to capture and digitize the movement of a body part.

Inputting Body Orientation and Position in Space.   When we move in the physical world, the visual relationships of the objects in a scene or a

---

[19]This gesture language was first developed by Warren Robinette of the University of North Carolina while working on NASA's VIEW project (Rheingold, 1991). Some form of this gestural code has become a part of many glove-based VR programs including those used by VPL, and labs at the University of Washington and the University of North Carolina.

TABLE 4.5
Kinematic Capture of Body Movements Used in Interpersonal Communication

General Research Area	Description of Movements	Input Devices Used To Capture and Digitize Movements
Proxemics	General body position and orientation, especially location of body relative to other bodies in space	Position trackers
Kinesics	hand, arm, head, leg, and torso movements	Position trackers (including 3-D mice), exoskeletons, data gloves (hand only), electromyography (EMG)
Facial expressions	motion of all expressive facial muscles	exoskeleton, electromyography (EMG)
Eye movement	eye movements, dilation	eye cameras, electromyography (EMG)

Note. This table assumes real-time capture only. The table excludes 2-D or 3-D video capture because neither is yet used for real-time control of a full 3-D animation of a user.

room change. As we move closer to a cup, for example, its image becomes larger on our retina. Also, as we turn our head, sound also changes: the sound of an object like a horn will change as each ear either faces or turns away from it. To create a convincing virtual space, the computer must keep track of where the user is looking and where the user is positioned so that the appearance and sound of scenes is changed appropriately as the user moves.

Position trackers are often used for this purpose (Meyer, Applewhite, & Biocca, 1992). Position trackers may use mechanical, optical, magnetic, or acoustic means to keep track of the physical location of a user's head, hands, or other parts of the body. One group of systems works by calculating the orientation and distance between emitters and the sensors. Depending on the type of system, the emitters or sensors may be worn by the user. In one popular magnetic tracking system (Polhemus trackers) the sensors are worn by the user and are quite small, about one cubic inch. Position trackers can report position along three dimensions of some small space such as a room, as well as the orientation of the device in space along three axes. (The so-called six degrees of freedom.) In this way, the computer can keep track of the location and movement of key parts of the user's body.

Keeping track of the location and orientation of the head is particularly important. The computer must be aware of what direction the user is looking to calculate the perspective relations of a scene that will be displayed to the user on the head-mounted display (Liang, Shaw, & Green, 1991), as well as to enable the computation of audio cues. The computer must continuously sense movement and change the visual scene and sounds to match the new position and orientation of the user's point of view.

Current position trackers can foster some limitations in virtual environment systems. Most trackers can only keep track of a user's movements in a relatively small space, and there are problems of accuracy, report lag, and other sources of distortion.

We can evaluate trends in the development of this technology using the evaluative scheme proposed by Meyer et al. (1992):

Resolution and accuracy. Current systems have adequate levels of resolution (the smallest change a system can detect) and accuracy (the range within which the reported position is correct). Good resolution and accuracy are desirable to detect such things as small movements of the head. Even small head movements can lead to significant changes in the visual scene. As VR systems will increasingly be asked to integrate real and virtual objects in a single illusion, the demand for higher resolution and accuracy are likely to increase.

Responsiveness. Current systems are often plagued by lags, the time between the moment a user makes a movement and the moment the computer responds to the movement. Part of this lag is attributable to the slowness of the position tracker and part is due to the time required to process the location information by the host computer. As lag increases, the sense of presence decreases to the point where it simply breaks down (Held & Durlach, 1991; Held, Efstathiou, & Greene, 1966). Lag also is suspected as a major cause of "simulator sickness" and nausea much like seasickness, sometimes induced by simulators. We can already see a tremendous emphasis on increasing the responsiveness of not only position trackers, but VR systems as a whole.

Registration. Does the position reported by the position tracker really match the position of the object in the physical space? Misregistration of your body parts, such as your hand, for example, can contribute to sensory conflicts and even simulation sickness (Biocca, 1993) when the virtual visual location of your body parts does not match their "felt" position (proprioceptive location). Like resolution and accuracy, good registration will become essential to the interaction of virtual and real objects in a single illusion.

Sociability. How many emitters (i.e., people or body parts) can a system keep track of? If VR systems are to become interpersonal communication environments where a number of people communicate in a task or game, then position trackers must be able to keep track of all the individuals and their movements. Some systems, like people, cannot "see" (detect) an object or person when they are occluded. But some communication applications, like virtual theaters (Lanier & Biocca, 1992) will require that the system keep track of multiple users engaged in rapid action. A "sociable" system also needs to have a large range of operation so that it can track positions in a large space. The most common systems used today have a limited range.

Robustness. Like snow on your TV set, position trackers are subject to interference from other environmental sources. Position trackers are subject to distortion from sources of energy similar to the sources used for position tracking by a particular system be it magnetic, acoustic, or optically-based.

Inputting Movements of Limbs: Gestures and Locomotion.   Although positioners keep track of the general position and orientation of body parts such as the user's head and hands, more information is needed by the computer. It is also valuable for the computer to know when the users flex their arms and fingers to pick up objects, or flex their legs to walk. Objects in the virtual world need to move when pushed by virtual hands, grasped by virtual fingers, or kicked by virtual legs. Users may also want to communicate with the computer through gestures. And finally, in telepresence applications the computer might use the digital record of a person's movements to guide the operations of a distant robot who then replicates the gestures in places such as deep under the sea, in a nuclear power plant core, or in space.

Exoskeletons.   One way a computer can keep track of our body movements is to have us wear something that can detect the flexing of our limbs when we walk or pick up objects. An exoskeleton is such a device. Earlier, we introduced the use of exoskeletons as output devices (see Fig. 4.17). But an exoskeleton can simultaneously be an input device (Little, 1988).[20] Strapped to the user's limbs, the exoskeleton's joints move when the user's joints move. By digitizing this information, the computer can know when we flex our fingers, arms, and legs (see Fig. 4.21).

Although exoskeletons can be bulky, they have the advantage that they can be used to both sense the movement of a user's limbs (input) and provide force feedback during movement (output) to help create illusions such as the resistance of hard surfaces like walls, springy surfaces like cushions, or movement through water. Exoskeletal devices are particularly important to telepresence applications such as the remote manipulation of

---

[20]Various exoskeletons are potential candidates for use with VR systems. Exos (Burlington, MA) produces such systems as the "dextrous hand master," "grip master," and their "exoskeletal arm master," and in 1994 introduced a new line of products. Sarcos Corp. (Salt Lake City, UT) produces expensive teleoperator exoskeletons including their "dextrous hand master."

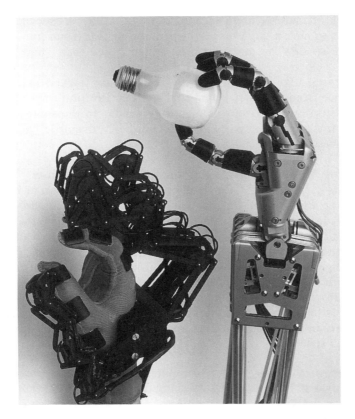

FIG. 4.21.   This exoskeletal-hand device (left) provides a means of inputting gestures in virtual environments. In purely virtual environments, it controls a computer graphic representation of the user's hand. In telepresence applications, it also controls the movements of a remote robotic hand (right). Courtesy of Sarcos.

robotic devices in space, military combat, microenvironments, or hazardous environmental applications.

Data Gloves.   As pointed out above, some exoskeletons can be heavy, awkward, or bulky. Although they can be precise, the bulk may not desirable if high precision or force feedback are not part of an application. Light, clothing-like input devices might be a more desirable means of keeping track of limb and hand movements.

The ubiquitous input glove (Zimmerman, 1987) is a popular means of inputting hand movement (see Fig. 4.22). VPL's data glove replaced the mechanical devices of an exoskeleton with thin fiber optic devices that can be stitched into a piece of clothing. When the hand is flexed, the fibers in

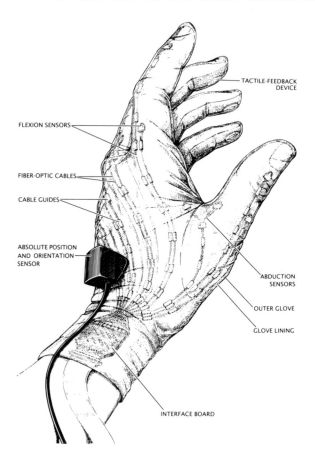

TACTILE-FEEDBACK DEVICE

FLEXION SENSORS

FIBER-OPTIC CABLES

CABLE GUIDES

ABSOLUTE POSITION
AND ORIENTATION
SENSOR

ABDUCTION SENSORS

OUTER GLOVE

GLOVE LINING

INTERFACE BOARD

FIG. 4.22.   The signature VR data glove uses inexpensive LEDs and fiber optic cables to input hand movements. The LED shines light down a fiber optic cable stitched onto the back of the glove. The fiber optic cable is altered slightly to be more sensitive to the flexing of the joints. When the hand is flexed, the cables are bent and less light is transmitted through the optical cable. A photo sensor detects changes in magnitude of light and the computer translates this information into an estimate of the flexion of a particular set of joints ($\pm 1°$). From "InterFaces for Advanced Computing" by James D. Foley. Copyright (1987) by Scientific American, Inc. All rights reserved.

the glove are bent and stretched at the joints. This flexion tells the computer about the movement of the fingers.

There are various ways to measure the flexing of the joints to get a computer graphic model of the user's moving fingers. Using small, inexpensive LEDs for light sources, the data glove shines light down fiber optic cables stitched onto the back of the glove. The fiber optic cables are altered slightly to be more sensitive to the flexing of the joints. When the hand is flexed, the cables are bent and less light is transmitted through the optical cables. A photo sensor detects changes in magnitude of light and the computer translates this information into an estimate of the flexion of a particular set of joints ($\pm 1°$) (Zimmerman, 1987).

When combined with a position-tracking device, the data provided by the input glove are translated into a three-dimensional representation of the user's hand. The virtual model of the hand moves and flexes in synchrony with the movement and flexing of the user's physical hand.

Other data glove designs measure the flexing of the user's hand using other means such as tension-sensitive switches at the joints. Mattel's Power Glove detected the flexing of the hand by monitoring changes in resistance in an electrical current running down a path of conductive ink printed on a flexible plastic strip attached to the back of each finger in the glove (Rheingold, 1991, pp. 163–164).

Data Suits.   If the developmental logic of the technology is to further increase the user's sense of presence into a virtual world, it is not surprising that the engineering principles behind the input glove have been applied to other body parts as well. VPL's work on the development of an input suit reflected the trend toward detecting and using the input from the movement of the whole body in the creation of virtual reality illusion. The greater immersion is attained at the cost of "suiting up." But critics like Krueger (1991) argue that this cumbersome need to put on so much equipment will restrict the use of devices like the input suit to a limited range of applications.

Inputting Smaller Body Movements: Facial Expressions and Eye Movements

Facial Expressions.   Facial expressions play a major role in interpersonal communication (Ekman, 1974). In a telecommunication application, a greater sense of "being there" (Brittan, 1992) might be achieved if VR systems could display representations of facial expressions.

Facial expressions can be captured with the use of exoskeletons. But such systems, such as those produced by Simgraphics, tend to be restricted to performance applications and one-time input of facial movement for modelling purposes. They are not practical for everyday interpersonal communication in cyberspace.

Although two-dimensional film representations of facial expressions are clearly achievable (e.g., picture phones), it is more difficult to provide a 3-D graphic model of facial expressions mapped inside a fully immersive virtual environment. There seems to be a trade-off between the more immersive head-mounted displays and the full capturing of facial expressions. Currently, most systems only can display a user's gross body movements. Output devices like head-mounted displays obscure much of the user's face, especially the user's eyes. Any simple input recording of facial expression is made difficult by the head-mounted display.

With flat-panel, windowed VR displays, this is less of a problem. But here, too, we can see some obstacles. Special glasses used to see some stereographic displays give all users that "sunglasses" look. The expressive eyes are masked. It is possible that some of the alternative display technologies may alleviate this problem.

The picture phone and teleconferencing facilities are examples of previous attempts to get facial cues into telecommunication between individuals. Some researchers are not willing to surrender this important communication channel when we go to 3-D displays. Rheingold (1991) discussed a very ambitious project at the Advanced Telecommunications Research Institute International in Japan. A goal of the institute is a large telecommunications environment in which virtual reality equipment may be used to create virtual meeting places, teleconferencing in 3-D. A key component of this project is to find ways to capture and communicate facial codes and display them in 3-D in these networked cyberspaces.

Facial codes could be carried on replicas of a user's face or used to animate computer graphic "masks," which may or may not resemble the face of the user. Some convincing examples of this approach have been produced (Morishima & Harashima, 1993). The exact means of incorporating and displaying facial codes in the current generation of virtual environments is not clear. Some point to the use of shape acquisition cameras (discussed later) as a solution to this problem (e.g., Krueger, 1991; Rheingold, 1991). But the refinement of this technology for use in real-time VR applications is still a long-term proposition.

Inputting Eye Movements.   In 1965, Sutherland stated the following: "Machines to sense and interpret eye motion data can and will be built. It remains to be seen if we can use a language of glances to control a computer. An interesting experiment will be to make the display presentation depend on where we look" (p. 506). This is exactly what has occurred.

Eye movement trackers have been part of military applications of virtual environments and are considered valuable input for future applications (Aviles et al., 1992; Rheingold, 1991). Eye movements can reveal where we allocate our attention over the visual space (Rayner, 1984). Just as another person may be very aware of the location of your gaze when the two of you are speaking, a computer with eye movement sensors can also make use of these behavioral indicators of a user's visual attention. According to Richard Bolt, a researcher in this area: "One reason for the system to watch the eyes is to open a new channel through which we can detect where the user's attention is directed. The effect can be compared to what children gain when they discover that where the parent is *looking* is useful to them in comprehending what is transpiring between them and their parent, and, in turn, with the world about them" (quoted in Rheingold, 1991, p. 231).

Eye movement can be digitally inputted in a variety of ways (Young & Sheena, 1975). Some of the more advanced eye location sensors use the corneal reflection of infrared light to track eye movements or computer analysis of video images of the eye. Other less expensive measures use eye muscle potential measures (electrooculographic techniques) (see Fig. 4.23). All these types of eye tracking have been used for various forms of

FIG. 4.23.   Illustration of a relatively inexpensive physiological input system. Various attachments can pick up electrical activity in the muscles, skin, or brain. The picture shows a user with a device that registers muscle movements in the eyes and face. When connected to a VR system, the input from such devices is used to (a) control computer functions through muscle movement, (b) signal changes in the user's attention, intentions, or other cognitive states, or (c) monitor the reactions of users to virtual experiences. Courtesy BioControl Systems.

computer input (Jacob, 1990) and flight simulation (Rolfe & Staples, 1986), and are likely to be part of high-level virtual environments (Aviles et al., 1992). As these eye tracking devices have become less expensive, we find them incorporated in other devices. For example, in 1993 Canon introduced a SLR camera that tracks the user's eye position, and then auto-focuses on the part of the scene at which the photographer is looking.

As Sutherland suggested, one way to use eye movement input in virtual environments is to change the kind of visual display presented within the foveal region of the visual field. These are called *gaze-responsive displays*. Some gaze-responsive displays make use of the fact that the eye's fovea needs a clear, crisp image, whereas our peripheral vision can make do with a fuzzier image. A maximum-resolution display is presented at the points where the user's vision is focused; a less resolved image is used elsewhere. (The CAE HMD mentioned earlier is this type of system.) This helps conserve the limited computing capabilities of the hardware and software. The computer saves computing time by not having to generate a highly resolved image over the full display but only where it is needed by the user, in the user's focal area.

Eye movements are voluntary and can be used to signal intention. Eye movements have been used to issue computer commands in the cockpits of fighter planes. MIT's famous "Put that there" demo combined eye movement and voice input to tell a computer to move items around a screen (Bolt, 1984; Brand, 1988). Japan's Advanced Telecommunications Research Institute is actively exploring the use of eye movement for both computer commands and input and for interpersonal communication within advanced virtual telecommunication systems (Rheingold, 1991).

Voice/Audio Input

The idea of human–computer interaction as a kind of conversation has been, until recently, the dominant metaphor in the design of human–computer interfaces (Walker, 1988). You type in a verbal command that approximates a human language like English (in the best of cases!) and the computer responds with language-like symbols. The science fiction literature of the 1950s to the 1970s is filled with images of computers that take voice commands and respond with metallic voices in a kind of pidgin syntax and monotonous rhythm. The conversant computer is best exemplified by the character HAL in the movie *2001: A Space Odyssey*.

Voice-input technologies have been developed to objectify this conversational vision of human–computer interaction (Waibel & Lee, 1990). A number of universities have major speech-recognition projects funded by the Advanced Research Projects Agency (ARPA) and there are significant commercial research projects at IBM, NYNEX, Texas Instruments, and elsewhere. A number of commercial voice-input systems exist that are potentially usable for VR applications (Duchnowski & Uchanski, 1992).

Although some speech-recognition systems are quite inexpensive, only a few virtual reality systems make significant use of voice input. For example, NASA's early virtual reality system included voice input (Rheingold, 1991, p. 141). However, more systems are incorporating voice I/O. These include IBM's Rubber Rocks demo system, and the Metaphor Mixer developed by Maxus Systems and Avatar Partners.

Voice input serves two purposes in a virtual environment: (a) to converse with other humans present in the virtual environment (a kind of virtual "walkie-talkie"), and (b) to converse with (command) the computer. The former use is technologically quite simple. The latter use of speech input is more troublesome. This discussion concentrates on voice input as a form of computer command.

Trends in the Development of Speech Recognition Systems.   According to Duchnowski and Uchanski (1992), speech-recognition systems for VR and other applications face three developmental hurdles to optimal performance:

1. *Continuous speech input.* When we speak, we make a continuous stream of sounds. Some systems can identify isolated words (discontinuous speech). But it is more difficult for computer systems to pick out the words in regular speech unless the user clearly stresses the words and pauses (100–250 msec) between words. It will be a challenge to develop a system that does not involve the compromises of discontinuous speech or special speaking styles for human-to-computer speech. But many would consider such compromises acceptable.

2. *Speaker independence.* Each one of us sounds different. We pronounce words in different ways. It is a challenge for a computer to recognize the common word among the many variations of sound produced by different speakers. Some speech-recognition systems must be trained to recognize one or a few voices. Although speaker-independent systems exist with acceptable error rates, the gain of speaker independence is achieved with a loss in vocabulary size (see the following) or continuous speech abilities.

3. *Vocabulary size.* Systems exist that can recognize from 10 to 50,000 words. Although the higher numbers seem impressive, we must remember that "recognize" does not mean the semantic understanding of words. Recognition often means nothing more than the ability of the system to successfully translate the sound of a word into its printed (graphemic) version.

Speech-recognition systems use dynamic programming algorithms to rapidly cut speech sounds (acoustic wave form) into speech units (words, syllable, phonemes, etc.), filter out a specific sound pattern, and match the pattern to stored patterns from prerecorded exemplars of the word ("dynamic time warping"). Statistical or stochastic models based on information theory and Markov models sometimes provide the rules for the matching process.

We are likely to see more complex models as faster processors with greater memory are available for speech recognition and incorporation of speech recognition capabilities into VR environments. Gains in accuracy and flexibility should develop from models that can use the discursive context to assist in speech recognition and understanding (Duchnowski & Uchanski, 1992), something that humans use to disambiguate speech. The use of neural network models may be useful for this and acoustic-phonemic modeling.

Other Haptic Input Devices

Computers have always used a wide variety of input devices, though many of these have been primitive (see Greenstein & Arnault, 1988). For example, the standard computer mouse is a system that detects 2-D position by monitoring the extent and direction of the movement of a track ball located in the underside of the mouse. The standard mouse has one to three buttons that can be used to issue all kinds of commands in tandem with options offered by the user's software.

The 3-D mouse[21] used with some virtual reality systems is a similar device equipped with a position tracking sensor to register 3-D position information (see Fig. 4.24). Such devices are very useful when the user is engaged in 3-D design applications such as those found in engineering, architecture, and computer animation. For example, a virtual reality system at the University of North Carolina uses a custom-designed device created by hollowing out a billiard ball and inserting two buttons and a position-tracking device inside the ball.

It follows that buttons and position sensors can be attached to all manner of virtual reality props including guns (e.g., Mattel), racquetball rackets (e.g., Autodesk), wands (e.g., Lincoln Labs), or any other object that may be a physical prop with a graphic equivalent inside a virtual environment. Input commands may be issued by virtue of the physical location of the prop (e.g., a virtual racquet hitting a virtual ball), the pressing of a button on the prop (e.g., a trigger on a gun), by moving a lever or knob (e.g., joysticks and dials), or by pointing a prop in a specific direction (e.g., pointing a wand). It is likely that we will see the development of all manner

---

[21]A number of companies have introduced a 3-D mouse device (e.g., SimGraphics, Logitech).

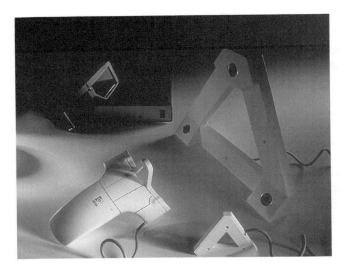

FIG. 4.24.   Example of typical 3-D mouse, which registers hand movement in 3-D space. Photo courtesy of Logitech, Inc.

of creative, useful, or frivolous input devices to be used in entertainment and training applications of virtual reality technology.

Psychophysiological Input

Psychophysiological input has been proposed for use in virtual environments (Krueger, 1991; Rheingold, 1991; Warner, 1992; see Fig. 4.23). Although psychophysiological measures have long been used to monitor user responses to mediated experiences (e.g., Cacioppo & Tassinary, 1990; Reeves et al., 1985; Stewart & Furse, 1982), rarely have such responses been used as "feedback," altering the nature of the mediated presentation. But most biofeedback applications involve tying psychophysiological inputs to some sensory display, be it differing tones, lights, or other indicators. Companies have even marketed so-called therapeutic systems that link a psychophysiological response to patterns on a computer display.

Virtual reality applications in training or entertainment can potentially take this one step further and tie various parameters of the environment (e.g., color, spatial characteristics, motion, activity of agents, etc.) to the digitized values of a psychophysiological measure. Such input could be used for medical reasons, personal mood management, interpersonal communication, or to evaluate training effectiveness. Consciously guided psychophysiological responses can also be used to control external devices (e.g., Keirn & Aunon, 1990). Some psychophysiological measures under consideration for use in virtual environments include heart rate, blood pressure, muscle tension (electromyography [EMG]), electrocardiogram [EKG], skin resistance (electrodermal activity [EDA]) and brain waves (electroencephalograph [EEG]) (see Warner, 1992).

Real-World Objects and Scenes with Shape Acquisition Cameras?

As immersive virtual environments are diffused to various segments of society, two critical technical problems are likely to become an issue: (a) how do we quickly import detailed models of physical objects into virtual worlds, and (b) how do we lessen and finally eliminate some of the devices such as gloves, suits, etc. necessitated by current immersive uses of the technology?

The first question is based on the notion that virtual worlds could be furnished by "3-D pictures" of real-world objects like chairs, cars, elephants, and so on. Most virtual objects must be built; their shape (polygon structure) must be drawn using CAD tools, the shading and texturing of surfaces specified, and physical and behavioral properties defined. The building of objects and worlds is still labor-intensive. Quarendon (1993) reported that the animation sequences in *Terminator 2: Judgment Day* required the sweat of 60 programmers and that the computer model of a starship in the animations of *The Last Starfighter* was pasted together from over 500,000 polygons. These are not objects that the everyday, garage VR user can assemble over the weekend. Building models like these is as tedious as assembling a toothpick model of the Brooklyn Bridge—only for people with money or time on their hands.

The goal is to make it easier for the least trained users to generate virtual worlds and populate them with objects. At this time there are few objects to populate all the virtual worlds on the planet. But the marketing of virtual objects is already in motion. A number of companies distribute a kind of virtual "clip art," cut-and-paste polygonal 3-D models of people and common objects. This is one way to make world-building easier.

Something even simpler would greatly help the general diffusion and usage of VR. The idea that one could take a 3-D "picture" of a person, object, or room and import it into a virtual world appeals to many (e.g., Rheingold, 1991). Shape-acquisition cameras that generate a digital 3-D map of the surfaces of an object would be of great value to quick construction of virtual worlds.

Technologies exist for mapping a 3-D surface using shape-acquisition methods (see Quarendon, 1993). Some use active sensing methods. For example, relatively inexpensive technologies exist for measuring the shape of objects using hand-held probes in combination with ultrasound imaging.

In some systems, for example, an object is touched with the pen and each time it is touched a vertex is acquired for the 3-D model. Eventually a full polygonal model emerges. But this process is slow and tedious for general use, although it is very valuable in engineering and industrial design applications.

Some visual active sensing systems shine linear, Moiré patterns over objects. The lines in the linear pattern distort when they are projected on bumpy surfaces like a face. The patterns of the lines reveals the shape. Some other active sensing methods use the time-of-flight of a laser light. The time it takes for the laser light to leave the emitter and bounce back tells the computer how far a surface is from the emitter (Connell, 1992). These technologies have been proposed for use in VR but they tend to be expensive or may not be easy to use.

Something closer to a "picture" of a 3-D object can be found in passive visual sensing systems. These systems use pictures or video and sophisticated algorithms to analyze the images to determine depth. For example, some use cues such as the different location of objects in stereo pairs of photographs. The 2-D forms of objects close to the camera tend to be further apart in the two stereo images. Other techniques use single moving cameras and measure the how quickly forms in the sequence move across the image plane. Due to motion parallax, forms closer to the camera move across the image plane faster than objects further away. But images are often ambiguous and image analysis is complex. All of these methods have different problems and none of them can assemble models in real time. But one of these may evolve into a general-purpose 3-D camera.

A shape-acquisition system that could measure not only form but also map colors, textures, and shapes would be most valuable for various VR applications. Teleconferencing applications are a good example. Some systems presently map the picture of someone's face onto a 3-D model of his or her head. The texture mapped model is animated to simulate convincing facial expressions (e.g., Moroshima & Harashima, 1993). This could be used to construct models of synthetic actors or representations that can act as "puppets," models of the users in the virtual world. Shape-acquisition cameras would also become the essential tool for quickly constructing models of physical environments for training and other applications.

A number of VR commentators and researchers hold out the hope for full, real-time shape-acquisition technologies. One calls for "gloveless VR" (Rheingold, 1991) and another calls for "come as you are" technologies (Krueger, 1991). The idea is based on the desire for input devices that use natural body movement without cumbersome equipment like gloves, suits, and exoskeletons, a system where anyone can simply walk in and use. In such scenarios shape-acquisition cameras would become the ideal, general input device if able to generate digital models of real-world objects in real time. Body movements and facial expressions could "simply" be digitally captured, transported, and represented anywhere else.

The telecommunications value of a full 3-D representation of a distant colleague, object, or environment is obvious. For example, NASA is particularly intrigued by the possibility of having ground-based specialists like geologists act upon virtual models of distant environments (McGreevy, 1991; Stoker, 1993). If, in the more distant development of this technology, researchers could successfully combine real-time shape-acquisition cameras with holographic display systems, then virtual reality technology would have taken a critical step to creating the kind of science fiction communication system such as the Holodeck of the *Star Trek* television series.

But like holographic display systems, shape-acquisition technologies are still in their infancy, a distant vision rather than a reality. Real-time versions of the prototypes are still off in the future. How far off? There is disagreement about whether the technologies are in the near or distant future. But it is clear that shape-acquisition input devices remain at the upper and distant end of the input devices discussed here.

Computer Platforms and Software Architectures

If the output and input devices are the "senses" and "limbs" of a virtual reality system, then the computer platforms and software are the "guts" and "brains" of the system. This technological area is probably the most dynamic and unsettled. A number of commercial programs exist for creating and controlling virtual environments. Virtual environments can be experienced on most computer platforms, but high-end experiences often require numerous specialized computers.

Among the more sophisticated virtual-environment computing systems are some advanced multicomputers that make extensive use of teams of specialized processors. These specialized processors are designed from the beginning with special "virtual construction" tasks in mind. Working in parallel, these multicomputers are like an assembly line of highly skilled workers, each constructing one aspect of a virtual world.

At the heart of most VR systems is a graphics computer. The graphics power of these configurations is often judged by rough measures such as the number of polygons produced (throughput) per second. A specialist in computer graphics technology, Alvy Ray Smith, estimated that the visual simulation of physical reality would require the production of approximately 80 million polygons per second (quoted in Rheingold, 1991). The best commercially available systems at the time of this writing rarely break the 2 million polygons-per-second threshold.

Virtual worlds are created from an endless series of computations that can be run on a number of computers. Computations take time. The more detailed and complex the virtual world, the higher the number of computations. Each added layer of sensory vividness, like detailed textures and multijointed simulated figures, takes additional computing power. Each layer of virtual world-modeling increases the complexity of the software.

Because calculations take time, users may experience a perceptual lag. For example, when users rapidly move their heads they may notice that the visual world lags behind their movements. Because perceptual lags can destroy the illusion of presence, it has been a major concern for developers. One solution is faster, more powerful, and more specialized computers. But because computing power is limited and software can only support limited levels of complexity, most virtual reality systems involve compromises.

Figure 4.25 displays the basic functional outline of a VR system. These functions may be carried out on a single computer or may be distributed to a number of computers operating in parallel and sharing information. Systems are often judged by (a) the perceptual complexity of the environments they support, (b) the speed of the system's responsiveness to user action, and (c) the number of users the system can support. These criteria

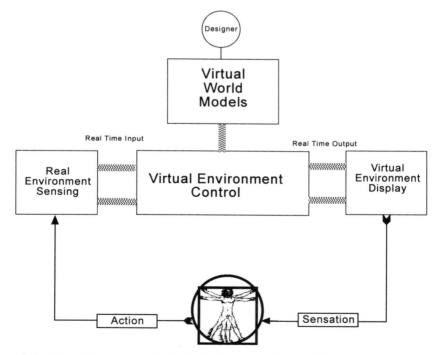

FIG. 4.25.   Diagram shows the basic functions carried out by VR computer hardware and software.

are all related and each is influenced by the combinations of hardware and software that make up the system.

Let us briefly describe some of these basic functions and development issues related to each one of the subsystems in Fig. 4.25.

Virtual Object and World Modeling.   Virtual worlds are composed of agents or objects: humanoid forms, animals, rocks, mountains, forests, and so forth. Everything in the world is artificial and must be created or imported by the designers of the world. Modeling software allows the designer, and sometimes the user, to create objects.

Modeling software is used to create objects. Objects are given properties: shape, color, sound, motion, and so forth. Graphic objects are most often created from polygons. Except for some of the unique stereoscopic computational issues, virtual environments share many of the same graphic-design processes found in other computer graphic and animation applications. Readers interested in technical issues in the creation of visually realistic virtual worlds should consult standard computer graphic reference sources (e.g., Foley, Van Dam, Feiner, & Hughes, 1990).

At a more complex level of world creation, objects may be given properties such as motion or dynamic internal properties such as hardness or springiness. This is sometimes referred to as kinematics. It is a form of automated 3-D animation — slick puppetering where the strings are replaced with programming commands.

Think of the many ways people and objects move in the real world. Motion can be simple like that of a rock thrown through the air, or it can be more complex, like the many motions involved in dancing — head, arms, torso, and legs moving harmoniously but in all directions. To simulate this motion the designer doesn't want a puppet with "200 knobs" on it. It is a computing challenge to create simplified programming instructions for realistic models of object motions (see Badler, Barsky, & Zeltzer, 1991).

One of the most significant modeling challenges is the creation of autonomous synthetic actors and agents. Here traditional modeling must include a certain amount of artificial intelligence. Among the most complex forms of animation is the generation of realistic expressions for humanoid agents (e.g., Morishima & Harashima, 1993). Synthetic actors must be given motion scripts, speech scripts, and must be fully animated. The actors must be programmed to respond appropriately to specified conditions in the virtual world such as the approach of a user, or the action of another object. The modeling, animation, and coordination of complex virtual worlds represents one of the most significant software challenges in the creation of interesting virtual reality experiences such as dramatic narratives (see Meyer, this volume).

Real Environment Sensing.   The computer must sense the user because the most important part of the real world is the user. Virtual environments are created for users. The computer must sense what the user is doing or intends to do to create satisfactory illusions. This part of the virtual environment program continuously collects information from input devices such as position sensors, data gloves, exoskeletons, and so forth. User actions are translated into numbers that the program can use to calculate appropriate responses.

Virtual Environment Display.   Virtual-environment display programs are the painters and illusionists of virtual reality. The world must be rendered up to the senses. Each of the user's senses must experience the virtual world in a different way. For our eyes, the virtual world is a set of changing colored pixels on a display screen. The image may look like a tree, but from the computer's viewpoint it is just a set of instructions that make a contiguous set of basic color pixels light up to produce green and brown light.

The computer must generate illusions for the other senses as well. For the ears the virtual world is changing pulses of sound from a set of speakers. For the hands, the virtual world is a set of tactors pressing on the skin. This part of the virtual reality programming translates the virtual world into instructions that generate the appropriate sensory illusions for each sensory channel.

Unlike television images, the illusion is tailored for each user. The world must look and feel different at different positions. Different users may be looking at the same virtual world but the display will match the perspective of the user. For example, the computer must determine whether a table overlaps a chair before it can render it realistically on the user's monitor.

Virtual Environment Control.   Virtual-environment control programs are the directors of the virtual world. They control the illusion and pass information back and forth among different computers or different functions of the virtual environment program.

FROM "CHEAP" TO "AWESOME": VARIOUS COMBINATIONS OF VR COMPONENTS

Immersive VR setups range from various "garage VR" systems using PCs, improvised software, the cheap Mattel PowerGlove and "home-brewed," head-mounted displays. At the high end we find costly research and military systems running on graphic workstations, like the Silicon Graphics Reality Engine, specialized image generators designed for simulation systems, such as the ESIG 2000, or powerful graphic engines, like UNC's Pixel Flow and Pixel Planes series.

In general, the nonspecialist can make some rough distinctions among the dizzying range of platforms and software architectures using a limited set of simple criteria. These general criteria are set out in Table 4.6. Each criterion is a construct. These constructs may be influenced by a host of technical variables. The table contains two kinds of criteria: (a) social constructs of user-friendliness such as diffusability and cost, and (b) constructs emphasizing the level of "presence" such as sensory vividness and sociability.

Using these simple, basic criteria we can divide the more immersive computer platforms and software combinations into three general classes.

TABLE 4.6
Basic Criteria for Evaluating VR Platforms and Software

Criterion	Description
Sensory vividness	The capabilities of the base hardware and software, and not just the output devices, contribute to sensory vividness, a key component of the sense of presence. Sensory vividness includes such considerations as: (a) the number of sensory channels supported, (b) the sensory resolution within each sensory channel, (c) the level of coordination between sensory displays and illusions, and (d) realism.
Interactivity	Interactivity is also critical to the sense of presence. In VR the criterion can be defined as: (a) the number and forms of input and output, (b) the level of responsiveness to conscious and unconscious user actions and states, (c) the range of interactive experiences (including applications) offered by the system, and (d) conformance to user expectations.
Sociability	Sociability is defined as the number of users a system can support. The lowest level of sociability is the single user interacting with the contents of a virtual world. An example of a highly sociable system is the large military simulations (e.g, Simnet) that support hundreds of sites and users.
Diffusability	Diffusability is the likelihood that a system can be adopted and used by various business, educational, and personal users. Variables that can raise or lower diffusability include: (a) *hardware compatibility:* systems that run on computers that are commonly available in organizations (e.g., PC's & low end workstations) as opposed to those that require highly specialized computers (e.g., Pixel Planes); (b) *software compatibility:* systems that can import existing 2-D and 3-D models (e.g., CAD based models) are more likely to be diffused; (c) *Tool integration:* integrated systems with hardware support, modular software (i.e., applications) and catalogs of virtual objects and worlds are more likely to be diffusable; (d) *user friendliness:* systems that allow world building with minimal to moderate computing skills.
Cost	Cost is influenced by all of the variables above. We can anticipate the same pattern of development seen elsewhere in the computer industry: cost dropping as low-end systems "inherit" high-performance features previously available only on the most costly systems.

Each is slightly different, trading off cost or performance in the drive to develop more convincing virtual reality or more available virtual reality illusions (see Table 4.7).

One approach tries to develop low-end virtual reality systems that can run on a single computer or a pair of commonly available video game players, personal computers and workstations such as the high-end Apples, IBM PC compatibles, or personal workstations like the Silicon Graphics Iris and Indigo. The advantage of these configurations is their widespread availability and low cost. Virtual reality applications developed on this hardware could be rapidly diffused throughout society. But the immersive quality of the illusion is less than optimal. The limitation and key disadvantage is the relatively low computing power of the common microcomputer platforms. But, as microprocessors rapidly gain power, we will see more acceptable performance from low-end systems.

Another approach is to divide the task of creating and maintaining the virtual environment among a large number of standard microcomputers or workstations (Appino et al., 1992; Bricken, 1990). For example, separate computers may serve the input and output devices, while others handle graphics processing, dialog managing, or other functions. This kind of distributed system is a form of parallel computing where a number of processors work in tandem. Although distributed computing and other multicomputing solutions raise the cost of the basic virtual reality platform, some configurations make use of common computers. Therefore, it is economically feasible for organizations to link a group of their computers together to support a multicomputer, virtual reality application.

At the higher end of the scale we may see systems using highly specialized components driven by one or more expensive parallel processing machines. Although these high-level systems may not be the mass media of virtual reality, they may fuel the most immersive displays and create the location where the sense of presence is most intense.

CONCLUSION

The computer is a protean technology; virtual reality is a protean medium. As virtual environments begin to diffuse throughout society, the range of these systems will be quite broad. The categories proposed here will certainly increase in complexity. The categories of components and the distinctions among systems will multiply as the virtual environment marketplace bursts into a kaleidoscope of applications and options. Like the microchip, a version of this medium may find its way into almost every form of mediated communication. From the low-end to the high-end system, various configurations of these components may grow to simulate every communication channel from a handshake, to a book, to the video image.

TABLE 4.7
Likely Range of Immersive Virtual Environments

Level	Characteristics
Low level	Sensory vividness: poor, nonimmersive or low resolution immersion mostly limited to visual and aural senses.
	Interactivity: poor to good, long lags, small movement volume, narrow range of input devices and applications.
	Sociability: most often restricted to a single user.
	Diffusability: tends to be good but will vary according to compatibility of the system and its user friendliness.
	Cost: relatively low, especially as the market matures.
	Possible markets and applications: arcades, video games, home consumers, "garage VR."
	Evolution: likely to disappear as capabilities increase and prices decline.
Midlevel	Sensory vividness: immersive, fair to good sensory resolution, especially in the visual and aural sensory channels, but poor in tactile and proprioceptive channels.
	Interactivity: good range of input devices, but with noticeable lag and limitations. Broad range of interactive experiences.
	Sociability: multi-user capability, possible telecommunications capability.
	Diffusability: fair to good depending on market segment, but may be narrowly targeted.
	Cost: moderate to high. Affordable for institutions but prohibitive for individuals. Rental agreements may make it affordable as an entertainment system.
	Possible markets: engineering, telecommunication, medicine and rehabilitation, education, high-end consumer or consumer rental (e.g., location-based entertainment).
	Evolution: likely to become minimal acceptable level.
High Level	Sensory vividness: good to very good, high end of range. Well integrated support for tactile, force feedback, and other proprioceptive illusions. Emphasis on simulation.
	Interactivity: wide range of input and output devices. Range of interactive experiences may be narrow due to high cost (e.g., high-end flight simulators).
	Sociability: good to very good but dependent on need in application.
	Diffusability: poor, likely to require highly specialized hardware, software, and programming support.
	Cost: high to very high.
	Possible markets: military and civilian flight simulators, military and industrial telepresence applications, high-end teleconferencing or location-based entertainment applications, scientific visualization, high-end medical and rehabilitation.
	Evolution: will become *standard* level of VR. New high levels will incorporate more proprioceptive cues and other sensory interfaces.

Note. In all cases capabilities are rapidly increasing as costs decline. There is little likelihood of this trend changing.

This tutorial has described the Model-T phase of virtual reality technology. The aerodynamic, Formula 1 version may have similar functional parts to the Model-T version; both may use steering wheels and rubber tires. But driving the later version may be as dissimilar as the difference between a bumpy chugging over a turn-of-the-century, dirt road and a pinned-in-your-seat, white-knuckle blast down some desert straightaway. Some see a distant destination, "perfect presence," barely visible on a hazy virtual horizon. Others fear that the destination itself is a virtual image, a mirage. But the medium has the left the lab and is already in motion. We will soon be better able to see where and how far this technology may take us.

ACKNOWLEDGMENTS

The writing of this chapter was partially funded by a publication grant from the University of North Carolina. An earlier version of this chapter appeared in the *Journal of Communication* (Autumn, 1992). The authors are grateful to Gary Bishop, Nat Durlach, Douglas Holmgren, Warren Robinett, and Mike Shimamoto for helping us get access to unpublished materials. The authors would also like to acknowledge the helpful comments of Gary Bishop, Glen Bleske, and Kenny Meyer. The authors must bear, of course, the burden of any errors or omissions that remain.

REFERENCES

Ackerman, D. (1990). *A natural history of the senses.* New York: Random House.

Alberti, L. B. (1966). *De pictura.* New Haven, CT: Yale University Press. (Original work published 1458)

Appino, P. A., Lewis, B., Koved, L., Ling, D., Rabenhorst, D., & Codella, C. (1992). An architecture for virtual worlds. *Presence, 1,*(1), 1–17.

Aviles, W., Durlach, N., Held, R., Pang, X.-D., & Spain, H. (1992). Visual and auditory displays. In N. Durlach (Ed.), *Virtual environment technology for training* (BBN Systems and Technologies, Rep. No. 7661). Cambridge: MIT. Virtual Environment and Teleoperator Research Consortium.

Bach-y-Rita, M. (1982). Sensory substitution in rehabilitation. In L. Illis, M. Sedgwick, & H. Granville (Eds.), *Rehabilitation of neurological patients.* Oxford: Blackwell Scientific.

Badler, N., Barsky, B. A., & Zeltzer, D. (1991). *Making them move: Mechanics, control, and animation of articulated figures.* San Mateo: Morgan Kaufmann.

Biocca, F. (1987). Sampling from the museum of forms: Photography and visual thinking in the rise of modern statistics. In M. McLaughlin (Ed.), *Communication yearbook 10* (pp. 684–701). Hillsdale, NJ: Lawrence Erlbaum Associates.

Biocca, F. (1988). The pursuit of sound: Radio, perception, and utopia in the early twentieth century. *Media, Culture, & Society, 10,* 61–80.

Biocca, F. (1993). Will simulation sickness slow down the diffusion of virtual environment technology. *Presence, 1*(3), 334–343.

Blauert, J. (1983). *Spatial hearing: The psychoacoustics of human sound localization.* Cambridge, MA: MIT press.

Bliss, J., King, B., Kotovsky, J., & Crane, H. (1963). *Tactual perception of visual information. Technical Documentary* (Rep. No. ASD–TDR–63–732). OH: Air Force Avionics Laboratory, Wright-Patterson Air Force Base.

Bolt, R. (1984). *The human interface: Where people and computers meet*. Belmont, CA: Lifetime Learning Publications.

Brand, S. (1988). *Media lab*. New York: Penguin.

Bricken, W. (1990). Virtual environment operating system: Preliminary functional architecture (Tech. Rep. No. HITL-M-90-2). Seattle: University of Washington, Human Interface Laboratory.

Brittan, D. (1992). Being there: The promise of multimedia communications. *Technology Review, 95*(4), 42-51.

Brooks, F. (1977). The computer scientist as toolsmith: Studies in interactive computer graphics. In B. Gilchrist (Ed.), *Information processing 77* (pp. 625-634). Amsterdam: North Holland.

Brooks, F. (1988). *Grasping reality through illusion: Interactive graphics serving science* (Tech. Rep. No. TR88-007). Chapel Hill: University of North Carolina at Chapel Hill, Dept. of Computer Science.

Brooks, F., Ouh-Young, M., Batter, J., & Kilpatrick, P. (1990). Project GROPE – Haptic displays for scientific visualization. In *Proceedings ACM SIGGRAPH 90, Computer Graphics, 24*(4), 177-185.

Burdea, G., Zhuang, J., Roskos, E., Silver, D., & Langrana, N. (1992). A portable dexterous master with force feedback. *Presence, 1*(1), 18-28.

Cacioppo, J. T., & Tassinary, G. (1990). *Principles of psychophysiology: Physical, social and inferential elements*. New York: Cambridge University Press.

Cadoz, C., Florens, J. L., & Luciani, A. (1984). Responsive input devices and sound synthesis by simulation of instrumental mechanisms: The CORDIS system. *Computer Music Journal, 8*(3), 60-73.

Cadoz, C., & Ramstein, C. (1988). Capture, representation, and composition of the instrumental gesture. In *Proceedings of ICMC 90*. Glasgow: ICMC.

CAE. (1986). *Introducing the visual display that you wear*. St. Laurent, Quebec: CAE Electronics, Ltd.

Chung, J., Harris, M., Brooks, R., Fuchs, H., Kelley, M., Hughes, J., Ouh-Young, M., Cheung, C., Holloway, R., & Pique, M. (1989). Exploring virtual worlds with head-mounted displays. In *SPIE Proceedings Vol. 1083 : Non-holographic true 3-dimensional display technologies*. Washington, DC: SPIE.

Comeau, C., & Bryan, J. (1961, Nov. 10). Headsight television system provides remote surveillance. *Electronics, 23*, 86-90.

Czitrom, D. (1982). *Media and the American mind: From Morse to McLuhan*. Chapel Hill: University of North Carolina Press.

Dennett, D. (1991). *Consciousness explained*. Boston: Little, Brown.

Dichgans, J., & Brandt, T. (1978). Visual-vestibular interaction: Effects on self-motion perception and postural control. In R. Held, R. Leibowitz, & H. Teuber (Eds.), *Handbook of sensory psychology, Vol. VIII: Perception* (pp. 756-795). Berlin: Springer-Verlag.

DiZio, P., & Lackner, J. (1986). Perceived orientation, motion, and configuration of the body during viewing of an off-vertical rotating surface. *Perception and Psychophysics, 39*, 39-46.

Duchnowski, P., & Uchanski, R. (1992). Speech recognition. In N. Durlach (Ed.), *Virtual environment technology for training* (BBN Systems and Technologies, Rep. No. 7661). Cambridge, MA: Virtual Environment and Teleoperator Research Consortium, MIT.

Durlach, N. (1992). *Virtual environment technology for training* (BBN Systems and Technologies, Rep. No. 7661). Cambridge, MA: Virtual Environment and Teleoperator Research Consortium, MIT.

Ekman, P. (1974). *Unmasking the face*. Englewood Cliffs, NJ: Prentice-Hall.

Ellis, S. (1991). Nature and origins of virtual environments: A bibliographic essay. *Computer Systems in Engineering, 2*(4), 321-347.

Ellis, S. R., Kaiser, M., & Grunwald, A. (1991). *Pictorial communication in virtual and real environments.* London: Taylor & Francis.

Englebart, D. (1962, October). *Augmenting human intellect: A conceptual framework.* (Summary report, contract AF 49(638)–1024). Stanford: Stanford Research Institute.

Feiner, S., MacIntyre, B., & Seligmann, D. (1993). Knowledge-based augumented reality. *Communications, 36*(7), 53–62.

Fisher, S., McGreevy, M., Humphries, J., & Robinette, W. (1986). Virtual environment display system. *Proceedings 1986 Workshop on Interactive 3D Graphics* (pp. 77–87). Chapel Hill, NC: Department of Computer Science, University of North Carolina.

Fitzmaurice, G. W. (1993). Situated information space and spatially aware palmtop computers. *Communications, 36*(7), 39–49.

Flexman, R., & Stark, E. (1987). Training simulators. In G. Slavendy (Ed.), *Handbook of human factors* (pp. 1012–1038). New York: Wiley.

Foley, J. D., Van Dam, A., Feiner, A., & Hughes, J. F. (1990). *Computer graphics: Principles and practice.* Reading, MA: Addison-Wesley.

Foster, S. (1988). *Convolvotron user's manual.* Groveland, CA: Crystal River Engineering.

Furness, T. (1989). *Creating better virtual worlds* (Rep. No. M–89–3). Seattle: University of Washington, HITL.

Furness, T. A. (1988). Harnessing virtual space. *Society for Information Display Digest, 16,* 4–7.

Gibson, J. J. (1966). *The senses considered as perceptual systems.* Boston: Houghton Mifflin.

Gibson, J. J. (1979). *The ecological approach to visual perception.* Boston: Houghton Mifflin.

Gibson, J. J., Olum, P., & Rosenblatt, F. (1955). Parallax and perspective during aircraft landings. *American Journal of Psychology, 4,* 27–35.

Gombrich, E. H. (1961). *Art and illusion: A study in the psychology of pictorial representation.* New York: Bollingen Foundation.

Greenstein, J., & Arnault, L. (1988). Input devices. In M. Helander (Ed.), *Handbook of human factors* (pp. 495–516). Amsterdam: North-Holland.

Haber, R. (1986). Flight simulation. *Scientific American, 237,* 96–103.

Hagen, M. (Ed.). (1980). *The perception of pictures.* New York: Academic Press.

Heilig, M. (1993). El cine del futuro: The cinema of the future. *Presence, 1*(3), 1–11 (First published in *Espacios* in 1955).

Held, R. (1970). Two modes of processing spatially distributed visual stimulation. In F. Schmidt (Ed.), *The neurosciences: Second study* (pp. 317–323). New York: Rockefeller University Press.

Held, R., Efstathiou, A., & Greene, M. (1966). Adaptation to displaced and delayed visual feedback from the hand. *Journal of Experimental Psychology, 2*(3), 171–191.

Held, R., & Durlach, N. (1991). Telpresence, time delay and adaption. In S. Ellis, M. K. Kaiser, & A. C. Grunwald (Eds.), *Pictorial communication in virtual and real environments* (pp. 232–245). London: Taylor & Francis.

Hochberg, J. (1986). Representation of motion and space in video and cinematic displays. In K. Boff, L. Kaufmann, & J. Thomas (Eds.), *Handbook of perception and human performance.* (Vol. 2., pp. 21:1–21:55). New York: Wiley.

Holmgren, D. E. (1992). *Laser displays for HMD.* Unpublished technical report. Chapel Hill, University of North Carolina at Chapel Hill, Department of Computer Science.

Jacob, R. (1990). What you see is what you get: Eye movement-based interaction techniques. In *Proceedings of the CHI'90: Human factors in computing systems* (pp. 11–18).

Jacobsen, S., Iversen, E., Knutti, D., Johnson, R., & Biggers, K. (1986). Design of the Utah/MIT dexterous hand. *Proceedings of the 1986 IEEE International Conference on Robotics and Automation,* 1520–1531.

Kaczmarek, K., Webster, J., Bach-y-Rita, P., & Tompkins, W. (1991). Electrotactile and vibrotactile displays for sensory substitution systems. *IEEE Transactions on Biomedical Engineering, 38*(2), 110–121.

Kalawsky, R. S. (1993). *The science of virtual reality and virtual environments.* Reading, MA: Addision-Wesley.

Keirn, Z., & Aunon, J. (1990). Man-machine communications through brain-wave processing. *IEEE Engineering in Medicine and Biology, 25,* 55–57.

Kilpatrick, P. (1976). *The use of a kinesthetic supplement in an interactive graphics system.* Unpublished doctoral dissertation, University of North Carolina at Chapel Hill.

Krueger, M. (1993). Environmental technology: Making the real world virtual. *Communications, 36*(7), 36.

Krueger, M. (1991). *Artificial reality.* Reading, MA: Addison-Wesley.

Lackner, J., & DiZio, P. A. (1992). Whole body displays. In N. Durlach (Ed.), *Virtual environment technology for training* (BBN Systems and Technologies, Rep. No. 7661) (IIIA53–IIIA65). Cambridge: Virtual Environment and Teleoperator Research Consortium, MIT.

Lanier, J., & Biocca, F. (1992). An inside view of the future of virtual reality. *Journal of Communication, 42*(2), 150–172.

Liang, J., Shaw, C., & Green, M. (1991, November). On temporal-spatial realism in the virtual reality environment. In *Proceedings of the Fourth Annual Symposium of User Interface Software and Technology* (pp. 19–25). Hilton Head, SC.

Loomis, J. (1992). Distal attribution and presence. *Presence, 1*(1), 113–119.

Matthews, N., & Martin, C. (1978). The development and evaluation of a g-seat for a high performance military aircraft training simulator. *Piloted aircraft simulation techniques.* Paris: Advisory Group on Aerospace Research and Development.

McGreevy, M. (1991). The presence of field geologists in Mars-like terrain. *Presence, 1*(4), 375–303.

McLuhan, M. (1966). *Understanding media.* New York: Signet.

McLuhan, M., & McLuhan, E. (1988). *Laws of media, the new science.* Toronto: University of Toronto Press.

Meyer, K., Applewhite, H., & Biocca, F. (1992). A survey of position trackers. *Presence, 1*(2), 173–200.

Minsky, M., Ouh-Young, M., Steele, O., Brooks, F., & Behensky, M. (1990). Feeling and seeing: Issues in force display. *ACM Computer Graphics, 24*(2), 235–243.

Morishima, S., & Harashima, H. (1993). Facial expression synthesis based on natural voice for virtual face-to-face communication with machine. In *Proceedings of the 1993 IEEE Virtual reality international symposium* (pp. 486–491). Seattle: IEEE.

Nagata, S. (1992). How to reinforce perception of depth in single two-dimensional pictures. In S. Ellis, M. K. Kaiser, & A. C. Grunwald (Eds.), *Pictorial communication in virtual and real environments* (pp. 527–545). London: Taylor & Francis.

Pollack, A. (1990, October 14). Coming soon: Data you can look under and walk through. *New York Times,* p. C1.

Quarendon, P. (1993). Toward three-dimensional models of reality. In R. A. Earnshaw, M. A. Gigante, & H. Jones (Eds.), *Virtual reality systems.* New York: Academic Press.

Rayner, K. (1984). Visual selection in reading, picture perception, and visual search. In H. Bouma & D. Bouwhuis (Eds.), *Attention and performance X: Control of language processes* (pp. 67–96). Hove, UK: Lawrence Erlbaum Associates.

Reed, C., Durlach, N., Delhorne, L., & Rabinowitz, W. & Grant, K. W. (1989). Research on tactual communication of speech: Ideas, issues, and findings. In N. McGarr (Ed.), *Research on the use of sensory aids for hearing impaired people.* Washington, DC: A.G. Bell Associates.

Reeves, B., Thorson, E., Rothschild, M., McDonald, D., Hirsch, J., & Goldstein, R. (1985).

Attention to television: Instrastimulus effects of movement and scene changes on alpha variations over time. *International Journal of Neuroscience, 25,* 241–255.

Rheingold, H. (1991). *Virtual reality.* New York: Summit Books.

Robinett, W. (1991, Fall). Electronic expansion of human perception. *Whole Earth Review,* 16–21.

Robinett, W., & Rolland, J. (1992). A computational model for the stereoscopic optics of a head-mounted display. *Presence, 1*(1), 45–62.

Rolfe, J., & Staples, K. (1986). *Flight simulation.* Cambridge: Cambridge University Press.

Salisbury, J. K., & Srinivasan, M. (1992). Haptic interfaces. In N. Durlach (Ed.), *Virtual environment technology for training* (BBN Systems and Technologies, Rep. No. 7661). Cambridge: MIT, Virtual Environment and Teleoperator Research Consortium.

Sedgwick, H. (1980). The geometry of spatial layout in pictorial representation. In M. Hagen (Ed.), *The perception of pictures* (pp. 33–90). New York: Academic Press.

Shaw, E. (1974). The external ear. In W. Keidel & W. Neff (Eds.), *Handbook of sensory physiology, Vol. 1, Auditory system* (pp. 455–490). New York: Springer-Verlag.

Sheridan, T. (1992). Musings on telepresence and virtual presence. *Presence, 1*(1), 120–126.

Shimoga, K. (1993a). A survey of perceptual feedback issues in dextrous manipulation: Part I. Finger force feedback. In *Proceedings of the 1993 IEEE Virtual reality international symposium* (pp. 263–271). Piscataway, NJ: Washington.

Shimoga, K. (1993b). A survey of perceptual feedback issues in dextrous manipulation: Part II. Finger touch feedback. In *Proceedings of the 1993 IEEE Virtual reality international symposium* (pp. 271–279). Piscataway, NJ: IEEE.

Stewart, D., & Furse, D. (1982). Applying psychophysiological measures to marketing research problems. In J. H. Leigh & C. Martin (Eds.), *Current issues and research in advertising.* Ann Arbor: University of Michigan Press.

Stoker, C. (1993). Telepresence and virtual reality for space exploration: Field demonstrations in Antarctica. In *Proceedings of Vision 21.* Cleveland, OH: Vision 21.

Sutherland, I. (1965). The ultimate display. *Proceedings of the IFIPS Congress, 2,* 757–764.

Sutherland, I. (1968). A head-mounted three dimensional display. *FJCC, 33,* 757–764.

Venkataraman, S., & Iberall, T. (1990). *Dexterous robot hands.* New York: Springer-Verlag.

Waibel, A., & Lee, K. (1990). *Readings in speech recognition.* San Mateo: Morgan Kaufmann.

Walker, J. (1988). *Through the looking glass: Beyond "user interfaces".* Sausalito, CA: Autodesk Inc.

Walser, R. (1990a). *Elements of a cyberspace playhouse* (Report). Sausalito, CA: Autodesk, Inc.

Walser, R. (1990b). *The emerging technology of cyberspace* (Report). Sausalito, CA: Cyberspace Project, Advanced Technology Department, Autodesk, Inc.

Warner, R. (1992). Physiological responses. In N. Durlach (Ed.), *Virtual environment technology for training* (BBN Systems and Technologies, Rep. No. 7661). Cambridge: MIT, Virtual Environment and Teleoperator Research Consortium.

Waters, J. (Director). (1981). *Polyester* [Film]. Los Angeles: New Line Cinema.

Wenzel, E. (1992). Localization in virtual acoustic displays. *Presence, 1*(1), 80–107.

Wenzel, E., Wrightman, F., & Foster, S. (1988). A virtual display system for conveying three-dimensional acoustic information. *Proceedings of the Human Factors Society, 32,* 86–90.

Young, L., & Sheena, D. (1975). Methods and designs: Survey of eye movement recording methods. *Behavior Research Methods and Instrumentation, 7*(5), 397–429.

Zimmerman, T. (1987). *DataGlove Model 2: Operating manual.* Redwood City, CA: VPL Research, Inc.

II | DESIGNING VIRTUAL ENVIRONMENTS

5 Communication Applications of Virtual Reality

Frank Biocca
University of North Carolina at Chapel Hill

Mark R. Levy
University of Maryland

Virtual reality's (VR) final destination may well be as a multipurpose communication medium — a combination of the television and telephone wrapped delicately around the senses. Even NASA scientists like Steven Ellis (1991a) admit that "Virtual environments . . . are communication media" (p. 321). Introductory VR books often describe virtual reality as the next logical step in the history of communication media (e.g., Hamit, 1993; Rheingold, 1991). A Delphi panel survey predicts that communication applications of virtual reality will amount to more than 60% of the marketplace when the technology matures (Miller, Walker, & Rupnow, 1992).

But what are virtual reality's communication applications? One could argue that *all* VR applications are communication applications. In some ways this is valid; after all, all applications involve man–machine communication and human-to-human communication. But, maybe we should ask a more confined question: What are VR's applications in the traditional domains of entertainment, news and information, and telecommunication? What shape might they take? What design challenges do they present?

As the opening chapters noted, the mid-1990s are full of turbulent change in the communication and computer industries. Virtual reality applications are being formed in this bubbling cauldron of activity. In this chapter we use the best available evidence and suggest the outlines of some key VR communication applications.

THE EMERGING MARKET

U.S. expenditures on communication technology and services account for between $7 trillion and $11 trillion, depending on what one counts as "communication." Also, three trends are evident: greater interconnectivity, greater information bandwidth between communication points, and greater information bandwidth between user and interface—the communication market is expanding.

The first trend—greater interconnectivity—has been going on for some time. For example, in the last decade cable television increased its penetration into U.S. homes by 300% and finally reached a majority of U.S. households (U.S. Dept. of Commerce, 1992). Evidence of communication expansion can also be seen by looking at past activity in the computer industry. According to the Software Publisher's association, entertainment software revenues rose by 29% and education software by 47% in 1992 (Gilder, 1993). At the same time sales of computers with modems increased by an amazing 1,000% and Internet burgeoned forth at the astounding growth rate of 15% per month. This is only the beginning. Only a small percentage of the general public has really been touched by this expansion of communication; whereas nearly every American household has a TV set (98%), little more than 40% of the households own a personal computer.

Where is all of this growth in mediated communication going? Let's consider the changes in communication interface only. In any media environment there is usually one communication medium (interface) that is dominant, one that most powerfully shapes how we communicate and see the world. In this century the newspaper, radio, and television have each risen to the top and then slowly declined in dominance, and with each new medium the cycle of rise and fall has accelerated (Shaw, 1991). The evolution of media technologies suggests that virtual reality may rise to become the next dominant communication medium. As some of the chapters in this volume point out (chapter 1, by Biocca, Kim, & Levy; chapter 3 by Steuer), the history of media is a history of interfaces that deliver information to more sensorimotor channels with increased sensory realism in each channel. At some point in the growth of communication services, it is probable that some form of immersive virtual reality will eventually become a general, home-and-office-based communication interface. By *general communication interface* we mean an interface used for interpersonal telecommunication, information retrieval, and information creation—a convergence of the telephone, television, and personal computer—the long-awaited metamedium (Kay & Goldberg, 1977).

Interactive mutlimedia systems are finally arriving at the nation's homes first. These multimedia platforms are evolving to incorporate VR-oriented input and output devices. For example, window-based, stereographic displays are already circulating in the marketplace at affordable prices (e.g., Simsalabim Systems, Stereographics, VREX). When will the home have some form of home-based reality engine? Predicting the exact pattern and diffusion rate of virtual reality technology is still hazardous and uncertain (see chapter 11, Valente & Biardini). But some patterns are emerging. At the time of this writing computer game companies had already anounced plans to network home-based, low-end systems together.

The shape of the virtual reality market has begun to emerge. Heading into the mid-90s the market for communication applications of virtual reality is still relatively small. The overall VR market in 1993 was estimated to be little more $110 million (Latta, 1993). Some believe that the market will grow slowly, rising to a modest $500 million by 1997. Others feel that the demand for VR technologies and services will grow at a much faster rate. But most analysts agree that the diffusion of virtual reality will be driven by communication applications, specifically, entertainment applications.

Playing with Virtual Reality

If entertainment applications of virtual reality take the lead, then we should expect to see virtual reality in the palaces of entertainment, the complexes of the location-based entertainment industry. The location-based market includes high-end entertainment experiences at large national and super-regional entertainment complexes, for example Disney World, Las Vegas, and various international Expos. These centers produce consumer-accessible, multisensory, entertainment experiences.

In the past multisensory experiences have been created by passive, cab-based simulators. The passive simulators use large-screen, 360°, or 3-D film for visuals, and high-quality audio, synchronized with motion platforms. Forty to 100 tourists are catapulted through a bone-jarring experience rarely lasting more that 10 minutes. As many as 500,000 to 3 million individuals experience some of these simulators every year. A classic example is Disney's Star Tours, which opened in 1987 (see chapter 6, Hawkins).

This sector of the communication industry is well positioned to introduce communication applications of virtual reality—it's a natural match. Companies such as Hughes, Spectrum-Holobyte, and Iwerks, to name a few, use technology to provide unique sensory experiences. These businesses are capable of assembling the capital and technology to build expensive VR systems and the settings to make it profitable. There are indications that theme park VR experiences are under development for theme parks in the United States, Canada, and Japan (see Hawkins, this volume). The entertainment at these sites might mature to develop more complex narrative experiences (discussed later; Meyer, this volume). Location-based entertainment is probably where most people will first experience high-end VR experiences.

VR entertainment needs to be a repeatable experience, not just a novelty at major tourist sites. The first[1] consumer-based applications of virtual reality emerged in the low-to-midrange segments of the location-based entertainment industry. These segments include complexes in regional entertainment centers and large shopping malls. Battletech™ by Virtual Worlds Inc. and various games by Virtuality[2] (Rowley, 1993) were among the first to incorporate interactive VR concepts into their entertainment (see Hamit, 1993; Hawkins, this volume; Heeter, this volume for consumer reactions). In these systems the user is immersed either in a cab-based VR unit or a head-mounted display.[3] Users are free to roam in a three-dimensional world inside a networked VR system that includes other people involved in competition or cooperation within themes of battle, exploration, or rescue. Such low-to-midrange VR entertainment experiences (see Biocca & Delaney, this volume) are closer to the user's home and more easily repeatable.

The full diffusion of communication applications of virtual reality crosses a threshold when significant VR experiences enter the home. The most likely platforms for the diffusion of virtual reality into the home are video game systems. In the early 1990s, 30% of U.S. homes and over 90% of homes with children already had some form of computer game. What many in the 1980s thought would be a small market generates from $4.5 billion to over $5 billion in yearly revenues.

Some virtual reality concepts have been introduced in the form of various new input and output devices for computer games. For example, in the early 1990s Abrams–Gentile Entertainment and Mattel introduced the Power Glove™ (Rheingold, 1991), a crude version of VPL's data glove (see Biocca & Delaney, this volume). In 1993 Sega, one of the largest manufacturers of computer games, announced a low-end, head-mounted display for only a few hundred dollars. The VR experiences it generated were of poor quality

---

[1]Determining the "first" consumer application of VR depends on what one considers to be virtual reality. Some consider *Explorama,* Morton Heilig's 1960s passive arcade ride, to be a likely candidate. But if one establishes the criteria that the VR systems must (a) be highly interactive and immersive, (b) involve free movement over a complex, computer-generated spatial display, and (c) involve some form of 3-D sensory representation, then only a few remain. The insistence on 3-D sensory representation, for example, would eliminate Battletech as a full VR experience.

[2]Formerly W-Industries.

[3]Cab-based systems are in some ways a technological step back because the experience fails to incorporate full visual 3-D depth cues. Some question whether such systems can really be called virtual reality. On the other hand, head-mounted displays present a number of problems for location-based entertainment applications. The head mounts can potentially spread bacterial infections or head lice among users. The head mounts take some time to put on and adjust to the individual. Some VR games require a human attendant. This may slow down the "thru-put" necessary for some of the location-based systems that require high volumes of users and speedy user entry and exits.

and often limited to a single user, but this technology is affordable and puts VR technology into the consumer's hands. These early forms allow new and future consumers to get used to VR interfaces and helps pave the way for the later arrival of higher quality computer platforms attached to input and output devices that generate more vivid experiences. Brought into the home for entertainment, these systems also open the door for informational and educational applications of virtual reality.

Indeed, communication applications will take a further qualitative leap when immersive, consumer VR systems can be affordably networked over large spaces. Cyberspace will then come closer to becoming a "consensual hallucination" (Gibson, 1984). Although some network communication systems claim to offer "virtual reality," truly immersive, networked virtual reality is likely to emerge in the later phases in the diffusion of virtual reality, the phase that ultimately ushers in a VR-based, general communication interface. Researchers affiliated with telephone companies such as NYNEX and US West tout the use of virtual reality for telecommunications. But networked, immersive virtual reality needs the bandwidth of high-end cable or telephone-based transmission channels.

Some scenarios for immersive, networked virtual reality count on the explosive popularity of interactive television and the emergence of a family of powerful graphic, multimedia computers ("black boxes") into the home. This must come first. For example, Bell Atlantic forecasts more than 1 million of these high-powered home terminals by 1997 (Cook, 1993). Silicon Graphics, manufacturer of some popular VR-oriented workstations, has entered into alliances with powerful cable companies to provide a screentop black box with the power of its graphic workstations for less than $300. According to this scenario (e.g., Biocca, 1993), some of these powerful interactive systems will eventually "grow" new input and output devices to support more immersive networked experiences.

Scenarios for home-based, immersive, networked virtual reality also assume successful installation of some form of "information superhighway." Such a network can provide the backbone for the massive data exchanges required. A national system of home-based, highly networked, fully immersive virtual reality would constitute the construction of a radically different communication system (see Biocca & Levy, chapter 2) and an unpredictable range of communication applications.

A few successful communication applications of virtual reality exist, although most are found in the location-based entertainment market. But the present generation of virtual reality communication applications are only crude outlines barely suggestive of applications to come. These immature applications are as similar to and as different from mature applications as Milton Berle's live 1950s TV show is to MTV, or as the first *Pong* game is to *SimCity 2000*. Thinking about communication in the age of virtual reality requires that we not be limited by last year's commercial success.[4] In the sections that follow we do not limit ourselves to existing applications, but rather consider the shape and design challenges of more mature applications to come.

"IMAGINE A PLACE LONG AGO AND FAR AWAY..."

Many forms of entertainment attempt to do one thing well: They take the listener/viewer/player/user into another world—a telepresence ride to the far reaches of the imagination. Successful novels, for example, "transport" you to distant locations in space and time or into the minds and motivations of people you meet only inside the medium. Like ancient tribal ritual spaces, story space is a constructed sociopsychological place. It is a liminal world where the user crosses a threshold and "suspends disbelief." Alone or with others the storyteller–audience enters the simulated "world of make believe" of the novel, play, film, or arcade game. Discussions of these applications often refer to two essential ingredients:

Imagination. The replacement of everyday sensory reality for user-generated illusions driven by cues from a medium: for example, words of the storyteller; a storybook picture; and an action-packed, car chase; and so forth.

Illusory Space. A mutually accepted make-believe space, a "consensual hallucination," where the fiction, game, or entertainment takes place— "long ago and far away." Entertainment terms that refer to this illusory space include: story space, film space, theatrical space, playing field, and so on.

These are ancient ingredients. Entertainment using virtual reality is in some ways no different from listening to an old shaman tell a creation myth around the tribal fire, or sitting on a cold, marble seat in ancient Athens at the first performance of Sophocles' *Oedipus Rex.* Immersion into the story space stimulates the inner psychological engines of identification, role playing, conflict, and the clash of deeply felt emotions. VR technology may be new, but the emotions it plays to are very old. But unlike older media, virtual reality attempts to realize some artists' dreams to make the creations of the imagination more literal. To quote an oft cited passage:

---

[4]Therefore, in our discussion of the communication applications, we do not dwell on specific companies, products, and projects. These change constantly. Such developments and other business ephemera are best tracked in monthly publications like the *CyberEdge Journal, Wired, Virtual Reality Report,* and *Virtual Reality World.*

Not till the poets among us can be
  "literalists of
  the imagination"—above
          insolence and triviality and can present

for inspection, "imaginary gardens with real toads in them," shall we have
it. (Moore, 1951)

Consider the "imaginary gardens" of dramatic narratives. Dramatic narrative is one of our most powerful forms of entertainment. How might a designer generate the emotional response of great storytelling in virtual reality? Some feel that virtual reality unleashes the possibility of an intensely rich and interactive storytelling. Laurel (1991), for example, speculated that an intelligent program, "an interactive playright," might write interactive narratives "on the fly," based on user actions. The interactive power of virtual reality seems to promise the possibility of great freedom for the user—he or she might be able to "go anywhere and do anything" in a VR story space. It has been suggested that the user may be the protagonist of a story, might choose to be any character, might change characters in the middle of a story, or might alter the sequence of events in a story. Others suggest that in VR storytelling, the user might not just experience the story but *live* it. Can virtual reality do this effectively in the near future? Maybe. Some pessimistic commentators suggest, however, that like early speculation about artificial intelligence, ideas about "go anywhere and do anything" storytelling seriously underestimate the complexity of programming storytelling environments. They argue that you cannot "go anywhere and do anything" because there are not a million roads to a emotionally powerful dramatic narrative, only a few.

In chapter 8, Meyer discusses the challenge of implementing classic dramatic narratives in virtual environments. He asks: How does a VR director orchestrate the dramatic narrative in virtual reality? Meyer points out various ways in which the use of virtual reality as a storytelling medium needs to be better understood. Consider, first, how a dramatic narrative works. Classic theories of dramatic narrative lay out how the emotional power and effects of a dramatic narrative rely on control over character motivation, plot structure, and timing of emotional effects. In a linear storytelling medium like books and film, *control* over these elements is more easily achieved. For example, think how story structure, timing, and emotional effects animate a mystery story whether it is told around a campfire, in a novel, or in film. The playright or director carefully controls the unfolding of the narrative and the amount of information available to the reader/viewer. The sequence and timing of events carefully stimulates emotional responses in the reader/viewer to create suspense. Can such effects be created in virtual reality if the user is completely free to roam around the story?

Unlike books or film, virtual reality is a nonlinear medium. The designer exerts a lot of control over all the *content* of the VR world but has limited control over the *sequence* of events. A freely roaming user inside a VR narrative can generate thousands of probable sequences of events. Artificial Intelligence (AI) storytellers must be ready to respond appropriately to all these sequences. Can AI story-making programs do this now or in the near future? Meyer (this volume) discusses the limitations of some of the early generation of AI narrative programs. Although the program may always produce *some* response, many may not be dramatically satisfying for the user. VR dramatic story makers are likely to face difficult trade-offs: Give the audience members too much freedom and the balanced effects of the story will suffer. Limit the choices of the audience member so that the user has a more emotionally orchestrated narrative experience, and you seem to underutilize the potential power of virtual reality. This is the paradox of VR narrative.

AI storytelling programs may be limited for some time to come. Even with better programs, a conflict may always exist between the need to control events and characters to effectively tell a dramatic story and the potential freedom of the "audience" member inside a VR story. When the user is free to alter all elements in a story, the user also becomes a playright. A basic contradiction exists. The user and the AI playright may be in conflict. User actions may disrupt the most effective timing of plot developments and emotional effects by the AI playright controlling the VR program. The result may be unsatisfactory dramatic narratives, nonnarrative sequences of events, or more anarchic story structures. These may still be narratives, but they may not be very good or emotionally satisfying.

Great VR storytelling is possible, of course. But as with the refinement of the arts in other media, VR playrights and directors will develop an understanding of both the possibilities and the limits of VR technology.

Managing, Altering, and Amplifying the Senses

There are some other interesting evolutionary connections between the needs of storytelling in older media and the likely needs of story making in virtual reality. Entering older story spaces often meant blocking information received from the senses (e.g., sitting in a quiet place to read or slumping in a comfortable, dark seat in a movie theater). Sometimes the imagination was released by suppressing the naysaying reality check of the senses. Phrases like: "This is not real" or "It's just a story," suggest the psychological tug-of-war between the compelling reality of the virtual story space and the physical reality surrounding the audience member. In successful moments of reverie, audience members ignore physical reality and project themselves into the story space. In the words of Coleridge (1817), "That willing suspension of disbelief for the moment, which constitutes poetic faith" (p. 87).

The blocking of sensory impressions from physical reality is a crucial part of the most compelling VR experiences. The senses are *immersed* in the virtual world; the body is entrusted to a reality engine. The eyes are covered by a head-mounted display; the real world is invisible. The ears are covered by headphones; ambient sound is muffled. The hands are covered by gloves or props: "touch only the virtual bodies." Virtual reality may share common elements with reading a book in a quiet corner, but this book has stretched in all directions and wrapped itself around the senses of the reader—the reader is swallowed by the story.

Instead of ignoring the senses, ancient story space sometimes altered or amplified them. This helped fire the illusion brewing in the imagination. Many forms of entertainment from shamanistic storytelling to Greece's dionysic festivals sometimes involved the consumption of drugs or alcohol, energetic ritualistic chanting or dancing, loud noises and flashing lights. With these the user could more easily enter the illusory space of the myth, story, or what have you. With a "magic" root or mushroom the user could "commune" with the gods.

In some ways, virtual reality continues in this tradition as well. The rhetoric of chemical and technological augmentations of experience permeate the pages of cyberspace-oriented magazines like *Mondo 2000*. This is not an accident. Neither is the fact that Timothy Leary,[5] LSD shaman of the 1960s, saw in virtual reality some of the same myth-making power he found in older chemical "media" (see Wooley, 1992). Awed by the possibilities of the technology for experiences he pursued by other means, he pronounced at one of the early virtual reality conferences: "I think this is one of the most

---

[5]For many VR workers, especially VR scientists, the presence of Timothy Leary at the early public promotion of virtual reality such as SIGGRAPH 1990 was met with much unease. For engineers and scientists in universities, the military, and major corporations, the 1960s jester was hot-dogging on a cresting wave created by years of their sweat. In a culture not comfortable with its use of drugs of modulate experience, people in the industry were eager to avoid public relations traps set by journalists and distance the technology from any hint of relationship with another technology of the imagination—drugs. But at a deeper level the two remained linked: one, drugs, an ancient, low-tech, hard-to-control means of altering sensory perception, the other, virtual reality, a silicon, sophisticated, increasingly capable engine for mind bending. In their private moments we would hear some of the VR scientists laughingly use the metaphors of drugs to describe certain aspects of the experience. But in their public performances all feared the sensation-seeking barbarians of the press and what they might do with the hints of connection—even a metaphoric one—between the two technologies.

important meetings ever held by human beings" (quoted in Woolley, 1992, p. 12).

Scientific discovery, artistic insight, and religuous epiphany may spring from a rearrangement of our sensory relations to the world. VR scientists often speak of the technology in terms of sensory rearrangement or intelligence augmentation, but in the same breath curse the day when the "pariah," Timothy Leary, embraced the technology. In this eager dismissal of Leary's self-serving "distractions," we may miss a deeper connection to a very old human tradition of using chemical and mechanical artifacts to alter mental functions.

VR pioneer Jaron Lanier tells anecdotes about virtual reality experiences where engineers at VPL experimented with reorganizing the relationship between bodily movement and sensory feedback. In a search for artistic effects, body parts were presented in different proportions in the virtual world for perceptual effect; body movements were linked to nonbodily activity. He even discussed the possibility of unusual sensory experiences only available in VR such as "crawling inside the mouth of a friend" (Lanier & Biocca, 1992). Lanier imagined linking such movements to events like the flying of birds or the eruption of volcanoes. Lanier speculated on linking physiological responses like emotion to visual changes: "if you were angry you could become a red lobster awhile" (Lanier & Biocca, 1992, p. 162). In some ways this seems less like the voice of modern technology and more like the voice of ancient shamanistic myth making. We should be excused if we detect a waft of ancient pipes and hear the chant of rituals in these anecdotes. This shape shifting is the modern equivalent of the animal and spirit costumes of primitive tribes. This is a virtual reality of masks, feathers, and mud-covered skin.

This electronic rearrangement and amplification of the senses suggests that the usage of virtual reality continues in the older traditions of sensory alteration and amplification. No doubt some will argue that perceptual amplification and the transformation of interaction with sensory stimuli yields "better learning" and "new insights." Maybe. If so, virtual reality will be called upon to make the senses raw and sensitive by altering the way we relate to the world.

Although virtual reality may incorporate all of the classic storytelling techniques, it is different. Like film, virtual reality facilitates the imagination not by depressing the senses but by immersing the senses in information from the illusory space. It will work most powerfully for entertainment when, like children's make-believe, it becomes in the words of Gibson (1984) a "consensual hallucination." Like all hallucinations, it will not be created solely by the evidence of the senses. VR technology merely calibrates sensory stimuli. Even the best VR technology will require the full cooperation of the imagination. As Heeter suggests in chapter 7, the ability to suspend disbelief (she calls it the Peter Pan principle) remains — and will forever remain — an important component of the enjoyment of VR entertainment.[6]

"AND NOW LET'S GO LIVE TO THE BATTLEFIELD..."

In this section, we engage in a brief *Gedankenexperiment* and try to imagine how virtual reality might affect the practice of journalism, say, 50 years from now, when communication in the age of virtual reality is in full bloom.[7] There is already much concern about the effect of interactive television on the delivery of news. We lay out a set of scenarios that extends emerging developments in interactive multimedia news systems and news simulations. For this discussion, we take as our general theoretical framework some standard notions drawn from media studies of popular culture. We take as given that important questions about communication can be identified and studied by seeing mass communication as a major site in which messages are created, reproduced and repaired and in which audiences create and share meanings based in substantial part on those mediated messages. We also assume that the study of journalism and the news has a special importance, because journalism and its messages is where the most significant aspects of social and political life are contested.

For virtual reality to have the impact we anticipate, it will be necessary for it to move out of the laboratory and to take on more of the characteristics of a mass medium. Some of those characteristics might well be borrowed from existing communication practices: the "live" coverage of world events brought to us by CNN; computer networks like Internet that have created virtual communities in cyberspace; interactive multimedia news systems and simulations; and electronic or hypertext publishing of academic journals and spicy novels — all offer codes, narrative structures, "models" for virtual news.

Telepresence and the Virtual News Environment

As a mass medium, virtual reality could fulfill the oldest dream of the journalist, to conquer time and space. Virtual news environments would

---

[6]As philosophers have pointed out for centuries, all experience, including the best VR experience, requires the constructive powers of the imagination.

[7]We are fully aware of the perils of predicting the future, especially the future of communication. A colleague of ours sat down in 1899 to predict the future of the newspaper in 1999 (Bird, 1899/1971). Although there are a few brilliant insights (e.g., the arrival of television), most of his speculations make for amusing reading today (e.g., the prediction of a national network of air tubes for news delivery). But if we accept that technology is socially constructed, then speculating about journalism's future and the relationship of that future to virtual reality might just contribute to the discourse that shapes journalism's present and VR's potential.

invest journalists with the ability to create a sense on the part of audiences of being present at distant, newsworthy locations and events. For over a century news has struggled to find ways to bring its audiences close to dramatic and historic moments. The very language of journalism suggests the goal of telepresence. Think of Edward R. Murrow's broadcast programs, *Hear it Now* and *See it Now.* Or Walter Cronkite's dramatized history with the prophetically cyberspatial title, "You are there." These phrases promise telepresence. Imagine what Murrow and Cronkite could have done with a virtual news environment. Instead of vivid language, they might have been better able to deliver the promise of telepresence inherent in the modern idea of news.

Indeed, as the chapters of this book and the visionary writings of the science fiction community remind us, the basic concepts and hardware also promise to take us "there" and more. In the influential novel, *Neuromancer,* Gibson (1984) conjured up what he called the "simstim" (simulated stimulation) deck, a virtual VCR through which the "viewer" experiences whatever has been taped for the deck or whatever the simstim communicator is experiencing "live." Gibson's simstim is clearly more immersive than today's VCR, but it is not really interactive. Still, one could imagine "jacking into" a simstim to experience a pre-recorded virtual documentary or a mult-sensory "story," reported by a trusted and/or celebrity journalist.

A mass telepresence system requires the development of: (a) remote, real-time cameras capable of transmitting a full 360° world, and (b) a digital model of such a world that can be simultaneously experienced by millions of people. Telerobotic systems work well for a single individual linked to a binocular camera system at some distant locations (see for example the linked systems offered by Fake Space Labs and Leep Optics). Figure 5.1 sketches the typical telepresence setup. But only one viewer is possible at a time, because the distant robot is slaved to the head movements of the human viewer — when the viewer looks to the right, the robot camera swings to the right. A million people cannot simultaneously don headgear and simultaneously control the viewing of a single remote binocular camera in

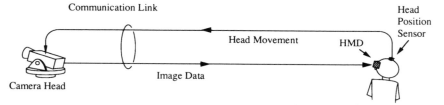

FIG. 5.1.   In a typical immersive VR telepresence system, a single user is connected to a distant slave camera. The camera moves to match the user's head movements. From Hirose, Yokoyama, & Sato (1993). Copyright 1993 by IEEE. Reprinted by permission.

some distant environment. If the mass audience must be forced to view passively, then this experience fails to deliver the full promise of virtual reality. It becomes just another form of passive television, even if it is stereoscopic.

The *virtual dome* system prototype produced at the University of Tokyo (Hirose, Yokoyama, & Sato, 1993) suggests one way to create a mass simulation, and provide active experience of a remote environment. Figure 5.2 shows the concept behind the virtual dome telepresence system. The system begins with a camera located at a distant location, let's say, for example, the lawn at the White House. Fixed on a tripod, the telerobotic camera rotates continuously around the scene (the prototype rotates at 6 rpm). The images are sent via a transmission line to a graphics workstation. The graphics workstation digitizes the images. The computer then pastes (texture maps) the images to the inside of a virtual dome (the prototype dome is composed of 75 polygons; see Figs. 5.3 and 5.4). With some additional processing, the system can also calculate the relative distance of surfaces on the distant image (using binocular slits and motion-parallax cues). In a clever piece of image matching, the virtual dome is deformed so that close surfaces protrude. Borrowing an idea from relief sculpture, the researchers cleverly distort the dome screen to generate 3-D effects (i.e., motion-parallax cues).

The virtual dome generates a 360° screen inside a virtual environment that preserves 3-D cues. The image is completely digital. In future prototypes it may be possible for multiple viewers to don headgear and "sit" inside the center of the dome. They could turn their heads in any direction

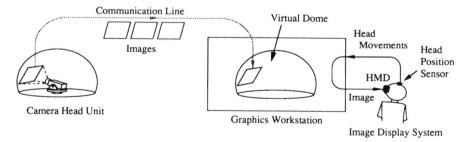

FIG. 5.2.   In the prototype VR telepresence system called the Virtual Dome, a remote rotating camera continuously pans the 360o views of a remote environment and sends images back to a computer workstation. These camera images are digitized and pasted (texture mapped) onto the inside of a virtual, computer-graphic dome and continuously refreshed as new images arrive. Using a head-mounted display users are transported to the center of the dome and can turn their heads in any direction to view the live 360° image of a distant location. A future system like this one may make it possible for mass audiences to freely experience live news events with full 360° views beamed from news locations all over the globe. From Hirose, Yokoyama, & Sato (1993). Copyright 1993 by IEEE. Reprinted by permission.

FIG. 5.3.   A simulation of a user viewing images inside a virtual dome. From Hirose, Yokoyama, & Sato (1993). Copyright by IEEE. Reprinted by permission.

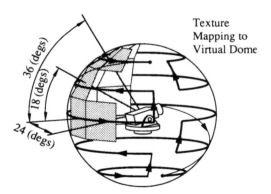

FIG. 5.4.   The figure displays the rotation pattern of the remote camera and how the images are pasted (texture mapped) onto the virtual dome. From Hirose, Yokoyama, & Sato (1993). Copyright by IEEE. Reprinted by permission.

and have the illusion of the 3-D scene that would surround them. Going back to our White House lawn example, multiple remote 3-D modeling cameras might be located there. Viewers could be free to "jump" from camera to camera, viewing the scene from a variety of vantage points and from a variety of angles. Pre-positioned telerobotic sensing systems could take us to the streets of Peking, the halls of Congress, or to a joint U.S.–Russian space station. Although the virtual dome demonstrates a number of interesting design concepts, there are many engineering obstacles to overcome before it can be turned into a mass telepresence system.[8] It is only one possible model among many of a mass telepresence system.

Now consider some of the questions the virtual dome scenario raises. Who, for instance, would own the telerobotic sensors? Who would pre-position them and based on what notions of newsworthiness? How does one edit a 3-D news story? Would reporters use some device to direct the attention of viewers to some part of the dome image? Is news from cyberspace the ultimate news from nowhere? At a later stage of development, could telerobotic sensor systems (or simstim decks for that matter) allow VR audiences to engage in virtual role-playing games, entering virtual environments for limited periods of time to see and hear and taste and feel what it's like to be a refugee in the sub-Sahara or a basketball star in the NBA finals? How would audiences judge the truthfulness or veridicality of the images and sound? (See Shapiro & McDonald, this volume.) What does it mean to say that viewers engage in a "negotiated" or "oppositional" decoding (Hall, 1973) in a virtual news environment?

What if we up the ante just a bit and include a higher level of interactive capability in this projected telerobotic system. Instead of passively receiving 3-D images and sound or interacting with simulations, what if audiences could interact with the people "in" the news, the journalists reporting the news and the social actors being "covered"? What would viewers do with this new capability? Does this become little more than a 3-D "call-in" show or something more? Would they, for example, seize the opportunity to engage in an even more intense kind of parasocial interaction (Horton & Wohl, 1956) with media personae? If they really are interacting – albeit through a mediated channel – is it parasocial or is it truly social interaction? The question of parasocial interaction of course is just one of many which come to mind when we consider the consequences of virtual news environ-

---

[8]The system is not presently designed for multiple users, but that is one of the next steps (Michitaka Hirose, personal communication). The image update rate for the dome is still too slow.

Camera rotation speed and image processing speed would need to be increased. At present, this is overcome by updating the image more frequently in the direction of the viewer. This is a good solution when there is only one viewer; it becomes less efficient as the number of viewers climb, although it is unlikely that even thousands of viewers would distribute their view randomly around a dome – they would likely follow the "action." The dome deformation takes time and is still somewhat inaccurate.

Because a news system could not allow that the viewers interact with the environment (e.g., interrupt the president's speech), signal delays can be introduced into live events to allow the computer more time to build the images. Pre-recorded events would also give the computer more time to construct the dome images and deform the dome for relief-like 3-D cues.

ments. There is no more important set of questions to ask than to inquire how virtual news environments might affect what its audiences know, think, and believe. As students of communication, we have always searched for communication effects, but with mixed success. If virtual news environments vividly engage many, perhaps all, of the human senses, then we might well hypothesize that its effects too will be heightened.

Just as virtual news environments will affect audiences, they will, we believe, also have substantial impact on the work of journalists. How, for example, will professional norms of "objectivity" be affected? What journalistic routines will be used when virtual news workers seek to demonstrate their lack of bias? And how will libel law be applied to news from virtual environments? Will "viewers" who interact virtually with people in the news be subject to libel action? (For one line of speculation, see chapter 14 by Harvey.) The questions of "objectivity" and "bias" bring us to the more troubling issue of simulation and its relation to the "reality" news seeks to represent.

VR News as Simulation

Behind the baroque of images hides the gray eminence of politics.
Thus perhaps at stake has always been the murderous capacity of images, murderers of the real, murderers of their own model as the Byzantine icons could murder the divine entity. To this murderous capacity is opposed the dialectical capacity of representations as a visible and intelligible mediation of the Real. . . . But what if . . . the whole system becomes weightless, it is no longer anything but a giant simulacrum—not unreal, but a simulacrum, never again exchanging for what is real, but exchanging for itself, in an uninterrupted circuit without reference or circumference
So it is with simulation, insofar as it is opposed to representation. Whereas representation tries to absorb simulation by interpreting it as false representation, simulation envelopes the whole edifice of representation as itself a simulacrum.
These would be the successive phases of the image:
—it is a reflection of basic reality
—it masks and perverts a basic reality
—it masks the absence of a basic reality
—it bears no relation to any reality whatsoever: it is its own pure simulacrum.
(Baudrillard, 1983, pp. 10–11).

After the fact, all news is a kind of simulation. Computer scientists Alan Kay and Adele Goldberg (1977) even argued that "Every message is, in one sense or another, a simulation of some idea. It may be representational or abstract" (p. 254). A newspaper journalist recreates an event using vivid language. A TV news crew "edits" a view of a demonstration. Sometimes the editing is pure fiction. For example, in 1910 a news reel crew completely simulated the coronation of Britain's King George V using actors and elaborate sets.

In television news, the modern version of pure simulation lives on in the current trend toward "reenactment" of new events. Sometimes, the reenactments attempt to deepen the ambiguity of the simulation by using the "real people" as actors. But this form of simulation violates "accepted" journalistic norms to a community of media workers uncomfortable with any practice that will loosen its claim to "real" representations. Even the innocuous "amelioration" of photographs is frowned upon in the journalistic community. Many journalists fear that any overt manipulation of iconic media like pictures or film casts into question the authenticity of all photographic news evidence.

Concern with the real is a concern with the authority of journalistic representations. Journalism's authority lies in the appearance of the presentation of reality, or at least of the earnest effort to recover reality. In a statement that seems quaint in the age of virtual reality, many journalists wonder: How will the audience know when something is real and when it's not? It's as if the community of journalists seeks desperately to an authentic claim to the real as Baudrillard's vision quoted earlier threatens to engulf them in the "gigantic simulacrum."

As a practical matter, virtual reality offers a means of providing richer interaction with news events through simulations. In a primitive way, simulations creep into many news reports. Consider the UN–Iraq war. All major news networks used graphic models that represented the movement of tank forces over a terrain. The model represented the "real" movement on the battlefield. News does not just carry information, it carries models of social events and processes.

Computer simulation is increasingly a valid way to present news. A number of news outlets are considering the use of computer simulations as a way of deepening knowledge about news. One simulation produced for Newsweek Interactive[9] models the natural environment. This would be a more news-oriented simulation than, for example, SimEarth. At the University of North Carolina a simulation of the federal budget and the economy was created for the *Baltimore Sun* newspaper.[10] Users made choices about budgetary allocations and the simulation responded with social outcomes. These simulations offer only limited interaction over a small, somewhat abstract domain. But they are a quite visible step in the direction toward richer computer simulation. Virtual reality offers only a

---

[9]Vernon Church, Newsweek Interactive (personal communication).

[10]A study is under way by Gary Rosenweig, graduate student at the University of North Carolina, involving an economic simulation created for the *Baltimore Sun* newspaper.

further point on the simulation continuum. But it is a point where the computer simulation may take on the added cognitive effect of sensory realism. It is news you can touch; it is news you can shape. Therefore, it becomes news you can create. The simulacrum of news reaches out and embraces the senses.

Vivid computer simulations present a number of problems in news environments. For example, there may be no such thing as an "objective" computer simulation—just as there may be no such thing as "objective" news. But the bias of the computer simulation is less visible that other forms of news bias; it sits deep inside the machinery of the illusion. The assumptions of a simulation lie buried in the guts of the program.[11] The face seems so real, but the heart is false. In advanced VR environments, a vivid—potentially seamless—realism might be displayed. A hundred hidden assumptions about time, motivation, causality, and sequence may lie largely unnoted in the unfolding simulation. The VR simulation's very transparency and apparent reality is the mechanism for its falsehoods.

On the other hand, it could be argued that simulations change little basically about news. Like news stories today, simulations will be suspect, ideologically marked. But symbolic interactionists (e.g., Blumer, 1969) might ask today's news reader: How many of you have set foot in Somalia? With no direct experience of the objects of news, how can you even be sure they exist? Is this not all a construction of sorts? Gross fabrications, of course, are unlikely now or in future news reports. The issue is not pure fabrication; the issue for decades has been the social construction of news events, people, and problems. As Baudrillard suggested, it is more rational to assume that a news report is not necessarily unreal, but a *simulation of the real*—with all the *incompleteness* that this suggests. Virtual reality further extends the power of our semiotic systems to filter and construct our views of the world around us.

Some suggest that some form of objectivity can be rescued with the use of multiple "points of view" and multiple scenarii that can be built into the simulation, just as different points of view are imported in the form of quotes from "opposing" sources. In this narrow sense, virtual reality offers the news organization opportunities for more varied representations, rich ways to extend existing professional practices.

But with "multiple simulations" the user of a VR news interface potentially enters a confusing news environment. The battle of the "film clip" becomes a battle of simulations. Multiple "realities" compete for his or her favor. The group that can stage the most experientially convincing simulation may conquer the hearts and minds of millions. Simulation gives rise to

---

[11]This issue already poses problems in legal cases where computer simulations are presented as "evidence."

more advanced semiotic forms of persuasion, a new *rhetoric of the senses*. Rather than creating a capacity for "mass persuasion" the power of this rhetoric of the senses is likely to be buried by the chaos of competing realities. In the age of virtual reality the "sound byte" will get replaced by the "experience byte," and users will be swallowed byte-by-byte into Baudrillard's "gigantic simulacrum."

News Space as Database

The cybersurfing digital journalist is a new, information-devouring creature in the age of virtual reality. Increasingly journalists need to be adept organizers of information and data, technical wizards filtering the nets and extruding patterns of human activity. Journalists access and manipulate government and private text and databases (e.g., Nexus–Lexis) or surf the Net in search of virtual sources of news. Sometimes called "data-based journalism," this kind of information spade work is an important part of modern news work.

The telling of news is also an act of database organization, and as such it requires the construction of categories — economic news, human interest, and so forth. News has a structure. Take, for example, the average daily newspaper, a seemingly "primitive" interface by comparison to the possible VR interface under discussion. But in many ways the newspaper is a user-friendly, print-based database. Information is organized in a 2-D space; certain categories of information — business, weather, sports — always appear in the same physical location, in a specific section or a page. Important information appears up front and higher on the page. Index words — headlines — are made big for easy user searches.

Like the newspaper, the virtual news environment is also a database. But unlike the newspaper it may have bottomless depth — a string of articles, pictures, and video receding backward in time and out to the infinite horizon. The cyberspatial news environment is a place of information richness — but also information confusion and overload. As we suggested in chapter 2, virtual reality interfaces offer a way to tame the likely information management crisis threatening cyberspace. The "globe-trotting journalist" becomes a "cyber-trotting" agent navigating cognitive space, seeing, editing, and even listening to vast data arrays (e.g., Kramer, this volume; Nilan, 1992). Returning from cyberspace with a rich trove of data, the journalist will have to decide what to share with his or her "readers," and how to display this news. Indeed, the routinization of news production forces the creation of simplified (i.e., edited) news spaces into which audiences could enter by using VR technologies.

Although some (see Hallin, 1992; Katz, 1992) have speculated about "the end of journalism," particularly in an age of virtual reality, we do not share that concern. Even though journalists are likely to be only one competing group among various savvy "information packagers," they are likely to endure the transition to this medium as they have the transition to radio, television, and multimedia. Conceptually, VR journalism may be no different than present-day journalism. Certainly the tools will change. But constructing a news space will increase the level of complexity of the news tasks by a power of 10. The added complexity of "deep" news environments is already being felt by journalists in the multimedia area. Creating links and structure among text, pictures, video, and simulation models will require new news routines and some form of increased news automation.

Undoubtedly, the art and science of journalism will change, as will its effect on public discourse. But even in cyberspace, there will be a need for good journalists—someone better skilled at "tweaking" and "riding" the nets. More than ever before, the information depth of cyberspace brings the editing function to the fore. Most audience members will have neither the time, nor the inclination. nor the experience to steer through the traffic jam of "news" which could gridlock the information superhighway. As today, journalists and editors will be at work, choosing and shaping the news. In the giant virtual simulacrum, there will still be some—maybe only a few— earnestly looking for the "real story."

"THE NEXT BEST THING TO BEING THERE"

The most interactive medium is the interpersonal medium—the fully interactive human being. The most interesting experience in virtual environments is likely to be other people.[12] Virtual reality technology is likely to build on the popularity of existing interpersonal communication media. It is the pleasure of interpersonal communication that breathes life into many other "cyberspaces" such as computer bulletin boards (CBBs), multiuser dimensional spaces (MUDS), teleconferencing systems, and multimedia (virtual) rooms and work spaces. France's teletext system, Minitel, would have died like many others were it not for the French intuitive sense for the pleasure of the "other."

"How Should We Talk: Natural or Augmented? "

"In a few years, men will be able to communicate more effectively through a machine than face to face" (Licklider & Taylor, 1968, p. 24).

---

[12]A moment of reflection reveals that all computer-based interactivity is a form of interaction with other humans, even when none are present. The human presence of the programmers and designers remains resident in the *logic and structure* of the artificial interaction.

This technoprediction was written in 1968, and it sets up one of the most critical questions for interpersonal communication in virtual reality: Can computer-mediated communication be more effective than interpersonal communication? If the answer to this question is yes — sometimes — then under what conditions and for what kind of interpersonal messages is it more effective? Both authors of this prediction, J. C. R Licklider and Robert Taylor, were at one time the heads of ARPA's Information Processing Techniques Office, a major force in development of technologies and concepts that led directly to development of virtual reality. Both men were instrumental in trying to make good on the promise of their prediction. Their promise of "more effective" interpersonal communication was written in the early years of "man–machine symbiosis" of the process of immersing the movement of human bodies into the computer (Bardini, Horvath, & Lyman, in press; Englebart, 1988).

In discussions of teleconferencing and cooperative work in virtual environments, one sees three competing design themes:

1. *Reproduction of interpersonal communication.* A design theme that emphasizes the desire to collapse space and reproduce in detail unmediated face-to-face communication.
2. *Augmentation of interpersonal communication.* A design theme that seeks to enhance or extend through artificial means the range of interpersonal communication (with an assumption that these can be more effective than unmediated interpersonal communication).
3. *Regulation of presence in interpersonal communication.* A design theme that acknowledges and tries to accommodate cultural rules that informally channel and regulate interpersonal communication behaviors.

A number of interesting and perplexing issues are likely to emerge as researchers seek to simultaneously simulate face-to-face communication and artificially augment interpersonal communication (in chapter 10 some of these issues are taken up by Mark Palmer). Is face-to-face communication the best way to understand someone's thoughts and intentions? Can mood-signaling behaviors like facial expressions be amplified? How?

This issue, natural versus augmented, is likely to focus on how we use interpersonal communication codes, whether a code is present (e.g., expressive hand gestures), absent (e.g., the direction of the other's eye gaze), or augmented (e.g., extreme close-up on the other's eyes). The more sensory channels are supported by the more advanced virtual reality systems the more possibilities are open to both naturalism and the augmentation. For example, consider the smile — natural or augmented? Is there some value of having smiling muscles change the color of virtual environment — red for smiles, blue for frowns? This simple example only begins to suggest the possibilities.

Less Is More: Interpersonal Regulation of Presence

Robert Lucky, former head of Bell Labs and later Bellcore, presents us with an interesting scenario. Reflecting on the checkered history of the picture phone in a TV interview, he suggested that maybe we may not necessarily want more presence in mediated interpersonal communication. In a television interview, he half-jokingly suggested that he wanted a "presence dial" on a future medium (Moyers, 1990). Each individual would determine the level of presence at which he or she experiences the other. For example, irritating salespeople would be dialed down to "reduced presence." Someone very close or important might be dialed up to "augmented presence."

Maybe, for certain kinds of interactions, "less is more." For example, the telephone highlights a set of audio codes but at the loss of all others.[13] This might serve the user better by buffering certain kinds of interaction like home shopping, registering a complaint, or lurking in some virtual environment. In certain interaction it is likely that users might find it helpful to restrict visual information. This might have cognitive benefits as when the audio channel carries most of the critical information (e.g., speeches or verbal instructions).

Communication might benefit from limited sensory stimuli, for example undivided attention to the audio channel. You might have noticed how individuals restrict their eye movements when they are attentively trying to decipher a distant or muffled sound or close their eyes when listening to a particularly pleasing passage in a symphony. In this case, blocking the visual sensory channel allows the individual to allocate more sensory resources to the aural channel.

There is a social dimension to how we use sensory channels. Obviously, access to sensory channels and codes is likely to be related to the intimacy of the relationship of two people meeting in cyberspace. As communication systems become capable of replicating and extending more of the sensorimotor channels and codes of face-to-face communication — including touch — conventions will emerge for establishing the "level" of code access each person has when communicating with another. These are likely to be extensions of our present interpersonal communication rules. For example, think of a crowded elevator and the unstated eye contact and touching rules that operate there. These social rules are likely to invisibly regulate interpersonal interaction in a mediated virtual environment as well.

---

[13]In some ways, the other codes are not "lost," they are "simulated" in the minds of the listeners.

But interpersonal communication rules involve assumptions about group membership and, inevitably, hierarchy. What will happen when individuals of unequal power meet in code-augmented cyberspace? By *code-augmented* we mean virtual environments where interpersonal codes are enhanced or amplified or where there may be more codes than are present in unaugumented interpersonal communication. Will the more powerful individual demand more access than the other (e.g., the ability to "see" the lower status individual while presenting only a "mask" to that person)? There is ample precedent for these kinds of rules in interpersonal communication. For example, the bowing greeting rituals found in some cultures are in part motivated by rules as to who is "allowed" to have full view of the other, and whether eye contact between a high-status and low-status individual is "permitted."

Interpersonal communication rules in the new medium are likely to be negotiated and constructed. Take for example, the experience of the telephone. When the telephone first made its appearance, it was considered "rude" to call people you didn't know. And, in the same context, some claim that the meaning of the word "phony" emerged from the tendency for some people to fake their identity or to be pretentious and falsely familiar when talking to others on the telephone.[14] One can only wonder how the meaning of words like "cyber" might change in the age of virtual reality.

The rituals of interpersonal communication are culturally derived. Work on multimedia teleconferencing systems has highlighted the importance of different codes and rituals that facilitate interpersonal communication in various task environments (Brittan, 1992). Teleconferencing system designs that fail to appreciate the rules and cultural nuances of interpersonal communication are likely to distort communication or fail to gain social acceptance and adoption. It is also likely that different tasks and contexts — for example, discussion of engineering specs versus hard business negotiation — will require different interface configurations and codes.

No matter which rules and rituals emerge, it is unlikely that the absolute reproduction of face-to-face communication will always be the best or most desired mode of interpersonal interaction. In some ways, the social or technological equivalent of Lucky's presence dial may emerge to regulate the intensity of interpersonal communication in virtual environments.

Reproducing Interpersonal Communication

If the goal in communication media is to completely reproduce interpersonal communication, as some theorists believe (see Ciampa, 1989), then virtual reality faces a number of major technological hurdles. The full

---

[14]Webster's dictionary notes that the origins of the word are unknown, but most early references to the term are American and appear to date from the early part of this century.

transmission of personal presence is not within the means of the present technology. But this technology is likely to communicate a greater sense of presence than any before it.

Transmitting 2-D representations of human expressions, for example, is now relatively easy—picture phones and teleconferencing systems do this daily. But mutual presentation of 3-D representations of facial expression is likely to be more difficult—maybe a lot more difficult. Real-time 3-D digitizers do not yet exist, therefore, 3-D "movies" of a face cannot be captured.

MIT's Media Lab demonstrated one possible solution. The solution involved the projection of a 2-D moving image of a face on a 3-D form. One early attempt to do this used cathode ray tubes molded to the contours of a human face (Brand, 1988). These molded TV tubes were to be mounted on dummies sitting around a conference table. But this was not a practical system; the small benefit was clearly outweighed by the cost and cumbersome design of the system. Yet, the effort to produce such a system clearly demonstrated the desire to generate interpersonal presence across mediated channels.

A similar concept has been carried over into the more malleable world of virtual reality. In virtual environments, the costs and feasibility restrictions are eased. In some visions of an interpersonal communication system 2-D images of a human face are bit-mapped onto 3-D wire-mesh models. In some cases the wire-mesh models are generic; in others, the models are digitized wire-mesh models of the actual face of the individual. These animated masks painted with realistic faces can be used to represent the individual.

A critical challenge occurs when we attempt to animate these models. Why not just show a 2-D video image of someone's face on a mannequin face in a 3-D world? In the present generation of immersive VR systems it is not even possible to easily video facial expressions. The most immersive environments use head-mounted displays. These cover the face, especially the expressive eyes. Therefore, it is not possible to video the face of the individual. Because the person's face is covered, a real-time video image of his or her facial expressions is not available to be mapped onto a wire-mesh model of the individual inside the virtual world. Even if it were available, it might not be satisfactory to see an animated, video-projected face on a motionless 3-D mannequin.

One solution is to fully animate the wire-mesh model using some electronic measure of facial movement and a digitized model of appropriate facial expressions. Facial muscle movement could be measured electronically using electromyographic sensors. Based on this measure, the 3-D wire-mesh model could be animated. Moroishima and Harashima (1993) displayed an example of a facial animation system that could be used for teleconferencing and facial animation of virtual actors. In this system, a 2-D image of a face is stretched (bit-mapped) over a 3-D digitized wire-mesh model of the individual's head. Using Ekman's (1974) work on facial expressions, the movement of facial muscles is simulated to create facial expressions. These can be timed to audio tracks of phrases, and the structure of speech itself can be used as a cue to facial expression. The resulting animations can display a rather impressive, convincing range of facial expressions with only slight but noticeable cues of the inauthenticity of the expressions. These are highly realistic, animated masks.

Unfortunately, animated masks—even highly realistic ones—face obstacles. We have evolved a very discriminating ability to read faces. The perception of inauthenticity is likely to be very high, and potentially off-putting in instances where the viewing individual knows the person intimately. In such cases, it is unlikely that the generic algorithms for animating the face will capture the nuances of the individual's own natural expressions. In real-time animations of interactions, it is also likely that the simulated facial expressions may not accurately express the emotion of the individuals and could contribute to the miscommunication of intention or emotion.

On the other hand, individuals may adapt and compensate for imperfections in such a system. For example, the miscommunication of emotion is common in telephone conversations where facial expressions are not visible and must be imagined. Vocal cues of emotion become more important. In sensory-impoverished environments like electronic mail, codes such as ":-)" have been constructed to communicate the irony and humor cued in conversation by facial expression, voice pitch, and rhythm. These examples show that users use other cues to compensate for the communication system's inadequacies. It is likely that the additional layer of expressiveness presented by emerging facial animation systems may add a highly satisfactory and feasible communication of presence. The slight miscoordination of facial codes and meanings may be compensated for—as they are on the telephone—by more explicit aural statements of intent and emotion. As in all interfaces, people's usage of codes interacts with the bandwidth and flexibility of the physical media.

There is one additional advantage to having a facial animation system based on measures of facial muscle movement rather than just simple video images of facial expression. The facial animation system described above makes use of a highly realistic *mask* of the individual's real face. If the data from the sensors can be used to animate one mask, it can be used to animate *all manner of masks*. For humor, ritual, or other forms of social expression, individuals may prefer to tie their facial movements to fantastic masks, masks of the faces of famous people, or other forms of visual display. This kind of behavior has already been observed in teleconferencing systems. In one prototype system developed at Xerox Parc individuals were supposed to place still images of themselves in boxes on a computer screen. These were used to represent them in their office. Soon users replaced the dull images with creative cartoons or animated pictures. In one case, a programmer put up an animated clip of Elvis' face instead of his own. In interpersonal communication within VR environments, such forms of expressive play may be given full vent.

Transmitting Kinesthetics, Proxemics, and Touch

A significant amount of communication is transmitted through the movement of the body (*kinesthetics*) and the location of the body relative to others (*proxemics:* see Hall, 1966). Multiuser VR environments can and do make use of such codes. At their crudest, VR war games express intent by movement to and away from enemies and by raised arms pointing weapons. At the moment, the most common models of physical movements in VR environments are somewhat wooden. This is due to the fact that individuals are often presented by only two position points, usually the head and the hand. A wooden, and largely inexpressive graphic puppet is attached to these points and represents the individual in the environment. When a data glove is used, most finger motion is captured and the hand can potentially communicate a modest range of expression. For example, gestural languages are used to communicate commands to the computer and with other users.

More complete exoskeletal devices (see chapter 4 by Biocca & Delaney) can capture and communicate a full range of kinesthetic and proxemic messages. Here more nuanced 3-D motions of the extremities and torso can transmit meaning. But, at present, most exoskeletal devices are cumbersome, especially those that are also used to provide force feedback. On the other hand, lighter exoskeletons like data suits, which use fiber optic sensors, are light and flexible enough to allow body motion as expressive as dance (but not yet precise enough to register dance). But as a practical matter, there is some question as to whether individuals will be willing to wear special clothing for common teleconferencing, a point frequently made by Myron Krueger (1991) who advocates his less intrusive, but also less immersive "mirror worlds." Full body motion is desirable for full interpersonal expression, but it is clear that common teleconferencing requires highly unobtrusive means of capturing this information.

Transmitting Touch.   Touch is the mark of intimacy. But most VR work on the transmission of touch is concerned with transmitting the sensation of distant or virtual objects like tools, rather than the touch of virtual humans (Shimoga, 1993a, 1993b). But it should be obvious that a technology developed for touching metal might also be used for touching skin. Touch is a very important part of intimate interpersonal communication, but only a small part of the more formal interpersonal communication of business and work communication. Most teleconferencing systems are designed for business and work communication—the likely markets for such expensive systems. Nonetheless collaborative work in such environments requires the joint handling of objects. Little is known about how users would accept and use mediated touch systems for interpersonal communication. Anyone who has spoken publicly on the topic of virtual reality knows that discussion of tactile feedback often leads VR enthusiasts to fantasize and joke about the possibility of "teledildonics," a term apparently coined by Ted Nelson for the remote, computer simulation of sexual contact (see Rheingold, 1991). But touch is more active in the imagination of virtual reality, than in the hardware and software.

Sometimes More is Better

"Perhaps the reason present-day two-way telecommunication falls so far short of face-to-face communication is simply that it fails to provide facilities for externalizing models. Is it really seeing the expression in the other's eyes that makes the face-to-face conference so much more productive that the telephone conference call, or is it being able to create and modify external models?" (Licklider & Taylor, 1968, p. 23).

Most intriguing is the potential expressive power of the development of flexible, augmented, interpersonal communication codes that exceed and enhance the range of codes available for personal expression, communication of intent, or interpersonal play (see Lanier & Biocca, 1992). These might help individuals communicate and construct more elaborate mental models[15] of interpersonal messages. In everyday communication, humans use artifacts to augment interpersonal communication codes. For example, women's makeup such as rich, red lipstick and striking eyeliner increase the salience and expressiveness of major communication "media," the lips and eyes. Clothing is often used to increase or decrease the salience of body shape or motion. In most cases, this is done to communicate aspects of sexuality, physicality, group membership, power, or status.

In virtual environments, the use of artifacts to augment interpersonal communication codes may be greatly enhanced. Artists often invent or explore these codes. McLuhan argued that "The artist is the person who invents the means to bridge between biological inheritance and the environments created by technological innovation" (McLuhan & McLuhan, 1988,

---

[15]Although many agree that mental models influence communication, not everyone agrees as to the structures of mental models. See Johnson-Laird (1984) for a seminal work on mental models. See Biocca (1991) for a theory of mental models of communication messages.

p. 98). This may be true of the development of augmented interpersonal communication codes. The exploration of augmented interpersonal communication is still unsystematic and largely the domain of VR artists like Krueger (1991). In Krueger's work we see some of the possibilities of interpersonal play using augmented codes. In one Krueger demo, giant hands nudge small bodies. In Krueger's "Tickle" the vibrating edges of a body radiate sound when touched. In another a moving body leaves behind visual "echoes" undulating in brilliant color. In such "experiments" we see possibilities for new ways to use the human body for expressive interpersonal communication.

The pursuit of augmented interpersonal communication strikes at some fundamental concepts of communication. As Licklider and Taylor suggested, all communication is about the construction, externalization, and reception of mental models (Biocca, 1991; Johnson-Laird, 1983). This is especially true of cooperative work. In cooperative work group actions must be based on some common communicated goals (e.g., agreement to construct a house) and some code-based model of the objects of collective action — the relevant things, actions, and world (e.g., the architectural plans for a house). Virtual reality can provide the tools to more easily express and share these models. The communication associated with architecture and construction is a good example because work at the University of North Carolina and elsewhere has already shown the value of virtual reality for the expression and communication of models of future living spaces.

Exploration of augmented interpersonal communication by interdisciplinary teams that include interpersonal communication researchers might provide more systematic insight into fruitful directions for human-to-human interaction and how VR interfaces might be designed to augment human communication.[16] But like the ill-fated attempts to design universal languages like Esperanto, it is unclear whether augmented human communication codes can be created by designers, labs, or committees. It is likely that the inventive imagination of artists and users will generate infinite variations of codes from specific needs of free play. In some ways, interpersonal communication in the age of virtual reality is likely to remain improvised and creative, as users define VR's communication norms (e.g., observe the emerging codes and norms in virtual communities such as the use of emoticons, e.g., (:-), see Rheingold, 1993).

---

[16]To some degree, this kind of work goes on in teams that explore cooperative work in various virtual environments at research centers like Xerox Parc, Bellcore, Media Lab, and others. While these are indeed creative centers, there is the possibility that the product development focus of the research might inhibit the exploration of apparently "frivolous," but ultimately more rewarding directions.

IF WE BUILD IT, WILL THEY COMMUNICATE?

We have touched upon only a few of the communication issues related to the development of VR applications. We hope we have given the reader a flavor of some of the creative possibilities potentially unleashed by this emerging medium. Experience of the more engaging forms of these applications remains at some point in the future. But the tapping of computer keys—the hammers and anvils of the computer industry—is busily stringing together the lines of code that will drive new communication applications. This creative tapping may start to sound like a deafening industrial clanging as more institutions and more individuals turn their talents to the crafting of VR communication applications. In the end we can only judge these applications by what they yield in our minds and for our society. It remains to be seen if virtual reality and its new communication applications will increase our understanding of human communication or human understanding of each other. Optimism usually greets the dawn of a new medium.

REFERENCES

Aukstakalnis, S., & Blatner, D. (1992). *Silicon mirage: The art and science of virtual reality.* Berkeley, CA: Peachpit Press.

Baudrillard, J. (1983). *Simulations.* New York: Semiotext(e).

Bardini, T., Horvath, A., & Lyman, P. (in press). The social construction of the microcomputer user: The rise and fall of the reflexive user. *Journal of Communication.*

Biocca, F. (1991). Viewer's mental models of political commercials: Towards a theory of the semantic processing of television. In F. Biocca (Ed.), *Television and political advertising: Vol. 1. Psychological processes.* Hillsdale, NJ: Lawrence Erlbaum Associates.

Biocca, F. (1992). Communication within virtual reality: Creating a space for research. *Journal of Communication, 42*(4), 5–22.

Biocca, F. (1993a). Communication research in the design of communication interfaces and systems. *Journal of Communication, 43*(4), 59–68.

Biocca, F. (1993b). Virtual reality: The forward edge of multimedia. In M. De Sonne (Ed.), *Multimedia 2000.* Washington, DC: National Association of Broadcasters.

Bird, A. (1971). *Looking forward.* New York: Arno Press. (Original work published 1899).

Blumer, H. (1969). *Symbolic interactionism.* Englewook Cliffs, NJ: Prentice-Hall.

Brand, S. (1988). *Media lab.* New York: Penguin.

Brittan, D. (1992). Being there: The promise of multimedia communications. *Technology Review, 95*(4), 42–51.

Ciampa, J. (1989). *Communication, the living end.* New York: Philosphical Library.

Coleridge, S. T. (1817). *Biographia literaria; or, Biographical sketches of my literary life and opinions.* New York: R. Fenner.

Cook, W. J. (1993). This is not your father's television. *U.S. News & World Report, 115*(22), 63–66.

Ekman, P. (1974). *Unmasking the face.* Englewood Cliffs, NJ: Prentice-Hall.

Ellis, S. (1991). Nature and origins of virtual environments: A bibliographic essay. *Computer Systems in Engineering, 2*(4), 321–347.

Ellis, S. R., Kaiser, M. K, & Grunwald, A. J. (1991). *Pictorial communication in virtual and real environments*. London: Taylor & Francis.

Engelbart, D. (1988). The augmented knowledge workshop. In A. Goldberg (Ed.), *A history of personal workstations*. Reading, MA: Addison-Wesley.

Gibson, W. (1984). *Neuromancer*. New York: Ace Books.

Gilder, G. (1993). Telecosm: Digital darkhorse newspapers. *Forbes ASAP.*

Hall, E. (1966). *The hidden dimension*. New York: Random House.

Hall, S. (1993). Coding and decoding in the television discourse. In S. Hall, Hobson, D.,**

Hamit, F. (1993). *Virtual reality and the exploration of cybserspace*. Carmel, IN: SAMS Publishing.

Hirose, M., Yokoyama, K., & Sato, S. (1993). Transmission of realistic sensation: Development of a virtual some. In *IEEE Virtual Reality Annual International Symposium* (pp. 125–131). Piscataway, NJ: IEEE.

Horton, D., & Wohl, R. (1956) Mass communication and para-social interaction. *Psychiatry 19*, 215–229.

Johnson-Laird, P. N. (1983). *Mental models: Towards a cognitive science of language, inference, and consciousness*. Cambridge, MA: Harvard University Press.

Katz, E. (1992) The end of journalism? Notes on watching the war. *Journal of Communication, 42*(3), 5–14.

Kay, A., & Goldberg, A. (1977). Personal dynamic media. *Computers & Operations Research, 10,* 31–41.

Krueger, M. (1991). *Artificial reality*. Reading, MA: Addison-Wesley.

Lanier, J., & Biocca, F. (1992). An insiders view of the future of virtual reality. *Journal of Communication, 42*(4), 150–172.

Latta, J. (1993, August 18). *Virtual reality: Technology in search of applications* (*Spectrum* Report). Waltham: Decision Resources.

Laurel, B. (1991). *Computers as theater*. Reading, MA: Addison-Wesley.

Licklider, J. C. R., Taylor, R. W. (1968, April). The computer as a communication device. *Science & Technology,* 21–31.

Lowe, A., & Willis, P. (Eds.). *Culture, media, language*. London: Hutchinson.

McLuhan, M., & McLuhan, E. (1988). *Laws of media, The new science*. Toronto: University of Toronto Press.

Miller, R., Walker, T. C., & Rupnow, M. (1992). *Survey on virtual reality* (Rep. No. 201) . Lilburn, GA: Future Technology Surveys.

Moore, M. (1951). *Collected poems*. New York: Macmillan.

Morishima, S., & Harashima, H. (1993). Facial expression synthesis based on natural voice for virtual face-to-face communication with machine. In *Proceedings of the 1993 IEEE Virtual Reality International Symposium* (pp. 486–491). Piscatawy, NJ: IEEE.

Moyers, B. (Interviewer). (1990). *Inventing the future with Robert Lucky, Parts I & II: World of Ideas with Bill Moyers* (Video). New York: Public Affairs Television.

Nilan, M. (1992). Cognitive space: Using virtual reality for large information resource management problems. *Journal of Communication, 42*(4), 115–135.

Rheingold, H. (1991). *Virtual reality*. New York: Summit.

Rheingold, H. (1993). *Virtual communities*. New York: Addison-Wesley.

Rowley, T. W. (1993). Virtual reality products. In R. A. Earnshaw, M. A. Gigante, & H. Jones (Eds.), *Virtual reality systems*. London: Academic Press.

Shaw, D. L. (1991). *The rise and fall of American mass media: Roles of technology and leadership*. Bloomington, IN: Indiana University.

Shimoga, K. (1993a). A survey of perceptual feedback issues in dextrous manipulation: Part I. Finger force feedback. In *Proceedings of the 1993 IEEE Virtual Reality International Symposium* (pp. 263–271). Picataway, NJ: IEEE.

Shimoga, K. (1993b). A survey of perceptual feedback issues in dextrous manipulation: Part II. Finger touch feedback. In *Proceedings of the 1993 IEEE Virtual Reality International Symposium* (pp. 271–279). Picataway, NJ: IEEE.

U.S. Dept of Commerce. (1992). *The national databook*. Washington, DC: Author.

Wooley, B. (1992). *Virtual worlds*. Oxford: Blackwell.

6 Virtual Reality and Passive Simulators: The Future of Fun

Diana Gagnon Hawkins
Interactive Associates

Virtual reality (VR), in which users enter and physically experience computer-generated worlds, has captured the imaginations of the populance through a flurry of conferences, articles, books, movies and TV documentaries. The first VR entertainment-based systems are now commercially available and are beginning to be implemented into sites around the world.

These early technologies and sites form the basis upon a which a new form of entertainment and supporting entertainment industry will be built. This chapter discusses the history behind this new industry; lays out the various technologies, and site concepts that are emerging; and explores some of the future directions that virtual reality entertainment applications may take.

THE TRENDS

A number of trends have come together to set the stage for the emerging new field of virtual reality public entertainment. These trends arose from the commercial availability of VR systems and the changing needs of the "out-of-home" entertainment industry; combined with a growing interest in interactive content development.

VR technologies that had primarily been the domain of the military flight simulator and research lab first became commercially available for public applications in the late 1980s. At this time, VR had received a great deal of press that created a public appetite for this intriguing new media.

The technologies, however, were not yet ready to be implemented in the home. The cheaper systems provided graphics that were too slow and crude, whereas the more powerful systems with texture-mapped graphics were too expensive.

At this same time, movie theater attendance had reached the lowest level in a decade. Through the use of VCRs and Pay Per View Television, many consumers were choosing to view movies in their homes rather than go to the theater. This trend created a need for a new form of out-of-home entertainment that could not be replicated in the home. The fact that virtual reality was perceived as a sexy new medium that could not be implemented in the home made it a prime technology to replace or supplement the ailing movie theater market.

Simultaneously, another trend was emerging in Hollywood. The traditional TV and film production community was being seduced by visions of a digital and interactive future that promised to soon be introduced through multimedia and interactive TV. Arcade games and VR represented the parallel out-of-home venue for this new interactive market.

The concept of joint production and cross promotion of interactive titles with movies had already been heralded by industry analysts as the next entertainment trend. *The Terminator 2*™ video game (which includes footage from the film) was the first clear example of this trend. During production of the film, a second crew was allowed on the movie set to sample the actors' voices and shoot images of the locations for inclusion in the arcade game. Many other arcade and home video games quickly followed suit, establishing a market for interactive game versions of both film and TV properties.

VR also offered producers and rights holders promises of a new auxiliary income and an opportunity to keep current with the youth market. Various hardware vendors and site developers were seeking the benefits of established titles to launch their new systems and were hoping to engage the Hollywood community in the production of future titles.

Developers of computer and CD ROM titles were also intrigued by the potential to produce content for the new VR market. VR represented a new venue that clearly would need first-class properties and software to feed what many began to believe might become a growing demand.

Many producers and rights holders of popular entertainment titles were faced with decisions about how and if they should enter this new interactive entertainment market, and whether or not they should license their valued properties, and if so, to whom.

The need for a new form of out-of-home entertainment, the commercial availability of VR systems, and the interest of the programming community in creating titles, set the stage for the development of VR public entertainment sites.

The entrepreneurs interested in offering VR to the public found that the first VR systems that were able to provide an appropriate level of graphics and response time were very costly. These higher end systems were too expensive for application in video game arcades, the only existing public interactive venue. On average, an arcade video game costs between $3,000 and $10,000, whereas the first commercially available VR systems cost $65,000 (for a single-player Virtuality unit) to over $1 million for multiple-player systems (e.g., Battletech,[TM] Visions of Reality,[TM] and Iwerks Virtual Adventures[TM]).

The fact that VR was too expensive to be supported in a traditional video game arcade was a catalyst for the evolution of a new type of out-of-home venue that was different from the arcade model. Early industry promoters dubbed this new type of site "location-based entertainment."

LOCATION-BASED ENTERTAINMENT

Various forms of entertainment have historically been an integral part of public spaces. The importance of entertainment in shopping centers began with the cinemas and expanded with the advent of the multiscreen theaters. As the public demanded more variety in entertainment, other tenants like video arcades and miniature rides appeared. The newest trend is in the development of location-based entertainment centers that incorporate aspects of arcades and theme parks in malls and shopping centers.

As shopping malls have evolved, four major types emerged, each distinctive in its own function: the neighborhood, the community, the regional, and the super-regional. The largest locations (the regional and super-regional) provide the most attractive settings for location-based entertainment sites.

There are close to 2,000 of these super-regional and regional shopping centers in the United States. They provide an excellent opportunity to fill the leisure gap in metropolitan areas without the attendance potential for a major theme park.

A range of family centers and miniparks began to spring up across the country. To exploit this opportunity Disney formed a new division to design miniparks in city center complexes. Other groups such as Edison Brothers and Rouse Enterprises organized entertainment divisions and opened a number of family entertainment centers and anchor attractions in malls. These small-scale entertainment centers were ideal locations to implement VR and other simulator technologies.

Simulators and VR represent the ideal new attraction because they occupy limited space, are cost-effective, safe, need limited maintenance, have relatively low power consumption requirements, have broad appeal and attract visitors. Above all, they are easy to re-theme to create a new attraction at a fraction of the original cost by simply changing the film or software.

Entertainment analysts agree that small-scale out-of-home sites may be the next significant entertainment concept; however their ideas of what should be in these sites vary. Overall the proposals for location-based entertainment sites can be divided into two types: (a) those that include passive film motion-based rides or theaters and (b) those that offer interactive VR or simulator systems.

Passive Location-Based Sites

Many entrepreneurs would like to develop sites that feature passive film simulators. This approach combines a film presentation with synchronized motion from a hydraulic motion base. Cabs, chairs, and entire theaters are moved in synch with short fast-action films. Although the users have no control of the action the high-quality visuals and sound combined with motion trick the senses into a believable and often thrilling "you are there" experience.

This approach is clearly an off spring of the speciality venue theater. Since the 1970s, special-venue theaters have provided a parade of advanced cinema concepts ranging from 70 mm, to 360-degree, to 3-D formats. These "larger-than-life" techniques rely on large screens, high resolution, and fast frame rates to envelop and surround their viewers within the action.

Early leaders in this field who all compete with various film technologies and products include: Iwerks Entertainment, Imax, Showscan, Hughes, and Omni films. This market has continued to concentrate on the speciality locations such as world fairs, museums, and theme parks, all of which are capable of investing several million dollars in construction and equipment.

The public has been very receptive to this form of entertainment, for its perceived "involvement" for the viewer; however, the missing ingredient has always been "motion." A number of suppliers finally added motion bases to their film presentations thus giving birth to the entertainment film simulator.

The field of film simulators is divided into high-capacity, medium, and small-scale units.

High-Capacity Simulators. High-capacity simulators usually offer seating for 40–120 and are targeted at theme parks. The intended audience is usually tourists with low-repeat visitation. As a result, they are usually heavily themed, fixed attractions within a larger venue (see Fig. 6.1).

Judging by exit polls, these high-capacity simulators have consistently been the top attractions at theme parks around the world. The Star Tours attraction at Disney Theme Parks is a good example of the phenomenal

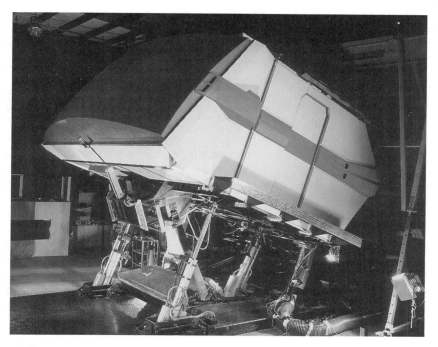

FIG. 6.1.   Large-scale passive simulator theater. Courtesy of Interactive Simulation, Inc.

success of this type of simulator. Six years after its introduction in 1987, it continues to draw crowds who stand in line for an average wait time of 45–60 minutes to experience this 4½-minute thrill.

This 40-seat simulator, featuring a spaceflight film developed by Lucas Films, takes viewers on a harrowing flight through space. The success of Star Tours compelled Disney to open a second simulation attraction entitled Body Wars.

The top audience grabber at MCA/Universal Tours was also a film motion-based attraction. The *Back to the Future* attraction takes two groups of 96 riders (8 in each of 12 Delorean cars) in a dome theater where they are exposed to a simulated time-travel trip through aerial battles and futuristic escapades designed by Douglas Trumbull.

A third example is the Tour of the Universe attraction, located in the CN Tower of Toronto. It consists of a themed ticketing area, a transition elevator that takes riders on a trip to the year 2019, and high-tech exhibits and interactive displays that lead to the boarding of a shuttle simulator. A cosmic film presentation with synchronized motion cues and digital sound is scheduled every 4–7 minutes, depending on the traffic. Riders then exit through a well-stocked gift shop.

There is no question that these high-end entertainment simulators have been strong audience attractors and will hold a prominent position in the amusement industry. The development of this type of attraction is expected to expand both within U.S. theme parks and across the globe.

Medium-Size Passive Simulators.   There is also a market for medium-size simulator units. These units cater to regional markets with medium repeat visitation. They usually take the form of unthemed motion theaters with changing films.

Unlike the high-capacity themed simulators, these units are smaller and employ seats usually in reconfigurable single or double units or in rows, which are synchronized to thrilling film sequences (see Fig. 6.2). The motion is "bumpy" at best but the novelty has captured the imagination of the public and the amusement industry.

Many of these simulator theaters have been placed inside various high-traffic public sites. These sites usually serve regional markets with medium repeat visitation and require a new film every 2 or 3 years. For example, Showscan has placed two units inside the Excaliber Casino in Los Vegas. These two 45-seat units (which charge $1.50 per ride) have met with great success. In 1993 the average attendance was estimated at 4,000–6,000 per day with annual admission revenue of $4.2 million.

FIG. 6.2.   Turbo Tours two-seat passive simulator. Courtesy of Iwerks Entertainment.

Small-Scale Passive Simulators.   The third type of film simulator is that of the small-scale units that appear in arcades, malls and touring shows. These simulators cater to resident markets with a high-repeat visit rate and as a result require frequent ride-film changes.

These small-scale simulators are beginning to appear in larger arcades, family centers, and in malls as stand-alone attractions and have even toured the country on the back of trucks. They consist of a small self-contained capsule theater, mounted to enable the entire structure to pitch and roll. The visual effect is projected by a film or laser videodisc onto a front screen. The physical motion, provided by a proprietary hydraulic platform, is synchronized to the film and sound effects. These units have less than 25 seats and feature low-budget films usually focused on reality-based experiences such as roller coaster rides, car chases, and so forth.

The first manufacturer of this type of simulator was Doron Precision Systems, Inc., based in New York. Doron markets a very reliable model that has been available worldwide for many years called the SR2. The SR2 is a 12-seat model that is easily reprogrammed to run a number of different off-the-shelf rides. Their newest system, the SRV, accommodates up to 15 or more people and incorporates one of over 25 land, sea, and air adventures (see Fig. 6.3).

Another early entrant into this market was Super X Ltd. of England whose first Prokon model was an instant success at Expo '88 in Brisbane.

FIG. 6.3.   SRV Small-scale passive simulator. Courtesy of Doron Precision Systems, Inc.

The Prokon is the first such simulator to employ video graphics and offer 10 different experiences.

In 1992, Sega Enterprises of Japan (the largest manufacturer of arcade video games) entered this market in Japan with a ride called Muggo's Revenge™ (featuring a film by Trumbull's Bershire Ridefilm). They also introduced a similar ride in the United States with a film featuring pop star Michael Jackson.

The same year, Hughes Training Inc. announced a system called the Venturer. This 14-seat entertainment simulator was the first to use a high definition television (HDTV) visual system. Hughes was successful in marketing this product to a variety of advertising sponsors such as Mountain Dew™ (see Fig. 6.4). In 1993, they introduced "McThriller"™ (a $2\frac{1}{2}$–3 minute ride) in a McDonald's fast food restaurant.

Numerous small-scale simulator developers have also introduced systems in this class. Vendors of these low-end simulators are targeting the resident market such as shopping centers, arcades, and cinema lobbies. These venues all have high repeat visitation and thereby necessitate new low-cost movies on a regular basis.

FIG. 6.4.   Mountain Dew-sponsored venturer. Courtesy of Hughes Training Systems.

The Pros of Film Simulators.   Overall, film simulators can be said to hold great promise as an out-of-home entertainment attraction. They provide high-quality visuals and audio, often surpassing what is currently found in theaters. The visuals (which often engulf the viewers' peripheral vision) combine with the motion to fool the senses into a believable and visceral "you are there" feeling that is unsurpassed.

The content, which is usually fast-action reality or science fiction, has a broad appeal and can draw from both the male and female movie audience. In many cases, these high-budget thrill rides equal or surpass first-run movies with their action-packed string of special effects.

To date, film simulators have proven to be the top attractions in theme parks and have been highly profitable in smaller venues as well.

The Cons of Film Simulators.   The main weaknesses of film simulator attractions have been the short format that makes it difficult to exist as stand-alone attractions, the often frantic and jerky motion, the lack of story, and the lack of interactivity.

Because the format for ride films has focused on short 4–6-minute thrill rides, many have questioned the viability of this format as a stand-alone attraction. Most out-of-home entertainment venues such as movies, concerts, and plays are all long-form. One might argue that when a person gets in a car and drives some distance, they might want to stay longer than 4 minutes.

Most ride-film sites propose some combination of attractions or a coupling of ride films with other activities such as restaurants, nightclubs, and shopping. Not only does this make entertainment sense, but it is also necessary to recoup the high cost of the simulator equipment and themed environments. In many cases, the food, beverages, and merchandising generate more revenues than the rides themselves.

In order to get the full effect of the motion, ride films have often utilized exaggerated jerky, and sometimes violent movements. These assaults on the body, although fun, can also be damaging and can cause various side effects such as motion sickness, sore backs, and vertigo.

The computer programs that move the hydraulic base are manually created after the movie has been shot. In the process of creating this motion program many movements are exaggerated and modified. Therefore, the motion the eye sees on the screen does not match the motion experienced by the body. This discrepancy often causes disturbances to the inner ear that result in sickness or dizziness.

Much more research is needed to fine-tune this relationship between the motion and the visual. To save on chiropractic bills, ride film designers might also try a few more graceful sweeps and less quick violent jerks. The fine art of designing "captivating" and "thrilling," yet "nondamaging" experiences clearly needs to be further explored.

Ride-film formats have also been lacking in the area of storyline and narrative. Most ride films are simple visceral yet dazzling thrill rides. To some degree they can be viewed as high-tech multimedia roller coaster rides. Rarely do they feature characters, stories, or narrative depth. Although audiences have long been attracted to thrill rides, they cannot compare to the level of obsession audiences have for other story-based media such as television, films, and books.

Film rides could be incorporated into longer story-based film formats or first-person action-based scenarios. This may allow for the manipulation of emotions as well as the body senses, creating an even more powerful experiential media format.

Although this format creates believable first-person experiences, it lacks the interactivity of real life. You are there, but you are only a passive viewer at the mercy of someone else's control. Adding user control in this format would clearly create the ultimate in virtual experiences.

Adding interactivity to a film-based system is currently technically difficult, if not impossible. Limited seamless video branching can be provided through the use of videodisc technology; however, until the video material is completely digital, users will not be afforded the level of interactivity currently achieved in common video games. In other words, users can be allowed to turn left and right along a limited path in a video world, but do not have free 360-degree movement as in virtual reality-based systems.

Interactive Location-Based Sites

As the Nintendo generation begins to age, many might argue that this interactivity will be key to sustaining younger audiences over time. Many believed video games would be a fad; however, they have continued to be a significant market resulting in over $4.5 billion a year in revenues, with hardware in over 30% of U.S. homes.

The interactivity wave has continued to spread to other home media. Remote controls and VCRs, which provided the first baby steps of user control, have penetrated a majority of homes and are now taken for granted as normal viewing practice. Multimedia has already been launched in the consumer market and there is no doubt that in the near future television itself will be digital, on-demand, and interactive.

Interactivity has also hit the out-of-home venue. A wide variety of out-of-home interactive sites have been tried. These range from simulated battles conducted in the woods with red-paint guns to more high-tech group battles conducted with lazar guns in science fiction sets.

Early Interactive Game Sites.   Photon was the first interactive lazar tag game introduced in the U.S. Photon was a participatory game that involved two teams of players (up to 15 per side) competing against each other in a highly themed space-age set of fog and props. Players carried an infrared gun to shoot their foes. These guns shot signals that were recorded on a small computer receiver imbedded in the chest plate of each player's suit, which registered kills and wounds. This simple high-tech "cowboys and Indians" game reported $10 million gross sales from 2 corporate and 19 franchised sites.

Wonder Wars, a similar concept, opened in a large shopping center near Tokyo, Japan in 1988. It was a self-participating attraction in which guests were invited to play the role of a hero gunfighter in a thrilling cosmic battle.

Amazing Square in Senju was a high-tech leisure land near Tokyo, Japan. Here, players participated in 12 areas of dimensional-space, laser beam attacks, and special effects to earn a computerized certificate of wins and losses. This game formed the main attraction in the Hitachi Pavilion at Expo 88, in Brisbane.

Blastar was yet another successful example in the realm of high-tech games. In this attraction riders enter a full-size space ship, surrounded by aliens, and test skills against target robots. Twelve players match wits with the robots for $3\frac{1}{2}$ minutes of action through hundreds of special effects.

Many different types of interactive shooting games have been tried. Some have suceeded although others have failed. Variations on this concept are still being introduced with new and improved hardware (e.g., Quzar,^{TM} Laser Storm,^{TM} etc).

Although these battle game scenarios are shallow and violent, they were successful in appealing to some younger, predominantly male, sections of the population. Most importantly, the success of these simple scenarios has proven consumer willingness to participate in first-person interactions with staged events as well as with other human beings.

Virtual Reality.   Virtual reality has been heralded as the next big step in interactive out-of-home entertainment. What is VR? There is no standard definition of VR. Broadly defined, VR or artificial reality is any medium that attempts to immerse the user into an artificially generated environment that fools the user's senses into believing that it is a real experience (Steuer, 1992). More narrowly, VR has come to refer to the current set of technologies that are used to achieve this goal, such as a helmet (with computer-generated display) and a data glove or other 3-D input device (see Biocca & Delaney, this volume).

Sophisticated VR systems attempt to simulate the real-world phenomenon of sight, sound, and touch through a combination of computer-generated input to the user's eyes, ears, and skin. Using head-mounted displays, gloves, body suits, or large projected images in simulator cabs, users can interact with artificially generated environments.

Current VR systems can be divided into vehicle-based systems, which use some form of vehicle; and immersion systems, which use a head-mounted display or helmet.

Vehicle-based systems allow the user to interact with an artificial world through the manipulation of a cab or vehicle. In this type of a system, real-time computer graphics are displayed on the windshield of the vehicle providing the user the illusion that he or she is driving a vehicle, tank, airplane, sub, or what have you in the computer-generated world. These cabs often use full theming with vehicle instrumentation, and spatial sound systems to recreate a believable vehicle.

The first publicly available vehicle-based experience was Battletech in Chicago. A few years later, a second commercial site called Fightertown was opened in Irvine, California.

BattleTech, Virtual World Entertainment Inc. The first VR cite to successfully launch was a vehicle-based game called Battletech. Opened August 1, 1990 at Chicago's North Pier, this 4,000-square-foot center features 14 networked VR cabs within a themed environment. At a cost of $2.5 million to develop, it managed to be profitable by maintaining a steady stream of repeat users (Latta, 1993).

Users pay $7 to drive a tank in a 100 square-foot computer-generated science fiction battlefield of the 31st century. Two teams of seven players climb into individual cockpits to control huminoid walking tanks called BattleMechs. The objective is to destroy enemy BattleMechs while dodging their counterattacks.

A color monitor in the cockpit serves as the players' window into the terrestrial landscape which changes to reflect the time of day and weather (see Fig. 6.5). The vehicle has more than 100 controls; however, new users can manage to control the vehicle with the use of under 10 controls. Each vehicle has an audio connection to the other vehicles on their team, so that the players may speak to each other and plot strategies.

Although BattleTech draws many one-time visitors, a strong 43% play more than one time (31% play 2–4 times, 10% play 5–20 times, and 2% play more than 21 times) (Heeter, this volume). Leagues of heavy repeat players have also developed. Some of these BattleTech fanatics have played an average of 228 games. There are some who have played more than 900 games (Heeter, this volume).

Overall, this site with its battle scenario and complicated controls appeals primarily to young males. The fact that 30% of the players call ahead to make reservations also suggests that many people are traveling to the mall for the explicit purpose of playing BattleTech. There clearly is an active market for this type of VR site.

BattleTech sites are beginning to be licensed around the world. Many of

A VGL™ pilot at the
controls of his virtual
reality pod. From here he
can engage opponents
in the ritual combat of
Battletech or the
Martian Death Race
on the Red Planet.
As all interaction in
the virtual worlds
between people
not computers, every
adventure is unique

VIRTUAL WORLD

FIG. 6.5.   Virtual Worlds Entertainment cockpit. Courtesy of Virtual Worlds Entertainment, Inc.

the sites have been opened under the name Virtual World Entertainment Center. These sites feature new content designed to appeal to a broader segment of the population.

The goal of the Virtual Worlds Entertainment centers was to create a place where both adults and children would feel welcome. Instead of focusing exclusively on hand–eye coordination, the new sites hope to focus on resource management, teamwork, and strategy.

The theme of the site is a futuristic explorer's club with various adventure experiences. The lounge features photos of great adventurers both real and fictional. The first Virtual World Entertainment Center opened in 1993 in Walnut Creek, California featuring Battletech and a second game called Red Planet.™

Fightertown.   The second VR site, called Fightertown,™ opened in June 1992 in Irvine, California. This site allowed users to experience a military flight simulator. Six realistic airplane cockpits (an F111, F104, F14, and two F16s) are networked together allowing the users to fly together in the same air space.

Users suit up in a flight jumpsuit and receive a 30-minute briefing given by a live instructor. They then enter their cockpit and are coached off the runway by a live operator in a flight control tower. Throughout the flight users are encouraged to communicate using authentic flight lingo.

The virtual world consisted of 180 X 100 miles including land, oceans, islands, and aircraft carriers (Latta, 1993). The image is projected onto a large screen in front of authentic trainer cockpits.

The price of admission to Fightertown was $27.95 rather then the $8 charged for Battletech. Fightertown also caters to a slighter older airplane enthusiast crowd. Overall this site too appeared to be a success.

Clearly, developing VR experiences with strong stories and characters will help to expand the audiences for this type of attraction. More sites will be developed with recognizable stories, perhaps based on other properties such as films and books. With this type of content, VR can become a serious storytelling medium whose first-person experiences will rival the more traditional vicarious media.

Marriage of Military Vendors and Entertainment Companies.   Many companies are hoping to enter the entertainment VR market. One successful business model seems to come from the marriage between military vendors and entertainment companies. Companies who had traditionally created military flight simulators have decided to couple with entertainment companies and modify their high-end technologies to create entertainment-based simulators. Examples of this include: Hughes and Lucas Arts; and Evans & Sutherland and Iwerks.

GM Hughes Electronics Corporation (with its British subsidiary Rediffusion Simulation) applied their many years of research and development on flight simulators to create a line of entertainment simulators. The first system, called Commander,[TM] was introduced in London at a price of $76,000 per unit.

The Commander was a two-seat cab unit that featured real time joystick control, dynamic motion base, CD-quality audio and high-resolution graphics. Each capsule was self-contained and equipped to run in environments without the presence of a human attendant. The unit contained a point of sale display, which included coin, card, or note validation system, an attract mode, and back-lit promotion and instruction display.

The Commander was intended to be a platform that would provide a wide range of games and experiences that were to be created and developed by Lucas Arts Entertainment. The partnership between Hughes and Lucas Arts also produced a higher end system called the Mirage.[TM] This system consisted of up to 64 two-person pods networked together (see Fig. 6.6).

In 1993, GM Hughes Electronics sold Rediffusion Simulation and along with it the rights to the Commander. The Mirage remained with Hughes

FIG. 6.6.   The Mirage networked VR system. Courtesy of Hughes Training.

Training, and the partnership between Hughes and Lucas Arts was disbanded.

Evans & Sutherland and Iwerks (a themepark attraction company) also formed a partnership to pursue entertainment VR. In 1993, they introduced Virtual Worlds Adventure. In this six-person underwater adventure, users work together to collect eggs from the nest of the Lock Ness Monster.

Many other small companies have also been formed to exploit this new market (e.g., Xatrix, Magic Edge, etc). These companies offer a variety of hardware solutions and software applications as well as work for hire (see Fig. 6.7).

It is clear that vehicle based VR is gaining great momentum. There are

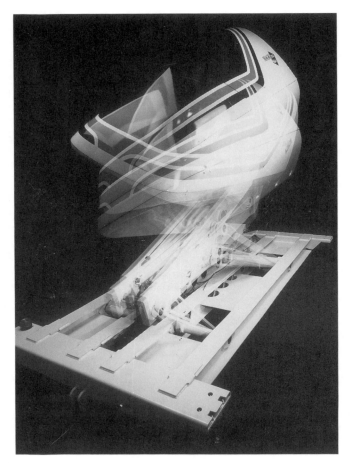

FIG. 6.7.   Hornet 1. Single-person motion-based cab. Courtesy of Magic Edge, Inc.

many vendors that offer systems, software, and site franchises that are finding their way into locations around the world.

Immersion Virtual Reality.   Immersion VR describes a system that surrounds the user's body within an environment. This type of system provides users with goggles or a helmet that feature small monitors positioned in front of the user's eyes. These monitors display 3-D stereo images that change in response to the direction the user looks. For example, if the user physically looks up, he or she will see a computer-generated image of the sky. If he or she looks down he or she will see an image of the ground.

This type of system also uses some form of input device so that the user can interact within the environment. This can range from a data glove that allows the user to grab and manipulate objects; to a full body suit that tracks the movements of the user's entire body into the computer generated world (Biocca & Delaney, this volume).

Some immersion systems also offer tactile feedback devices that allow the user to grab an object in the computer world and feel the shape of the object through a glove. This type of feedback is usually provided by computer-controlled air pressure.

Like the vehicle-based VR units, these devices can also be networked so that more than one person can enter the world at the same time and interact with each other in the same environment. They can also have a microphone so users can talk to each other and a tactile feedback device so that they can shake hands or engage in various games or activities.

It is this vision of groups of people entering and physically experiencing fictional worlds that has captured the imaginations of all who have learned of its potential. People have espoused the possibilities of everything from virtual sex to total addiction and mass withdrawal from reality (Shapiro & McDonald, this volume).

The reality of VR is a long way from these images. The first-person real-time response provided by immersion VR systems is technically more demanding than cab-based VR systems. This approach not only requires real-time graphics generation but also requires well-designed input devices that are safe and comfortable.

VPL Research Inc. was an early entry that gained significant notoriety in this market. However, they went out of business before having sold a single entertainment system. W Industries was the first company to successfully offer commercial immersion systems for the entertainment industry. In 1993, other companies such as Visions of Reality began to offer competing systems.

VPL Research Inc. and MCA.   VPL research was the most high-profile of the various VR companies. They introduced their first VR systems in 1989. Although VPL had focused primarily on high-end medical and research markets, they attempted to introduce a system called the Micro-Cosm, which they hoped to market to the entertainment industry.

This VR system ran on a Macintosh and featured a data glove and unique display device. Unlike other head-mounted displays, which were helmets that fit over the user's head, this unit was held up to the face like an opera glass.

Inside the display unit were speakers and a set of controls on the handle to control the direction of movement through the environment. The unit also had an optional strap that allowed the user to wear the headpiece, thereby freeing up the use of the hand. This system was never commercially launched.

VPL had also joined with MCA to develop a plan for a VR theater. Unlike any other VR sites, this plan called for a combination of audience participation and first-person interactivity. An audience of approximately 36 members was to be seated in a circular theater. Each seat was to be fitted with a head-mounted display (resembling a beauty parlor hair dryer) and a hand input device attached to the arm of the seat.

Two players were intended to interact on the stage using an ambulatory headmount display and glove. They were to be led by a third suited actor who guided them through a VR adventure that could be described as a cross between a story and a game. Random audience members were also to be given some limited opportunity to interact at various points.

Although this project was never implemented, the idea of audiences passively viewing a VR experience was unique and generated a great deal of interest from the VR community.

W Industries.   W Industries, founded in 1987, offered the first commercial line of immersion systems, accessories and software. Their units included a sit-down unit with an open cab (see Fig. 6.8) and duel joystick (1000sd); a stand up unit with a pull-down padded ring, helmet, and hand-held joystick (1000 cs); (see Fig. 6.9) a networked option in which two of these units were hooked together, allowing users to enter the same environment (head2); and a Virtuality Center that hooked four or more units together with a full range of theming accessories (such as ceiling and floor panels, monitors for spectator viewing, and a checkered platform).

The ergonomics of many of the components such as the helmet and padded ring offered a safer and better design for public spaces than any other immersion system at that time. In short, it was the only immersion VR system that was viable for placement into public environments. Other VR immersion systems are not designed to endure this rugged environment and had not undergone the strict safety and sanitary tests that Virtuality had.

W Industries also had the largest number of experiences developed for their systems. Their titles included: Vtol™ (a Harrier jet simulator), Total Destruction™ (a stock car racing simulator), Battlesphere™ (a space battle), Exorex™ (a robot warrior battle) and Dactyl Nightmare™ (a cyberspace combat experience). These titles appealed to the same male youth market as BattleTech.

In 1993, other small companies began to offer competing entertainment immersion systems. For example Visons of Reality Corp. licensed the rights to the Kaiser Electro-Optics Inc.'s head-mounted display and offered an immersion experience that consisted of six networked units. The helmets

FIG. 6.8. Virtuality sit down immersive VR system. Courtesy of Edison Mall Entertainment.

were attached to a sit-down unit and the user controlled the motion with joysticks and directional foot peddles (see Fig. 6.10). Other small vendors also offered various forms of head-mounted display, but did not offer full turn-key immersion systems.

EVALUATION OF VIRTUAL REALITY SYSTEMS

Although there are many companies involved in various aspects of the VR business there are few companies that can be seen as serious contenders in the entertainment arena. To date only a few have launched their systems and many have failed in the process. In order to evaluate the potential success of these various VR systems a number of variables should be taken into account such as technological capabilities and software.

FIG. 6.9. Virtuality stand up immersive VR system. Courtesy of Edison Mall Entertainment.

Technological Capabilities Comparison

The current battle for who is best in the VR world is a technical tangle of features and promises. In order to evaluate these systems, one must first ask what are the current graphic and input capabilities. The components that make up the systems are quickly improving, thus one must also ask how these capabilities will be improved over the next few years.

To the layman's eye, the quality of the VR system is based on the following:

1. The details of the graphic. Does he really look like a relatively believable robot? Is this an aesthetically pleasing and compelling environment?

FIG. 6.10.   Cybergate: Immersive VR application. Courtesy of Visions of Reality.

2. The responsiveness of the image. Do objects move in real time to match my gestures? When I reach out, is there a delay before my computer-generated hand reaches out? If I turn my head, how quickly does the view follow?
3. The safety and comfort of the helmet. How uncomfortable and safe is this thing you are putting on my head? How dirty is it? Can I wear my glasses? Does it fit? Can I get out of it if I get claustrophobic?
4. The ease of use of the input device. How coordinated do I have to be to use this thing?

Judging by these criteria, each system appears to have its strengths and weaknesses.

Display Graphics.   The quality of the graphics is a result of both programming capabilities and hardware features such as the resolution of the display, the method used for displaying foreground and background, and the computer that is used.

Resolution.   The resolution of the display varies across systems. All of the early systems utilized relatively low-resolution displays and planned to increase the resolution significantly in their next generation of equipment.

The newest trend is to include higher resolution displays such as HDTV screens and collimated monitors.

Scaled Bit Maps Versus 3-D Polygons.   One significant way that the systems vary is in the method they use for creating the foreground objects and the background environment. Some systems like BattleTech use a two-dimensional bit-map method for displaying the scenes while others like W Industries use a three-dimensional polygon system.

In the bit-map method, hand-drawn or computer-generated background elements are scanned or entered into the computer and stored. The images are then called up and displayed. As the user moves closer to the background the objects are scaled and a new picture with larger objects is drawn. The foreground objects are then recalled from a library of possible positions scaled and then presented on the screen.This approach is commonly used in video games.

This bit-map approach provides for greater detailed images that give a heightened sense of reality to the adventure. It does, however, have its drawbacks. This method requires a great deal of storage capabilities and is limited in its ability to provide various points of view. Bit-mapped graphics are most appropriate for game scenarios that stay on a flat surface with limited points of view, such as adventure games.

In the polygon approach, numerical representations of the background or foreground objects are stored as polygons (triangles or other geometric shapes). They are then drawn in real time as solid shaded objects on the screen. This approach requires less storage space on the computer and allows quick-changing views to be displayed. The drawback is that the images lack detail and appear as blocky solid forms. This approach is necessary for applications like flight simulators where users are moving fast and must have the ability to go in any direction.

Texture maps are now being used to improve the detail of the polygon surfaces. Texture maps allow for a sample image to be applied as a pattern over a geometric shape. For example, a picture of a brick can be entered into the computer and replicated onto a plain surface to create a full brick wall. Images of 2-D objects can be mapped onto 3-D objects to create 3-D effects. For example, a rock surface can be placed onto a cone to create a mountain. This allows for greater realism and detailing in polygon-defined applications.

Stereoscopic Imaging.   The immersion units that feed images to a helmet use stereo images presenting a different image to each eye. This kind of display can cause some problems. Since the computer must supply two views at the same time, they are either one half the standard frame rate or require stronger computers. Cab-based units present only one image and can therefore either double the frame rate or increase the visual detail.

Some believe the 3-D stereoscopic effect enhances the experience; other disagree. It is clearly a subjective judgement. It is also important to note that 10% of the population cannot merge the two images into one 3-D image and as a result do not see a 3-D effect. This is a consideration when creating a mass appeal attraction.

Computer.   The graphics are also influenced by how powerful the computer is and how quickly it can generate real-time images and control and synchronize the input information.

The initial Virtuality system used a 68030 processor with 320 × 240 color helmet display system. A TI 34000 coprocessor was used to speed up the graphic allowing real-time polygon rendering. This 3-D rendering allows for quick movement and viewing in all directions. In two of their games they also include scanned bit-mapped backgrounds.

The units were networked via Ethernet allowing players to share experiences in the same room and, eventually, across nationwide connections. A magnetic detection system reads hand movements and head position, and the system renders 5,000 flat shaded polygons per second.

W Industries plans to add a special-purpose high-speed graphics processor that can present 500 textured polygons per frame. Inside the helmet the current screen will be replaced with a 512 × 480 display, and the system response time with be hastened to 2 milliseconds. A tactile feedback glove that allows the user to feel the objects may also be added. Although this system uses polygons with texture maps to provide detail, it is still limited in its ability to present objects.

The initial BattleTech system was based on a 68020 processor with a 320 × 240 screen. The backgrounds were recalled from an optical disk drive allowing for a pan-and-scan-based terrain system. Similar to the Virtuality system, the networking was achieved on Ethernet. The electromagnetic joysticks have limited resolution and only provide for movement in two dimensions (forward, back, right, left). The foreground characters were recalled from precomputed possible positions and scaled. This system has been updated and the new system has been installed in all the licensed sites.

Similar to the current Virtuality system, the next generation BattleTech system will use a 68020 with 320 × 240 display. It will also add a TI34000 coprocessor to speed up the graphics and allow for real-time polygon rendering with texture maps. BattleTech's approach combines bit-mapped and polygon rendering and promises to offer superior graphics.

Many systems are beginning to use significantly more powerful computers such as Silicon Graphic's Reality Engine, enabling a new level of graphic texture, light, and shading. These capabilities will continue to advance with each generation of equipment.

Response Time.   How quickly the system responds to the user's movements is important in creating the "you are there" feeling and in keeping the user from getting disoriented and dizzy. Because the user is immersed in the system with his or her peripheral vision covered, his or her sense of balance can be severely influenced by the coordination between his or her movements and the images.

The current response time for most systems appears to be approximately 40 milliseconds. Many vendors claim to have lowered this to 2 milliseconds, a feat that should significantly enhance the experience.

Safety and Comfort of Helmet.   To create 360 degrees of immersion, most VR systems require the user to have monitors in front of their eyes. In the future this type of display will be provided by goggles that are as lightweight as a pair of sunglasses; however, today this requires a bulkier helmet set-up. The design of this helmet is an important element in the overall comfort and ease of use of a VR system.

The W Industries' Visette was the first commercially viable helmet. This slick high-tech design is a significant improvement over the heavy noncounterweighted designs of the past.

It features a unique "Ergolok" design that makes it easier to get on and off and has passed stringent health and safety requirements in the areas of electrical safety, noise safety, neck stress, and bacterial transfer. The smooth plastic materials are used to stop the spread of head lice.

Newer helmets are focusing on smaller lighter-weight designs with detachable headbands that the users can take home as souvenirs. These disposable bands allow for theming, as well as advertising or sponsorship opportunities.

Input Device.   Users of VR systems incorporate input devices to both direct their movement within the environment and to conduct various manipulations of objects within the space. Most systems use either a joystick or glove. Some research systems use full body suits to map the entire body into the system; however these have not been used in commercial environments (see Biocca, 1992, for review).

As a general rule, cab-based units allow for more versatility in the interface device. This allows the designers to theme the vehicle. For example, BattleTech, which is a form of tank, has two foot pedals for steering similar to what one would find in a real tank. Unfortunately, when designers are too literal, they often create simulations that are too difficult for the average user.

Software Comparison

One of the largest concerns with VR systems is the fear that once users try the system and get over the "novelty effect" they will not want to play again. It will be the software or the experiences on the system that determines both who will be attracted to try it in the first place, and whether or not they will come back again. Once the technological issues are worked out, software is the single strongest determiner of initial and long-term success.

The software on VR systems is one of the weakest factors in an otherwise promising picture. Compared to other interactive and game software, it is safe to say that VR software has been sorely lacking. Other than Battle-Tech, no system has been installed long enough to endure the test of time. Most systems are relying solely on the novelty of the equipment and shortness of the experiences (usually under 3 minutes, most of which is spent learning how to move and use the controls).

In the early years of VR, almost all software was male-oriented (flight simulators, battles, car races, shooting and killing, etc). BattleTech presented a futuristic battlefield in which users duke it out against their fellow players in tank-type robots. Fightertown was a military flight simulator experience.

W Industries provided users with Exorex, a robot warrior battle where you kill other people who pose as Cyberdroids; Vtol, a flight simulator where you shoot other people's jets; Total Destruction, where you are driving a stock car in a race; and Battlesphere (no, not BattleTech, it's *sphere*), a dog flight battle in space.

A few experienced vendors acknowledge a strong desire to draw a broader audience. Virtual World Entertainment's approach is to create adventures rather than battles, with clearly identifiable goals. They plan to focus on strategy, teamwork and resource management skills, allowing players to work together rather than simply annihilate each other. Iwerks Virtual Worlds Adventures also shares these goals. This is the correct software view if they are able to implement it.

Depth.   In addition to the continuous focus on fight or flight, VR experiences have all presented shallow scenarios devoid of characters, emotional involvement, or stories. BattleTech is one exception to this rule.

Unlike the other titles, BattleTech is based on a fully developed story and set of properties that are licensed in the form of books, games, and action figures. Although there is tremendous depth of story, the story elements do not come through in the VR experience. More advanced players who buy the book will learn incredible details about the background, story and vehicles they drive. Unfortunately, this depth does not come across in the experience or preshow.

BattleTech has focused their depth in the detailing of the vehicle (the vehicle has 100 controls). Although the desire to learn how to master the vehicle has created a subculture of young male fanatics, a large number of novices are intimidated. For many people this desire for mastery must be fueled by an emotionally appealing goal.

Sound.   Sound is another factor that will impact the effectiveness of the VR titles. It is no secret to film and TV producers that sound adds to the emotional impact of a story and can be used as a valuable tool for emotional manipulation. One thing many of the VR systems have done right is to include high-quality sound capabilities, however few have effectively used it.

W Industries has the strongest record to date for using music to create a mood for their experiences. Both Virtual World and W Industries have included microphones in their systems. This person-to-person communication is extremely valuable in creating the "you are there" experience, and will facilitate the ability to include player cooperation features into games.

VR titles can learn a great deal from the rules of good video game design. For many years video games have fine-tuned a formula "easy to learn but hard to master" that has created the current generation of game addicts. Not until stories and characters are added to this formula will these addictive features achieve cross-over to the mass audience. Virtual reality with its first person experience has the potential to become the ultimate storytelling medium.

To date, few of the VR companies have produced titles that would even compete with the poorest of video games. When the novelty of the equipment wears off the one who has firmly planted themselves in the software chair will be the winner.

EVALUATION OF LOCATION-BASED SITE PROPOSALS

Given the plethora and variety of location-based entertainment sites that have been proposed it is difficult to evaluate the comparative merit of each. It is therefore important to examine similarities and differences in order to determine which model to support.

In considering a location site proposal one must ask:

Is the site a virtual reality site or a passive simulator site?
Is the virtual reality immersion- or vehicle-based?
Is the site themed?
What capacity does it handle?
Do the parties have the facilities and skills needed to successfully launch
    sites?

Virtual Reality Versus Passive Simulator Sites.   In comparing a VR site to a passive simulator there are many pros and cons to consider. Each option has its own strengths.

Passive simulators provide broad-appeal, high-resolution film images with the kind of robustness that consumers expect. The real images allow for the inclusion of characters and celebrities; film and TV tie-ins and coproduction; and the high emotional impact of film-based storytelling. The physical motion makes it novel and experiential. This format also allows larger numbers of people to pass through in a shorter period of time.

VR is a concept that triggers the imagination. It has generated a great deal of hype that will intrigue many people to try it at least once. It offers a much more intense personal experience in which the user actually controls the events and interacts with the environment. Because the systems can be networked they also provide a social aspect that adds to the appeal. If the interactive experience is good, users will want to play again and again to master it.

Perhaps one solution is to create sites that include both a passive simulator (which has broad audience appeal, and large capacities) and a VR site (which has a strong novelty draw, will soon improve in quality, and is more likely to draw repeat users).

Immersion Versus Vehicle-Based Virtual Reality.   In assessing VR reality sites it is important to consider whether the site is an immersion- or vehicle-based site. Each of these approaches has its relative strengths and weaknesses.

In choosing which type of VR system to use, it is clear that the practicality of the vehicle-based systems must be weighed against the novelty draw of the helmet. Which one is best may depend on the other elements of the site.

Themed Sites and Site Capacity.   Sites also vary according to whether they are themed or nonthemed and what capacity they allow for. Non-themed sites usually are modeled after a multiplex that brings in new experiences the way a movie theater brings in new movies. It does not rely on one theme, but focuses attention on the individual experiences themselves without the packaging.

Themed environments add to the overall excitement, novelty, and fantasy of the moment. They make the site itself feel more like a place to be. Because many of the attractions provide short experiences, it is important to create a site where the customers will linger and spend money on other items such as food and merchandise. Creating an attractive theme makes the site itself into an event.

The different sites vary in the number of people they can accommodate. Interactive sites can accommodate fewer people than passive sites. Vehicle-based VR can accommodate more people than immersion units. The level of personal interactivity is traded off against the number of people that can be run through and the amount that can be charged for the experience.

Overall, the strongest site would be one that includes: a number of types

TABLE 6.1
Strengths and Weaknesses of Immersive Versus Vehicle VR

Immersive Virtual Reality Systems	
Weaknesses	*Strengths*
Require the use of a helmet that poses many health and safety considerations	It is a novel and exciting experience that people want to try
Require a full-time attendant to get the users in and out of the equipment	It is surrounded by a great deal of hype and mystique
Loading and unloading users from the equipment takes valuable time	The technologies will quickly get better, improving the graphics and creating lighter weight and safer helmets
The stereoscopic images cannot be seen as 3-D by 10% of the population	
The graphics provided do not reach the level of detail provided by a common videogame	
Many users get sick and dizzy	

Vehicle Virtual Reality Systems	
Weaknesses	Strengths
They do not provide as intense a first-person experience as a helmet	Are more comfortable and safer than a helmet system
Can be perceived by some as high-end videogames especially given the current content	Can easily be themed to increase realism
	Can be networked to include many people at the same time or can give different roles to people within the same vehicle
	Do not use stereoscopic images
	Can be easily loaded and unloaded

of attractions (both passive simulator and virtual reality); broad-appeal content with stories based on popular film properties or music; a themed environment with changing-attraction software; and a restaurant/bar and merchandizing outlet.

FUTURE DIRECTIONS

It is clear that VR is well on its way to becoming a public form of entertainment. With each generation, the technology and software will improve. In the near future we should see significant advances in:

1. Input devices.
2. Interactive story lines.
3. Networking.
4. Real-time sound scores.
5. Virtual life programming techniques.

Input Devices.   The input devices in VR entertainment applications have primarily focused on allowing users to control their movement through virtual space or allowing them to shoot at targets. A number of devices that provide tactile feedback are now in the labs and will eventually become commercially available (Biocca & Delaney, this volume; Mogal, 1993).

These tactile devices will provide a range of sensations allowing the user to feel feedback from the environment. For example, the users will be able to feel the size and texture of objects that are grabbed. Forced feedback devices such as rackets, clubs, and weapons are already in development. Eventually full bodysuits could be employed to provide a feeling of complete physical contact with the virtual world.

In addition to moving and feeling, users must be able to communicate. Many VR experiences already provide microphones for users to talk to other players and to the game operators.

As VR begins to incorporate stories, there will be a further need for input that allows the user to communicate to the system and advance the plot. Graphical menus and buttons which are used in other interactive applications are inappropriate for VR because they interfere with the "you are there" feeling.

In order to suspend disbelief and create a real experience, it will be necessary to incorporate methods of communication that are used in real life such as talking, pointing, and looking. Voice recognition, gesture input, and eye tracking will most likely be used to provide the user with this more natural means of communicating to the system.

Interactive Stories.   VR entertainment to date has focused primarily on simple fight or flight content with little depth and no characters except the other players. These applications usually provide a simple scenario in which the user can act. In BattleTech, for example, you are in a vehicle and must shoot all the other players. There is no character development or events that happen or story that progresses.

In order to appeal to a broader audience VR must add characters and story elements that engage our emotions and thoughts. The traditional story formats of TV and film must be reinvented into a new interactive form that puts the user into a first-person experience while still retaining the excitement and integrity of a story.

In addition to providing a scenario, place, and other players, VR may begin to offer a series of events that evolve based on the users' actions. These elements would interweave in real time to create a unique first-person story. The players may encounter computer-generated characters, earthquakes, birthday parties, weddings, or any other plot element. Eventually programs may even be developed to coordinate these events to create real-time stories of aesthetic appeal (Bates, 1992; Laurel, 1991; Laurel, 1987; Meyer, this volume).

Networking. Networking methods will also see many advances in the near future. Most VR sites are networked to allow multiple players to interact within the same environment. Players can see computer representations of the other players and can communicate through built-in microphones.

In the near future these representations can be photo-real images of the players instead of computer graphics or alternatively players can be allowed to select their own fanciful images. The networks will also extend between sites and across the country. Players in a New York site will be able to join players in a California site all in one global virtual world.

Sound Track. Interactive sound scoring will also become more sophisticated in the near future. Currently, interactive soundtracks for video games, mulitmedia and VR consist of musical loops. For example, while the player is in the castle hall he or she will hear one sound loop that will repeat until he or she moves to another room. If the sound loop is constructed well, it may not be immediately evident. In less powerful applications like hand-held games and some video games the monotonous electronic loops can be quite maddening.

A new form of layered soundtrack must be developed that is composed in real time based on the situation. For example, in an underwater environment the various depths may have a base soundtrack that is associated with the different depths. The surface layer of water may have a light humorous sound while the deeper levels may have a scary or mysterious soundtrack. On top of this base sound, various context-specific sound effects would be added.

A program would trigger the appropriate sound effects based on what is happening to the user. Similar to a movie sound score, discordant tones could be added to predict impending danger or laugh tracks to accent a funny situation. In this way layers of context-specific sounds would be assembled creating a real-time sound score. Computer programs would eventually be developed to coordinate these various sounds into an aesthetically appealing musical score.

Virtual Life Programming. As VR begins to include computer-generated characters the appeal of virtual life programming techniques becomes more evident. In current video games characters are driven by simple programs that are often randomly generated and in some cases influenced by the user.

Vitual life programming techniques provide a full set of internal attributes to the characters themselves. For example, in a jungle scenario the animals could be programaed to be hungry at certain times, have emotional states and moods, make their own inferences and decisions, and, in general, act unpredicably, like real animals.

In the near future VR will come closer and closer to depicting a virtual world. Technological advances combined with engaging stories and characters promise to catapult the medium into a popular form of entertainment. It is this author's opinion that VR may well represent the future of fun.

REFERENCES

Bates, J. (1992). Virtual reality, art and entertainment. *Presence, 1*(1), 133–138.

Biocca, F. (1992). Virtual reality technology: a tutorial. *Journal of Communication, 42*(4), 23–72.

Latta, J. (1993). *At the cutting edge: Fightertown and Virtual World Entertainment.* Alexandria, VA: 4th Wave, Inc.

Laurel, B. (1991). *Computers as theater.* Menlo Park, CA: Addison-Wesley.

Laurel, B. (1987). *Toward the design of a computer based interactive fantasy system.* Unpublished doctorial dissertation, Ohio State University.

Mogal, J. (1993). VR technologies: Full immersion. *Iris Universe, 25,* 29–32.

Steuer, J. (1992). Defining virtual reality: Determining telepresence. *Journal of Communication, 42*(4), 73–93.

7 Communication Research on Consumer VR

Carrie Heeter
Michigan State University

This chapter is about consumer-oriented virtual reality (VR), which in the early 1990s includes a handful of commercial entertainment experiences such as Virtual World's BattleTech™ Center, Virtuality's mall-based science fiction games, and FighterTown's™ military simulators. Other start-up companies are working to open their own VR entertainment centers in malls or amusement parks. Museums will be another source of VR experiences, offering entertaining educational content. Virtual travel centers will allow people to visit (and shop at) faraway places. Health clubs will offer workout programs and physically challenging virtual games in exotic virtual environments. Eventually schools and even homes will have VR technology, and interactive distribution of experiences will occur over phone and cable lines. Virtual communication environments will bring friends and strangers together for communication experiences.

Although consumer VR will include a diverse set of experiences, those experiences will share some common parameters. Humans will enter these virtual worlds with the intent of engaging in a synthetic experience, with a goal of experiencing the synthetic world instead of or in addition to the real world for a period of time. Some VR will be individual experiences but most will link two or more people into the same virtual environment. Unlike dreams, these experiences will exist on computers, external to the minds of the participating humans. Each human will experience that external world from his or her own point of view, usually under his or her own control.

Data from five Comm Tech Lab studies of virtual reality are used to revisit classic mass media effects issues (such as uses and gratifications, cultivation theory, effects of violence, etc.) in the context of consumer-

191

oriented VR. The Methods section describes the studies and the VR systems they are based on. The Discussion section identifies traditional areas of mass media inquiry, suggests ways VR may change the focus of the issue, and, where appropriate, cites data from the studies.

METHODS

There were 787 respondents who offered their reactions to and opinions about four different VR experiences. Two were studies of entertainment VR installations (one based on science fiction fantasy and the other based on the U.S. military), two were of second-person VR prototypes tested with convention participants; and one was a study of college students who had never experienced VR (see Table 7.1).

BattleTech (Chicago, Illinois)

Since August 1990, the BattleTech Center[1] in Chicago has been transporting visitors to the year 3025, placing them in control of BattleMech robots at war in a computer-generated terrain amidst computer-generated weather conditions. For $7 per person, uniformed crew members guide six players at a time through a training and strategy session and then escort them to individual cockpits with multiple viewscreens and more than 100 controls to navigate the terrain and fight each other's Mechs for 10 minutes. Somebody wins, others lose, and detailed statistics on the battle are provided after (and during) the game. Figures 7.1 and 7.2 show BattleTech robots in action.

For four weekdays and one Saturday in September 1991, players were given questionnaires developed at Michigan State University when they purchased playing times, to be turned in after the game. Demographics about the "inhabitants" of this 1-year-old virtual world, their reactions to it, and their reasons for playing were studied. There were 312 completed questionnaires collected, for a completion rate of 34%. (One questionnaire was collected per person; at least 45% of the 1,644 games sold during the sample days represented repeat plays within the sample period.) BattleTech differentiates three classes of players: novices, who have played 1 to 10 BattleTech games ($n = 223$); veterans, who have played 11 to 50 games ($n = 42$); and masters, who have played more than 50 games ($n = 47$). Novices only play against each other, to assure that skill levels are somewhat matched. The novices surveyed had played an average of 3 games; veterans averaged 23 games; and masters had played an average of

---

[1]The BattleTech Center in Chicago is located at North Pier Mall on Illinois Avenue. For more information, call (312)-243-5660.

TABLE 7.1
Survey Summary

	Sample	Year	VR Experience	% Male	Age Range	Average
BattleTech (Chicago)	312	91	cockpit	93%	7 to 67	23
FighterTown (Irvine)	85	92	cockpit	97%	14 to 64	32
CyberArts (Pasadena)	87	91	2nd person	74%	17 to 55	34
SIGGRAPH (Chicago)	176	92	2nd person	74%	11 to 79	30
College (East Lansing)	127	92	none	55%	17 to 32	20
Total	787					

FIG. 7.1.   Mech robot at BattleTech.

228 games. Ninety-three percent of the BattleTech players surveyed were male. Age range was 7 to 67, with an average age of 23.

FighterTown (Irvine, California)

FighterTown[2] officially opened in August 1992. At FighterTown, you climb into and fly state-of-the-art military flight simulators that feature realistic

---

[2]FighterTown is located at 8 Hammond, Suite 100 in Irvine, California. For more information, call (714)-855-8802.

FIG. 7.2.   A Mech robot exploding.

aerodynamic models, functional glass cockpits and avionic panels, and stick and throttle controls. Multiple aircraft are linked in the same virtual world, which each pilot sees from his or her own perspective projected on 11-foot by 10-foot screens. Pilots can operate from land bases or take off and land from aircraft carriers to fly day or night in variable weather conditions, guided by a (human) air traffic controller who helps teach them to fly and guides them through their preplanned mission. Missions include military operations and general flight training experiences as well as combat (once a pilot has learned to fly well enough) against live or synthetic opponents. Cost for a 1-hour experience ranges from $27.95 per hour to fly the F-104 to $49.95 for the F-111. In addition to one-time and ad hoc flights, FighterTown offers year-long squadron memberships that involve monthly team flying experiences with the same group of people every month. Figures 7.3 and 7.4 show views from a FighterTown cockpit.

During early fall 1992, when the center first opened, ad hoc FighterTown participants were given exit poll questionnaires. Eighty-five completed questionnaires were collected. It is impossible to calculate a completion rate, because during busy times (of which there were many), surveys were frequently not distributed. In general, when they were distributed, FighterTown employees reported a high return level.

Ninety-seven percent of the FighterTown fliers who filled out surveys were male. Ages ranged from 14 to 64 with an average age of 34. Twenty

FIG. 7.3.   Planes at FighterTown.

percent had some military experience. Nearly half had flown a (real) plane at some time. No respondent had flown a FighterTown simulator more than five times, and the majority (81%) had just completed their first flight. All but one respondent indicated that they intended to return to FighterTown to fly again.

ENTER 3-D Second-Person VR at CyberArts

At CyberArts International in Pasadena for 4 days in November 1991, ENTER™ Corporation[3] and the Michigan State University Comm TechLab exhibited 3-D interactive second-person VR demos and conducted research on participant reactions. In second-person VR, you know you are there because you see yourself as part of the scene. On one side of the room, you stand in front of a blue background. You face a monitor and TV camera. On the monitor you see yourself, but instead of being in front of the blue background, the self you see is inside of a graphic or combined video/graphic virtual world. Edge detection software keeps track of your location and movement and allows you to interact with graphical objects on the screen. Rather than mimicking real-world senations, second-person VR

[3]ENTER Corporation is headquartered in Larkspur, California. For more information, call (415) 924-4512.

FIG. 7.4.   Another FighterTown view.

(also called "mirror worlds") changes the rules, and relies strongly on a "seeing is believing" argument to induce a sense of being there.

At CyberArts, second-person VR participants wore 3-D glasses and stood in front of a blue curtain. The camera that was pointing at them was chromakeyed[4] over 3-D motion video scenes, so that they saw themselves on a large screen across the room inside of a motion video scene. People were able to interact with graphical objects that appeared alongside them on the screen. Participants could choose to swim undersea and befriend unusual sea creatures, dance or wander peacefully through a Japanese garden, or transform into Godzilla to terrorize downtown Tokyo while aliens from outer space tried to stop them. A loose nonverbal narrative story unfolded, with opportunities for the participant to interact. Figure 7.5 shows a screen shot from the undersea experience.

Approximately 160 individuals entered one or more of these ±3-minute virtual experiences. One hundred and ten were given questionnaires to fill out (in particularly busy moments, questionnaires could not be distributed). Eighty-seven completed questionnaires, for a response rate of 79%. Three

---

[4]Chromakeying one video signal over another involves use of a chromakey-capable video switcher that strips a predefined or user-defined subset of the overall picture chromanence of one of the two signals, and replaces all parts f the image that were comprised of that chromanence setting with the other video signal. Typically the color used is blue.

FIG. 7.5.   MSU-Enter's 3-D Octopus Encounter Undersea.

fourths of CyberArts respondents were male. Average age was 34, ranging from 17 to 55.

ENTER 3-D Second-Person VR at SIGGRAPH: Once Upon a 3-D Time

At the Association of Computing Machinery's (ACM) 1992 annual international Special Interest Grouping Graphics (SIGGRAPH) convention in Chicago for 5 days in July, ENTER™ Corporation and the Michigan State University Comm Tech Lab exhibited a new interface for 3-D interactive second-person VR demos and conducted research on participant reactions. As before, participants wore 3-D glasses and stood in front of a blue curtain. The camera that was pointing at them was chromakeyed over 3-D motion video scenes, so that they saw themselves inside of the video worlds.

In this installation, we experimented with second-person VR interfaces, trying to build on what we learned from the initial prototypes. The exhibit was called "Once Upon a 3D Time." Instructions were built into the experience, delivered in the form of a spoken story narrative, as if describing something that happened in the past, for example: "When the sorcerer touched the ball, the scene would change . . ." The crystal ball and the 3-D motion Viewmaster are interfaces where it is natural to be able to touch parts of them to change the video scene. In both cases, you manipulate a portal to the video world, interacting by controlling the video rather than being immersed in it. As the story progresses, you enter one of the video worlds. Figure 7.6 shows this 3D viewmaster from "Once Upon a 3D Time."

Approximately 300 individuals tried the three minute experience. One hundred seventy-six completed questionnaires, for a response rate of 59%. Three fourths of SIGGRAPH respondents were male. Average age was 30, ranging from 11 to 79.

FIG. 7.6. MSU-Enter's 3-D Viewmaster.

College Students Contemplating Entertainment Virtual Reality

College students were surveyed to address the industry-wide issue of gender differences in the appeal of virtual entertainment. The findings are based on a preliminary fall 1992 sample of 127 students enrolled in an introductory telecommunication course at Michigan State University. These students completed the survey before attending any formal lectures about virtual reality. The questionnaire began with an introduction: "Suppose there were an entertainment virtual reality experience which adults could sign up to go play at a local mall . . .". Hypothetical questions about the desirability of different kinds of experiences were then asked.

Of the respondents, 55% were male. Ages ranged from 17 to 32, with an average age of 20. When this study is referred to in the chapter, the respondents are described as "prospective VR users."

The study results that are cited are exporatory—primarily descriptive data and bivariate statistics. The goal is breadth of attention to a range of issues, with some actual data from today's consumer VR centers.

DISCUSSION

As an emerging communication technology, consumer VR will allow social scientists to reexamine the historical body of research on mass media and consider certain paradigm shifts in light of unique features of this new medium.

Reality and VR

The interaction of reality and virtual experiences is complex. Like movies and novels only far more so, enjoyment of virtual experience is higher if you feel like you have entered another world. Theorists speak of creating a suspension of disbelief in theater audiences that allows viewers to get involved in the drama. VR seems to require a more intense involvement — engagement of belief, perhaps. In part this feeling depends on technical and artistic aspects of the experience, and in part it depends on your ability and willingness to act and feel as if a virtual world is real.

We tried to develop questions to assess how much participants had been able to engage belief. For the second-person VR survey, here are related questions: How real did the overall experience feel? How real did the 3-D feel? To what extent did you feel a physical response when your screen self touched other objects? To what extent did you feel an emotional response when your screen self touched other objects? Which felt like the real you — the being on the screen or the one the camera was pointed at? (See Table 7.2.)

The first five questions used a 7-point response scale, with possible answers ranging from 1 (not at all) to 7 (very much). The last question could be answered with "the being on the screen," "the being the camera was pointed at," or "both." This was an exploratory study, attempting to shed light on how to design better second-person VR experiences and how to ask better survey questions. Looking at correlations among these six questions, how much respondents reported feeling like they had entered another world

TABLE 7.2
Feeling of Entering Other World Compared with Other Variables

Entered other world?			
Yes	No	p	Question
5.4	3.4	.00	How real did the overall experience feel?
4.6	3.7	.00	How real did the 3-D feel?
5.5	4.2	.06	To what extent did you feel a physical response when your screen self touched other objects?
4.8	3.4	.00	To what extent did you feel an emotional response when your screen self touched other objects?
90%	50%	.00	The being on the screen or both felt like the real you.
6.8	5.8	.06	On a scale of 0 to 10 where 10 is *very much*, how would you rate your enjoyment of the experience?

was highly correlated with each. I split responses at the medium, putting the respondents who indicated stronger than neutral agreement with that statement into one group and the rest into a second group. *T* test comparisons of means between those two groups were significant for every variable in the group, even with a small sample size of 85. The degree to which CyberArts participants reported feeling as if they had entered another world strongly related to every other measure of enjoyment of the virtual experience. The findings described in Table 7.2 inspired ongoing research into what factors contribute to a sense of presence in virtual worlds, reported in more detail elsewhere (Heeter, 1992).

The Peter Pan Principle

Both studies of second-person VR found similar proportions of participants reporting three kinds of reactions: 29%–31% of the people who tried it felt as if the "being on the screen" was their real self; 26%–29% felt that the physical body the camera was pointing at was their real self; 40%–42% felt as if both were real. The percentages were surprisingly consistent across different audiences and different virtual experiences. This may be a personality characteristic related to propensity to get involved in virtual experiences. To extend the reactions to second-person VR, it seems that about one fourth of the population is easily able to "engage belief" and get involved in a virtual experience (in fact, they may have a hard time staying in the real world generally). About one fourth of the population is so strongly situated in the real world and their real body that they have a difficult time becoming involved in a virtual world. The rest are more balanced. Second-person VR requires a rather outrageous leap of faith, to transfer your sense of self into a world on the screen. But perhaps that leap is a powerful first step to experiencing a virtual world. Like Peter Pan thinking a happy thought, once you make that initial leap, reality becomes plastic and you can fly. Some people have an easier time thinking a happy thought than others. . . .

Perceived Reality

In defining synthetic experience, Robinett (1992) differentiated four sources of VR models:

1. *Models can be scanned from the real world.* Teleoperation uses video cameras (one for each eye) to scan the real world at a remote site. Binaural sound recordings (one microphone for each ear) scan an audio model of the real world. Remote sensing data scans the real world using different senses.

2. *Models can be computed mathematically.* One of NASA's VR experiences represents air flow around the wind of a jet with visible colorized moving patterns that are generated by a mathematical formula. In some cases, a thing rather than a place is modeled, such as an individual molecule.

3. *Models can be constructed by artists.* Polygonal CAD models are created with complete coordinate structures, allowing new views to be computed dynamically. These models can be based on actual or imaginary spaces (e.g., an exact replica of a real laboratory or an imaginary kitchen). The models are not necessarily 3-D. Battle-Tech, FighterTown and other virtual reality games show participants 2-D displays of the 3-D worlds they are flying or driving through.

4. *Models can be edited from a combination of scanned, computed and constructed content.* ENTER-MSU second person VR combines 3-D motion video scanned from the real world with live motion video of the participant and computer-generated models of other entities to interact with. VR worlds may add mathematical forces such as gravity, force feedback or magnetism to constructed or scanned models. Ixion Corporation[5] combines a physical dummy and modified laproscope with interactive videodisc to model the experience of conducting laproscopic survery in the gastrointestinal tract, complete with the force feedback doctors feel during laproscopy.

FighterTown and BattleTech use "cab simulator" VR technology. FighterTown is like the real world. Pilots sit in real fighter plane cockpits (without the rest of the plane) and watch the virtual world projected in 2-D onto the white wall in front of them. Surrounding darkness focuses attention on the projection and reduced awareness of anything else in the room. Pilots wear military flight suits, and the air traffic controllers address them in military-speak, using the same language and speech patterns as are used in the military. The pilots fly through a synthetic, made up world, using much of the same simulator technology that actual pilots are trained on. FighterTown pilots like the real world parallels. They say it is important that FighterTown is based on real planes (1.6 out of 7, where 1 is *very much* and 7 is *not at all*). They express a desire for technological improvements to make it more real—motion simulators, 3-D images, visuals on all sides. They want to see a more realistic world—preferably even to fly through the real world, with more realistic responses when they blow things up. And

---

[5]Ixion Corporation is headquartered in Seattle, Washington. For more information, call (206)-547-8801.

they do *not* want the FighterTown designers to make it a science fiction-fantasy world nor to change the laws of physics for variety. FighterTown developers recently added a motion simulator platform, in response to high demand.

In contrast, BattleTech is wholly imaginary, including when and where you are, who and what you are fighting and why. The BattleTech cockpit resembles nothing in the real world. A primary screen shows the virtual world in 2-D from the perspective of the robot you are driving. A secondary screen shows selectable other perspectives, such as 50 feet in the air looking down, or internal views of damage to the robot.

BattleTech players were asked what kinds of features they would like to see added to the game. They are less interested in motion simulators or 3-D images than are FighterTown pilots. They want to play for longer periods, with more people at a time. On a masters-only write-in question asking what they would change about BattleTech, the suggestions tended not to address fundamental alterations in the game or how it is played. One third of the 25 responding masters proposed improvements in maintenance and customer relations. One third asked for more of the same (more different kinds of robots, more terrain, more players, more missiles). Only two masters asked that BattleTech management work on "improving the reality."

Thus, both reality-based and fantasy-based consumer VR systems have been commercially successful. Perhaps as long as the experiences are well designed, people will pay to experience either kind. Or perhaps the two centers are attracting different audience segments who would not overlap if they were in the same city.

Unlike the BattleTech players, CyberArts and SIGGRAPH participants wanted goggles and more realism. They already were experiencing themselves in 3-D photorealistic motion video space for the first time, and they wanted more. Respondents were asked whether they would prefer to experience themselves in the 3-D world by wearing glasses and looking at the screen as they did at CyberArts, or by wearing goggles that fill their vision with what is on the screen, no matter which direction they look. This question is complicated. It was intended to begin to address the constraint of having to look straight ahead to see a screen all the time. The vast majority of respondents (74%–84%) indicated they would prefer to wear goggles and be able to turn their head in any direction, even though the video world they were seeing would stay still, and they would watch themselves turning in a world that did not move. None of them have actually tried this—it creates its own complications because you cannot see the real world you are moving around in when your entire field of vision is taken up by a virtual world. You enhance presence by removing competing real-world perceptions, but complicate presence by making the experience even less like reality. Goggles versus single screen would be an interesting second-person VR experiment.

What is and what isn't VR has been debated with great frequency and duration on online forums and at conferences. Scientists and businesses involved in traditional immersive VR with head-mounted displays, computer-generated 3-D worlds, and head and hand tracking tend to argue that theirs is the only true virtual reality technology. Virtual reality conferences, showrooms and exhibits contain a broader array of technologies, and experts and journalists talk about taxonomies of VR that include many different technology configurations, all of which strive to create the illusion of a virtual world (Tomorrow's Realities Gallery Catalog, 1992). The question of what elements of an experience are necessary and sufficient to invoke that illusion carries theoretical, practical, artistic, and financial implications.

Second-person VR write-in suggestions were numerous, with more inter-activity mentioned by more than 70%. More realism was requested in write-in responses by about half of the sample, including 3-D graphics, real photos instead of graphic objects, making the 3-D sound, tactile feedback, and so forth. Greater perceptual richness was definitely desired. (These people were attending a VR trade show. . . .)

Virtual travel will someday be able to transport you to Paris, or to an imaginary city. A visual representation of abstract information (such as the stock market) may bear little relationship to any reality humans have experienced, but it may still provide a form of spatial environment which can be navigated and experienced.

Shapiro and McDonald (1992) expressed concern about people being unable to distinguish virtual experiences from reality. Although technology may someday be so powerful that it is hard to distinguish, in many ways differentiating reality and virtual experiences is irrelevant. Unlike dreams and daydreams, VR experiences do exist outside of the mind of the human being. Those that include other people offer an externally verifiable shared experience. In other words, VR experiences are not necessarily unreal. On many important levels, there is little difference between the reality of a tennis match and the reality of a round of BattleTech. Both are shared, competitive experiences that a number of different people experience together. In the end they are probably as likely to agree on what happened during the game. Certainly something happened, whether in the physical world or not. Furthermore, some VR experiences actually affect the real world. A telepresence component of the Monterey Bay Aquarium lets you control and watch the output of a camera that is located in the ocean.

The important distinctions will be more subtle than an either/or "am I in the real world or am I connected to a VR system?" Instead, participants may consider questions like: Is this representing reality in real time or in the abstract? Are my actions able to affect the real world? Who is watching me? Which beings represent real consciousness and which are artificial life? If the virtual world is purely imaginary, to what extent are elements in it based on aspects of the real world?

TV effects researchers have surveyed perceived reality of fictional television in general (e.g., how real do you think soap operas on TV are) and specific aspects of fictional television (how real do you think the problems people have on TV soaps are) and have sought to link perceptions of such reality to viewing levels and to people's own experiences. As a snapshot of consumer VR in 1992, here are answers to typical perceived reality questions. How real does the BattleTech world feel? 2.96 out of 7, where 1 is *very real* and 7 is *not real at all*. To what extent does the BattleTech world respond like the physical world? 3.59. How much do you feel like you are the 'Mech when you play? 3.39. Curiously, for Fighter-Town, experienced pilots and those who had never flown a real plane were not significantly different in their estimates of how real the FighterTown simulators felt (2.75, using the same scale as BattleTech).

Cultivation Theory and VR

Another branch of media effects research related to perceptions of reality is *cultivation theory,* which assumes that "the repetitive pattern of television's mass produced messages and images forms the mainstream of a common symbolic environment." Television is the common storyteller of our time, and viewers cannot avoid absorbing or dealing with TV's recurrent patterns (Gerbner, Gross, Morgan, & Signorelli, 1986). Instead of immediate change in viewer attitude or behavior as a result of viewing a specific program one time, they posit that "massive long-term and common exposure of large and heterogeneous publics to centrally produced, mass-distributed, and repetitive systems of stories" (p. 18) will help form people's perceptions of what the world is like.

Obviously VR entertainment is not yet common or pervasive. It is as if there have been one or two TV shows produced so far, so their effects can be more carefully studied without having to turn to Eskimo or other far away cultures to find humans not exposed to VR. However, even one VR center is likely to have a stronger impact than one violent TV show. In the two VR centers studied, entertainment VR is a repetitive experience. After 1 year of BattleTech Center operation, one of the frequent BattleTech players had played more than 800 times. He spent at least 8,000 minutes in 1991 inside of the BattleTech world, blowing up other people's Mechs. FighterTown members fly once a month for at least a year. In addition to being a repeated experience, VR is much more of an active, direct experience than is being a passive audience member for traditional mass media.

Cultivation impacts will depend on the content of virtual experiences. CyberArts respondents were given a list of different kinds of experiences which could be created using this technology, and asked to rate their likely enjoyment of each genre, where 10 is *highly enjoyable* and 0 is *not enjoyable at all*. Ratings are shown in Table 7.3.

The list of content preferences suggests that there will eventually be a rich body of VR content from which social perceptions of the world will be unconsciously generalized as part of people's world view. Cultivation analysis researchers count acts of violence per hour in representative samples of TV shows every season. Acts of violence at BattleTech are reported on a computer printout at the end of the 10-minute game, and can number in the hundreds.

The strong interest in multiplayer experiences and involvement with live events points to a second factor that may impact on real-world generalizations: The other human players, not just the programmed content, will become part of people's experience of what the rest of the real world's inhabitants are like.

Violence in Virtual Entertainment

The consumer VR centers that exist today are based on combat or military themes. Designers of VR entertainment are cognizant of possible social and media backlash about the violence, and their language and world designs

TABLE 7.3
Genre Preferences for VR

Experiences	Ratings
Multiplayer experiences	8.5
Interactive live events	8.3
Interactive art	7.9
Science fiction story	7.7
Interactive Star Trek	7.6
Adventure game	7.5
Science "infotainment"	7.3
Cultural "infotainment"	7.0
Participatory drama	6.6
Travelogue	6.5
Interactive MTV video	5.3
Interactive spots	5.0
Exercise	3.9

These respondents were artists attending a computer art show. Sports and exercise may be rated higher by other populations.

reflect that awareness. Humans never die—at BattleTech they eject to safety at the last minute and reappear in a new Mech; at FighterTown they parachute to safety. System operators also carefully avoid making the virtual enemy be associated with a particular nationality or ethnicity (except when real humans are playing against real humans in real time)—instead the virtual enemies are futuristic robots, imaginary people or aliens. Players sometimes ask whether the enemy can represent some real-life foe (e.g., during the recent Persian Gulf war, people asked to have the enemy targets be Iraqi). System operators have every desire to avoid promoting ethnic strife, getting bad press, and alienating potential customers by presenting them as the enemy. Consistent with military-speak, at FighterTown one does not "blow people up"—one successfully "engages enemy targets." These nameless, faceless, unreal enemies are different from action adventure TV and movie antagonists, where the bad guys are human actors with visible physical and social characteristics.

Some people are very interested in engaging in violent virtual acts. Prospective VR players expressed a desire to shoot at attacking enemies—an average of 5.5 out of 7 where 7 is *very much*. (Two thirds of males and 16% of females would like this very much—the average for males is 6.2 compared to 4.6 for females, significantly different by t test at $p < .001$). Prospective players also expressed a desire to see explosions in realistic detail when ships are blown up (5.5 out of 7, where 7 is *very much*).

BattleTech players enjoy blowing people up—the average degree of enjoyment is 1.5 out of 7, where 1 is *very much*. This was significantly different by gender, but both sexes enjoyed blowing people up. Slightly more than one third find it more fun to blow up good friends (35%) or acquaintances (3%) than strangers (5%), but the majority (57%) say it makes no difference.

In open-ended responses to a question of what they would like to experience in VR, 47% of male and 13% of female prospective players volunteered that they would like to experience sex or violence. There was little overlap. One fourth of the males were interested in "war, combat, death, and destruction"; one fourth wanted sex; and 4% wanted both. Ten percent of the females were interested in "fighting and conquering"; 5% mentioned sex or love; one female wanted both.

Although there is still disagreement after decades of research into whether television violence causes aggression in the real world (Tan, 1986), there is general consensus that TV violence can cause short-term arousal and modeling effects.

Bandura's social learning theory (Bandura, 1977) has often been applied in studies of the effects of TV violence on children's behavior. According to social learning theory, when an observer sees a modeled event that is positively reinforced (particularly if the observer is in an aroused state), the modeled behavior may be remembered and reproduced. Reproduction of modeled behavior is most likely when the observer is in a circumstance similar to the observed occurrence. This suggests that the danger of modeling aggression is greatest during those times when players find themselves inside of robot or fighter plane cockpits. Following social learning theory, the less close to reality, the less likely violent behavior in VR will be replicated in real life.moreRather than merely observing a violent behavior, in VR you engage in violent behavior. Bandura defines aggression as "behavior that results in personal injury and physical destruction." At today's VR centers, no humans are shown being injured. So, there are resons to postulate a more intense effect of violent VR than violent TV, and also reasons to postulate a less intense effect. Advances in VR technology may be accompanied by more hard-core VR violence, with stronger negative effects.

Callousness Toward Violence and Sex

Desensitization is one of the impacts of media violence and sex. A literature review by Fenigstein and Heyduk (1984) concludes that as people are exposed to more and more media violence, they become less emotionally responsive to violent acts (Cline, Croft, & Courrier, 1973; Thomas, Horton, Lippincott, & Drabman, 1977). Unlike VR violence where no humans really get hurt, in virtual sex humans presumably become aroused. A study by Zillmann and Bryant (1982) found that massive viewing of pornography led to a loss of sensitivity toward rape victims, expressed in the form of more lenient sentences recommended for rapists. Participation in pornography may have stronger impacts than observation.

As VR becomes more realistic and pervasive, researchers will surely revisit these issues.

Positive Effects of Violent VR Games?

VR experiences are active and involving, unlike television viewing. The experiences are challenging and motivating for the players. Although few studies have been conducted about video games, they do suggest positive impacts. Kubey and Larson (1990) studied 483 children who carried pagers and reported on their activities and emotions when the pagers beeped at random times during the day. They found the children reported significantly higher attention, arousal, and motivation levels while playing video games than they reported while watching television. Graybill, Kirsch, and Esselman (1985) were surprised by their own findings when they compared elementary school children who had just played violent video games to those who had just played nonviolent video games. Using Rosenzweig's picture–frustration scale, the subjects responded to cartoon-like depictions of everyday frustrating situations. Those who had just played violent video games were more likely to attempt to seek solutions to the problem, whereas those who had just played a nonviolent video game were more likely to react to frustration with ego-defensiveness. In my own informal interviews, BattleTech players told me that playing BattleTech was a great way to relieve stress. And that blowing someone up was a great way to make new friends.

Catharsis was defined by Aristotle (1954) as "the release of emotion evoked by the action represented in a play." VR consumer games do not provide the kind of theatrical, gut-wrenching, sensitive, intelligent explication of good, evil, and justice as was intended with the word catharsis. But some kind of powerful emotional release seems to occur. Playing Battle-Tech has a similar feel to real-world athletic competition.

Learning from VR

Gagnon (1985) conducted early research on learning from video games. She wrote about video games producing subtle changes in cognitive skills, increases in attention span and concentration, and improving spatial visualization and eye–hand coordination. Her exploratory study randomly assigned college students to two groups. The experimental group practiced playing video games for 5 hours. Both groups were tested on spatial skills and hand-eye coordination, and significant correlations were found between scores on the videogames and scores on the spatial skill and hand-eye coordination.

FighterTown is based on flight simulators used to train military personnel to learn to fly. The experience that people pay to enjoy is very much like what the military is required to do for their jobs. Learning certainly occurs. At FighterTown the learning has a relationship to the real world. At BattleTech, even masters who have played an average of 200 games believe they will be able to improve. The learning may or may not extend explicitly to other walks of life. There are at least three classes of learning that occur during VR entertainment experiences: (a) learning skills or facts or gaining experience in things directly related to real life; (b) learning skills or facts related to the specific game; (c) incidental learning of things like spatial skills, hand–eye coordination, persistence, teamwork, aggression, and so on. Each of these three kinds of learning may involve learning generally considered to be socially positive, negative or neutral.

Social Interactions and VR: Intimate Strangers?

If participants have their way, VR will be a very social technology. BattleTech, CyberArts, and SIGGRAPH data identify consistently strong desires for interacting with real humans in addition to virtual beings and environments in VR. VR will bring new forms of computer-mediated social interaction. To understand the social possibilities of VR, consider for a moment your own hypothetical preferences. If you were jogging or walking in a virtual exercise path, would you prefer to encounter other real people who are also exercising, or would you prefer it to be empty of other sentient beings? If other real humans did appear and could see and talk to you, would you prefer that they be people you know, people who are at the same physical site, or people from around the world? Would you prefer to see and be seen by others as your real self, or as some fantasy representation of yourself (such lobsters Jaron Lanier discussed; Lanier & Biocca, 1992)? If you go to a VR entertainment center with family or friends or a date, would you want to stay with them throughout the virtual experience, or meet afterward to leave together?

FighterTown plans to network different locations around the country into the same world, so that pilots from around the United States will be able to see each other flying by (and engage in friendly or combat maneuvers together).

In BattleTech, playing against and with other people was very important. Just 2% of respondents would prefer to play against computers only. 58% wanted to play against humans only, and 40% wanted to play against a combination of computers and humans. In general, respondents preferred playing on teams (71%) rather than everyone against everyone (29%).

The BattleTech study results are corroborated by the CyberArts findings mentioned earlier. The desire to have other, real people in second-person VR worlds with you is strong. Sixty-nine percent of respondents rated having multiple players in the virtual world as highly enjoyable (9 or 10). The second highest desired experience was to participate in live events interactively, rated highly enjoyable by 61%.

The majority of people very much want to experience virtual environments with other people. Only 14% of prospective players indicated they would prefer to play alone against and with computer generated beings. On the other hand, it matters very little whether those other people are friends or strangers. When asked how much it mattered whether BattleTech players played with people they knew, the response was 5.27 on a scale where 7 was *not at all.*

Although science fiction sometimes portrays people becoming addicted to VR experiences to the point where they ignore the real world and starve to death, our data suggest that virtual worlds and virtual reality interfaces are likely to connect people to other people and to world events in new ways. Communication in virtual environments may have interesting differences from face-to-face interactions. Lanier discusses postsymbolic communication and Moulten describes VR communication scenarios elsewhere in this book.

Media (and Real-Life) Displacement

When a new medium becomes available, time spent using the new medium has to come from someother leisure-time activity. Today's consumer VR fanatics are still heavy users of other media. The typical frequent Battle-Tech player is a heavy consumer of other media. He is a 22-year-old unmarried male who lives an active media life. He reads newspapers about 4 days a week, reads four to five books and seven to eight magazines a month. He watches about 3 hours of television per day, including 30 minutes of MTV and listens to 4 or 5 hours of radio per day. He goes out to theater movies 2.5 times and rents six or seven home videos per month. BattleTech-related behavior includes spending about 5 hours a month with online services, playing arcade video games 5 to 11 times a month, playing video games at home 15 to 21 days per month, and playing fantasy games 26 times in 1991 (as of September). On the average, he plays BattleTech 12.4 times per month.

In the case of BattleTech, virtual reality entertainment does not appear to extinguish other media behaviors. BattleTech regulars consume lots of other media. They are, however, mostly single, childless, and not involved in a romantic relationship. There may or may not be a causal relationship between VR game fanaticism and lack of (interest in? or time for?) a romantic life.

Players who had played more than 50 BattleTech games were given a list of 13 activities and asked to rank each on a scale from 0 to 10, where 10 meant they liked doing the activity very much. Playing BattleTech was the top-rated activity (8.4), deemed more enjoyable than reading science fiction, going to parties, going to the beach, playing fantasy games, going to the museum of science and industry, rafting, working, going to the art institute, going to Great America amusement park, snorkeling and going to cubs games. The choices are listed in order of decreasing preference. Great America, snorkeling, and Cubs games were very low on the list.

Gender Differences

Gender differences are frequently found in the realms of television content preferences and viewing styles. For example, females more strongly prefer soap operas, dramas, and sitcoms, whereas males more strongly prefer sports and action adventure programming. Males are frequent zappers, who channel surf and avoid commercials, whereas females are more likely to watch an entire show from start to finish.

Gender differences are evident in the extreme for today's consumer VR, which appears to hold little appeal for the female half of the population. Ninety-seven percent of the FighterTown pilots surveyed were male. At

BattleTech, 2% of masters, 5% of veterans, and 9% of novices were female. The small group of females who actually chose to play BattleTech might be expected to be more similar to the males who play BattleTech than would females in general. Even so, gender differences in BattleTech responses were numerous and followed a distinct, stereotypical pattern.

On a scale from 0 to 10, female novices found BattleTech to be: *less relaxing* (1.1 vs. 2.9, $p < .01$) and *more embarrassing* (4.1 vs. 2, $p < .01$) than did male novices. Males were more aware of where their opponents were than females (63% vs. 33%, $p < .05$), of when they hit an opponent (66% vs. 39%, $p < .01$).

Females enjoyed blowing people up less than males did, although both sexes enjoyed blowing people up a great deal (2.4 vs. 1.5, $p < .01$, out of 7, where 1 is *very much*). Females reported that they did not understand how to drive the robot very well (4.6 compared to 3.1, $p < .01$, for males where 7 is *not at all*). Fifty-seven percent of female novices said they would prefer that BattleTech cockpits have fewer buttons and controls, compared to 28% ($p < .01$) of male novices.

Seventy percent of males preferred to play BattleTech in teams, whereas 53% ($p < .01$) of females preferred everyone against everyone.

What can consumer VR offer to appeal to women? Jordan Wiseman, President of Virtual Worlds Entertainment which founded BattleTech, discussed his company's thoughts on that topic. He said they had concluded that to be aggressive, men just needed a place, but women needed a reason. Thus, if the game is to continue its basic theme of blowing up other people's Mechs, the Mechs you blow up may need to have done something terrible to you or a loved one to motivate the violence.

Uses and Gratifications

Rubin (1986) described uses and gratifications research as a "receiver-oriented approach" where the focus is on what people do with mass media rather than what mass media do to people (Klapper, 1963, cited in Rubin, 1986). Media use is assumed to be goal-directed and purposive. Media are used by individuals to satisfy felt needs. Individuals initiate media selection.

VR use today is a very purposive (expensive, inconvenient) activity. Models of media impacts have moved from the original hypodermic needle view of injecting opinion and information into passive viewers, to a more receiver-oriented perspective, and even to a "participant" type of model of effects. VR pushes that transformation even further, such that the human becomes the center of the universe (or, if there is more than one human, each is one center in a multicentered world). The kinds of gratifications that humans seek, even from today's limited VR entertainment centers, is distinctly different from the needs viewers of more passive media are hoping to satisfy.

Typical gratifications sought from television, based on Greenberg's original 1974 study and confirmed and modified by Katz, Blumler, and Gurevitch (1974) are:

1. Arousal.
2. Relaxation.
3. Habit or Pass Time.
4. Escape.
5. Companionship.
6. Learning.

The first three are the most salient, or strongest reasons people cite for watching television.

An analysis of BattleTech as an optimal experience using Czikszentmihalyi's (1990) theory of "flow," happiness, and optimal experiences found that BattleTech fit well a set of six criteria that most often characterize experiences individuals consider optimal (Heeter, 1993).

Playing BattleTech is hard but fun for those who choose to play. Players at all levels (novice, veteran, and master) all strongly agree that they will eventually be able to significantly improve their skill at the game. There is room for improvement even after the basics are mastered. BattleTech is a game of skill. In addition to being challenging, BattleTech is enjoyable. BattleTech was rated nearly off scale challenging, fun, exciting, unique (9 or higher on a scale of 0 to 10, where 10 is *very much*), creative, competitive, intense and absorbing (between 8 and 9 out of 10).

Factor analysis of ratings of how well 18 positive and negative adjectives describe "what BattleTech is like for you" resulted in five factors with loadings above .5 of two or more adjectives. Factor loadings, percent of variance explained, alpha reliability of the scale and average response on a scale calculated by summing the high loading factors and dividing by the number of items are listed in Table 7.4.

Given the way the question was asked (how well do the following words describe how BattleTech is for you), these might be considered gratifications *received,* as opposed to gratifications *sought.* INVOLVEMENT was the highest rated factor, averaging 8.7 out of 10. INVOLVEMENT brings together fun, exciting, competitive, addictive and intense. An evaluation of a QUALITY DESIGN of the virtual experience, combining unique, creative and realistic, was also highly rated (8.4). The propensity for BattleTech to SOAK UP money and attention averated 7.6, but the reliability of this scale was low (.34). Feelings of OVERLOAD: not relaxing, confusing, and overwhelming, were experienced much more strongly by novices (6.1) than

TABLE 7.4
BattleTech Gratifications Factors

Factors and Loadings	Percent of Variance Accounted for and Alpha Significance
Factor 1: QUALITY DESIGN (average 8.4 out of 10) .74 creative .72 realistic .69 unique	20% of variance alpha .63
Factor 2: INVOLVEMENT (average 8.7 out of 10) .74 intense .63 fun .63 competitive .60 addictive .54 exciting	13% of variance alpha .69
Factor 3: Social DISCOMFORT (average 2.5 out of 10) .81 embarrassing .77 silly .52 intimidating	9% of variance alpha .61
Factor 4: OVERLOAD (average 5.6 out of 10) −.70 relaxing (not) .64 confusing .57 overwhelming	6% of variance alpha .50
Factor 5: SOAK UP (average 7.6 out of 10) .83 expensive .50 absorbing	6% of variance alpha .34
Factor 6: CHALLENGING (just 1 item—ignored factor) .76 challenging	6% of variance

by 10–50 game players (4.7) or 50+ game players (3.2). Social DISCOM-FORT such as feeling silly, intimidated, and embarrassed was the lowest rated factor, averaging 2.5 and not varying significantly with experience. The three negative factors are not normally part of TV gratifications, because gratifications usually ask why people watch TV. Social discomfort is experienced only by a small set of players. Overload varies by experience, and the tendency for BattleTech to absorb (soak up) time and money is most strongly felt by those who spend a lot of time and money playing it. . . .

In the next survey, this one at FighterTown, a set of 21 reasons for flying the simulators were asked, in an attempt to assess gratifications sought from the experience in a manner more closely paralleling uses and gratifications research for other media. The scale was 0 to 10. Factor loadings, percent of variance explained, alpha reliability of the scale, and average response on a scale calculated by summing the high loading factors and dividing by the number of items are listed in Table 7.5.

Factors that emerged included CHALLENGE (average 7.8 out of 10), which combined "because it's challenging," "to learn new skills," and "for a

TABLE 7.5
FighterTown Gratifications Sought Factors

Factor 1: AGGRESSION (average 4.6 out of 10)	31% of vaiance alpha .81
.84 as an outlet for aggression	
.75 to compete with others	
.70 to engage enemy targets	
.62 because it's addictive	
.57 to prepare for a pilot's license	
Factor 2: VARIETY (average 5.2 out of 10)	12% of variance alpha .80
.79 to try moves I couldn't try in a real plane	
.67 to cooperate with others	
.61 because it's different every time	
Factor 3: EXPERIENCE (average 7.2 out of 10)	10% of variance alpha .81
.83 because I've always wanted to fly	
.87 to experience what it's like to be a pilot	
.67 to experience virtual reality	
Factor 4: CHALLENGE (average 7.8 out of 10)	7% of variance alpha .76
.76 for a sense of accomplishment	
.75 to learn new skills	
.68 because it's challenging	
Factor 5: CHEERS (average 6.6 out of 10)	7% of variance alpha .34
.94 because it's exhilarating	
.92 for the camaraderie	
Factor 6: ESCAPE (average 6.5 out of 10)	6% of variance alpha .56
.83 because it feels good	
.72 to get away from the real world	
Factor 7: FUN (average 8.7 out of 10)	5% of variance alpha .59
.90 because it's fun	
.52 because it's challenging	

sense of accomplishment." EXPERIENCE (average 7.3) linked "because I've always wanted to fly," "to experience what it is like to be a pilot," and "to experience virtual reality." CHEERS (average 6.6) reflected a kind of social exuberance: "because it's exhilarating" and "for the camaraderie/friendship," but the scale had low reliability (alpha = .34). ESCAPE (6.5) was closest to the typical TV gratification of the same name, combining "to get away from the real world" and "because it feels good." VARIETY (5.2) represented a combination of "because it's different every time," "to use my imagination," "to try moves I couldn't try in a real plane," and "to cooperate with others." AGGRESSION (4.6) included "as an outlet for aggression," "to engage enemy targets," "to compete with others," and "because it's addictive." Although the averages for VARIETY and AGGRESSION are near midrange, they are both roughly trimodal, with about one third of respondents rating each very high (10), about one third rating them very low (0) and one third in the middle. Most of the other gratifications were much closer to normal distributions.

Returning to the comparison with TV gratifications, VR entertainment experiences are not relaxing. They are not something people do out of habit, to pass time—they are too expensive and inconvenient, not to mention challenging and arousing. Arousal needs are common to both TV and VR, but the levels of arousal VR affords are presumably much higher. Escape shows up for both media, although TV presumably distracts and numbs the mind, whereas VR is a more literal escape from the real world into another world, still as a proactive entity or central processing unit (CPU). TV offers a substitute for companionship, whereas VR brings friends and strangers together to share experiences, providing real companionship. Learning is typically the lowest rated TV gratification. Involvement, challenge, and experience are the strongest VR entertainment gratifications. Watching television is extremely different from playing VR games. Players seek and obtain a sense of accomplishment as they seek to improve their skill at a challenging experience. Even the most experienced BattleTech master believes he can and will significantly improve his performance over time. FighterTown offers the chance to experience what it is like to fly a plane, with sufficient realism and challenge.

Television is bemoaned as a passive medium. Active viewers change channels and take control over what they view. Another form of active viewer is the critical viewer who consciously processes and critiques incoming messages. VR players are an almost ideally active media consumer. In many ways, VR entertainment today is not very different from video games, in part because VR is so crude today. Even so, the presence of other humans and the fact that you are playing against or with other humans rather than just a computer seems to make a difference in player's perceptions of VR compared to video games. It will always be difficult to differentiate video games and VR, because eventually they will be one and the same.

In general, prospective players want the game to be somewhat educational, so that they learn something while they play (5.2). They would like the game to have meaningful parallels to real-life situations, that help them understand their own life (5.1). Females are more likely than males to want to learn something while they play (5.6 vs. 4.8, $p < .019$) and to have it parallel real-life situations (5.7 vs. 4.7, $p < .001$). Of females, 52% compared to 34% of males would like the experience to involve "very much" learning (as compared to "some" or "none"), $p < .008$.

Competition and Play

Traditional television offers little opportunity for competition. VR often presents a competitive physical and/or mental challenge. One can win or lose. Regardless of winning or losing, one can play well or poorly on a particular day. Zillmann and Bryant (1986) explored the entertainment experience of television viewing, concluding that people can be very deliberate in their entertainment choices. Television can be used to produce excitement, particularly when someone's initial state is a relatively low level of excitation. Entertainment can also soothe and calm those who areuptight, annoyed, or otherwise disturbed. The proposal that people form mood-specific preferences based on their current affective circumstances is supported by research (Bryant & Zillmann, 1984.) Great enjoyment follows great distress, as long as there is a happy ending. A competitive VR situation opens the possibility of greater catharsis because of the physical involvement, but also greater possibility for frustration at losing or playing poorly.

BattleTech players were asked how satisfied they were with the way they played their last game. The response was near the middle—3.4 out of 7 where 1 was *very satisfied* and 7 was *not at all*. Players claimed it was not essential that they win—asked how much it mattered, the average was 4.2 out of 7. Even among those who had played 800 games, there was a belief that they would improve if they kept playing (1.67 out of 7). Despite or because of the competition, BattleTech was quite universally considered fun, challenging, exciting and competitive (all rated an average of at least 9 out of 10, where 10 means the word describes BattleTech *very well*). FighterTown is also considered very fun—an average of 9.4 out of 10. And FighterTown pilots (including those who have actually flown a plane) feel motivated to do well flying and to improve (2.1 out of 7, where 1 is *very much*).

Experience of Self

Unlike mass media where people are merely "viewers" who watch or listen to content, virtual reality experiences place you inside of the content. People want to be able to experience a strong sense of self in the virtual worlds. They want to be able to see their real hands, perhaps their real bodies. They want to be able to interact with the environment and with other people in as many ways as possible. They want to be in control, to have an effect, and to clearly understand the causal link between their actions and the effects of those actions.

Prospective VR entertainment players would like others to be able to see their real face in the virtual world (57% reacted positively, with an overall average of 4.8 out of 7). But they are even more interested in seeing other people's real faces (78%, with an average of 5.7). And they want to see the "real" faces of computer-generated agents or characters (82%, with an average of 5.9).

They are divided 50:50 on whether they would prefer to be represented by their real face or a fantasy face. (Women are more likely to prefer a fantasy face; men are more likely to prefer their real face; the difference is statistically significant at $p < .006$.) Asked whether they would prefer to wear their regular clothes or a special costume, 48% strongly preferred a costume, while 25% strongly preferred regular clothes. Gender differences were not statistically significant.

For whichever of the three experiences a CyberArts participant tried (Undersea Adventure, Japanese Garden, and Tokyo Godzilla), he or she were asked to rate his or her enjoyment, on a scale from 0 to 10 with 10 being very enjoyable. Those who experienced only their shadow on average rated the experience 5.8, compared to average ratings of 8.0 for those who saw their real self. Otherwise identical experiences were considerably more enjoyable when you got to see your real self in the world.

VR experiences that use a power glove or data glove frequently show users a computer-generated hand to represent their real hand movements. SIGGRAPH participants were asked whether they would prefer to see a computer-generated hand or their whole, real body. Eighty-seven percent would prefer to see their real body. Seeing your real self makes VR seem more real and more enjoyable.

Today's consumer VR centers are only a hint of things to come. Even this brief survey of possible VR effects suggests that it will be a richly new societal phenomenon with impacts distinctly different than any previous communication medium.

REFERENCES

Aristotle. (1954). *The poetics* (I. Bywater, Trans.). In F. Solmsen (Ed.), *Rhetoric and poetics of Aristotle.* New York: The Modern Library.

Bandura, A. (1977). *Social learning theory.* Englewood Cliffs, NJ: Prentice-Hall.

Bryant, J., & Zillmann, D. (1984). Using television to alleviate boredom and stress: Selective exposure as a function of induced excitational states. *Journal of Broadcasting, 28*(1), 1–20.

Cline, V., Croft, R., & Courrier, S. (1973). Desensitization of children to television violence. *Journal of Personality and Social Psychology, 27,* 360–365.

Czikszentmihalyi, M. (1990). *Flow: The psychology of optimal experience.* New York: Harper & Row.

Fenigstein, A., & Heyduk, R. (1984). Thought and action as determinants of media exposure. In J. Bryant & D. Zillmann (Eds.), *Selective exposure to communication* (pp. 113–140). Hillsdale, NJ: Lawrence Erlbaum Associates.

Gagnon, D. (1985). Videogames and spatial skills: An exploratory study. *Educational Communication and Technology Journal, 33*(4), 263–275.

Gerbner, G., Gross, L., Morgan, M., & Signorelli, N. (1986). Living with television: The dynamics of the cultivation process. In J. Bryant & D. Zillmann (Eds.), *Perspectives on media effects* (pp. 17–40). Hillsdale, NJ: Lawrence Erlbaum Associates.

Graybill, D., Kirsch, J., & Esselman, E. (1985). Effects of playing violent versus nonviolent videogames on the aggressive ideation of aggressive and nonaggressive children. *Child Study Journal, 15*(3), 199–205.

Greenberg, B. (1974). Gratifications of television viewing and their correlates for British children. In J. G. Blumler & E. Katz (Eds.), *The uses of mass communications: Current perspectives on gratifications research* (pp. 71–92). Beverly Hills: Sage.

Heeter, C. (1992). Being there: The subjective experience of presence. *Presence, 1*(2), 262–271.

Heeter, C. (1993, Winter). BattleTech Masters: Emergence of the first U.S. virtual reality subculture. *Multimedia Review,* pp. 65–70.

Katz, D., Blumler, J., & Gurevitch, M. (1974). Uses and gratifications research. *Public Opinion Quarterly, 37,* 509–523.

Klapper, J. T. (1963). Mass communication research: An old road resurveyed. *Public Opinion Quarterly, 27,* 515–527.

Kubey, R., & Larson, R. (1990). The use and experience of new video media among children and adolescents. *Communication Research, 17*(1), 107–130.

Lanier, J., & Biocca, F. (1992). An insider's view of the VR future. *Journal of Communication, 42*(4), 150–172.

Robinett, W. (1992, Spring). Synthetic experience: A proposed taxonomy. *Presence, 1*(2), 229–247.

Rubin, A. (1986). Uses and gratifications and media effects research. In J. Bryant & D. Zillmann (Eds.), *Selective exposure to communication.* Hillsdale, NJ: Lawrence Erlbaum Associates.

Tan, A. (1986). Social learning of aggression from television. In J. Bryant & D. Zillmann (Eds.), *Perspectives on media effects* (pp. 41–55). Hillsdale, NJ: Lawrence Erlbaum Associates.

Thomas, M., Horton, R., Lippincott, E., & Drabman, R. (1977). Desensitization to portrayals of real-world aggression as a function of exposure to television violence. *Journal of Personality and Social Psychology, 35,* 450–458.

Tomorrow's Reality Gallery Catalog. (1992). Introduction. Presented at annual SIGGRAPH convention, Las Vegas.

Wiseman, J. (1992, September). Panel on Entertainment Applications of Virtual Reality at the Meckler Virtual Reality Convention, San Francisco.

Zillmann, D., & Bryant, J. (1982). Pornography, sexual callousness, and trivialization of rape. *Journal of Communication, 32,* 10–21.

8 Dramatic Narrative in Virtual Reality

Kenneth Meyer

Dramatic narrative has been part of the storytelling tradition since antiquity. It has been adapted into the familiar forms like plays, movies, novels, and situation comedies. These new forms evolved to accommodate the peculiar opportunities and constraints of new media. The advent of virtual reality (VR) marks another new medium; one that will give rise to yet another kind of dramatic narrative (see Table 8.1).

Rudimentary efforts to define the new form have begun. VR narrative is a principal goal of the Carnegie Mellon OZ project (Bates, 1992). Bates, the project leader of OZ, said he expects "VR to join the novel, cinema, and television as a broadly successful artistic medium" (p. 134).

This discussion explores the nature of a VR drama and how it differs from other narrative forms. The principle underlying this discussion is that VR creates a world that may be occupied in a way not possible in other media. In particular, VR allows the audience to walk on the stage of the drama and interact with the fictional world. This interactive quality conflicts with the exacting structure of drama, and the conflict between structure and interactivity is a decisive factor. The interactivity must be constrained to preserve the dramatic structure; in other words, *being audience to a VR drama is essentially passive* with respect to the story. However, the audience may interact with many other elements of the world of the story. This level of limited interaction will give rise to VR drama's unique narrative qualities.

The following description of a VR drama is theoretical in character. Because of the novelty of VR and the limitations of existing technology, nothing of the sort has yet been created. A VR drama requires a platform

219

TABLE 8.1
Types of Narratives

Dramatic Narrative: Sequence of events with dramatic structure	Non-Dramatic Narrative: Sequence of events
• Theatrical Plays • Novels • Short Stories • Feature films • Ratio dramas • TV sit-coms • VR dramatic narrative	• Interactive fiction (adventure game, or strategy based story) • Arcade games (Twitch games) • Fantasy role playing games • Computer aided instruction • Improvisational theater • Standup comedy

that supports fully interactive, real-time animation[1] that allows users to experience a sense of presence, or "being there." Presence has been discussed by Sheridan (1992), Zeltzer (1992), Biocca (1992), Heeter (1992), and others. Additionally, the system will need sufficient graphic resolution to communicate emotion through expressive behavior. Photorealism may not be essential. Most of the necessary system components currently exist. However, improvements in position tracking, displays, 3-D graphics, and computer animation technology are needed before a suitable platform is available. Advances in the technology may take 3 to 10 years.

The subject of VR drama touches on a range of literatures including drama, film theory, cognitive science, computer animation, and artificial intelligence. Biocca rightly pointed out in comments to an early version of this article that the discussion "treaded lightly over great bodies of literature and omitted discussion of others." The comment is especially true regarding the literature of narrative perception. But, a line had to be drawn because an account of all relevant subjects is beyond the present scope. Similarly, VR dramas are discussed to the exclusion of other narrative forms, not to suggest that they are undesirable or inferior, but to limit the scope. The purpose here is not overarching scholarship but to describe a new art form, the VR drama.

ELEMENTS OF A DRAMATIC NARRATIVE

Before all else, a VR drama is a drama. This section describes dramatic structure in order to make clear the elements that separate drama from other kinds of narrative. Basically, a *narrative* is a recounting of a sequence

---

[1]See Biocca's chapter, "Virtual Reality Technology: A Tutorial," for details on the components of a VR system.

of events. Holman (1975) broadly defined *narrative* as "an account of actual or fictional events" (p. 336). A dramatic narrative, or drama, is a narrative that has been molded and porportioned to communicate a theme through a compelling story.

The Western tradition of drama evolved from Greek religious ceremonies of the Hellenistic era when Euripides, Aeschylus, Sophocles, and Aristophanes were producing their classic works. The form flourished throughout antiquity, then all but disappeared with the decline of Rome. Dramas were reinvented in Medieval times as mystery and morality plays, and the art continued to flourish throughout Europe in the 14th and 15th centuries. During the English Renaissance the form hit a high-water mark before the Puritans closed the theaters. Drama was revived in the 18th century's restoration, and has continued to prosper till the present day (Holman, 1975).

Contemporary drama is quite different from either classical or Renaissance drama, but the basic elements have remained unchanged. There is a long history of commentary on the components of a successful dramatic story. Although no single analysis has been broadly embraced, there are several structural elements repeatedly identified as key to a successful drama. These elements would be part of a successful VR drama in much the same way that they are key to successful movies, novels, and plays.

Narratives, Interactivity, and Drama

A narrative can take a variety of forms. It can be as loose-knit as a rambling dinner-time tale of office shenanigans or as commonplace as the recitation of one's medical history. Computers add to narrative the extra dimension of practical interactivity. The gamut of narratives no longer need be conceived only for a "passive" reader or audience. With the aid of the computer, the narrative may change in response to user input. For example, interactive help programs are a familiar form of interactive narrative. Perhaps less familiar but equally well established are the mazes of interactive fictions (sometimes called adventure games) or the evolving simulations generated by genetic algorithms.[2] The notion of an interactive narrative is a powerful

---

[2]Heitkoetter (1993) described a *genetic algorithm* as "a model for machine learning which derives its behavior from a metaphor of the process of evolution." This learning is based on the principles of natural reproduction. Random binary strings, which are actually programs, are mated. The full strings act as chromosomes; substrings act as genes. The new generation of binary strings are subjected to a survival test to assure their suitability for the task. Those strings that survive can mate with other surviving strings and give rise to a third generation. The process continues through multiple generations with the evolved strings becoming better programs.

one, and traditional narrative forms, like newspapers, may be greatly enriched by an interactive multimedia transformation.[3]

However, not all narratives can be translated successfully into interactive forms. Dramatic narratives pose a particular problem because they are fragile structures that depend on specific outcomes. It is the structure of dramatic narrative that makes the form compelling—the structure makes it a drama. A well crafted dramatic narrative can entertain even after multiple tellings. The same cannot be said for yesterday's news or last week's SimCity session. Gasperini, the author of the successful computer games Hidden Agenda and Star Trek, put it this way: "Even the best interactive fiction, once all the puzzles have been solved and the plot is revealed in all its naked linearity . . . is like a punctured balloon. . . . There is little reason to go through it again" (Gasperini, 1990).

The Elements

> The story, as an imitation of action, must represent one action, a complete whole, with its several incidents so closely connected that the transposal or withdrawal of any one of them will disjoin and dislocate the whole. (Aristotle, 1941, p. 1463)

Stipulating the essential ingredients of a good story verges on folly. A coterie of commentators going back to Aristotle have attempted to distill a reliable formula for successful drama. No single analysis has become the last word. Nevertheless, many of the commentators divide the form into similar components. The following discussion is a representative breakdown of a dramatic narrative's key components: premise, conflict, orchestration of characters, and rising action—which together form the structure of the drama.

Premise. A good drama needs a central motivating idea, or a premise, that captures some truth about the human condition. Dramas without a premise disintegrate into disconnected episodes. The 19th century French dramatist Dumas the Younger explained it this way, "How can you know which road to take unless you know where you are going?" (Baker, 1919, p. 73). Or as Laurel (1991) pointed out, dramas have "a strong central action as compared to the episodic action of other narratives" (p. 76).

In fact, all the elements of a well-conceived drama devolve from this central premise. The characters, the conflict, the rising action, and the confluence of all these ingredients, the plot, are all driven by the tension inherent in the premise. As Baker (1919) observed, "Though [the play-

---

[3]In July 1993, Cox Newspapers and Prodigy Services announced an interactive newspaper network. The goal is to allow newspapers to combine print and electronic services.

wright's] mind is full of dramatic material . . . his plot is at a standstill. The trouble is that he has not sifted his material by means of the purpose he has in mind" (p. 87).

Not all premises are equally suited for dramatic invention. A suitable premise must be dialectical. The drama is the struggle to reconcile the opposing forces. Egri (1942) offered many examples of classic dramas that embody dialectical premises. The premise of *Romeo and Juliet* is that "great love defies a tradition of hate and even death" (p. 3). The premise of *Othello* is "jealousy destroys both itself and the object of love" (p. 4). The premise of Molière's *Tartuffe* is "he who digs a pit for others falls into it himself" (p. 280), and of Ibsen's *Doll House* is "inequality of the sexes in marriage breeds unhappiness" (p. 100).

Orchestration of Characters.   A drama's principal characters should embody the polarities of the premise. "The premise should show the goal, and the characters should be driven to this goal" (Egri, 1942, p. 164). The characters will then be compelled toward a conflict where no compromise is possible. If the characters are orchestrated to struggle, the events of the story will then spring naturally from the characters. So it is that Cassio in *Othello* pursues Desdemona in order to regain his reputation, and on that incident hangs Iago's scurrilous plot. According to Egri, "This unbreakable bond between parties will ensure rising conflict, crisis, and climax. The crisis was inherent from the very beginning of the play; the choosing of these particular characters predicated it" (p. 225). Or as Holman (1975) said, "The plot translates character into action" (p. 396).

When characters are badly orchestrated, the plot is subject to gratuitous turns for the sake of action. Instead, the action should grow from characters responding to the dramatic circumstances. "If you wish to create jumping conflict, you have only to force the characters into action which is alien to them" (Egri, 1942, p. 148). Characters who behave without motivation seem unnatural, and their stories seem dull. Baker (1919) advised that "usually it is not through incident or episode . . . but through character . . . that one presents what is . . . dramatic." Egri explained it this way: "Crime is not an end in itself . . . the reasons behind the events interest us" (Egri, 1942, p. 148). And Lessing (1985) admonished that "The misfortunes of those whose circumstances most resemble our own, must naturally penetrate most deeply into our hearts, and if we pity kings, we pity them as human beings, not as kings" (p. 7).

Conflict.   Dramatic conflict is prescribed by the dialectic of the dramatic premise and is a fundamental consequence of that tension. "Conflict comes from a conscious will striving to achieve a goal that was determined by the premise of the play" (Egri, 1942, p. 137). Conflict is the prime mover of the story. It is responsible for interest and suspense. It motivates the dialog. "No dialogue, even the cleverest, can move a play if it does not further the conflict" (Egri, 1942, p. 137). Without conflict, a story is dull.

Rising Action.   The rising action is composed of a series of continuing crises growing from the struggle between well orchestrated, opposing characters. Every episode of the story must move the play to its climax. The action should rise, continuously building to a pitch that culminates in a final crisis and demonstrates the contention of the premise.

Some commentators have suggested that rising action is the principal ingredient in dramatic structure. Freytag (1863) proposed a diagrammatic outline of dramatic action for a five-act play. His outline is plotted as a symmetrical inverted "V" with the climax at the apex and catastrophe at the bottom of the trailing edge (see Fig. 8.1). He called episodes on the leading leg the rising action, and the trailing leg the falling action. Freytag recommended equal portions of rising action and falling action.

Modern dramas tend to ignore Freytag's five act structure. The falling action is typically truncated. Field (1979) wrote a successful "how-to" book on writing Hollywood screenplays. Field's overly prescriptive paradigm even specifies page numbers for specific plot points. The introduction, including the main character, the premise, and situation must be concluded by page 10. On page 25 the plot should change direction. And so on. Field maintains his paradigm is inflexible, and that every good screenplay must conform to it.

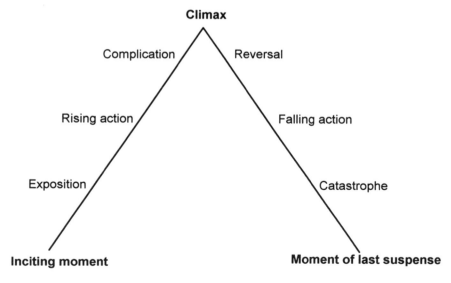

FIG. 8.1.   Freytag's Pyramid. A diagram of the structure of a five-act tragedy.

Freytag's and Field's structures can be regarded as outlines for action in an overall scheme of rising action. Egri (1942) summed it up this way, "There is no moment in a play which does not grow from the one before it" (p. 233).

THE PROBLEM WITH INTERACTIVE DRAMA

We will want to tell the stories that demand interaction. But what does that mean? What is the story that can best be told with your meddling? (Crockford, 1992)

The idea of an interactive narrative is terribly exciting. Participating in our favorite story is the fulfillment of a childhood fantasy. How wonderful it would be to save our favorite characters from their woeful fates — imagine guiding Hansel and Gretel home or warning Sleeping Beauty of the apple.

Laurel (1991) discussed the prospects of such an interactive story system. She imagined a computer "playwright" that creates a new plot in response to the action of audience members who "march up onto the stage and become various characters, altering the action by what they say and do" (p. 16). The playwright would calculate new actions until it finds a good match for the current situation. This task of generating new stories on the fly with a computer poses difficult problems.[4]

This task of generating new stories on the fly with a computer poses difficult problems.[5] The computer playwright must be able to generate stories that preserve the delicate balance of dramatic elements while responding to the ad hoc actions of the user.

This section surveys Artificial Intelligence (AI) research related to generating stories with computers. None of the approaches discussed can

---

[4]A thorough study of the subject of VR drama should include a reading of Laurel's (1986) dissertation "Toward The Design of a Computer-Eased Interactive Fantasy System." Her work is one of the earliest and most thorough discussions of the subject. Regrettably, Laurel's dissertation is not covered in this chapter.

[5]The grand question of whether a computer can be creative remains moot (McCorduck, 1979; Penrose, 1989). Fortunately creativity is not primary to this discussion because creativity alone is not sufficient to produce an interesting story. All humans can be creative, but not all humans can create good stories. Whether creativity is necessary for tasks like the selection of a theme, or a pertinent detail is unclear, although it does seem likely. Nevertheless, even if a computer could solve a problem considered "creative," its place as a creative intelligence is open to dispute for critics might claim the so-called creative problem was misunderstood and never a "creative" problem at all. These critics, who are the advocates of weak AI, argue that creativity requires consciousness and natural intelligence. In this sense, whether a computer can be creative or not is beside the point. For this reason, the main discussion focuses on problems that are difficult to solve with or without a "creative" computer.

generate dramatic narratives in response to ad hoc user actions. In fact, the research suggests that generating a compelling story with a computer is extremely difficult. The obstacles confronting interactive story generation are discussed after the survey.

Story Generators and Computer Protagonists

During the past three decades there have been efforts by cognitive scientists to formalize the structure of simple stories such as folk tales and fables (Black & Bower, 1980). Story grammars have been developed by a number of researchers including Thorndyke (1979), Johnson and Mandler (1980), Lakoff (1972), and Rumelhart (1975).[6] Thorndyke's (1979) grammar is representative. His formula is story = setting + theme + plot + resolution.

An effective story grammar could provide a foundation for a computer playwright. However, story planning is inadequate to produce good stories (Turner & Dyer, 1986), and the proficiency of story grammars tends to break down with multiple characters or broken narrative threads (Black & Bower, 1980). No story representation can make a full account of an elegantly simple tale like those told by O'Henry, Saki, or Gogol. More complex stories like those commonly seen at the cinema are even more problematic. A useful formal description of movies like *Chinatown, The Sting,* or *Ordinary People* is beyond the scope of present cognitive research.

Alternatively, there is a class of story "generators" that assist an author with the construction of dramatic structure.[7] Typically, these applications generate a sequence of questions that are intended to guide a writer in the selection of plot and character. And because they are not automated, they cannot produce interactive story lines.

A different strategy abandons the effort to distill story into components and adopts a scheme where a narrative emerges from the activity of an AI computer protagonist. In this approach, an autonomous computer protagonist is imbued with a set of goals that causes activity culminating in a dramatic narrative. The system does not manipulate a protagonist but, rather, *is* the protagonist (see the section on Denizens for further discussion on artificially intelligent characters). The following describes several relevant examples.

Meehan's TALESPIN program generates episodic narratives about woodland creatures (Meehan, 1981). The actions that constituted episodes

---

[6]For additional sources see Thorndyke's (1980) useful bibliography of material related to story processing.

[7]*Dramatica,* a commercial product of this class, is soon to be published by Screenplay Systems of Burbank, California. Screenplay Systems describes Dramatica as a storyforming and analysis tool.

were picked by a plan generator to satisfy a character goal—for example, to satiate hunger. However, Turner and Dyer (1986) reported that the TALESPIN narratives "could not produce interesting or memorable stories."

Vere and Bickmore's (1990) Homer is a robot submarine that lives in a 2-D world simulation called Seaworld. Homer is an example of an integrated AI agent that is designed to act, reason, and reflect on its experience. Vere and Bickmore intended this work to be a precursor for work outside simulated worlds. It was not developed specifically as a story generator, but its function is similar (Okada & Endo, 1992).

Homer incorporated several AI components: a task planner-reasoner, a plan interpreter, an episodic memory and reflection system, a natural language parser, and a lexipedia (lexicon plus encyclopedia). These gave Homer the ability to communicate to users with an 800-word vocabulary, remember events, decide on a plan of action, and act on the plan. Vere and Bickmore claim to be the first to combine these components into a single integrated agent. During the experiment, the researchers typed instructions for Homer and waited to see what it would do. Here's an edited sample of the results:

> Vere: What's in front of you.
> Homer: A log.
> Vere: Turn away from the log.

While Homer is turned away from the log, Vere moves the log to a new location with a mouse.

> Vere: Turn back.
> Homer: I've lost the log.
> Vere: Go to the rock (another destination in Seaworld).
> Homer: OK.

Homer generates a plan for the next actions.

> Homer: I'm going to the rock.

Vere accelerates time to next day. In route to the rock, Homer finds the log.

> Homer: I've found the log.
> Vere: Tim wants the log that you lost yesterday.
> Homer: OK.

Homer picks up the log and swims to a stick figure of Tim Bickmore.

> Vere: This is Tim.
> Homer: Oh.
> Bickmore: Where were you last night?
> Homer: At the rock. (Vere & Brickmore, 1990)

Admittedly, the narrative is not dramatic, but Homer demonstrates how the behavior of an autonomous agent composes a narrative.

Okada and Endo (1992) have undertaken a similar strategy in the MULTRAN project. They set out to recreate Aesop's fable "The Fox and the Grapes" as an integrated simulation using an AI Fox as the protagonist. The Fox lives in "a natural environment" called Aesopland. He is assigned goals and makes plans to achieve them. He takes actions based on those plans. He perceives the results of his efforts and then makes intellectual and emotional judgments. Then, if necessary, he modifies the original plan. All of these processes are reported to the experimenters in natural language.

The Fox was built on a "structure of mind" model that resembles Minsky's Society of Mind (Minsky, 1985). Minsky's approach might be simply described as a representation of the mind that is composed of multiple components sharing data. The mental processes of Okada and Endo's Fox are simulated by a battery of modules, or "domains of mind," that act on a shared knowledge base and input stimuli. The Fox was endowed with eight mental domains including desire–instinct, sensation–perception, emotion–character, and plan–creation.

The narrative, as agent behavior, arises as a sequence of actions spawned in the Fox's pursuit of his programmed primitive drives. In the initial condition, the Fox's degree of thirst is over the threshold. The desire–instinct module sends a "thirsty" message to the plan–creation module that, in turn, creates a plan to relieve thirst. The plan–creation module then decides the best place to look for water is the mansion. At the mansion, the sense–perception module senses the grapes, and then the plan–creation module decides jumping is the best way to get them. This behavior is the story.

The authors discuss a few shortcomings of the system. Among those they list is "the generated story is too monotonous" (Okada & Endo, 1992, p. 154). Okada and Endo prescribe more varied language, specifically onomatopoetic words, as a cure for the monotony.

But the reason for the lackluster story runs deeper than a limited vocabulary. The problem is more fundamental. A good story requires a premise, conflict, and characters orchestrated for struggle. While a model of a mind may be able to produce episodes of realistic behavior, episodes alone are not sufficient for a dramatic story.

The Oz Project at Carnegie Mellon University (CMU) is developing a technology for an artistic form of "dramatic" virtual worlds based on interactive fictions. According to Bates, "the primary task in building a world is to transfer artistic knowledge, of both general and specific kinds, into the machine" (Bates, 1992, p. 134). Three areas of research have been identified as key to the project: agent behavior, dramatic content, and presentation style.

A notable objective of the Oz project is to enable a user to have the subjective experience of being a fictional character. The user would *become* a "user character" who enters the story and "can go anywhere and do anything" (Bates, 1992, p. 136). The researchers speculate that an Oz user might have "significant aspects" of the character's subjective experience (Smith & Bates, 1989).

Bates specifies that Oz needs a "director" or "computational theory of interactive drama" to "leave the user with an undiminished feeling of free-will." The director makes use of general story knowledge and generates a drama in response to user activity. The knowledge is composed of information the director acquires about character traits and the causes of "desired moods and attitudes." Bates suggests that computer chess is an analogy for the Oz director. In computer chess, the user and computer operate by turns; the user "acting as free agent" and the director "pushing the elements of the world in various ways" (Bates, 1992, p. 136).

In the current stage of development, the Oz group is building an autonomous agent named Lyotard,[8] the cat. Lyotard is built on the Oz agent architecture called Tok. Tok has two key components: a plan generator called Hap, and an emotion modeler called Em (Bates, Loyall, & Reilly, 1992; Loyall & Bates, 1991; Reilly & Bates, 1992). Em develops emotions by comparing external events to goals, actions to standards, and objects to attitudes. Happiness or sadness results when goals succeed or fail. Em's "emotional" element then influences Hap's planning.

Lyotard can demonstrate some captivating behavior. Bates et al. (1992) described the following example of Lyotard's behavior. Lyotard explores a room in search of amusement. He discovers a plant and nibbles a leaf. After a time, Lyotard decides to find a comfortable place to sit. He finds a chair and begins to lick himself. Later, a disliked human user enters the room. Lyotard takes note and starts to feel hate toward the user. When the user approaches, Lyotard jumps off the chair and runs from the room. In this manner, narratives generated by Tok characters resemble Homer and Multran; the narrative emerges from their behavior. Similarly, the work suffers from a "certain flatness" (Smith & Bates, 1989).

Turner and Dyer (1986) outline a system called MINSTREL[9] for generating stories based on the psychological process of writing. In their view, human authors compose stories from recalled experiences and the themes intrinsic to those experiences. Similarly, MINSTREL is designed to generate stories from themes and is distinct from systems that generate narratives from the episodic behavior of characters. The researchers specifically

---

[8]Lyotard is named after the French political activist and social critic J. F. Lyotard.
[9]Turner's completed dissertation, *Minstrel: A computer model of creativity and storytelling,* was published by the UCLA Computer Science Department, January, 1993.

wanted to avoid generating "the wandering, pointless stories of TALE-SPIN" (p. 4).

Turner and Dyer use grouped themes based on Schank's method of representing common patterns of goal interaction[10] (Schank, 1982). Dyer calls these theme groups Theme Abstraction Units (TAUs) and incorporates them in his story-understanding system called BORIS (Dyer, 1983). TAUs are characterized by adages offering story advice; for example "be kind to strangers" or "don't chase moonbeams." TAUs are similar in spirit to Egri's premises (Egri, 1942). Rather than use TAUs to generate stories from scratch, Minstrel searches a knowledge base for an existing story from the same theme group and borrows the plot and characters.

Using the borrowed story line as a foundation, Minstrel develops a new plot and characters. The episodes of the plot are embellished by a plan generator, similar to TALESPIN. Characters are modified to match characters in the knowledge base. In one instance bankers become knights. Suspense is injected by amplifying the urgency of the character's goals to increase the reader's anticipation of an imminent outcome. For example, a dragon might be introduced to threaten the knight.

While Minstrel's method of borrowing from the existing literature might produce more interesting stories than those of Homer, Multran, or Oz, it does not undertake to resolve the question of interactivity. In principle, the TAU search for similar stories starts anew with every user action. As events progress, these searches become progressively more restrictive until at last a new story line is required.

The Fragility of Structure and the Art of Selection

A realization of a go-anywhere-do-anything VR drama system is beyond the reach of existing story generation research. A larger question prevails: Are the deficiencies of story generators for interactive plot creation merely a reflection of the state of the art, or are they indicative of an essential quality of good drama that prevents it from being interactive?

Previous sections described the delicate interworkings of premise, conflict, orchestration, and rising action. Each is part of a whole whose balance cannot be carelessly disrupted. The climax must be tightly bound to the rising action; the protagonist to the antagonist; the theme to the action. Break these relations apart, and the result will be a dull story with an arbitrary conclusion.

Three issues in particular raise doubt about the feasibility of an interactive AI playwright: (a) the inadequacy of rules for drama, (b) the necessity of the ending, and (c) the art of selection.

---

[10]Schank called these patterns Thematic Organization Packets, or TOPs.

Inadequacy of Rules. "It is certain that there are laws for drama, since it is an art; it is not certain what these laws are" (Pierre Corneille, French dramatist, quoted in Egri, 1942).

Deriving a formula for good drama is at best extremely difficult — iron-clad rules are destined for inadequacy. A good example is the attempt to enumerate the basic dramatic situations. Best known is Polti's *Thirty-six Dramatic Situations* (1868/1977). Polti's list includes such sure-fire plot ideas as "crime pursued by vengeance," "revolt," and "self-sacrifice for a kindred." Polti's theory of plots was based on the 19th-century "discovery that there are in life but thirty-six emotions . . . and no more" (p. 9).[11]

Polti was not the first to fix a figure on the number plots. Count Carlo Gozzi (1420–1497), who wrote the play *Re Turando* (the basis of the opera), was the first to assert there were thirty-six situations. Frederich von Schiller (1759–1805), the German dramatist, attempted to verify Gozzi's number, but came up short. Another commentator, the French playwright Gerard de Nerval (1808–1855), used the seven deadly sins to identify only 24 plots. The effort to count the number of basic situations is unresolved. Perhaps Baker's (1919) comments effectively sum up the effort: "It may be possible to agree on the smallest number of dramatic situations possible, but disagreement surely lies beyond, for according to our natures, we shall wish to subdivide and increase the number" (p. 63).

Similar difficulties confront rules that would prescribe the balance of character and plot, or the proper use of narrative voice. Lessing advised, "The strictest observation of the rules cannot outweigh the smallest fault in character" (Egri, 1942, p. xv).

No self-evident or compelling formula for a good drama exists. Guidelines of the sort previously described merely help understand why some dramas are good and others are not. They are analytical, not generative. Generations of aspiring dramatists have been familiar with the dramatic elements, but few have produced memorable stories. There is no known substitute for that intangible knack called *talent.*

The difficulties are compounded for a computer playwright. Because computers rely on formal systems, a dramatic algorithm is required. As no reliable generative rules exist, the quality of the resulting stories will be unpredictable. More troubling is the limitation of formal rules for forming judgments (Penrose, 1989, p. 110). In a formal system there are propositions that cannot be proven true but are known to be true on reflection. Penrose explained it this way: "There could be many perfectly acceptable results in our mathematical literature whose proofs require insights that lie far from the original rules and axioms of the standard formal systems for arithmetic." Penrose said these insights are based on the *reflection*

---

[11]It's worth noting the similarity between Polti's 36 dramatic situations and Minstrel's TAUs.

principle. He described the reflection principle as a type of seeing that requires an understanding "that is not the result of the purely algorithmic operations that could be coded into some . . . formal system" (p. 110). In other words, we can know a good story when we see it, but we cannot prove it's good. On the other hand, the computer playwright knows only what it can prove and may not be able to distinguish a bad story from a good one. Penrose said, "Algorithms, in themselves, never ascertain truth!" (p. 412). The principle holds for dialog, description, orchestration of character, or any other element of dramaturgy.

The Necessity of the Ending.   "The ending is the first thing you must know before you begin writing" (Field, 1979, p. 56).

The ending of a good drama is the realization of the dramatic premise. Endings that do not realize the dramatic premise tend to be weak or contrived (Field, 1979). A case in point is the 1985 film *Clue.* In the first run, the producers released three versions, each with a different ending. The alternative endings were designed to encourage the audience to puzzle through the assortment of clues and solve the murder. The story development was weighted down with exposition (i.e., story development) needed to justify the different homicide scenarios. Riordan (1993) noted a similar problem with the heavy exposition required in each scene of the multimedia title *Voyeur.*[12] The *Clue* ending was meant to be a surprise; however, because each audience saw only one version, every ending had to stand on its own. More important, no matter which ending was presented, the narrative details used to develop the alternative endings became superfluous. The results were not good. Halliwell said of *Clue,* "those not in on the joke may tend to be restless" (Halliwell, 1989, p. 208). Ayn Rand's unsuccessful play *Night of January the 16th,* which let the audience determine the guilt of the accused criminal, suffered similar shortcomings.

For a drama to be compelling, every element must contribute to the rising action. The path to the ending should be an expression of the premise. If the destination changes, so must the premise. Because all elements derive from the premise, it must be fixed. A change in premise forces a change in character, conflict, and rising action. Consequently, any change to the ending obliges a reworking of the story. In other words, a change to the ending without adapting all the dependent dramatic elements leads to an unsatisfactory result. A compelling drama depends on a harmony of the elements.

The need for an indeterminate ending presents a fundamental problem for a go-anywhere-do-anything VR drama. If the users are permitted to arbitrarily affect the outcome, the resulting story will be unsatisfying.

---

[12]*Voyeur* is published by Phillips POV.

The Art of Selection.   "Before he finishes he may discard what originally seemed important . . . because he comes to see an interest that will be stronger for the audience" (Baker, 1919, p. 77).

The plot in a good drama is a distillation of events, rather than an exact image of life. All plot episodes and details of character or setting should contribute to rising action. Even seemingly ordinary events contribute dramatic tension by revealing some source conflict. Egri (1942) commented, "Art is selective, not photographic" (p. 240).

The playwright must select from a welter of possibilities, choosing only those that further the story. The selection requires an indeterminate sensibility that might best be called artistic judgment. The ability to make unusual and interesting selections is certainly the mark of talent and perhaps the greatest challenge facing the designer of a computer playwright. Penrose (1989) described the problem this way: "Enough information is in principle available for the relevant judgment to be made, but the process of formulating the appropriate judgment, by extracting what is needed from the morass of data, may be something for which no clear algorithmic process exists — or even where there is one, it may not be a practical one" (p. 412). In fact, Penrose was skeptical that computers will ever be able to make aesthetic decisions. "The judgment-forming that I am claiming is the hallmark of consciousness is itself something that the AI people would have no concept of how to program on a computer" (p. 412).

Interactive Alternatives

Given these difficulties, a story generator that supports a dynamically interactive plot does not appear feasible. Dramatic narratives are too fragile to support go-anywhere-do-anything interactivity. Watching a VR drama is essentially a passive pursuit. However, if the goal of interactivity is reformulated, a level of interactivity is possible, namely, one that preserves the dramatic structure. This alternative view, a VR drama with limited interactivity, is described in the next section.

INTERACTIVE VR DRAMAS

A VR drama takes place in a virtual world that can exist outside the story. This world may be occupied by users as well as the characters of the story. This co-occupancy suggests a variety of narrative devices that leave the dramatic structure unperturbed but allow interactivity.

The following section describes these narrative devices. The discussion in not intended to be formal or exhaustive. It is very early in the game. Metz (1974) reminded us that the evolution of cinematic language took 20 years.

Nonetheless, an analysis based on methods of existing media, like cinema, can be instructive. Eisenstein (1942) pointed out that passages in Milton's *Paradise Lost* anticipated the techniques of *montage* (especially for battle scenes). The goal here is to capture something of the style of a VR drama's *mise en scene*. Entirely novel methods will, no doubt, evolve as VR dramas are produced.

Point of View

The audience of VR drama is free to roam the virtual world and observe anything of interest. Because an audience knows only what is observed, the VR dramatist must take steps to ensure that the audience has knowledge of relevant dramatic details. This artistic challenge is compounded by the absence of a cinematic frame to focus the audience's attention.

The mobile audience marks a radical departure from the point of view of traditional dramatic forms.[13] A novelist is assured of the reader's knowledge because the reader's only experience of the story is from the narrative point of view. A playwright knows the audience is positioned before a stage and can observe anything that happens there. A motion picture director has more control of the audience than either the novelist or the playwright. The motion picture is always seen from the same point of view with the episodes strictly ordered. Fowles (1977) said of the cinema, "the final cut allows no choice, no more than one angle; no creative response; no walking around, no time for one's own thought" (p. 90).

In VR drama, alternative means are needed to focus the audience on the dramatic action. The most obvious method is to have a character guide the user. Lanier described a guide called a "changeling," which was planned for the Universal Studios Voomie (Lanier, 1992; Lanier & Biocca, 1992). The guide fills a range of functions from usher to narrator. An usher might simply keep the audience in the proper place. A narrator might be knowledgeable and exhibit traits that lend a literary quality to the story.

Another approach is to restrict the user's position. This strategy has been successfully used in theme park attractions like the Disneyland's *Pirates of the Caribbean*. The world of pirates is a comprehensive illusion from the confines of the cab; but, outside the cab, behind the flats, the illusion is destroyed.

---

[13] *Point of view* refers to the perspective from which the author presents the actions of a story (Holman, 1975). Biocca (1991), in his discussion of mental models in television, distinguishes point of view from *point of sight* where point of sight is the position in space as suggested by the camera position. Biocca says that point of view is a composite of point of sight and narrative cues, called *modes of address,* which urge the viewer to adapt attitudes toward story elements. The audience's viewpoint in a VR drama is a mobile version of a TV viewer's point of sight.

Krizanc's (1989) play, *Tamara,* uses an elaborate twist of the same technique. The play is staged in a multiroomed facility dressed as a 1930s-era Italian villa. There is no proscenium. The audience joins the actors in the rooms of the villa. In the opening scene, the audience receives instructions on how to view the play from the characters Finzi, the Fascist police officer, and Dante, the valet.

> Finzi: There are ten people that live here. You follow just one of them.
> Dante: Is that an order, Capitano?
> Finzi: No, it's a strong suggestion, if you like order. If you are an anarchist you may switch from person to person.
> Dante: You're very kind Capitano.
> Finzi: If you are not following a person, you are breaking the law . . . Anyone found wandering around on their own will be deported. (Krizanc, 1989, p. 24)

Additionally, the audience is admonished not to chase after noises, open doors, or follow characters who shut a door.

The point of view can also be confined by restricting the user's perspective to the viewpoint of select characters. This viewpoint might be through the eyes or over the shoulder of the character. This is a variation of cinematic montage. The technique has been used recently in the multimedia title *Wrong Side of Town* (Diamond, Escoffier, Goldstein, & Roach, 1993). *Wrong Side of Town* plays as a traditional film[14] except that the user can click on the head of a character and see the story from a camera angle that corresponds to that character's point of view. The technique is enhanced by varying the characterizations to match the perception of the selected character. For example, a businesswoman is presented as caring and sympathetic from her own perspective, but is portrayed as callous from the perspective of a homeless woman. Later, the same businesswoman is presented as prim from her own viewpoint, but from the standpoint of a male waiter, she appears seductive. Coover has called this *multivocalism* or alternating points of view (Stansberry, 1993).

A more promising dramatic alternative is to beguile the audience into following the action. For example, it would be natural to follow a sympathetic character, or examine an object that had come to our attention. Consider a scene where a character appears and warns us of a foreboding possibility. The character vanishes, but leaves a message in an envelope. Natural curiosity would compel most users to read the message whose content might advise where the dramatic action is likely to resume.

Regardless of the method applied to focus attention, the risk remains that

---

[14]Roach, who wrote and directed *Wrong Side of Town*, calls the approach *virtual cinema*.

a viewer may miss an important dramatic development or even lose the story's thread. However, knowledge of every event is not necessary. Incomplete information may add suspense, or dramatic irony. For example, distractions may intentionally divert the viewer's attention at crucial moments with a dramatic sleight of hand. Or, partial information may add urgency to the viewer's quest to discover missing facts of the story. The artful practice of revealing information may prove a valuable dramatic technique.

Another benefit is that freedom of movement may enhance the audience's emotional involvement in the story. Gasperini (1990) pointed to a similar effect in interactive fiction. "Since the audience of an interactive work no longer sits to one side judging how the protagonist meets various challenges, authors can build emotional resonance on the player's sense of direct responsibility for how those challenges are met."

Narrative Threads

A VR drama may have a multithreaded narrative with events occurring simultaneously on parallel tracks. Plots need not be revealed serially as in novels, movies, and traditional plays. For example, *Tamara* is plotted along parallel narrative tracks. The play is divided into 21 different sections. Each section represents a unit in time. A number of the scenes occur simultaneously. The characters criss-cross the narrative lines. It is not possible to see the entire play in a single performance.

A multithreaded narrative offers interesting possibilities for storytelling. The narrative may not be complete until it is viewed from several tracks. In essence, the user may have to assemble pieces to understand the whole story. Roach used a similar technique in *Portals,* as does Riordan in *Voyeur.*[15] Or, the narrative lines might reveal the plight of characters prior to their appearance at the scene of the dramatic action. Perhaps the unhappy fate of the Misfit could be told prior to his encounter with Bailey's family in O'Connor's short story "A Good Man Is Hard to Find." Similarly, overlapping narrative lines of related stories from the same world might cross. Consider a mystery in which Sherlock Holmes discovers a clue leading to the discovery of a crime in another mystery — a crime committed during the course of the current mystery.

Although intriguing, the existence of multiple narrative threads complicates the task of ensuring that the audience is privy to narrative events.

---

[15]*Portals* is a collection of interactive narratives scheduled for release in winter 1993. *Voyeur* is a multimedia title scheduled for release about the same time.

Time and Space

> All stage clocks are temporarily out of order lest they mark too distinctly the discrepancy between pretend and real time (Baker, 1919, p. 132).

Because the world of VR drama is fictional, it need not be bound by the rules of the physical world. Dramatic time and space can be molded for dramatic effect. A flashback can be used for exposition. A flashforward can be used for foreshadowing. An edit can transport characters across continents in an instant. A beat can be dilated to build suspense, or constricted to quicken the pace.

In conventional dramas, the facts of time and space are fixed; episodes occur at an appointed time and place. Time and space in interactive drama may be altered at show time. The VR dramatist may develop dramatic techniques not available to dramatists of other forms. A similar opportunity led to the development of the multiangle montage in film.

Time.   "There is the time of the thing told and the time of the telling . . . this duality . . . renders possible all the temporal distortions that are commonplace in the narratives" (Metz, 1974, p. 18).

A drama may progress by the passage of actual time or by the passage of fictive events. This passage may be distorted by dilations, contractions, and rifts for dramatic purposes.

A football game progresses by the passage of actual time. In the theater, when the duration of the action is condensed to equal the time on the stage, the play is said to have unity of time. Aristotle argued that unity of time increases dramatic tension. Consider a hero brushing his teeth while a bomb ticks away in the shower. Similarly, the use of actual time can be used to raise tension in an interactive fiction.

In *Prince of Persia,* a popular computer game, a player has a brisk hour to solve a maze and defeat a swarm of swordsmen or a princess will be lost to an evil king. In a VR drama, if story progress is tied to the passage of actual time, the user must keep up or be left behind. The effort to keep up engenders active participation. On the other hand, inappropriate use of unity of time can drain dramatic tension. Consider a lengthy episode of a hero routinely brushing his teeth because that's how he starts his day. The midday soaps suffer from a dearth of rising suspense because scenes, regardless of dramatic intent, are played out in actual time.

By comparison, baseball time progresses by events. Each out is an event; 27 outs per side and the game has elapsed. The actual playing time of a baseball game varies. The same is true of interactive fictions like *Zork*. Events in *Zork* progress as a user solves problems or triggers actions. A single game may last weeks, even months. If a puzzle is too difficult, the action bogs down. Gasperini depicted the problem with a quote from Porson: "Life is too short to learn German."[16]

In this respect, interactive fictions offer an example for interactive drama: progress of the drama may be delayed or expedited in response to a user's action, determining, in effect, the pace of a story. Users might become allies or adversaries by facilitating or retarding the fulfillment of the character's goals. User interaction might be as rudimentary as turning on a light, or as complex as passing information to a character. Interaction is limited only by dramatic structure. Since users participate in actual time, interactive opportunities occur in actual time. Effective interaction requires a dramatist's knack for storytelling.

Distortions of time are used for transitions that communicate ellipses in the action. In the theater, a transition most commonly takes the form of scene change or blackout. Film has a wider vocabulary of transitions: cuts, jump-cuts, cross-fades, and segues are but a few of the available devices. A new variety of transitions will characterize VR dramas. For example a gray-out might transport a user from one time to another, or a suggested motion may suggest time travel. Transitional devices may be necessary to move a user seamlessly between narrative threads.

Unlike other dramatic forms, the world of a VR drama may persist between tellings. Depending on the venue (discussed later), events may proceed without a user. For example, there may be a schedule of performances, and users may be required to catch a "show time." A parallel circumstance exists in instances where dramas proceed along parallel threads. Perhaps the VR dramatist will provide a "newspaper" for users to catch up on missed events.

Space. A VR drama occurs in a definite space with position, distance, and adjacency. This space is the primary consequence of the VR medium. Without the invocation of a virtual space, there would be no VR drama.

The use of space in a VR drama is more like theater and less like film. In theater, actors must negotiate the positions and distance of the stage. The users of a VR drama will likewise occupy the space of the story. In film, definite space is less crucial because of the ease with which disparate places can be juxtaposed.

Although a VR drama space need not be a replica of the physical world, it should be consistent and readily understandable. An inconsistent or confusing space impedes ease of use because a user may not understand how to interact with the system. However, the virtual space may have qualities

---

[16]The quote is actually from Peacock's novel *Gryll Grange*. Peacock routinely used thinly disguised contemporary figures as his characters, in this case Porson.

unlike the physical world. Like time, space may be dilated or contracted for dramatic purpose. Similarly, it may have novel, even Escheresque, adjacencies.

Venue

"Think of a playhouse as a hybrid theater, gymnasium, school, sports arena, and conference center" (Walser, 1990).

The most distinguishing trait of a VR drama is that the audience is on the stage occupying the world of the story. Since it is a world, it need not be limited to the story—the story only happens there. Walser called that place a "cyberspace playhouse."

The VR playhouse should be understood as having geography in both physical and virtual domains. Since the user is necessarily in a physical location, the user's interaction with virtual objects must cross the physical-virtual boundary. In effect, the venue should be understood as a composite.

Consider a Location-Based Entertainment (LBE) facility housed in a shopping mall. Users would go to a VR LBE much like they go to a theater. The drama might be staged in a space dressed with props appropriate to the VR drama. The setting might be an interior replica of *Star Trek's Enterprise,* Tolkien's Middle Earth, or Doyle's 221 B Baker Street. Users might don a transmissive head-mounted display (HMD) or carry a "Looking Glass"[17] and observe the drama superimposed on physical surroundings. Or perhaps the LBE will resemble Fightertown or Battletech[18] where users enter "vehicles" with views into a virtual world.

There are many permutations, but the approach used by Kalawski for the RAVE HMD is especially interesting. The RAVE HMD has two video cameras mounted on the front of the helmet over the position of the eyes. The user sees the immediate surroundings as stereo video. The physical surroundings incorporate blue surfaces, for example windows, where virtual objects are matted. The user views the physical and virtual as a composite (Bevan, 1992). A similar technique was developed at the University of North Carolina for superimposing real-time ultrasound images on a patient (Bajura, Fuchs, & Ohbuchi, 1992).

Combining the physical and virtual worlds gives rise to hybrid stagings in

---

[17]A "Looking Glass" is a hand-held display with a position tracker attached. A Looking Glass permits the user to view virtual objects. An example of the Looking Glass was built for the Silver Surfer exhibit at SIGGRAPH '91. Ganapathy also mentioned the Looking Glass at Wescon '92.

[18]Fightertown users sit in mockups of fighter cockpits and fly combat operations against an opponent. *Battletech* users sit in *Mech* pods and battle opponents for control of strategic ground.

which real actors interact with virtual counterparts. In effect, animated characters walk on the stage of a live theater. Likewise, live actors might perform in virtual settings that can change instantaneously to juxtapose disconnected times or places.

Additionally, because the world of the drama exists outside the story, users might interact with the objects of the virtual world. Interaction with the characters is possible to the degree that they are autonomous. Also, the world may be filled with interactive puzzles or games that are merely props. Perhaps a puzzle must be solved outside the story in order to view a narrative thread at show time. For example, a user must solve a riddle to learn the password to a new region. However, this kind of puzzle solving may disrupt the dramatic pacing, and the solved puzzles lose their appeal on repeat encounters.

Interaction between entities of the physical and virtual domains can be summed up as follows: virtual entity operating in virtual domain, virtual entity operating in physical domain, physical entity operating in virtual domain, or physical entity operating in the physical domain. Each situation offers an opportunity for a dramatic device (see Table 8.2).

The venue need not be conceived as a physical location. It can be a network-based playhouse existing merely as a virtual location. Users and characters might be geographically dispersed; the settings exist only as computer-generated constructs.

TABLE 8.2
Types of Interaction Between Physical and Virtual Domains

Type of Interaction	Examples
Physical entity operating in the physical domain	• Actors on stage. • Hammer, nail, thumb.
Physical entity operating in virtual domain	• Physical light switch activates virtual light. • Looking glass. • Goggles and gloves. • SimGraphic's PAS system.* • Remote manipulator sensor.
Virtual entity operating in physical domain	• Virtual light switch activates room light. • Virtual key opens physical lock. • Homer in the Pacific. • Remote manipulator effector.
Virtual entity operating in virtual domain	• Whales of virtual Seattle. • Pterodactyls from Pterodactyl Nightmare. • Multran Fox.

*The Performance Animation System (PAS) is a facial armature that can be used to control the facial expressions of a computer-generated character.

A similar approach is used in a multiple-user dungeon (sometimes, multiple-user dimension) or MUD. A MUD is a network-based computer program that allows users to interact with each other in a simulated (usually text-based) world. Users are represented by a character. This user-based embodiment can perform a variety of functions such as walking around, chatting with other characters, or taking objects. Users can participate from anywhere a network connection is available.

Morningstar and Farmer (1992) described Habitat, a commercial prototype MUD. Habitat players logged on from a home computer into the Habitat host. The players were represented as animated figures called avatars. Avatars could move around, manipulate objects, gesture, and talk to other players with word balloons. Each avatar had a house. Houses were organized into cities with traffic and shopping malls. Cities were separated by wilderness areas. In time, a social structure evolved among the avatars: a church was founded and social mores were instituted.

The shared spaces of Habitat could provide a stage for dramas with users and characters occupying the same space. Interacting with other users in the story space might supply an added element of interest. Morningstar and Farmer did not report any dramas in Habitat, but they did describe an unsuccessful interactive fiction called D'nalsi Island.[19]

Denizens

The world of a VR drama is populated by both characters and users. Characters, unlike users, may be under either computer or human control. In either case, characters must exhibit sufficiently complex behavior to fulfill the goals of the drama. Creating computer-controlled characters, or synthetic actors, with complex behavior requires the use of integrated-agent architectures such as those described by Bates (Bates et al., 1992) and Okada and Endo (1992). The term *denizen* is used to refer to integrated agents that are situated in a virtual world.

Denizens are complex technical entities that combine AI and computer-graphic components. A typical denizen architecture has four layers (see Table 8.3).[20] At the bottom layer, the agent is merely an array of graphical objects, such as polygons, that move in a coordinated manner. At the next layer, the agent is a skeletal model of linkages and joints whose movement can be dynamically described with inverse kinematics or physically based

---

[19]Morningstar and Farmer spent months developing D'nalsi Island. Their hope was to provide a contest that would engage subscribers for months. Unfortunately, the puzzle was solved in a few hours, and D'nalsi Island quickly fell into disuse.

[20]Calvert divides his "ideal system" into three levels: detailed movements for each limb as a function of time, detailed script, and natural language (Calvert, 1991a). Zeltzer divides agents in four levels of abstraction: agent, function, procedure, and structure (Zeltzer, 1991).

TABLE 8.3
Layers of Denizen Architecture

Layer of Architecture	Description
Autonomy Layer	• Determines the degree of autonomous intelligent behavior. • Incorporates multiple functions including action selection (planning), environment sensing, learning, and/or natural language interpretation.
Instruction Layer	• Supplies instructions for movements prescribed by a plan generator or script. • Acts on environment. Environmental changes may encourage or inhibit other actions.
Dynamic/Kinematic Layer	• Supplies rules for movement of graphic primitives. • Incorporates inverse kinematics, physically based modeling, constrained modeling or linkage database.
Graphic Layer	• Provides the aggregation of graphic primitives (e.g. polygons) that compose the denizen. Graphic model used by renderer.

modeling (Calvert, 1991a).[21] On the third layer, the agent is a set of instructions for movement and action (Badler, Webber, Kalita, & Esakov, 1991). At the top level, the agent is the mechanism for intelligent action. This top layer, or *autonomy* layer, determines the behavior and intelligence of the denizen; and accordingly is of special interest to the VR dramatist.

Mechanisms for intelligent action have been the focus of both robotic and AI research. Although a detailed discussion is beyond the present scope, a sketch of some basic AI issues may help to understand the problems of creating denizen behavior.

Designs for generating intelligent action fall along a continuum defined by two technical approaches: *physical symbol systems* and *physical grounding systems* (Lewis, 1992).[22] The symbol system architecture was first described over two decades ago by Simon and is considered the

---

[21]*Kinematics* (as used in animation) is the branch of mechanics that describes motion as the rotation of joints and linkages. *Inverse kinematics* describes the combination of linkage and joint movements required for an end-point to traverse a path. Neither accounts for the effects of force or energy on motion. *Dynamics* is the branch of mechanics that describes motion as the forces acting on each joint. *Physically-based* movement incorporates dynamics; it is based on the effects of the external forces on joints and linkages. Physically-based movement provides the most realistic movement, but, "generating proper torques for a locomotion cycle is complicated by such problems as balance and co-ordination of the legs. However, kinematic approaches are inflexible and produce weightless unrealistic animation" (Calvert, 1991a).

[22]For additional reading on physical symbol systems, see Allen, J., Hendler, J., and Tate, A. (Eds.). (1990). *Readings in Planning.* San Mateo: Morgan Kaufman. [For additional reading on physical grounding systems, see Maes, P. (Ed.). (1990). *Designing Autonomous Agents.* Cambridge, MA: MIT Press.]

classical approach (Simon, 1969). A symbol system is governed by a programmed set of procedures that give rise to agent behavior. This symbol system is called a *plan* and the process of selecting actions is called *planning*.

A typical plan might operate as follows: The agent is assigned a repertoire of goals and associated actions for fulfilling the goals. These goals may be arranged in a hierarchy so that the agent can assess the appropriateness of a selected goal or pursue intermediate goals in pursuit of higher goals. For example, an agent may plan a path in order to reach a destination. These top-most goals are called *intentions* or *meta-goals* (Pollack, 1990). Goal selection is based on the perception of the environment. These perceptions, sometimes called *beliefs,* may be erroneous. For example the denizen may look at an apple and see an orange. In some agents, beliefs are assumed to be the de facto result of actions; in which case, the agent has no provision for failed actions. For example, if an obstacle blocks a denizen's path, the denizen will not know it failed to reach its desination. In more complex agents beliefs are based on observation (through sensors) so that goals can be adapted to failed actions and environmental changes. For example, the Multran Fox might stop planning jumping actions when the grapes fall. The use of the terms *intention* and *belief* stem from the effort to model symbol systems on human thinking. Badler (1991) called this approach *plan as mind*; Rao and Georgeff (1992) name agents with belief and intention *rational agents.*[23]

In practice, symbol systems have proved brittle. Procedures predicated on a symbolized world model are prone to failure when the world model is incorrect or incomplete. Developing complete worlds that support robust agents has proven to be difficult (Brooks, 1992).

In the mid-1980s grounding systems were proposed to overcome the problem of symbolizing a domain which, like the real world, is unstructured and unpredictable. In a grounded system, the world is not symbolized. All knowledge is extracted directly from the environment with sensors. In effect, sensations replace symbols and the world serves as its own model. Furthermore, there is no overarching set of rules. Agent behavior emerges in response to environmental conditions because the sensors are tightly coupled to procedures. For example, when a food sensor detects food, a procedure associated with food detection gets triggered.

Like symbol systems, physical grounding agents are limited. In particular, they tend to be less successful at sophisticated tasks like puzzle solving or path planning. Brooks (1990) commented that, "nouvellers [are] roman

---

[23]A certain amount of caution is needed not to mistake *intention* and *belief* for their psychological equivalents. Nonetheless, these researchers are trying to model their systems on human mental attitudes.

tically hoping for magic from nothing while classists are willing to tell their systems almost anything and everything in the hope of teasing out the shallowest of inferences" (p. 4).

The degree to which an agent can behave intelligently is a consequence of its autonomy layer. For the dramatist, the method that behaviors are implemented is secondary to the degree of autonomy conferred. The degree of autonomy, in large part, determines the role a denizen may play. The degree of autonomy may be broken down as one of four levels: *fully autonomous, automatic, reflexive,* and *proxy* (see Table 8.4).[24]

A *fully autonomous* denizen comes closest to a realization of machine intelligence. It incorporates mechanisms for intention and belief as part of the goal-directed reasoning of action selection. It can respond in real time to world changes that mandate a change of plan, even while planning is in progress. It can discern whether actions are successful, and adjust to failure. It can make allowances for the plans and actions of other agents. With these capabilities, a fully autonomous agent is able to respond to a broad range of user interactivity. Homer and Lyotard are limited examples of fully autonomous denizens.

An *automatic* denizen, like a fully autonomous denizen, uses goal-directed reasoning. However, an automatic denizen has no belief mechanism so it cannot test the success of an action and assumes all actions are successful. Furthermore, it cannot adjust to world changes during planning, adapt to the intentions of other agents, or operate with real-time constraints. A denizen that only periodically observes the world is automatic. For example, an irrigation denizen may start watering during a thundershower if the soil was dry when it made its plans. Or a commuter denizen might miss a bus because it was planning to board when the bus pulled away.

A *reflexive* denizen has no awareness of the world and responds to a stimulus in a predetermined way. A reflexive denizen is a finite-state automaton; all possible states are determined. For example, light switches and locks are examples of reflexive denizens. Yet, reflexive denizens are capable of complex behavior. Traditionally animated characters are reflexive since all character states are predetermined. Reflexive denizens can also be suited to interactivity. The Guides of the Grolier Encyclopedia project offered suggestions of relevant cross-references to novice users (Oren, Salomon, Krietman, & Don, 1990). Similarly, the narrator of an

---

[24]Badler identifies three types of AI agents: intentional, mechanistic, and world. Mechanistic agents can act only when acted on by intentional agents. (Badler et al., 1991). Zeltzer identified a continuum of control from "programming" to "guiding" (Zeltzer, 1991).

TABLE 8.4
Degrees of Denizen Autonomy

Level of Autonomy	Description
Fully Autonomous (Machine intelligence)	• Goal directed reasoning responds to anomalous situations. • "Belief" mechanism to perceive world and test success of actions. • "Intention" or metaplanning goal hierarchy determines action selection. • Responds to dynamic environment during plan formation and execution. • Adapts to the plans and actions of other agents. • Operates within real-time constraints. Resource bound. • Loosely coupled to user.
Automatic	• Goal directed reasoning responds to anomalous situations. • "Intention" or metaplanning hierarchy determines action selection. • Unable to test the success of an action. All actions presumed successful. • No response to dynamic environment during plan formation and execution. • No adaptation to the plans and actions of other agents. • No capacity to operate within real-time constraints. Spends as much time as necessary planning for actions. No ability to stop planning.
Reflexive	• Predetermined behavior closely coupled to specific stimulus. Finite state automata. • Unaware of the domain.
Proxy (Natural Intelligence)	• An object which represents a human user in cyberspace. • Tightly coupled to user.

interactive fiction is reflexive; yet it accompanies the user through any sequence of the world of the fiction.

A *proxy* denizen represents a human user in a virtual world. It acts with belief and intention that reflect the judgment of the human occupant. The human user occupies the proxy agent through an act of transmigration. The familiar virtual hand and the VPL/MCI changeling (Lanier, 1992) are examples of proxy denizens.

The characters of a VR drama may be embodied in any of these forms. Characters need only as much autonomy as necessary to fulfill the needs of the story. Consequently, a VR drama may be staged without fully autonomous denizens. Fully autonomous characters would be needed only where highly complex user interactions are required. Otherwise, simpler denizens may suffice. In some cases, a proxy might offer an excellent alternative to a fully autonomous denizen. Tools like the SimGraphics Performance Animation System enable humans to drive proxies (Brill, 1992).

Nondramatic Elements

The virtual world can include activities besides the drama. The activities may include other narrative structures like interactive fictions, "twitch games," or computer-aided instruction. Twitch games are exercises in eye–hand coordination (Gasperini, 1990). Similarly, the world may incorporate nonnarrative elements like tools for data visualization. These classes of activity are not mutually exclusive, and may co-exist in a single world as local, or disconnected, events. The user might engage in these activities independently of any ongoing drama. (A drama may in fact pass through the space occupied by a user who is engaged in another activity.) The following section describes various classes of activity that might be part of the world of the story.

Narrative Elements (Nondramatic). The virtual world may include plotted and unplotted narratives. Interactive fictions are plotted; improvisational narratives like go-anywhere-do-anything fictions and voomies are not. Neither have dramatic structure.

In an interactive fiction, the narrative arises as the user solves a sequence of interconnected puzzles as a way of unraveling a plot. The dramatic pacing is desultory. The principal motivation must be the player's desire to solve the puzzles. In this respect the player is the protagonist.

Improvisational narratives are generated spontaneously. Go-anywhere-do-anything fictions may generate highly engaging results, especially if the user becomes the director or playmaker (Smith & Bates, 1989). *SimCity* and other game applications that use genetic algorithms to simulate behavior will also produce spontaneous narratives with considerable entertainment value. Likewise, voomies (Lanier, 1992) incorporate vaudevillian methods used by magicians and stand-up comics and can produce engaging and theatrical results, but only as long as the content is witty. All of these narrative forms suffer on retelling since their interest stems from novelty. In fact, replaying a sequence of one's own creation (say *SimCity*) is less entertaining than doing something new.

NonNarrative Elements. Nonnarrative elements such as design and visualization tools can be in the world of the story. The mixture of the actual with the fictional has traditionally been a source of verisimilitude in fiction.

Since a VR drama is interactive, the story may be updated to reflect current conditions. A story about a stockbroker may include real market data, or a story about an engineer may include a simulation of flow through a pump, and so on. Characters and users may use the same analytical tools. Tools for achieving these results in VR are under development (Coull & Rothman, 1993; Digital Image Design, 1992; Reveaux, 1993).

Real-world tools may be used to produce virtual world artifacts. The Sun Lathe (Deering, 1992) simulates the function of an actual lathe and may be used to create furniture or hand props. This type of interaction is common in MUDs where users have access to programming tools. Likewise, more complex tools like the Personal Assistants described by Pan and Tenenbaum (1991) may be used for functions like narration.

Overview: What You Might See at the VR Theater

The interactive opportunities for a VR drama arise because the user can occupy the world of the fiction. This world can be occupied by multiple users and filled with activities extraneous to the drama. For example, the world of the story may function as a MUD, include ancillary interactive fictions, or provide tools with real-world application.

VR dramas are distinct from conventional dramatic forms in two significant aspects: users are free to move about, and the plot line may run along simultaneous and parallel threads. Since the audience's experience cannot be predetermined, the VR dramatist must craft the action so that the audience is privy to essential information.

Characters and setting can reside in either the physical or virtual world. Characters may be under either computer or human control. Computer characters, or denizens, may be endowed with various levels of autonomy. Viewers may interact with denizens who are suffecently autonomous. The interaction with either denizens or setting must not disturb the dramatic structure.

Observing a VR drama is fundamentally a passive pursuit. In this respect it resembles other narrative forms: the events of the narrative are predetermined, the telling of the story incorporates techniques from theater and film, use of space resembles theater, and discontinuities of space and time resemble film.

A single world may serve as a setting for multiple dramas. The stories may take a serial form like a soap opera, where new episodes are created daily by an authoring team working from a completed story outline. Or, stories may be connected by character and place like those of Faulkner's Yoknapatawpha County, except that the stories may run concurrently so that the user may switch in mid-telling from one tale to another.

CREATING VR DRAMAS

VR playwrights will need conceptual devices and production tools to create their dramas. These devices will radically influence the content and peculiar quality of a VR drama. It is notable that a VR drama, like a novel or short story, could be the work of an individual. Theater and film are necessarily collaborative. Artistic collaborations tend to be expensive and prone to compromise. Once the production tools are refined, creating a VR drama will be no more expensive than writing a novel and potentially as prevalent and varied.

The following section discusses the types of tools a VR playwright might use.

Conceptual Devices

The techniques used to create a VR drama will borrow heavily from existing dramatic forms. Eisenstein (1942) found archetypes for cinematic montage in the works of Da Vinci and Milton. The exact nature of the devices will be realized only when the form matures, but some examples will suggest how the emerging form resembles existing ones.

A VR drama resembles a play in the use of space because actors must physically move across the stage. The ellipses commonly edited into film to bring about discontinuities in time or space are inappropriate within a VR scene because the user's time and space are the same as the character's. Intercutting causes an apparent dislocation of the user, or a disruption in the continuity of the dramatic time. Roach's *Wrong Side of Town* is a case in point. When viewers click on the head of a new character, the change from one narrative perspective to another is jarring. It disrupts the flow of the story, dissipates dramatic tension and strains the suspension of disbelief.[25]

A less troublesome and potentially more useful device is the instantaneous set change. These transitions happen as gray-outs, black-outs, or segues where the surroundings dematerialize and then rematerialize into a new place.

VR drama resembles film in that sound and visual effects are tightly bound, conveying a synaesthetic sense of place. An alarm clock ticks at a bedside. A viola vocalizes its part to the right of the cello, but to the left of the second violin. A dog barks outside a window. In a VR drama, the potential for binding is stronger since the proprioceptive senses may be involved. A user may reach over and stifle an alarm.

VR drama resembles literary drama in that a narrator, in the form of a

---

[25]It's worth noting that the option to select an alternative point of view may grow less desirable as the quality of the drama improves. A comparison can be made to the continuous-data measures taken by audience response systems. Typically an audience stops operating the continuous-data input device when fully engrossed in a program, and the resulting data do not reflect rising scores during the most interesting segments. Likewise, a viewer will not select alternative points of view during engrossing dramatic action.

denizen, may guide or accompany the user through the course of the story. These narrators exhibit all the qualities of a literary narrative voice. They may be savvy. They may be unreliable. They may have an active role in the action. They may merely be retellers of what they've heard. They may be familiar with missed narratives' threads and acquaint a user with those narrative details needed to understand the action.

Some devices have no precedent in other dramatic forms. Here are some examples.

In a VR drama, the user is responsible for keeping up with the action. Suppose we have followed a single character through the story's narrative thread. The character turns a corner and suddenly vanishes. What next? Suppose another character appears and beckons us to pursue another course. Suppose our narrator–companion admonishes us against the advice of the newcomer and advocates a different course? This type of decision lends interactivity to the drama while contributing to its urgency. For those users who prefer a more passive role, a narrative trolley might cruise through the story like a jungle boat in Adventure Land. This device might be useful as an overture to the world and its denizens.

In a VR drama, the user has a local view of events. Choosing to listen to a whispered conversation means missing the comments of other characters. Similarly, seeing events in one location means missing events in another. An omniscient point of view is not possible.

Interludes may be built into the dramatic action for users to explore a location. The unprompted discovery of facts of the world may contribute an element of foreshadowing or dramatic irony. Consider an unoccupied office with a desk, chairs, and hat rack. When the desk drawers are investigated, a gun is discovered—a gun that could figure prominently in later events.

Not all elements of the world of the story need be determined. An indefinite or uncertain element may be incorporated so the world is never quite the same from telling to telling. Indeterminacy may arise from the actions of fully autonomous denizens or users that change the state of the story world. Consider a slot machine that can be played by both viewers and characters. If a user gets lucky and hits the jackpot, a character who later plays the same machine may win but a pittance. The missed fortune might trigger a subplot driven by the need for cash. On the other hand, if the character hits the big jackpot, the money might trigger a subplot triggered by a bout of profligate spending.

Production Tools

Production tools are needed to implement a VR drama. The most important tools are those for scripting, training and directing synthetic actors, pre-production, cinematography, editing, and scenic design.

Scripting Tools. "When you take up a playbook, it strikes you as being a very trifling thing—a mere trifle beside the imposing bulk of the latest six-shilling novel. Little do you guess that every page cost more care, severer mental tension, if not more actual manual labor, than any chapter of a novel" (Baker, 1919, p. 518).

A screenplay or a playbook merely outlines the intent of the author. The actual play or movie is realized only in production. There are poor productions of good plays, and good productions of poor plays. A good play captures the subtleties of motive and behavior in action. Descriptions of emotional states or physiognomy are frequently excluded because they seldom communicate subtlety and tend toward cliché. In practice, a pithy suggestion is far more effective than an elaborate description. Zeltzer (1991) discussed the same problem with regard to the control of synthetic actors.

The script of a VR drama should provide enough detail so that the behavior of the characters can be inferred and interpreted. The full drama is not realized in the script. The full drama would be realized only when all the components are brought together in a particular realization.

A VR script describes parallel plot threads. Scripts of this sort have been written, but they are difficult to understand. *Tamara* (Krizanc, 1989) is organized as a sequence of simultaneous scenes. Reading straight through the playbook is equivalent to reading sections at random; a reader has no sense of the action sequence because adjacency on the page has no relevance. To follow the action of a character through the script, a reader must riffle back and forth through the pages. This process must be repeated for each character in each scene. By degrees, the reader builds up a mental picture of the events of the story. Although this approach is awkward, it works, but only because all the scene changes are progressing in lock-step. A less structured sequence of events scripted with this method would be unintelligible.

Others have described scripting difficulties. Riordan (1993) used a hypertext tool that is "readable but hard to follow." And Escoffier (Diamond et al., 1993) used blank walls with index cards connected with string and "silverware."

An alternative scripting method needs to be contrived to help the dramatist keep track of motives, beliefs, props, settings, and all the other varied elements of the story—perhaps a scripting application that uses multiple views of the action in conjunction with diagrams to show the progress of the characters, plus annotations to describe the location and dialog. Similar approaches have been applied to animation control in the COMPOSE system (Calvert, 1991a; Calvert, Welman, Gaudet, Schiphorst, & Lee, 1991b), and Pixar's interactive animation software (Ostby, 1989). This scripting application might use gant charts for tracking the characters and props, pert charts for tracking motives, or Petri nets for tracking the locus of dramatic action from point to point in the world. Development of a scripting application is a subject for further research.

Training and Directing Synthetic Actors

The Art of Acting. Actors train to use themselves as instruments for the expression of character in much the same way a musician uses a musical instrument. The body, as an instrument, is highly complex and expressive. An actor who attempts to communicate emotions by control of individual muscles is doomed to produce clichéd and amateurish results. Consider the performer who portrays anger by only frowning and shouting — the results will soon test the patience of any audience.

Actors learn to control the instrument as a *gestalt,* a single organic entity. In training, an actor learns a set of techniques to trigger behaviors that can be used to render a characterization. These techniques can be images, intentions, colors, recalled emotions, or any mental construct that gives rise to a particular creative impetus. They are *not* universal; their use is highly personal. Images produce different results in each and every actor, and not all images work for everyone. There is no single language of image, color, or intention. When training is complete, an individual knows which images will produce which results.

When actors have completed enough training to act with control, they can undertake the task of interpreting dramatic material. This interpretive process requires skills distinct from the training process. In order to be successful, an actor must grasp the truth of the human condition portrayed in the drama and select behaviors that fulfill their assigned role. An actor dissects the material beat by beat, determines the intent beneath the dialog (subtext), and selects techniques from his or her repertoire to produce character results matching the needs of the scene. Because it is difficult for an actor to observe the success of the selections, an objective view is furnished by a director who typically participates in all aspects of the interpretation.

Training and Directing Synthetic Actors. "The importance of abstraction for hiding irrelevant detail . . . the human figure has over 200 DOFs, yet providing the user with 200 knobs for interactively controlling joint rotation doesn't seem to be the answer" (Zeltzer, 1991, p. 5).[26]

The technique of preparing actors for theatrical performance is a useful

---

[26]DOF is an abbreviation for degrees of freedom. Each degree of freedom refers to a way a system might change. Any position of a human figure may be described by specifying all rotations of every joint. If a separate knob was used to control each rotation in every joint, over 200 knobs would be required.

model for training the synthetic actors of a VR drama. Animated characters currently require an expert human hand to create expressive behavior appropriate for dramatic action. However, animation techniques are becoming more automated, principally by directing synthetic actors from higher layers of the agent architecture (discussed previously). In effect, more complex behavior can be generated with fewer instructions to smarter denizens (Zeltzer, 1991).

Specifying complex movement with simple instruction requires an underlying database of movement dynamics. The databases are created by a number of techniques including attaching responsive position trackers (Meyer, Applewhite, & Biocca, 1992) to actors and recording their movements (Ginsberg, 1983; Maiocchi & Pernici, 1990).[27] More recently, facial armatures have been used (Brill, 1992). Another approach is to define the actor as an aggregate of objects with physical properties whose movement can be calculated when acted on by external forces. This includes specifying particulars like joint friction and muscle and ligament elasticity (Calvert, 1991a). In either case, the movements are converted to dynamic models including physical attributes like mass and stiffness to generate more realistic results (Zeltzer, 1991).

Several means have been developed to animate synthetic actors. A simple approach borrowed from traditional animation is *keyframing*. In keyframing, an animator specifies a sequence of body positions and the computer extrapolates a sequence of intermediate positions (called "tweening" for "in-betweening" in traditional animation). The COMPOSE system uses keyframing to choreograph dancer movements (Calvert, 1991a). A more powerful method is to use a specialized programming language for bundling pre-packaged routines. The Human Factory is an interactive animation environment based on this approach (Thalmann & Thalmann, 1990). For example, an animator animates a speech by creating keyframes of mouth shapes for each phoneme. A script of phoneme keyframes is tweened to create speech-like mouth movement. The animator interacts with the synthetic actor on the instruction layer.

Specifying expressive behavior requires an additional type of instruction. Morawetz's GESTURE uses secondary movements to add subtlety to gestures making them expressive (Calvert, 1991a). To add a gesture, the animator assigns a name to a movement between keyframe positions. The name refers to all the body model components involved in the gesture. A catalogue of the gestures comprise a body language vocabulary that would give a synthetic actor a personality.

A more sophisticated approach enables interaction at the autonomy

---

[27]Motion capture is becoming available in the commercial marketplace. Several products were demonstrated at SIGGRAPH '93.

layer. The synthetic actors can be given instructions and then permitted to act independently. Homer and Multran (described previously) are examples of this kind of denizen but they have minimal graphical components. However, several systems integrate kinetically based graphics with agent architectures. The Director system of Maiocchi and Pernici (1990) provides the animator with a "movement grammar" for generating a scene without intervention. Badler (1989) developed a system called Jack for instructing synthetic actors using motion verbs. Zeltzer described similar work in an MIT package called BOLIO. Ridsdale's Director's Apprentice permits animators to stage and block character movements (Calvert, 1991a).

None of these systems generate behavior expressive enough to communicate the nuances of character without human intervention. Presently, expressive characterization requires an animator to specify the posture, limb position, and facial expression for each and every action.

Serious obstacles confront the development of a system that automatically generates expressive movements. A fully independent system has to make artistic judgments. Expressive behavior should produce dramatic results that advance character and story. Selecting an appropriate behavior requires an understanding of the subtleties of body language and vocal expression. Matching behavior to character and story requires an understanding of the dramatic subtext and a plan for interpreting it. Given the difficulty of devising an algorithm for artistic judgment (discussed previously), it seems unlikely a fully independent system for the generation of expressive behavior is within the reach of existing technology.

However, a directing tool that generates expressive behavior, which has been selected by a human director, may be feasible. The tool would resemble Director, Jack, or BOLIO except that the results would be expressive. In practice, a director, having determined the needs of the subtext, would specify both an action and an expression for a fully autonomous or automatic denizen.[28] In response, the denizen would generate a movement that was appropriately expressive. But natural language, being ambiguous and highly sensitive to context, is too imprecise to specify a particular expression. It is not adequate to say that a character is nervous, delighted, or afraid. All these traits call on the peculiar and diverse nature of character. Each character is emotional in a different way. No character is always emotional in the same way.

A useful approach for specifying expressive behavior might be to adopt the strategy used to train actors for the theater. A VR playwright could train

---

[28]In proxy denizens the interpretive action selection is performed by a human host. In reflexive denizens action selection is determined by the world state; so the interpretive choice must be elsewhere. Both fully autonomous and automatic denizens have the means to select a particular action from a repertoire of actions.

actors to respond in specific ways to evocative images, colors, or intentions. In other words the VR playwright would create his or her own language for directing the synthetic cast. Such a language would be part of the denizen's autonomy layer. The denizen would not need a deep understanding of natural language. Once the actor is trained, the VR playwright could use this expressive language to direct the synthetic actors in performance. Development of a training and directing tool is a subject for future research.

Admittedly these directing and training tools do not solve the fundamental problem of creating expressive behavior autonomously. In fact they only reposition the problem; true autonomy will require a technological breakthrough. Until that time, the use of training and directing tools may provide a useful layer of abstraction for hiding some of the burdensome detail needed to produce expressive behavior.

Other Tools.   Pre-production tools are needed to manage the burden of detail accompanying any dramatic production. Some of these tools are of the standard project management variety. Set and prop design may be accomplished by standard CAD tools. Cinematographic tools are needed to control camera angles for those special circumstances of a movie within the VR drama. For the most part, however, cinematographic control is not needed because the user controls the point of view. Issues concerning control of the user's point of view were discussed by Ware and Osborne (1990), and Chapman and Ware (1992). An editorial tool for creating transitions between discontinuities in time or place should be integrated into the scripting application.

SUMMARY

The preceding discussion characterizes dramatic narratives as they might be translated into the new medium of VR. VR dramas are distinct from other narratives because they allow an audience to walk into the virtual world of the story. The viewer's presence in the virtual world makes possible an interactivity not available in traditional forms. However this interactivity must be limited so that the dramatic structure is preserved. Serious difficulties confront the development of a story generator that can create an interactive plot and yet preserve dramatic structure.

VR drama's distinctive qualities arise from this limited interaction. Although many qualities were discussed, viewer mobility and multithreaded narrative are particularly important. Also, because the world can exist outside the story, nondramatic and nonnarrative components may be part of the world.

Finally, creating VR dramas will require new tools for scripting the story and directing the denizens. The development of these tools is the subject of future research. Meanwhile, an experimental version of a VR drama could be produced using proxy denizens.

It will take some years before the art of VR drama matures. At that time it will have the mass appeal of cinema, the literary qualities of great literature, and the visual aesthetics of the visual arts. In the last analysis, VR is merely a communication medium and, in its best use, it will be a vehicle for the expression of ideas.

ACKNOWLEDGMENTS

I would like to extend my thanks to Bonnie Lund, Frank Biocca, and Hugh Applewhite who took the time to read the various drafts and offer their invaluable comments. A special thanks to Frank Biocca for taking my nattering about dramatic narrative seriously. Without his encouragement, this chapter would never have been written. Finally, I would like to thank a funding organization, but unfortunately there was none.

REFERENCES

Aristotle. (1941). The Poetics. In R. McKeon (Trans.), *The basic works of Aristotle.* New York: Random House (Original work written 335–322 B.C.)

Badler, N. (1989). Artificial Intelligence, natural language, and simulation for human animation. In N. Magnenat-Thalmann & D. Thalmann (Eds.), *State-of-the-art computer animation, proceedings of computer animation '89* (pp. 19–31). New York: Springer-Verlag.

Badler, N., Webber, B., Kalita, J., & Esakov, J. (1991). Animation from instructions. In N. Badler, B. Barsky, & D. Zeltzer (Eds.), *Making them move: Mechanics, control, and animation of articulated figures* (pp. 51–93). San Mateo, CA: Morgan Kaufman.

Bajura, M., Fuchs, H., & Ohbuchi, R. (1992). Merging virtual objects with the real world: Seeing ultrasound imagery with a patient. *Computer Graphics, SIGGRAPH '92 Conference Proceedings, 26*(2), 203–210.

Baker, G. (1978). *Dramatic technique.* New York: Da Capo Press. (Original work published 1919)

Bates, J. (1992). Virtual reality, art, and entertainment. *Presence: Teleoperators and virtual environments, 1*(1), 133–138.

Bates, J., Loyall, A., & Reilly, W. (1992). *Integrating reactivity, goals, and emotion in a broad agent.* Manuscript submitted to AAAI-92, July 12–16, Menlo Park. [Available as technical report CMU-CS-92-142 from the Computer Science Department, CMU, Pittsburgh, PA].

Bevan, M. (1992, August/September). BAe merges real and virtual environments. *VR News, 1*(7), 7.

Biocca, F. (1991, May). Mental models of television: Toward a theory of the semantic processing of television. Paper presented to *Information Systems Division of the International Communication Association,* Chicago, IL. [Available as technical report from the Center for Research in Journalism and Mass Communication, UNC, Chapel Hill, NC.]

Black, J., & Bower, G. (1980). Story understanding and problem solving. *Poetics, 9*(1) 223–250.

Brill, L. (1992, April). Facing interface issues. Computer Graphics World, 15(4), 48.

Brooks, R. (1990). Elephants don't play chess. In P. Maes (Ed.), *Designing autonomous agents: Theory and practice from biology to engineering and back* (pp. 3–15). Cambridge: MIT Press.

Calvert, T. (1991a). Composition of realistic animation sequences for multiple human figures. In N. Badler, B. Barsky, & D. Zeltzer (Eds.), *Making them move: Mechanics, control, and animation of articulated figures* (pp. 35–50). San Mateo, CA: Morgan Kaufman.

Calvert, T., Welman, C., Gaudet, S., Schiphorst, T., & Lee, C. (1991b). Composition of multiple figure sequences for dance and animation. *The Visual Computer, 7*(2–3), 114–121.

Chapman. D., & Ware, C. (1992). Manipulating the future: predictor based feedback for velocity control and virtual environment navigation. *Proceedings of 1992 Symposium on Interactive 3D Graphics, Cambridge, MA,* pp. 63–66.

Coull, T., & Rothman, P. (1993, August). Virtual reality for decision support systems. *AI Expert, 8*(8), 22–25.

Crockford, D. (1992). *The multimedia conference: Quest into the unknown.* Whole Earth 'Lectronic Link computer conference system. Sausalito, CA.

Deering, M. (1992). High resolution virtual reality. *Computer Graphics Proceedings, SIG-GRAM '92, 26*(2), 195–202.

Diamond, J., Escoffier, S., Goldstein, K., & Roach, G. (1993, July 24). *Interactive creation, creative interaction.* Unpublished panel sponsored by Writers Guild of America, International Interactive Communications Society in cooperation with UCLA extension, Department of Entertainment Studies, Los Angeles, CA.

Digital Image Design. (1992, April 10). InScape product description. [Trade literature].

Dyer, M. (1983). *In depth understanding.* Cambridge, MA: MIT Press.

Egri, L. (1942). *The art of dramatic writing.* New York: Simon & Schuster.

Eisenstein, S. (1942). *Film sense.* New York: Harcourt Brace.

Field, S. (1979). *Screenplay: The foundations of screenwriting.* New York: Dell.

Fowles, J. (1977). *Daniel Martin.* New York: Signet.

Freytag, G. (1985) Technik des dramas. In M. Herzfeld-Sander (Ed.), *Essays on German theater* (pp. 97–121). New York: Continuum. (Originally published 1863)

Gasperini, J. (1990, December). An art form for the interactive age. *Art-com, 10*(10).

Ginsberg, C., & Maxwell, D. (1983). Graphical marionette: Motion: Representation and perception. *Proceedings of acm SIGGRAPH/SIGART Workshop,* pp. 303–310.

Halliwell, L. (1989). *Halliwell's film guide.* New York: Harper & Row.

Heeter, C. (1992). Being there: The subjective experience of presence. *Presence: Teleoperators and virtual environments, 1*(2), 262–271.

Heitkoetter, J. (Ed.). (1993). *The hitch-hiker's guide to evolutionary computation: A list of frequently asked questions (FAQ).* Usenet: comp.ai.genetic. [Available via anonymous ftp from ft.fm.mit.edu in pub/usenet/news.answers/ai-faq/genetic/part1. Also parts 2 & 3.]

Holman, C. (1975). *A handbook to literature* (3rd ed.). Indianapolis: Odyssey Press.

Johnson, N., & Mandler, J. (1980). A tale of two structures: Underlying and surface forms in stories. *Poetics, 9*(1), 51–86.

Krizanc, J. (1989). *Tamara.* Toronto, Canada: Stoddard Publishing.

Lakoff, G. (1972). Structural complexity in fairy tales. *The study of man.* CA: University of California, Irvine, School of Social Sciences, 1, 128–190.

Lanier, J. (1992). Virtual reality: A status report. In L. Jacobson (Ed.), *Cyberarts: Exploring art and technology* (pp. 272–279). San Francisco: Miller Freeman.

Laurel, B. (1986). *Toward the design of a computer-based interactive fantasy system.* Unpublished doctoral dissertation, The Ohio State University, Columbus.

Laurel, B. (1991). *Computers as theater.* Reading, MA: Addison-Wesley Publishers.

Lessing, G. (1985). Hamburg dramaturgy. In M. Herzfeld-Sander (Ed.), *Essays on German theater* (pp. 1–19). New York: Continuum. (Original work written 1767–1768)

Lewis, L. (1992, August). Reviews: Designing autonomous agents, theory and practice from biology to engineering and back. *SIGART bulletin, 3*(3), 14–15.

Loyall, A., & Bates, J. (1991) Hap: A reactive adaptive architecture for agents. (Tech rep. CMU–CS-91-147.) Pittsburgh, PA: CMU, School of computer science.

Maiocchi, R., & Pernici, B. (1990). Directing an animated scene with autonomous actors. *The visual computer, 6*(6), 359–371.

McCorduck, P. (1979). *Machines who think.* San Francisco: Freeman.

Meehan, J. (1981). Tale-spin. In R. Schrank & C. Reisbeck (Eds.), *Inside computer understanding* (pp. 197–226). Hillsdale, NJ: Lawrence Erlbaum Associates.

Metz, C. (1974). *Film language, a semiotics of the cinema.* New York: Oxford University Press.

Meyer, K., Applewhite, H. & Biocca, F. (1992). Survey of position trackers. *Presence: Teleoperators and virtual environments, 1*(2), 173–200.

Minsky, M. (1985). *The society of mind.* New York: Simon & Schuster.

Morningstar, C., & Farmer, R. (1992). The lessons of Lucasfilm's Habitat. In M. Benedict (Ed.), *Cyberspace: First steps* (pp. 273–301). Cambridge, MA: MIT Press.

Okada, N., & Endo, T. (1992). Story generation based on dynamics of the mind. *Computational Intelligence, 8*(1), 123–160.

Oren, T., Salomon, G., Kreitman, K. & Don, A. (1990). Guides: Characterizing the interface. In B. Laurel (Ed.), *The art of computer–human interface design* (pp. 367–381). Reading, MA: Addison-Wesley.

Ostby, E. (1989). Simplified control of complex animation. In N. Magnenat-Thalmann & D. Thalmann (Eds.), *State-of-the-art computer animation, proceedings of Computer Animation '89* (pp. 59–67). New York: Springer-Verlag.

Pan, J., & Tenenbaum, J. (1991). An intelligent agent framework for enterprise integration. *IEEE transactions on systems, man, and cybernetics, 21*(6), 1391–1408.

Penrose, R. (1989). *The emperor's new mind.* New York: Oxford University Press.

Pollack, M. (1990). Plans as complex mental attitudes. In P. Cohen, J. Morgan, & M. Pollack (Eds.), *Intentions in communication* (pp. 77–103). Cambridge MA: MIT Press.

Polti, G. (1977). In L. Ray (Trans.), *The thirty-six dramatic situations.* Boston, MA: The Writer Inc. (Original work published 1868)

Rao, A., & Georgeff, M. (1992). An abstract architecture for rational agents. In B. Nebel, C. Rich, & W. Swartout (Eds.), *KR '92, principles of knowledge representation and reasoning* (pp. 439–449). San Mateo, CA: Morgan Kaufman.

Reilly, W., & Bates, J. (1992). *Building emotional agents.* Manuscript submitted to AAAI-92, July 12–16, Menlo Park. [Available as technical report CMU-CS-92-143 from the Computer Science Department, CMU, Pittsburgh, PA.]

Reveaux, T. (1993). Virtual reality gets real. *Newmedia, 3*(1), 32–41.

Riordan, D. (1993, July 1). *Interactive narrative — are interactive movies possible?* Unpublished paper presented at a USC Multimedia and Creative Technologies Center seminar, Los Angeles, CA.

Rumelhart, D. (1975). Notes on a schema for stories. In D. Bobrow & A. Collins (Eds.), *Representations of understanding: Studies in cognitive science.* New York: Academic Press.

Schank, R. (1982). *Dynamic memory.* Cambridge: Cambridge University Press.

Sheridan, T. (1992). Musing on telepresence and virtual reality. *Presence: Teleoperators and virtual environments., 1*(1), 120–125.

Simon, H. (1969). *The science of the artificial* (2nd ed.). Cambridge: MIT Press.

Smith, S., & Bates, J. (1989). *Toward a theory of narrative for interactive fiction.* (Tech report CMU–CS-89-121.) Pittsburgh, PA: CMU, School of computer science.

Stansberry, D. (1993, May). Hyperfiction: Beyond the garden of the forking paths. *New Media, 3*(5), 53–55.

Thalmann, N., & Thalmann, D. (1990). *Synthetic actors in computer generated 3D films.* Berlin: Springer-Verlag.

Thorndyke, P. (1980). Story processing bibliography. *Poetics, 9*(1), 329-332.

Turner, S., & Dyer, M. (1986). Thematic knowledge, episodic memory and analogy in minstrel, a story invention system. (Technical report csd-860078). CA: UCLA, Computer Science Department.

Vere, S., & Bickmore, T. (1990). A basic agent. *Computational Intelligence, 6,* 41-60.

Walser, R. (1990, March 19-22). Elements of a cyberspace playhouse. *Proceedings of the National Computer Graphics Association '90. Anaheim.*

Ware, C., & Osborne, S. (1990). Exploration and virtual camera control in virtual three dimensional environments. *Computer Graphics Proceedings of SIGGRAM 1990,* pp. 175-183.

Zeltzer, D. (1991). Task-level graphical simulation: Abstraction, representation, and control. In N. Badler, B. Barsky, & D. Zeltzer (Eds.), *Making them move: Mechanics, control, and animation of articulated figures* (pp. 3-33). San Mateo, CA: Morgan Kaufman.

Zeltzer, D. (1992) Autonomy, interaction, and presence. *Presence: Teleoperators and virtual environments, 1*(1), 127-132.

9 Sound and Communication in Virtual Reality

Gregory Kramer
CLARITY, Santa Fe Institute

Audition, like vision, is fundamental to our understanding of the world. However, in the design of virtual worlds, audition has been a poor cousin to vision, having largely been relegated to trivial enhancements of visualizations. Considering virtual world design from the standpoint of Biocca's (1994) "Communication Design Matrix" (a means of evaluating communication media; see Table 9.1), auditory display techniques can touch every aspect of a comprehensive communications system. This chapter investigates sound and the immersive interface from this comprehensive perspective.

As we acknowledge the importance of audition in everyday life, so should we accept the importance of audition for communication in virtual reality. VR is, after all, sensed and processed by the same perceptual systems as those which apprehend the physical world. Biocca has noted a number of qualities inherent to any comprehensive communication system, including: extending our creative thought processes, amplifying experience, acting in concert with others, and making physical transformation more perceivable. Visible representations play a role in a number of these. So do audible representations. That audio has been heretofore overlooked to the extent that it has is more a comment on the visual bias of many system designers, rather than any reflection on the utility of audio for communication.

In our evaluation of the role of sound in a VR system, we will use Biocca's criteria. As we shall see, auditory display touches some of his elements lightly although it offers to others the potential for profound extension.

Current audio implementations in immersive worlds can be categorized into three basic technologies: namely, sample playback, synthesized sound effects, and spatialization. All three have as their primary goals enhancing the realism of the modeled world and providing alerts for the system user.

Sample playback is the playback of digitally recorded sounds, usually initiated by some action on the system user's part. For example, when the subject knocks on a virtual door, (i.e., when the hand crosses a threshold in space that the computer recognizes as the door boundary) a sound of wood being struck is played back from the computer's memory. Thus the user feels as if he or she has just struck a door. As the subject enters the room, the computer plays back a soundfile of the new auditory environment, such as the sound of a restaurant or factory.

Synthesized sound effects are widely used in entertainment environments, such as games, to signify a simple event such as a "laser gun" blast or the landing of a space craft. Sound synthesis may also be used to save memory space or CPU time in cases where a passable imitation of a sound can be generated by a mathematical function rather than played back from sample memory.[1] For example, a burst of "white noise," like the sound of radio static, may be efficiently generated mathematically and used to imitate a crowd, the sea, or rain on a street. Users of more general computing environments will recognize the simple beep of the PC or the musical sequence of tones in a computer notification or a game as examples of synthesized sounds.

Spatialization, or 3-D sound, is the effort to bring externalization and directionality to sound by using the computer to synthesize the auditory cues we get from a natural acoustic environment (Wenzel, 1992). These cues include the different amplitudes, phases, and frequency spectra of the sound arriving at each ear of the subject. If all of these cues are properly employed, the resultant sound, even when heard through headphones, will appear to originate outside the hearer's head and it will be localized not just from right to left, but also up and down and, when combined with room reverberation characteristics, forward, back, near and far. Significantly, as the subject moves his or her head, the sound will behave veridically. That is, a stationary sound will appear to remain stationary when we turn our head to the side; if it started out in front of us, when we turn to the left the sound now appears to emanate from the right.

As mentioned earlier, these three techniques have as their primary goals enhancing the realism of the modeled world and providing alerts for the system user. We can see in most video games the combination of the first two techniques, sample playback and sound synthesis. Spatialization is currently too costly for these applications, although new spatialization algorithms and signal processing hardware are making these techniques

---

[1]For extensive literature on sound synthesis techniques, see issues of the Computer Music Journal, MIT Press.

more affordable. A combination of sample playback and spatialization can be found in current high-end experimental virtual reality systems.

In all of the aforementioned implementations, the enhancement of realism occurs in what we might call direct and indirect ways. Directly, the sound functions exactly as it does in the real world; an object drops to the floor and a crash is heard, for example, or the jet goes faster and the sound of the engine increases in loudness as the pitch area goes up. This is by far the most common use of sound in VR.

Indirect enhancement comes in the form of synesthesia, wherein sound is used to replace (or augment) the missing stimulation of another sense, typically the sense of touch. It is not uncommon, for example, to have a VR system wherein an object makes a noise when touched (Begault, 1992). This noise may have little to do with the realism of touching an object (e.g., how often does your drinking glass make sound when you pick it up?). However, in the absence of the tactile feedback that we have in fact contacted the object, the sound informs us that we have done so. The door knocking example above is both a direct and synesthetic representation; it sounds like a door *and* it lets us know we've touched the boundary of the room.

Over time, the technology for spatializing sound has improved and will continue to improve. Physical modeling techniques of sound synthesis will likewise improve and are likely to replace the simple sample playback systems now in use. A modicum of interactivity will almost certainly be implemented. Even these simple advancements will have a substantial impact on VR as a communication medium. They will make possible sound implementations that respond veridically and in real time to the actions of the user and changes in the environment.

If we approach the design of immersive interfaces exclusively from the standpoint of designing realistic representations of the physical world, then the approach to sound currently being taken may be adequate. However it is the developments along other, less obvious trajectories that will allow VR to more radically *extend* our ability to communicate (Kramer, 1992), particularly when it comes to communicating those ideas whose real meaning lies below the obvious discursive surface.

EXTENDED TECHNIQUES: AUDIFICATION AND SONIFICATION

The techniques described previously provide a good start at implementing the aural aspect of a multisensorial, immersive, interactive communications system. In order to understand the possible contributions sound can make to a more highly developed system, we must consider other, perhaps less obvious but nevertheless important techniques.

Audification

Audification is the direct audible playback of data, the "making audible" of that data (Kramer, 1994a). An example of audification is shifting the frequency range of seismic data (Hayward, 1994) and then playing back the result. In this way we can hear earthquakes. Other examples include the playback of radio telescope data and equation generated-waveforms (Mayer-Kress, Choi, & Bargar, 1994). Audification can allow us to create realities that extend beyond our normal perceptual abilities. We cannot normally hear seismic or radio telescope data. The sound of an equation that has been audified has no other auditory correlate. Can we learn something about the data by using audification? Can we learn something about chaos mathematics by listening to waveforms generated by chaos equations? These questions are currently being considered by auditory display researchers.

Audification techniques are also applied to simulations, wherein the simulation is designed to replicate an event or process that would generate sound based upon mechanical interactions. For example, a mathematical simulation of a rotor in an engine would produce a sound identical to the physical rotor if the model were perfectly designed and the samples representing the pressure waves generated by the simulation were output to a D/A converter and amplifier (McCabe & Rangwalla, 1994). In this type of audification we have clearly taken a jump in veridicality from a noninteractive sample playback system. Simply stated, multivariate changes in a multivariate system can be attempted and the results of the changes heard.

Sonification

Sonification involves the use of data to control a sound generating system for the purposes of comprehending the data or monitoring the process represented by the data (Kramer, 1994). By the use of sonification techniques, the universe of numerical data can be encoded in sound. This results in an information channel between the computer (VR system) and user (subject) that is wider than vision-only channels and can employ the pattern-recognition capabilities of the auditory system to extract meaning from data.

A sonification device with which most of us are familiar is the Geiger counter. A number, the radiation measurement, is used to control an auditory variable, the speed of clicks. We can monitor a process that has no auditory correlate by using the values to control a sound.

More advanced sonification systems have been developed that allow a researcher to move a cursor through a data visualization and, as each point is traversed, the data values that point represents are sent to the control inputs of a sound generator. These systems have been used to display gas plasma (Smith et al., 1990) and turbulent systems (Bargar, 1993) amongst other data sets.

Another closely related sonification approach is the sequential readout of a data file, injecting the data values of the n-dimensional data set into a sonification "map," or router. These values are scaled, translated into the appropriate format, and sent to a sound-generating target. Chaotic data (Bidlack, 1992; Kramer & Ellison, 1991), census data (Madyastha & Reed, 1993), data from the Magellan Venus fly-by (Kramer & Ellison, 1991), computer debugging and analysis (Jackson & Fancioni, 1993; Jameson, 1993), and other sonifications have been implemented. Additionally, real-time data from medical monitoring (Fitch & Kramer, 1994), automobile gauges (Fubini et al., 1988), and printing presses (Kaiser & Greiner, 1980) have been sonified.

If there were no advantages to auditory presentation of data over visual or textual presentation, the work described here would amount to just more monitoring and analysis techniques in a field full of techniques. A brief look at the advantages auditory displays offer over and above (or in combination with) other displays will show us that at the very least they are a meaningful adjunct to visual or statistical techniques.

Auditory display techniques offer several obvious benefits over visual displays. Auditory displays leave the eyes free to perform other tasks, they maintain temporal relationships that may be inherent in the data that static visual displays cannot maintain, and they may have the capacity to display very high-dimensional systems (Kramer, 1994b). In a paper on auditory imagery and sonification, the author also suggests that auditory display techniques, boldly applied, offer tools for extending our conceptual capacities. For a more in-depth consideration of these issues, please see the literature on sonification and audification cited elsewhere in this paper.

AUDIBLE OBJECTS

The author's work with *audible objects* provides an example of how the display medium can alter our modes of interaction in such a way as to demand a rethinking of our sensory ecology. Audible objects are the aural correlate of visible objects. Like other objects, the audible object is fabricated, it can be encountered and re-encountered, and it can be manipulated and interacted with, not unlike computational objects and physical objects. Audible objects are an instance of how feedback in a VR system can enable radically different interactions with a modeled world or data set.

An experience of an "audible object" may go like this. You have your 3-D visualization system on (these days a helmet or glasses of some sort), and your earphones. Your body and head movements are kept track of with a 3-D tracker. You see computer-created objects in the visual display system. Either you walk through them or encounter them with your gloved hand. If they emit a sound when encountered, they are visible and audible objects. You walk or reach elsewhere and hear a sound of another object. You do not see it. This is an audible object. It is not visible.

Based upon our description of current sound implementations in VR, this may appear to be simply a generalized definition of auditory notification of boundary crossings. However, the author has been defining *and* extending the domain of audible objects to include data objects controlling a sonification system. So, when encountering an audible object we may simply be triggering a sampled sound that has been associated with that object or we may be hearing an audible representation of the *data* associated with the region in question.

Walking through a virtual reality you encounter a visible object. You move your hand through the object (or place your head inside it). The computer is notified of your presence and the data associated with this object is injected into the map in the sonification system and that system is "turned on." You hear a sound that represents quantitative information about that object.

In this scenario, the data being represented could be associated with a real-world object, for example temperature and pressure readings in a piece of machinery or a human heart. It could also be data that has no inherent spatial quality or physical manifestation, for example data associated with an isomorphic surface generated by a data visualization system or amusing objects in an immersive game.

In informal experiments, the author has been working with audible objects that have no visible correlate. Encountering such an audible object is more akin to discovering a previously unknown entity or palpating space itself. Using audible objects, the system user is able to navigate a database, with each object being a sound with n variables (brightness, roughness, pitch, etc.) and representing the data in an n-dimensional cell. In this way we have been able to differentiate a small number of data objects using entirely abstract auditory variables.

A significant aspect of audible objects is their combining haptic and auditory involvement in the data-exploration task, which is to say, the senses of proprioception and audition are combined in the creation of an audible object. The haptic sense is reaching out to "touch," and the consequent response is "auditory." While either auditory or haptic cues, by themselves, will be difficult to use as data navigation tools, investigating a data object by allowing the system user to touch it "audiotactually," has yet to be explored as a source of valuable synergy. Using motor involvement to perform a task has been shown to improve learning (Biocca, 1994). Sonification also looks promising as a learning aid (Kramer, 1990).

About a century ago the electronic storage, manipulation, and transmission of sound changed our world. Prior to these innovations, we identified many events in our world primarily by audition. We heard animals in the woods, wind, rain, streams, street vendors, and ships offshore. Radios, portable music players with headphones, prerecorded music services in stores and elevators, and a steady noise floor of traffic have served to isolate us to some extent from nuances in our auditory environment. As a result, our civilization has brought with it a desensitization as regards our auditory perceptual abilities. Identifying objects solely by their sound may, in fact, rejuvenate listening skills that have been largely ignored in modern times. It is interesting to speculate whether sensitive uses of sound at the human–machine interface will bring valuable classification skills to the recognition of audible objects.

AUDITORY DISPLAY AND BIOCCA'S COMMUNICATION DESIGN MATRIX

Biocca (1994) suggested that in our effort to construct VR applications, we consider essential communication goals and needs rather than adopting the conventional vantage point employed in film, television, newspapers, and arcade games. He asked, "What should we look for in an ideal metamedium?" In response he developed the Communication Design Matrix as a tool for systematic evaluation of the VR interface. As we can see from Table 9.1, the matrix consists of five communications "dimensions," or functions, and four levels of testing and evaluation.

The general functions of a communication system are listed by Biocca as:

- Information encoding.
- Information decoding.
- Coordination of social action.
- Creation of social reality.
- Transformation of physical forms.

The levels of testing and evaluation include:

- Cognitive.
- Instrumental.
- Normative.
- Expressive.

TABLE 9.1
Biocca's Communication Design Matrix

Levels of Testing and Evaluation	Individual Processes		Social Processes		Physical Processes
	INFORMATION ENCODING: Objectification of Thought	INFORMATION DECODING: Reception and Mental Modeling	Coordination of SOCIAL ACTION	Creation of SOCIAL REALITY	Transformation of PHYSICAL FORMS
Cognitive	Facilitates, reflects and extends creative thought processes	Extends or amplifies experience	Group action plans easily created and understood	Communication and experience clearly transfers across users	Makes physical transformation more perceivable
Instrumental	Satisfies strategic/reflexive goals	Satisfies information skill or mood management needs	Motivates and directs sustained and successful action	Facilitates persuasion and negotiation of social reality	Achieves desired measure of physical transformation
Normative	Satisfies group/social codes and norms of expression	Facilitates acquisition and modeling of group norms	Actions create or are regulated by norms	Establishes or reinforces group/social rules and norms	Confirms structure and harmony of natural or cultural order
Expressive	Provides uers with a wide range of expressive tools and codes	Expresses wide range of user mental states, moods and attitudes	Facilitates a wide range of group actions	Engages wide range of existential relations	Transforms nature into culture

INFORMATION ENCODING:
OBJECTIFICATION OF THOUGHT

Gestural languages, such as dance and music, are means of encoding both qualitative and quantitative information. They allow both thought and feeling to be communicated. Similarly, auditory display provides a tool for representing both kinds of information. Auditory communication by encoding extends creative thought processes, as evidenced by the virtual torrent of (data-driven) music that has taken advantage of computer-extended performance and synthesis techniques. These expressions, at their best, involve communicative norms, not unlike the norms one finds in a good jazz ensemble. Lanier's and Vincent's work with VR as musical instrument is a logical extension of these techniques into immersive worlds.

However, it would be a mistake to see only the expressive nature of the objectification of thought. Auditory display also satisfies strategic goals by providing an enhanced display medium for hard data. With sound tools ranging from event notification and object description to aurally encoded data, the user of an auditory display system is experiencing the objectification of conceptual material.

Information Decoding: Reception and
Mental Modeling

Information decoding, or the reception and mental modeling of data structures, is the area in which sonification can make its most significant contributions to VR as a communications medium. Until recently, computers and related systems were designed as if the system user were more or less deaf. Except for the occasional alert sound, the user's auditory abilities were entirely ignored. At its core, sonification is designed to expand the information-carrying capacity of the transmission medium (computer, VR system, machinery, etc.) to more closely match and exploit the capabilities of the human sensorimotor system.

As described earllier, auditory display techniques address this information capacity mismatch between man and machine. Sonification, in particular, has the capacity to widen the information conduit at this juncture and, in so doing, allow the system user to conceptualize richer models based upon richer perceptual input.

A Case Study

A project conducted in cooperation with Apple Computer's Apple Classrooms of Tomorrow (ACOT) group (Kramer, 1990) is illustrative of how audio may be used to enhance mental modeling. ACOT had been working with high school students to determine new ways in which the computer could be used to help the students form mental models of different processes and so better understand those processes. A predator/prey model was selected because it contained just a few simple variables but produced a complex, nonlinear and not immediately obvious result.

The three dynamic variables in the simulation were:

1. Prey population (deer).
2. Predator population (wolves).
3. Prey food (grasses).

In addition to these three dynamic variables, the student could also set fixed values for Deer Tags (which reduced the prey population), Bounty (which reduced the predator population), and food imported by the park ranger (which increased the Prey food).

The sensory feedback provided to the students consisted of pictures, or icons, that would grow and shrink as the number of predators, prey, and food increased and decreased. Students could also refer to a graph that plotted the change in values of each variable over time.

A problem consistently encountered in ACOT's early work was that the students approached the ecomodel much as they would approach a video game. The results of each run of the model become the basis for the next run, with very little understanding of the "big picture" or the value of a methodical inquiry. The animated icons were found to be very compelling and students based their conclusions on the concepts formed as the model unfolded. If their conclusions did not match the graphs generated by the software, the students discounted the graphs, not their conclusions.

This suggests that the moment of the simulation's unfolding was the most compelling, not an analytical or reflective period following the "real" event. We hypothesized that if multimodal techniques were used to make the moment of unfolding more information-rich, that the student might be better able to create an accurate mental model of the underlying simulation dynamics.

The author proposed that sonification may have the capacity to help the student gain an intuitive understanding of the data as it changes in time. By tapping a purely aural or musical mental capacity rather than visual or speech capacities, the power of aural perceptual processing is called into play (which, it was proposed, would engender substantially improved pattern recognition). We also proposed that certain students that are deficient in other areas may have strong, if overlooked, aural data-processing capacity.

Additionally, it is easy to ignore the graphs that are generated as the simulation is run. With audible feedback providing constant updates on the status of the system the student would have more stimulation available and could be more fully apprised of all the system variables. Also, we suspected that sensory interactions might result in a synergy of the two different sense modalities. During the course of this research one thing we hoped to discover was the ability of the students to benefit from the increased perceptual capacities that auditory processing afford.

Finally, we hoped that sonification would have the capacity to be perceptually compelling, just as the animated icons in the original model were. We thus hoped to develop a system that could provide enhanced neural stimulus and a set of tools to be used in conjunction with visual feedback. Research by Bly (Bly, 1982) and others has proven that combining visual and aural feedback greatly increases the ability of system users to understand complex data.

Two sonification techniques were employed, namely, using realistic sounds and abstract sounds. The realistic sound implementation was simple—more prey was indicated by more deer sounds (drinking, hoofs, walking through shallow water), more predators by more wolf sounds (howling, barking, and growling), and more prey food was indicated by more/louder insects (since grass sounds were not too compelling). The abstract sounds included a pulsing sound that got faster with prey population and higher in pitch with predator population, whereas brighter with faster onset times indicated increased food supply.

Preliminary sessions with students at ACOT suggested that the sonified predator/prey model seemed to be more compelling than the simulation without an audible component. Although ACOT has not run a large number of subjects and quantified the results of this research, several possibilities suggested themselves based upon anecdotal feedback and our own, subjective experience with the system.

Increased engagement is not a trivial advantage. After using the sonified model, one's experience of the simulation seemed flat and uninteresting without the sonification. It would seem possible that a more compelling experience may also be one that generates a more vivid mental model.

With the realistic sounds it was possible to close one's eyes and experience the aural environment. Affective responses to sounds included fear associated with the growling sound, excitement with faster pulses and rising pitch (more predators and more prey), and an inviting sense of a natural environment associated with the "food" ambiance (hearing crickets and other insects while deer walked through the water). It was beyond the scope of this project to ascertain the amount or character of mental imaging that was taking place, but the "soundscape" created by the sonification did seem to engender a qualitatively different experience of the essentially quantitative information.

The experience of using abstract sounds to represent data was alien to the students. For this reason it may have been difficult for them to ascertain how the sound was actually being used and specifically what data variables were mapped to what auditory variables. This very factor, however, may possess the potential of leading them (or us) to *conceive* of the model differently because we *perceived* the model differently.

Other Relations to Mental Modeling

Other elements of the information-decoding aspect of Biocca's Communication Design Matrix are navigation of the medium and the effect of this navigation on comprehension. Although conclusive data is not available, the author's work with the sonification of spreadsheet/database data subjectively indicates that it is possible to form an overall image of a large data set by moving around within the data using aural feedback. Without a doubt this technique is very poor at providing precise numerical information. However, it seems possible that a generalized mental model of the data can be formed and, with various techniques, different features of the model can be investigated. The reader is referred to Kramer (1993) for more information on this work.

Another role of a communication system in information decoding is its ability to extend or amplify one's experience. Just as microphones, hydrophones, telephones and audio recorders have expanded and redefined our aural reality, sonification and audification clearly extend our perceptual experience. For example, without sonification and audification how could you hear stock market or census data or the macrostructure of an earthquake? In what other environment could one encounter an invisible but audible object that has spatial extent?

Biocca includes mood management as another factor in information decoding. Music is one element of auditory display that has an obvious impact on a system user's mood. A less obvious element is what I refer to as *affective association*. Affective association represents an effort to associate how we respond emotionally to an auditory display based on what we expect would be a characteristic emotional response to changes in the underlying data. For example, a sound may get uglier as defoliation occurs in an ecosystem model. A sound may become more "clear" (less noisy) as air pollution is reduced. (For a more thorough consideration of affective association see Kramer, 1994a.)

Attentional and behavioral issues in response to content are key issues in sonification, as they are in any mental modeling medium. How does directing our attention to a sound (which is representing data) effect our comprehension of the information encoded therein? When attending to one auditory stream, what information can we absorb from other auditory streams? How does attending to an auditory display effect the efficacy of the visual display and vice versa?

Although it is beyond the scope of this paper to address these issues in detail, it is worth noting that any attempt to provide a richer information display must confront the issues related to the user's saturation point for information absorption. How do we select the salient information from a complex display when forming our mental models of the processes being represented? Is there such a thing as too much sensory input or do our perceptual systems simply take what they need and ignore the rest? As more sophisticated auditory displays are developed and integrated with other display modalities, answers, or at least heuristics, will no doubt be forthcoming.

COORDINATION OF SOCIAL ACTION

Although this paper has focused on the role of nonspeech audio in VR as a communication medium, the preeminent communicative device for the coordination of social action is speech. The subtleties of speech audio are important and on the verge of significant expansion, as speech recognition and synthesis algorithms improve and as better audio is integrated into more group work platforms. It is hard to imagine a fully functional group meeting without the benefits of speech inflection. Additionally, the localization of speech sound in a telepresence environment aids in speaker identification, stream separation and veridicality.[2] Furthermore, speech need not be just with other humans. Speech audio as a means of communicating with a software system or higher level software 'agents' maps well to our everyday behaviors. When we want something, for example, we ask for it, usually with speech.

In a cooperative data-exploration task, a wide range of group actions can be coordinated by several users manipulating a common sonification to explore a subject data set. In this case, each of the users is both hearing and effecting the sonification, arriving at a cooperative understanding of how to best represent the data. For example, a group of scientists exploring a complex simulation via networked workstations may individually manipulate elements of the sonification map. Each member of the group benefits from hearing the results of the other member's actions and is then able to elaborate.

---

[2]Please refer to the sound examples produced by R. Begault to accompany Wenzel (1994).

CREATION OF SOCIAL REALITY

Language is a fundamental element of social reality. When a language is richer, the power and subtlety of communication reflects this. Construction of a social reality that encompasses extended auditory display techniques should contribute to the creation of a richer social language and environment. The language of sonification may not be utterable by most humans, but it can enrich and inform our concepts of qualities and quantities. These then become common references, part of the expression of otherwise unperceptualized data and of the shared imagination.

When common sonification techniques evolve, they will provide a new set of analogies with which we understand and speak about our world. Just as the XY graph gave us the phrases, "off the charts" and reinforced the concept of "he's at his peak," sonification could provide us with analogies based upon auditory qualities. "Interest rates are bright," or "inventory has a real thump to it" could convey associations with a higher spectral centroid or faster onset time, either of which could become standards that any sonification system user would understand. In this way concepts and language associated with our internal auditory imagery can augment the already rich palette derived from visual imagery.

TRANSFORMATION OF PHYSICAL FORMS

Telepresence and teleoperation is mentioned by Biocca as the quintessential physical transformation of reality. Audition is an integral element in our everyday perceptions. Therefore, the auditory aspect of telepresence makes this variety of physical transformations more compelling and ecologically congruent.

Our normal sensory capabilities provide the necessary and sufficient means for a realistic telepresence, given appropriate input to our sensory channels. Our sensory capacities can also be extended by means of auditory display. Durlach's research into superlocalization, in which a subject is given paranormal localization cues (Durlach & Pang, 1986) is one such extension. Sensitive microphones installed at a remote site and amplified, thereby providing super hearing for a telepresence system user, is another example of sensory extension. Synesthetic representations that provide the system user with the ability to hear what is visible or tactual (and conceivably hear what is normally smelled or tasted), are more radical physical transformations. If in the process of crossing modalities there is amplification of the sensory experience, the transformation becomes even more extreme (e.g., a delicate touch makes a loud sound).

Audible objects, described earlier, can be understood as a type of physical transformation possible via a VR system. In this case, data representing either physical objects or numerical values are transformed into auditory experiences. When manipulation of auditory reality reaches this stage, it gains expressive potential. Rather than limiting the fabricated world to sounds normally occurring, the sounds or their data precursors can be extensively controlled. In this event, nature becomes culture. The found object becomes the made object.

Sonification can also transform our world by simply keeping us better informed as to the status of its components. For example, the sonification of a production line, such as a paper pulp processing plant, enables an operator to use the equipment more efficiently. If the mix is too viscous or the chemical balance is off, the sonified parameters signal the operator to adjust levels accordingly, with the added benefit of leaving the operator's hands and eyes free for other tasks. Feedback is provided to the machine user, keeping him continually updated as to the status of his efforts to transform the world.

TESTING AND EVALUATION CRITERIA

Biocca's design matrix divides the testing and evaluation of communication media into four levels: cognitive, instrumental, normative, and expressive. Each of these levels represents an important set of values to be satisfied by a medium. The salient *cognitive value* to auditory display resides in its capacity for expanding the thinking process by rendering data via previously unexplored sensory modality, offering the opportunity for expansion of our comprehension and insight into the data.

The *instrumental values* of auditory display techniques include: engagement (which enhances motivation); affective coherence (which make a display medium more intuitively meaningful and leads to ease of task completion); and the reduction of problem-solving task completion times (by providing a wider information conduit that taps a broader set of pattern recognition skills).

The *normative values* enhanced by auditory display are to be found in a sharing of rules or understandings by various users. This will be increased as auditory display research develops. At this time there are few, if any, underlying design philosophies in auditory display. Gaver's focus on realistic sounds (Gaver, 1993) is an example of a possible normative factor, but many display techniques do not even have this level of specificity. Certainly most sonification techniques that employ abstract sounds lack the common language that will make them easy to learn and effective vehicles for shared understandings.

We clearly need new tools to enhance and encourage creative thinking.

Sonification can present a thoroughly nonintuitive information display in which the data requires rather than requests a novel approach. In this way, the very weaknesses of sonification can be turned to its advantage, introducing the subject into a novel landscape, presenting a fresh viewpoint, and possibly highlighting insights that might otherwise have passed unnoticed.

Finally, the same *expressive value* of audition found in music, speech, and our affective responses to environmental sounds appears also in auditory interfaces and sonification. An ugly or aggravating sound is likely to influence user objectivity (see discussion of *affective association*). Although it may be true that the goal of auditory data display is usually comprehension rather than expression, the user of a sonification system or an auditory interface designer is still employing tools of nonverbal *expression* of abstract concepts. In the context of auditory display, the dividing line between affect and concepts can be easily blurred. We will do well to appreciate the complexity of our experience in an immersive world. When we actively manipulate an immersive environment, the line between exploration and expression may frequently be crossed.

CONCLUSIONS

The author hopes that from the above discussion it is clear that auditory display techniques are essential to the communicative properties of immersive media. The current state of the art of sound in VR is very underdeveloped. As such, it offers a rich field for progress in pure research and applications.

The current use of sound, mostly limited to sample playback, simple synthesis, and spatialization, is progressing steadily towards more realistic and ecologically valid interfaces. Taken by themselves, these developments will enrich the VR experience considerably by making the modeled world aurally reflect the real world.

So far as auditory display is concerned, it is the extensions of reality, represented by synesthesia, audification, sonification, and audible objects that stand to most profoundly extend VR's communicative powers. All of the evaluation criteria in Biocca's Communication Design Matrix are impacted positively by these extended techniques. The greatest impact, we believe, will be on information decoding, particularly mental modeling, amplifying experience, and the expression of a wide range of user mental states.

We experience VR in the same way that we experience reality—via our senses. The more transparent the boundary between human and machine, the richer the information flow. When we employ this information flow in service of realism we stand to fully engage the system user and create a compelling communication tool. When we further employ this information flow to create new ways of perceiving, we extend the entire concept of communication.

ACKNOWLEDGMENTS

The author gratefully acknowledges R. Jonathan Kramer for his editorial assistance. Early stages of this research were supported by research awards from Apple Computer's Apple Classrooms of Tomorrow group. Ongoing research in this area is supported by the Santa Fe Institute.

REFERENCES

Bargar, R. et al. (1993). *Auditory image* (Computer program). Champaign-Urbana, IL: National Center for Supercomputing Applications.

Begault, D. (1992). An introduction to 3-D sound for virtual reality. In *VR becomes a business, the proceedings of VR '92* (p. 6). Westport, CT: Meckler Corp.

Bidlack, R. (1992). Chaotic systems as simple (but complex) compositional algorithms. *Computer Music Journal, 16*(3), 33–47.

Biocca, F. (1994). *A framework for evaluating communication designs.* Unpublished manuscript, University of North Carolina, Center for Research in Journalism and Mass Communication, Chapel Hill.

Bly, S. (1982). *Sound and computer information presentation.* Unpublished doctoral dissertation, University of California, Davis.

Durlach, N. D., & Pang, X. D. (1986). Interaural magnification. *Journal of the Acoustical Society of America, 80*(6), 1849–1850.

Fitch, T., & Kramer, G. (1994). Sonifying the body electric: The superiority of an auditory over a visual display in a complex, multivariate system. In G. Kramer (Ed.), *Santa Fe Institute Studies in the Sciences of Complexity: Vol. 18. Auditory display: Sonification, audification and auditory interfaces* (pp. 307–325). Reading, MA: Addison-Wesley.

Fubini, E., De Bono, A., & Ruspa, G. (1988). *System for monitoring and indicating acoustically the operating conditions of a motor vehicle* (U.S. Patent #4,785,280). U.S. Patent and Trademark Office.

Gaver, W. (1994). Using and creating auditory icons. In G. Kramer (Ed.), *Santa Fe Institute Studies in the Sciences of Complexity: Vol. 18. Auditory display: Sonification, audification and auditory interfaces* (pp. 417–446). Reading, MA: Addison-Wesley.

Hayward, C. (1994). listening to the earth sing. In G. Kramer (Ed.), *Santa Fe Institute Studies in the Sciences of Complexity: Vol. 18. Auditory display: Sonification, audification and auditory interfaces* (pp. 369–404). Reading, MA: Addison-Wesley.

Jackson, J., & Fancioni, J. (1994). Synchronization of visual and aural parallel program performance data. In G. Kramer (Ed.), *Santa Fe Institute Studies in the Sciences of Complexity: Vol. 18. Auditory display: Sonification, audification and auditory interfaces* (pp. 291–307). Reading, MA: Addison-Wesley.

Jameson. (1994). Sonnet: Audio enhanced monitoring and debugging. In G. Kramer (Ed.), *Santa Fe Institute Studies in the Sciences of Complexity: Vol. 18. Auditory display: Sonification, audification and auditory interfaces* (pp. 253–265). Reading, MA: Addison-Wesley.

Kaiser, W., & Greiner, H. (1980). Warning system for printing presses (U.S. Patent # 4,224,613). U.S. Patent and Trademark Office.

Kramer, G. (1990). *Audification of the ACOT predator/prey model* (Unpublished report). Apple Computer's Advanced Technology Group, Apple Classrooms of Tomorrow. Portland, OR: Clarity.

Kramer, G. (1992). Sonification and virtual reality I: An introduction. In *VR becomes a business, the proceedings of VR '92* (p. 85). Westport, CT: Meckler Corp.

Kramer, G. (1993). Sonification of financial data: An overview of spreadsheet and database sonification. In *Virtual Reality Systems 1993*. New York: VRS Publications.

Kramer, G. (1994a). Some organizing principles for representing data with sound. In G. Kramer (Ed.), *Santa Fe Institute Studies in the Sciences of Complexity: Vol. 18. Auditory display: Sonification, audification and auditory interfaces* (pp. 185–221). Reading, MA: Addision-Wesley.

Kramer, G. (1994b). An introduction to auditory display. In G. Kramer (Ed.), *Santa Fe institute Studies in the Sciences of Complexity: Vol. 18. Auditory display: Sonification, audification and auditory interfaces* (pp. 1–77). Reading, MA: Addison-Wesley.

Kramer, G., & Ellison, S. (1991). Audification: The use of sound to display multivariate data. In *Proceedings of the International Computer Music Conference* (pp. 214–221).

Madyastha, T., & Reed, D. (1994). A framework for sonification design. In G. Kramer (Ed.), *Santa Fe institute Studies in the Sciences of Complexity: Vol. 18. Auditory display: Sonification, audification and auditory interfaces* (pp. 267–289). Reading, MA: Addison-Wesley.

Mayer-Kress, G., Choi, I., & Bargar, R. (1994). Musical structures in data from chaotic attractors. In G. Kramer (Ed.), *Santa Fe institute Studies in the Sciences of Complexity: Vol. 18. Auditory display: Sonification, audification and auditory interfaces* (pp. 341-367). Reading, MA: Addison-Wesley.

McCabe, K., & Rangwalla, A. (1994). Auditory display of computational fluid dynamics data. In G. Kramer (Ed.), *Santa Fe institute Studies in the Sciences of Complexity: Vol. 18. Auditory display: Sonification, audification and auditory interfaces* (pp. 327-340). Reading, MA: Addison-Wesley.

Smith, S. et al. (1990). *Stereophonic and surface sound generation for exploratory data analysis*. Paper presented at the proceedings of CHI '90, Seattle.

Wenzel, E. (1992). Localization in virtual acoustic displays. *Presence: Teleoperators and virtual environments, 1,* 80–107.

Wenzel, E. (1994). Spatial sound and sonification. In G. Kramer (Ed.), *Santa Fe institute Studies in the Sciences of Complexity: Vol. 18. Auditory display: Sonification, audification and auditory interfaces* (pp. 127–150). Reading, MA: Addison-Wesley.

10 Interpersonal Communication and Virtual Reality: Mediating Interpersonal Relationships

Mark T. Palmer
Northwestern University

Technological advances in the forms of human communication will un-doubtedly be listed among the major achievements of the 20th century. Widespread growth in computer, telephone, and broadcast networks has generated a process by which society is redefining itself in terms of the information age. An increasingly larger share of the population is spending work and leisure hours creating, transforming, transmitting and consuming a man-made resource—information. The study of communication is be-coming the science of information transfer. Yet an inescapable and essential part of social life is the formation and maintenance of interpersonal relationships.

In the information age, humans come to know one another and form bonds in a variety of contexts and through a variety of media. Individuals are finding ways to adapt the essential features of interpersonal relation-ships to the changing features of available media technologies. This interaction has never been so important as now when conducting personal and private relationships with others via computer-based channels is not a remote possibility, but a current reality. The advent of virtual reality (VR) promises to create a communication environment that transcends the limitations of all other media developed in the information age. This new technology will bring the immediate and sensually rich domain of the face-to-face encounter into direct contact with the imaginative, artificial, and control-oriented domain of the computer.

This chapter defines a perspective on interpersonal communication and describes how that perspective views the interaction of interpersonal communication and communication technology in general, and virtual reality in particular. The chapter begins by describing a cognitive-affective-behavioral approach to interpersonal communication and the assumptions on which it operates. Next, a brief discussion follows on how the defining features of interpersonal communication map onto characteristics of mediated communication. Finally, the conclusions of these first two sections are applied to a fully-developed and idealized form of virtual reality.

A COGNITIVE-AFFECTIVE-BEHAVIORAL MODEL OF INTERPERSONAL COMMUNICATION

Interpersonal communication is a transactional process in which humans negotiate the nature of their relationships with others. Through the back-and-forth exchange of interactive and interdependent behavioral messages, individuals create mental representations of themselves, others, and the relationship between them. Thus, interpersonal relationships reside in the minds of relational partners but are transacted through observable exchanges of behaviors (Cappella, 1987; Watzlawick, Beavin, & Jackson, 1967). As pointed out by Heim (1993), the Greeks conceptualized the process similarly: "In ancient times the term interface sparked awe and mystery. The archaic Greeks spoke reverently of prosopon, or a face facing another face. Two opposite faces make up a mutual relationship. One face reacts to the other, and the other face reacts to the other's reaction, and the other reacts to that reaction, and so on ad infinitum. The relationship then lives on as a third thing or state of being. The ancient term prosopon once glowed with mystic wonder" (p.78).

While the "mystic wonder" of the interpersonal process may be tempered with "scientific" rationality in our modern technological world, the essential elements of interpersonal communication remain the same. The defining features of interpersonal communication are:

1. Interaction between humans.
2. The formation of cognitive and emotional bonds.
3. Interactive and interdependent negotiations of personal and interpersonal perceptions and cognitions.
4. A process in which nonobservable cognitive and affective phenomena are linked to observable behavioral interactions.

I will briefly describe each of these features in order to better discuss how media technologies (including VR) affect interpersonal communication.

Human to Human Communication

Interpersonal communication is communication about relationships between human beings. This is not to deny that relationships can exist between people and machines or between people and animals, nor that such relationships may appear to be "interpersonal" in some respects, but rather it is to accept a useful vanity describing the focus of theory and research among scholars and lay persons alike. I will address this issue again when discussing how interpersonal communication can be mediated by computers.

Interpersonal Relationships and Communication

Of all the possible functions accomplished through the transmission of messages between people, the interpersonal functions concern themselves with the creation, modification and dissolution of affective and cognitive bonds. Appearing on nearly every list of fundamental human activities are seeking or giving affection, creating intimacy or inclusion, and developing a sense of belonging to another person (see Bowlby, 1969; Burgoon & Hale, 1984; Cappella & Street, 1985; Hinde, 1982; Patterson, 1983). These activities and others like them are relational in nature and define emotional and cognitive associations that create the phenomenological sense of being bonded to another.

I will further claim that in *every* human interaction, the participants can not fail to communicate some sense of how they feel about themselves, about their partners, and about the relationship between them (Watzlawick et al., 1967). This claim suggests that in every interaction there are relational negotiations taking place, even if the relational transaction is not the explicit or consciously held purpose of the interaction. Even in a simple meeting between strangers in which one is expressly interested in finding directions from the other, partners will demonstrate their willingness to engage, predisposition to seek and provide help, and their personal idea of who they are (i.e., their "face" as the Greeks would say; see also Goffmann, 1959). From such a simple encounter as this, individuals come away with a sense of how much they liked the other and whether they would be willing to meet with them again. Thus, relational communication is pervasive in our social encounters.

Interdependence and Interaction

Another defining feature of interpersonal communication is that it represents an interdependent exchange or negotiation of relational information (Cappella, 1985; Leary, 1955; Palmer & Lack, 1994; Watzlawick et al.,

1967). This perspective assumes the back-and-forth exchange of relational messages between interaction partners constitutes a process by which an interpersonal relationship is defined and redefined. For example, Person A observes the behaviors of Person B, and based on what A already knows about B, about how the behaviors are typically used, and the social context of the interaction, A will infer something about the relational value of the behaviors. This inference will then guide A in selecting behavioral responses that seem appropriate. B will then observe A's responses and engage in a similar process resulting in new responses from B, and so on. With each behavioral message one partner is making a relational bid that represents his or her view of the relationship. The other then must accept, reject or modify this bid by producing a behavioral response influencing the state of the relationship (Watzlawick et al., 1967). Thus, interpersonal communication is interactive and transactional in nature, and the exchange of messages is interdependent.[1]

Cognitions and Behaviors

From this perspective, interpersonal relationships reside in the minds of relational partners and behaviors gain meaning when partners perceive, identify, and interpret those behaviors. Such interpretations or inferences provide mental models of the current state of the relationship that can be compared to desired goal states. On the basis of such comparisons, behavioral responses may be selected in an effort to modify the current state to bring it in line with expectations or desires. Representations of the relational partners and the state of the relationship may also guide ongoing interactions or be stored in long-term memory to be accessed at some later time.

This claim is not to imply that human interactants are always *consciously* involved in interpretation and behavioral selection processing. Indeed, it is widely believed that a large portion of social behavior, including communication behaviors is automatically triggered and enacted (Bargh, 1989; Kellermann, 1992; Palmer & Simmons, 1993). Often, the actual transaction of a relationship is occurring through behavioral exchanges that are not observable in a verbal transcript, but must be attended to in other channels. Subtle, nonverbal behaviors (including eye gaze, smiles, hand gestures, posture, speech duration, speech rate, head nods, and more) are the channels by which a large share of affectively changed relational information is conveyed. For example, no matter what the topic of conversation, increases in eye gaze and smiles will show increases in positive regard

---

[1]For definitions of interaction based on probablistic models, see Cappella (1987) and Rafaeli (1988).

(Palmer, Cappella, Patterson, & Churchill, 1990; Palmer & Simmons, 1993). These exchanges often occur outside of the conscious awareness of interactants rendering the relational transaction automatic.

In a recent study, we asked pairs of strangers to have a discussion about anything they wanted to talk about (Palmer & Simmons, 1993). After about 5 minutes we separated the partners and secretly recruited one of them to carry out an interpersonal task. We asked one person to try to demonstrate more or less friendliness toward their partner in a second interaction with the same partner, and we asked them to do this *without actually saying out loud* how they felt about the other. Results showed that after the second meeting, targets tended to increase or decrease their liking for the confederate in accordance with the confederate's intention. Also, the confederates consistently used a set of nonverbal behaviors (i.e., increases and decreases in eye gaze, smiles, talk duration, and gesturing) to carry their intention, while targets used the same behaviors to decode those intentions. However, when asked to list the behaviors they used to communicate their intentions, only about 50% reported using nonverbal behaviors. Of this 50% less than half (about 25% of the total) were accurate in reporting how they used the nonverbal behaviors. In other words, conversational partners who were clearly aware of their interpersonal goals were very often unaware of the subtle manipulation of behaviors by which those goals were accomplished.

I have tried to describe an approach to interpersonal communication that considers interpersonal relationships to be the product of a cognitive-affective-behavioral process. This approach assumes that interpersonal relationships reside in the minds of relational partners as mental representations of the relationship that include declarative, procedural, and emotionally charged information. it also assumes that these mental representations are the result of an inference-making process based on the information available in behaviors displayed in back-and-forth exchanges of verbal and nonverbal behaviors. Furthermore, these back-and-forth exchanges constitute a negotiation of the relationship and are characterized as interdependent and interactive. The question now arises as to how these features map onto media technologies.

INTERPERSONAL COMMUNICATION AND MEDIA TECHNOLOGY

There is an important distinction that must be made between the concepts of "interpersonal communication" and "media technology." An interpersonal relationship is an abstract, nonobservable object that exists in the minds of relational partners and is created and manifested through interdependent exchanges of behaviors (i.e., interpersonal communication). Media are observable physical channels that provide the means by which behavioral messages are exchanged. If communication is about relationships (explicitly or implicitly), and is based on the interactive and interdependent exchange of messages between humans, then interpersonal communication may logically be carried out through any medium. In its most simplistic form, the discussion is reduced to comparing the features of interpersonal communication with various forms of media to determine how well the media facilitate interpersonal interactions. Therefore, the interaction of media with interpersonal communication is the crossing of the features of interpersonal communication with the features of media. Or, to make the issue more specific, media are suited to interpersonal communication to the extent that their features are isomorphic with the features of interpersonal communication.

This section develops this view of the media–interpersonal interaction by first describing how the face-to-face (FTF) medium has become the "ideal" or paradigmatic medium for interpersonal communication. Next the discussion attempts to demonstrate *in principle,* how the closer media come to replicating the features of FTF, the closer they come to creating an immediate, interactive, and private communication environment where individuals can feel involved in an affective, emotional and involving relational transaction.

The Face-to-Face Ideal

Although it is logically true that any medium may properly facilitate interpersonal communication, I believe it is fair to say that most researchers and scholars tend to consider face-to-face interaction as the paradigmatic social context and medium in which interpersonal processes occurs (Schudson, 1978; but see Rafaeli, 1988). The reasons for this focus have to do with the way individuals develop into social actors and the nature of affective, relational transactions.

First among many possible reasons for this focus may be the fact that FTF contact is the very first mode of interaction known to all humans. Within moments of birth, indeed in the birthing process itself, nonverbal channels (e.g., touch and voice) are communicating subtle relational messages of affiliation between neonate, mother, and attending adults. This social interaction continues in the FTF mode through infancy and toddler years (Stern, 1985). The rich and emotionally charged domain of nonverbal communication is the primary environment through which humans first learn to communicate their desires and needs, including material and affective bonds (Bowlby, 1969; Cappella, 1991). Thus, face-to-face interaction is a primary and prototypical form of communication.

Another reason why FTF modes may be considered to be the paradigm of interpersonal interaction is that individuals rely heavily on the subtle, multichannel display of nonverbal behaviors to glean relational information from their partners (Schudson, 1978). As individuals develop language skills, the range of expression in face-to-face modes of interaction are expanded to include the broad, conscious and explicit forms of expression made possible by language. For the first few years of life, years in which interpersonal as well as instrumental goals are critical (e.g., getting food, making friends, and learning to maneuver safely through life's dangers), individuals learn to use a full range of verbal and nonverbal behaviors to manipulate and maintain their interpersonal and material worlds. As described earlier, the verbal forms tend to become the focus of conscious attention perhaps due to their ability to express complex details of instrumental and task-oriented information. However, the nonverbal behaviors first learned in infancy do not diminish in their importance for communicating emotion and affect and thus remain a critical part of interpersonal communication.

The most intimate messages are often carried nonverbally by tone of voice, facial expressions, or other channels (e.g., Burgoon, Buller, Hale, & deTurck, 1984). The close physical proximity of the face-to-face mode provides the greatest opportunity to experience the maximum number of these subtle channels. Some of the most intimate expressions of affiliation are carried through physical contact or touching and clearly FTF interactions present the best opportunity for this kind of communication.

Also, the multichannel nature of the FTF mode provides opportunities for high redundancy, which means that multiple behaviors can carry the same or similar information. Typically, nonverbal behaviors operate in sets. For example, individuals may communicate liking toward their partner by increasing gaze, smiles and head nods toward them during an interaction. Thus, partners may scan incoming messages from a variety of sources, allowing efficient processing of relational information as well as the often complex and engaging explicit verbal content of the interaction. Moreover, the well practiced nature of nonverbal communication and language use, make the multiple channels of typical FTF interactions virtually "transparent" to the users. The creation and interpretation of relational messages may occur at less than conscious levels, but still efficiently and effectively (Palmer & Simmons, 1993). Thus, individuals gain a sense of directly encountering others and their relational "minds" in FTF encounters.

The multichannel aspects of FTF communication, however, may sometimes be intrusive, creating relational consequences. In some instances, different channels may carry conflicting information simultaneously. For example, when trying to deceive or create irony, smiles showing positive regard may not agree with a tone of voice revealing disdain (Ekman, 1992).

However, any attention drawn to the mixed messages will be interpreted relationally, as in "my partner is lying" or "my partner is making a joke." These inferences in turn are relational in nature and not focussed on the way or manner in which the mixed messages are created. (More on the conscious intrusion of media will follow.)

Thus, the multichannel nature of FTF interactions leads individuals to directly engage their partners with little concern for the physical medium they are using. Partners in FTF encounters have a sense of being part of a relational event. Popular descriptions of ideal encounters might use terms like, "I was really into it" or "he is really *there* when he talks to you," and so on. These terms describe an experience in which the mode is transparent and the relational and informational content of the interaction appears to occur without effort outside of simply "thinking" and "feeling" it. Conversational partners engaged in such interactions are creating a sense of intimate and close bonding with the other.

Interpersonal scholars have developed such concepts as "immediacy" (Andersen, 1985; Mehrabian, 1972), "intimacy" (Argyle & Cook, 1976), and "involvement" (Cappella, 1983; Cegala, Savage, Brunner, & Conrad, 1982) to describe the degree to which conversational behaviors may display relational bonding and engagement. Although these terms are typically used to describe behaviors, it is not difficult to imagine that they also describe a cognitive state in which individuals feel more or less directly "present" in the interaction and in the process by which relationships are being created. This approach implies that the behavioral exchange that constitutes a FTF interaction carries with it a sense of an immediate and intimate sharing of private information. The interaction is a process of self-disclosure of personal information that tells each partner something about the internal state of the other and brings the mental representations closer together to be shared or sometimes rejected (Altman & Taylor, 1973).

Thus, the FTF medium ideally fits the general features of interpersonal communication and has the advantage of being learned early and practiced often throughout our lives. Live, FTF interaction presents a medium conducive to the rapid and often subtle exchange of verbal and nonverbal behaviors that represent the cognitively driven negotiation of relationships. FTF communication provides a sense of immediate and direct involvement with another person, with their thoughts and with their behaviors.

Other Media

As early mediated forms of communication technologies developed in our society they offered individuals a chance to communicate across space and time. Messages could be stored or delayed in their delivery, and they could be sent to individuals removed from the immediate, FTF context. In this way, mediated communication allowed individuals to communicate and form relationships that were otherwise impossible. In exchange for these advances, earlier forms of media technology restricted the interpersonal communicator in terms of available channels of communication. Writing eliminated the visual and vocal nonverbal channels, thus limiting interpersonal expression to what could be explicitly stated in the content, what could be written "between the lines" by manipulating the language (as in a poem), and what could be put into graphic design. Writing as a medium also slowed the response time, thus making interactivity less immediate. Telephones regained the vocal channel and increased the immediacy of responses but eliminated (until recently) the visual channel. Video technologies (VCR, TV, etc.) added the visual to the audio channels but on the whole prevented immediate interactive communication. Touch, which is perhaps the most intimate form of nonverbal communication has been absent in all forms of media technologies to date.

Furthermore, mediated communication has typically represented communication of one-to-many, rather than one-to-one. Face-to-face communication has the ability to reduce interpersonal communication to a private environment shared by two individuals. The interpersonal negotiation of relational bonding often takes place between two people who, for various reasons, desire that the process be secret. For example, intimate, personal information may lead individuals to feel vulnerable or embarrassed, and private tête-à-tête's may be seen as more secure.

Also, conventional media may become intrusive and distract individuals from the smooth and transparent (even nonconscious) processing of relational information. In general, we expect the media to be transparent in interpersonal communication. This means we expect that the media will not be intrusive and the full effect of the relational message can be experienced. Should the media become intrusive and call attention to itself, then attention is shifted from relational-inference making. To the extent that media reflect or match the defining characteristics of interpersonal communication, the likelihood that they will become intrusive is reduced and the more likely human communicators will express interpersonal behaviors and make interpersonal inferences.

In FTF communication we take the medium for granted. We attend to the "delivery" of a message only if some feature of the physical form or structure of the message intrudes on our cognitive processing of the content. For example, if a conversational partner has difficulty using the language, the disruption in the medium will call attention to itself. If this attention leads to interpersonal attributions about the source (for example an inference that the source is angry with us), the transaction of the relationship is not discontinued but is enhanced by this information. In other words the medium and the way it is used can be part of the message. However, if we attribute the disturbance or intrusiveness of the media to a failure of the technology (as with electronic technology or the difficulty of the language itself) then we become distracted from the interaction partner and the interpersonal negotiation.

Let me give an example. Sitting in Soldier Field, watching the Bears and Giants playing football, I glanced up and saw an airplane circling the field towing a banner that said, "I Love You, Sally. Will you marry me? Bill." The novelty that struck and amused me was the fact that this medium (airplane banner), which is usually used to carry persuasive messages (advertising), was being used to carry an interpersonal message. In this case, I was surprised by the mismatch between medium and message and thus, the medium became intrusive. However, the mismatch in this case pointed out the importance of the message and so the medium became part of the message. If I were distracted from processing interpersonal information by attention to the channels themselves (e.g., the words were misspelled or the sign was torn), then the medium would not be transparent and the attributions would have been directed at the medium and its operation rather than the source and the relational consequences. Thus, most forms of mediated communication appear to "distance" individuals from one another by placing restrictions on the channels available to interactants or by distracting users from processing relational information by requiring attention to maintaining or controlling the medium. Advances in communication technologies have been useful in closing distance and time, but on the whole tend to remove individuals from direct access to behavioral transactions in which multiple verbal and nonverbal cues are interactively and transparently orchestrated in real time.

Theoretically speaking, any medium is capable of carrying relational information and adopting capabilities that serve one or more of the features of interpersonal communication. Face-to-face communication would appear to remain the *idealized* form of interpersonal communication, embodying all the features that humans developed to facilitate the rapid, explicit, and implicit negotiation of relational information. Most media, as we have known them, have been capable of carrying interpersonal information and of facilitating interpersonal relationships, but the features of interpersonal communication have evolved directly out of the FTF environment.

Computer-Mediated Communication

Theorists and researchers concerned with computer-mediated communication (CMC) also generally view FTF as the ideal form of interpersonal communication. Most of the approaches to studying this mode of communication have assumed that computer interaction is written; that is, messages created on a computer keyboard and read on a CRT. Consequently, scholars and researchers often focus on the social aspects of computerized communication by directly or indirectly comparing CMC to face-to-face communication (Brittan, 1992). For example, CMC is considered to restrict "social presence" (Culnan & Markus, 1987; Short, Williams, & Christie, 1976), have less "media richness" (Trevino, Daft, & Lengel, 1990), and lack "social context cues" (Sproull & Kiesler, 1986) when compared to FTF modes. To summarize, it is believed that CMC restricts the number of channels, specifically nonverbal vocal and kinesic ones, and thus limits interpersonal and social information. The increased real-time, interactive capabilities of the medium are not generally considered to be important *interpersonally*. In accordance, experiments have shown that compared to FTF, CMC is often described as cold and unsociable (Hiltz, Johnson, & Turoff, 1986), less preferable for developing relationships and resolving conflict (Rice, 1984), and more prone to negative emotional content (Kiesler, Zubrow, Moses, & Geller, 1985; Rice & Love, 1987). In general, most theorists have suggested that CMC is the chosen vehicle for task-oriented communication and problem-solving (Phillips & Santoro, 1989; Rice, 1984).

However, this view may be extreme in its claims. Individuals use CMC formats that have interpersonal or relational effects (see Walther, 1992). Some evidence does exist indicating that humans find the means to carry on interpersonal transactions in the CMC format. For example, e-mail participants may "carbon copy" superiors when trying to exert influence over their mediated discussions with peers (Phillips & Eisenberg, 1989). Also, some individuals who are more experienced and practiced in using CMC, rate CMC as "richer" than other media, including FTF (Steinfield, 1986), and over time, report more strongly developed impressions of their communication partners than in other media (Walter, 1993). Anecdotal evidence (Rheingold, 1993) and participant observation studies (Bruckman, 1992; Bruckman & Resnick, 1993) also demonstrate how individuals involved in short-term and long-term interactions via computer networks develop "personalities" and interpersonal relationships with others.

Rheingold (1993) has recently published a personal account of his experiences with The Well, a public computer network. He amply demonstrates the existence of an electronic community of individuals who exchange information, create and destroy friendships, provide material help and assistance, and even announce their intentions to commit suicide through their ongoing interactions via computerized mail. The computer network in this instance has been commandeered from the purely instrumental task of transferring task-relevant information and transformed into a "virtual community." Rheingold (1993) described his feeling about The Well in this way: "There's always another mind there. It's like having the corner bar, complete with old buddies and delightful newcomers and new tools waiting to take home and fresh graffiti and letters, except instead of putting on my coat, shutting down the computer and walking down to the corner, I just invoke my telecom program and there they are. It's a place" (p. 24). Thus, humans are social by nature and communication *by any means* may offer an opportunity to develop social relationships. As long as two humans are using a CMC medium, even if it is limited in channel capacity to written forms, they will find ways to make the medium interpersonal. Thus, CMC can mediate interpersonal communication, but in its most widespread form it does not approach the FTF ideal in providing access to the full range of interpersonal communication features.

The Interface

When the Greeks discussed communication as an "interface," or *prosopon* (Heim, 1993), they meant to describe a process where individuals created relationships through the exchange of messages about their own and their partners' self-images. For the Greeks the interface between people was the FTF interaction. For modern scholars and technicians, an "interface" usually is the means or medium by which humans access computers. The conclusions we have reached about CMC thus far are based on the extent to which users adapt it to an interactive, interdependent relational transaction; NOT to the extent to which computers can mimic human behaviors. Humans do not have interpersonal relationships with computers, but with other humans.

It can be argued that human behavior is so dominated by a social orientation that they will attempt to form relationships and communication "interpersonal" with any *object* that presents a sense of interactivity or interpersonal intentions. For example, Rafaeli (1987) reported that people prefer to solve problems with partners who are more interactive than not, whether those partners are humans or computers. Also, Nass (Nass & Steuer, 1993) recently demonstrated that anthropomorphizing computer responses increases the likelihood that human operators will develop attitudes, social orientations and preferences among computers. Thus, humans have a propensity for interpersonal and interpersonal-like reaction and may be prone to transforming man–machine interactions into "interpersonal-like" contexts when media present subsets of cues or features resembling the features of interpersonal communication and FTF interaction. In other words, humans are social animals with well-developed instincts for social interaction that naturally respond in kind to cues resembling social communication.

Designers of computers and computer-assisted systems have attempted to capitalize on the human propensity for social interaction by anthropomorphizing the interfaces between humans and machines. "User-friendly" interfaces tend to exploit humans' natural language or iconic recognition abilities in trying to create interfaces that fit human expectations of how communication works. Artificially intelligent machines ultimately must communicate with humans in modes that are readily understood and manipulated by a species that is adept at natural language processing and symbol manipulation. However, to date there are no computers that are capable of initiating interactions with humans for the purpose of satisfying "personal" needs for affective bonding. Although forms of human–machine interaction may resemble interpersonal interactions when interfaces are patterned after human communication, this resemblance is not sufficient to define interpersonal communication.

In assessing the degree to which media are compatible with interpersonal interaction, *all* of the features of interpersonal communication must be kept in mind. Interpersonal relationships exist between people and are negotiated in interactive exchanges of behaviors in which both parties are consciously or nonconsciously processing information based on behavioral displays. A human-like interface means only that designers are accommodating the human propensity for social interaction and symbolic communication. It may mean that humans will appear to have a relationship with a computer, but it can not mean that the computer will have a relationship with the human. In the end, there is no genuine negotiation of a relationship through a transactional exchange of relationally charged messages. Consequently, creating an interface that mimics human-to-human interaction is not the ultimate criteria for interpersonal communication.

Having established the face that human–machine communication is not interpersonal communication, it is safe to say that there are certain advantages to "interpersonalizing" the interface. Clearly, humans will find the interaction with computers more comfortable and perhaps more appealing if the machines adapt human interaction patterns and behaviors (Nass & Steuer, 1993). Adding multiple channels of access to the computer's "mind" and multiple channels by which the computer can "talk" to the user will provide greater "user-friendly" benefits in terms of ease of use and productive interactions.

There are also potential dangers to developing human-like interfaces. As computer presentations become more well-developed it will be possible to simulate all forms of human communication. Voice-responsive computer systems are now available for the office and home market, and of course there is the coming of VR. When interfaces become indistinguishable from interaction with humans, the phenomenon Bates (1992) called the "Eliza Effect" will be more prevalent. This phenomenon was demonstrated in the well known studies in which humans came to believe they were interacting with a "real" human when in fact they were interacting with a computerized set of outputs engineered to be similar to human responses.

The danger in the Eliza Effect is that there is a real potential for abusing users' rights to free choice and privacy when the interaction is being represented as human-to-human rather than what it is, human-to-machine. In these cases, programmers may practice deceptions that take unfair advantage of the human user. Such deceptions are not unknown in human-to-human communication since individuals naturally conceal ideas and feelings from one another all the time. When a computer provides complete control over the communication channels, individuals are deprived of the opportunity to detect the many and varied verbal and nonverbal cues that are nonintentionally leaked by deceivers in FTF interactions (Ekman, 1992). Thus, the natural inclination of humans to engage in social interaction may lead users to readily accept a computer response as originating from another person when in fact, the computer responds by selecting or synthesizing a message unrelated to interpersonal or instrumental needs of the user. Under these conditions, users must beware of the computer's potential to be the consummate charlatan, magician, liar and dishonest salesperson.

Yet one product of the quest for this same anthropomorphic interface is the VR media, which may create a total environment capable of true and genuine interpersonal communication that rivals, if not surpasses, the FTF mode! The differences between a well developed interface and interpersonal communication through virtual reality, lie in the application of the multi-channel, real-time interface to human-to-human interaction. Thus, VR mediates interpersonal relationships by providing a human-like, anthropomorphized interface bringing two *people* together, rather than machines and people.

VIRTUAL REALITY, CYBERSPACE
AND INTERPERSONAL RELATIONSHIPS

With the dawning of the age of virtual reality, media technologies are appearing that promise to transform interpersonal communication to the very extent of our imaginations. VR will provide the traditional benefits of electronic media by bringing people together across space and time and will also provide all of the features of interpersonal communication by faithfully simulating the ideal FTF medium. Designers and developers of virtual reality environments are developing a medium that will do more than be isomorphic with the features of interpersonal communication. VR will eventually provide the means by which interactants will transcend the real and create communication environments that are hyper-real.

The mediation of interpersonal interaction in virtual environments is *in principle* no different than interactions that occur through any other medium. VR is compatible with interpersonal communication to the extent that individuals can encounter another "social presence" or person (Heeter, 1992) in a virtual environment, and effectively negotiate a relationship through an interdependent, multichannel exchange of behaviors. Therefore, virtual reality can be evaluated as a medium of interpersonal communication in the same way all media have been evaluated.

Like other media, VR allows individuals to communicate and conduct interpersonal exchanges across time and space. It is an interactive, multichannel communication environment and therefore allows a wide range of verbal and nonverbal interpersonal messages to be created. However, the expansion and control over those channels will transform media from a way to link two individuals in *different places,* to a way to put two individuals *in the same place.* That place is *cyberspace,* a simulated environment where communicators in different places and different times can meet "face-to-face."

The main difference between VR and conventional media is in VR's ability to realistically simulate the elements of face-to-face interactions by providing sensual stimuli that are *vritually* equivalent to those in verbal and nonverbal channels. High-fidelity audio channels will present the human voice with all of the subtle intonations in pitch and volume that carry information about the internal emotional states of the interactants (Scherer, 1988). Enhanced video will show detailed representations of facial displays that also reveal nonverbal information relating to emotions and important cues about deception and interpersonal attraction (Cappella & Palmer, 1991; Ekman, 1982). Also, VR may someday include the ability to communicate touch and thus allow the medium to carry the most intimate and powerful of all nonverbal indicators of relational involvement (Thayer, 1986; see Rheingold, 1991).

Also the VR environment has the potential to provide these multiple communication channels in real time, in an interactive setting. In other words communication partners will be able to enact and observe the full range of conversational behaviors as they occur immediately. Patterns of interaction and mutual influence are critical to interpersonal communication and are never so important as they are in the rapid exchange of conversational behaviors in face-to-face interaction (Cappella & Street, 1985). Thus, VR users engaging in communication mediated through virtual space will be carrying on a FTF interaction in every way isomorphic with an actual interaction except that all the sensations of their bodies in the environment are simulated. Thus, VR as a medium promises to create a means of conducting interpersonal negotiations that is most like face-to-face interactions, and therefore most "interpersonal" among all media.

Of course this line of reasoning assumes that VR will continue to be developed as a fully operating sensory interface, and that it will be used for communication between humans, rather than only between humans and machines. If users will conduct interpersonal communication in the VR environment, they will be conducting FTF interactions as conducted person-to-person in "real" space. In VR, the interface is interfacing people (as proposed by the Greeks) and not interface people with machines.

One result of increasing the richness of sensory stimulation is an increase in the levels of subject involvement experienced by participants. Increasing this sense of involvement has been a goal of VR developers who envision a medium that enhances users' experiences of "telepresence," or the feeling of actually being in a virtual environment (Biocca, 1992; Sheridan, 1992; Steuer, 1992). As defined by Sheridan (1992), this presence is "experienced by a person when sensory information generated only by and within a computer and associated display technology compels a feeling of being present in the environment other than the one the person is actually in" (p. 279). The success of "telepresence" in VR is determined by the degree to which real-environmental sensations can be simulated while keeping the medium and its technologies transparent in the experience (Held & Durlach, 1992). To this end, designers, engineers, programmers and psychologists talk of users' "immersion" in the environment (i.e., total sensory contact with the environment) and their ability to "navigate" or move themselves and other objects, in the virtual world (Rheingold, 1991; Sheridan, 1992b; Zeltzer, 1992). VR creates a sense of physical closeness with the environment in which communication takes place, including a sense of being in the presence of other users.

Therefore, one of the promises of VR technologies is to create the completely transparent interface. Individuals will control their communication and the instruments creating that communication by simply performing the "normal" communication behaviors in the normal way. For example, to communicate a smile, hand gestures, and touch, one would only have to smile, gesture, and reach out to touch the other. The technology would take care of simulating the actions faithfully, *and* providing the expected responses — a smile, a gesture, and touch from the partner. The sense of "presence" created by this medium may eventually be unencumbered by extra-communicative behavior such as finding objects that only approximate a desired action among a menu of other available and approximate actions. Current communication technologies also have the ability to become transparent after users become experts. For example, most of us do not think about the keyboard as we type letters on e-mail. Yet it is still relatively easy to tune into the click of the keys and to notice the transposition of letters as we hastily try to capture a fleeting idea. There is still little if any isomorphism between moving the fingers on the keyboard to form one letter at a time, and the complex multichannel creation of spontaneous speech.

The enhanced interface of VR will bring users the same transparent, automatic and easy facility that they already possess in the FTF mode. Appropriately designed technologies will free communication at a distance from the intrusion of special computer skills or even elementary knowledge of the devices that make it possible. Therefore, VR technologies will present the most advanced form of interpersonal media yet developed by providing multichannel, multisensory and real-time interactive capabilities simulating all of the features of interpersonal interactions in FTF encounters.

However, the most challenging and important aspects of VR lie in the ability of the medium to create realities that are *different* than the "true" reality experienced or known by the user. VR is based on technologies that will ultimately be able to re-create any environment down to the smallest detail by rendering that environment into computer-controlled images and machine-induced sensations. For example, two people located in different northern cities during the worst blizzard in a decade, may decide to hold a conversation in the virtually warm simulated sunshine of a southern city. Furthermore, those people may decide that they should represent them-selves as dressed in beach clothes to suit the virtual weather. Or, these same people may decide that they should show themselves suitably tanned for the occasion. Nothing, in fact, prevents the VR user from presenting him or herself in any physical form. A complete physical alias is possible for the competent user, including morphological shapes ranging from extraterres-trial to human (Rheingold, 1991). In other words, the power of the computer to digitize and simulate VR environments will provide the opportunity for users to be creative and adaptive in their forms of expression. From the interpersonal perspective, the ability to transform one's self means a greater latitude and freedom in choosing a self-image to present to an interaction partner.

Expressing a concern for self-image and self-presentation is clearly a very human trait (Goffman, 1959). Social actors expend considerable conscious energy attempting to manage and present acceptable images of themselves through their forms of dress, personal habits and manner of speech. Managing a personal image is part of all interpersonal transactions, and this means part of nearly all social encounters. Individuals who spend their time interacting on computer networks know the power of being able to manipulate others' perceptions and create new identities that may enhance their own self-image or perhaps better project their personal messages. Some online networks already invite personality constructions and aliases (Bruckman, 1992; Rheingold, 1993; Walther, 1993). With the advent of VR, users will no longer be limited to creating self-images in written formats, but will have the opportunity to make three-dimensional, fully interactive and fully aware (i.e., sensing) simulations of any image they would care to project. The limits on the type of image presented will be defined only by the limits of the imagination of the user.

This discussion of VR's enhanced power to manipulate images and create realistic presence will undoubtedly recall the questions of responsibility and ethics in interpersonal communication raised earlier. The ability to deceive and manipulate others by providing false impressions of one's self will be available with every VR communication machine. With some practice, those who may not be good at controlling their FTF behaviors will have professional help from designers and programmers in creating flawless, albeit deceptive, self-images. In VR environments that are so real users will forget that they are operating in virtual space, the potential to lead and mislead others is heightened by the ability to control and suppress cues that might otherwise leak important interpersonal information. VR, with its powerful multichannel ability to create telepresence, increases the potential for losing awareness of the artificiality of the situation. At this level of "transparency," the medium has the greatest potential for abusing power and more users are at risk of falling victim to traps and deceptions that they will undoubtedly encounter.

On the other hand, consider the advantages of producing images that are not truthful representations of the "natural" state of affairs. If one goal of communication is to create relationships in the "real world" that conform with our ideal mental models of those relationships, then the power of VR is made to order. In the movie *Annie Hall,* the hero, played by Woody Allen, tells his girlfriend that he "lerves" her, because "love" is a word totally inadequate to describe his true feelings. To the extend that VR provides the user with control over the shapes, forms, and textures of his or her world, there may be less frustration at finding adequate means to express mental and emotional states that transcend the "simple," conventional modes of communication. As Rheingold (1991) pointed out, computers are machines that "extend" the mind by allowing users to manipulate symbols (and "thought") in forms that can be directly applied to the external world and to other beings. VR promises to extend the mind into levels of object-based abstractions that most language-based modes cannot allow.

Also, the environmental control offered by VR may allow individuals who have communication deficits and disabilities to discover interfaces that let them regain power over the physical modes of expression that they have been denied. Others who may have no physical handicaps, but find it difficult to express themselves in "mere" words will be provided with a multidimensional palette with which to "paint" their messages free of the restrictions of language. VR may provide us with a rich environment that finds common ground across differences in age, culture, and linguistic orientation.

In short, VR will provide a communication environment in which the dangers of deception and the benefits of creativity are amplified beyond the levels that humans currently experience in their interpersonal interactions.

The possibilities for positive and negative outcomes are still the same in terms of the human process of creating and transacting interpersonal relationships. What will be different are the means to effectively enact those transactions. Still, it is not clear that the potential will be always used or even welcome.

In spite of the expressive power of VR, it is possible that social actors will not indiscriminately choose VR to conduct all their interpersonal business. There is some evidence that users of CMC are making choices about when to use current computer communication technology. For example, Rheingold's (1993) e-mail community, which accomplishes so much interpersonal communication via the Well, finds it important to meet face-to-face at least once each year to see what their communication partners are like in those situations. Also, some studies have shown that individuals in work situations might begin to discuss new plans and new ideas through multimedia networks, but prefer to further develop the details of these plans in face-to-face meetings (Brittan, 1992). Thus, FTF interaction appears to be preferred over conventional audiovisual modes at some point in the development of interpersonal or work relationships.

The choice of when to use VR for interpersonal communication will be more complex. It is my guess that strangers and intimates will be the least attracted to VR as a standard mode of communication. Strangers and those who have reason not to trust their conversational partners may feel concerns about possible manipulation and deception aided by VR's potential for control. On the other hand, intimates who have every reason to trust their partners may find that even the best VR environment with the finest sensory features still does not produce the same physical and mental qualities they find in the FTF mode. Relationships may begin and continue to be maintained in VR communication, but when there is real risk to the relationship, or when there are threats to the individuals, or when the communication is critical, partners may wish to "see with their own eyes and hear with their own ears" face-to-face. Even when partners trust each other, for historical, evolutionary, or other reasons, important relational communication is often reserved for FTF transmission. Our culture (the majority) may find it difficult ever to accept machine-mediated interaction as a substitute for intimate, face-to-face encounters.

On the other hand the appeal of VR to begin, maintain, and develop our interpersonal relationships will be undeniable for the majority of our interpersonal interactions. VR will provide an opportunity for individuals to experiment with modes of self-presentation that will be particularly useful when trying to explain to others what we feel about ourselves or about them. For those who have a clear "base-line" knowledge of their VR partner, creative license taken with manipulating self-images and the environment will be seen as another form of expression in which partners can re-create themselves in contrast to what is expected and already known about them. In this case, there is no deception. In fact, the added power of expression will ultimately enable interpersonal problems to be "seen" and acted out in cyberspace where they can be "tinkered" with and manipulated by both parties.

Of course, any interaction in which the multichannel display of verbal and nonverbal behaviors is interactive, immediate, and interdependent will engender a negotiation of an interpersonal relationship. Regardless of the intention with which individuals will take up VR communication, the result will in some way be interpersonal. Relationships will be formed whenever two people meet in cyberspace. Hence, the ultimate power to control expression will be in the hands of anyone willing to learn the interface.

This book is about the dawning of an age brought on by a medium in which users may directly create and experience multidimensional messages which take on the proportions of "reality." In the new age, the primitive needs and goals of humans will not have changed, nor will the importance of interpersonal interaction in achieving those goals. However, what will be different is the power of expression brought to bear on the interpersonal task. In the age of VR, face-to-face communication may no longer appear to be the richest or most immediate form of interpersonal communication. After all, any person who is allowed to use a medium that will provide total freedom of expression by becoming an extension of their own mind and their own personality may find the restraints and restrictions of face-to-face communication too confining. But it is becoming less profitable to spend much time discussing whether individuals will use VR or not, for if it exists, they will certainly use it. Time is better spent in creating forums such as this book in which communication scientists begin to extend their thoughts and theories to include a form of communication that changes the "face" of human interaction.

REFERENCES

Altman, I., & Taylor, D. A. (1973). *Social penetration.* New York: Holt, Rinehart & Winston.

Andersen, P. A. (1985). Nonverbal immediacy in interpersonal communication. In A. W. Siegman & S. Feldstein (Eds.), *Multichannel integrations of nonverbal behavior* (pp. 1–36). Hillsdale, NJ: Lawrence Erlbaum Associates.

Argyle, M., & Cook, M. (1976). *Gaze and mutual gaze.* London: Cambridge University Press.

Bargh, J. A. (1989). Conditional automaticity: Varieties of automatic influence in social perception and cognition. In J. S. Uleman & J. A. Bargh (Eds.), *Unintended thought* (pp. 3–51). New York: Guilford.

Bates, J. (1992). Virtual reality, art, and entertainment. *Presence: Teleoperators and Virtual Environments, 1*(1), 133–137.

Biocca, F. (1992). Communication within virtual reality: Creating a space for research. *Journal of Communication, 42*(4), 5–22.

Bowlby, J. (1969). *Attachment and loss.* New York: Basic Books.

Brittan, D. (1992). Being there: The promise of multimedia communication. *Technology Review, 95*(4), 42–50.

Bruckman, J. A. (1992). *Identity workshop: Emergent social and psychological phenomena in text-based virtual reality.* MIT Media Laboratory.

Bruckman, J. A., & Resnick, M. (1993). *Virtual professional community: Results form the MediaMOO Project.* MIT Media Laboratory.

Burgoon, J. K., Buller, D. B., Hale, J. L., & deTurck, M. A. (1984). Relational messages associated with nonverbal behaviors. *Human Communication Research, 10*(3), 351–378.

Burgoon, J. K., & Hale, J. L. (1984). The fundamental topoi of relational communication. *Communication Monographs, 51,* 193–214.

Cappella, J. N. (1983). Conversational involvement: Approaching and avoiding others. In J. M. Wiemann & R. P. Harrison (Eds.), *Nonverbal interaction* (pp. 113–148). Newbury Park, CA: Sage.

Cappella, J. N. (1985). The relevance of the microstructure of interaction to relationship change. *Journal of Social and Personal Relationships, 1,* 239–264.

Cappella, J. N. (1987). Interpersonal communication: Definitions and fundamental questions. In C. R. Berger & S. H. Chaffee (Eds.), *Handbook of communication science* (pp. 184–238). Newbury Park: Sage.

Cappella, J. N. (1991). The biological origins of automated patterns of human interaction. *Communication Theory, 1,* 4–35.

Cappella, J. N., & Palmer, M. T. (1991). Attitude similarity, relational history, and attraction: The mediating effects of kinesic and vocal behaviors. *Communication Monographs, 57,* 161–183.

Cappella, J. N., & Street, R. L. (1985). Introduction: A functional approach to the structure of communicative behavior. In R. L. Street & J. N. Cappella (Eds.), *Sequence and pattern in communicative behavior* (pp. 1–129). Baltimore: Edward Arnold.

Cegala, D. J., Savage, G. T., Brunner, C. C., & Conrad, A. B. (1982). An elaboration of the meaning of interaction involvement: Toward the development of a theoretical concept. *Communication Monographs, 49,* 229–248.

Culnan, M. J., & Markus, M. L. (1987). Information technologies. In F. M. Jablin, L. L. Putnam, K. H. Roberts, & L. W. Porter (Eds.), *Handbook of organizational communication: An interdisciplinary perspective* (pp. 420–443). Newbury Park, CA: Sage.

Ekman, P. (1982). *Emotion in the human face.* Cambridge: Cambridge University Press.

Ekman, P. (1992). *Telling lies: Clues to deceit in the marketplace, politics, and marriage.* New York: Norton.

Goffman, E. (1959). The presentation of self in everyday life. Garden City, NY: Anchor.

Heeter, C. (1992). Being there: The subjective experience of presence. *Presence: Teleoperators and Virtual Environments, 1*(2), 262–274.

Heim, M. (1993). *The metaphysics of virtual reality.* NY: Oxford University Press.

Held, R. M., & Durlach, N. I. (1992). Telepresence. *Presence: Teleoperators and Virtual Environments, 1*(1), 109 112.

Hiltz, S. R., Johnson, K., & Turoff, M. (1986). Experiments in group decision making: Communication process and outcome in face-to-face versus computerized conferences. *Human Communication Research, 13,* 225–252.

Hinde, R. Q. (1982). Attachment: Some conceptual and biological issues. In J. Stevenson-Hinde & C. M. Parkes (Eds.), *The place of attachment in human behavior* (pp. 60–76). New York: Basic Books.

Kellermann, K. (1992). Communication: Inherently strategic and primarily automatic. *Communication Monographs, 59,* 288–300.

Kiesler, S., Zubrow, D., Moses, A. M., & Geller, W. (1985). Affect in computer-mediated communication. *Human Computer Interaction, 1,* 77–104.

Leary, T. (1955). The theory and measurement methodology of interpersonal communication. *Psychiatry, 18,* 147–161.

Mehrabian, A. (1972). *Nonverbal communication.* Chicago: Aldine-Atherton.

Nass, C., & Steuer, J. (1993). Voices, boxes, and sources of messages: Computers and social actors. *Human Communication Research, 19*(4), 504–527.

Palmer, M. T., Cappella, J. N., Patterson, M. L., & Churchill, M. (1990, June). *A multifunctional-multibehavioral analysis of nonverbal behaviors in conversational settings.* Paper presented to the International Communication Association Annual Meeting, Dublin.

Palmer, M. T., & Lack, A. M. (1994). Topics, turns and interpersonal control: using serial judgment methods. In J. E. Aitken (Ed.), *A reader in intrapersonal communication processes* (pp. 259–274). Pittsburgh, PA: Mellen Press.

Palmer, M. T., & Simmons, K. B. (1993, November). *Interpersonal intentions, nonverbal behaviors and judgments of liking: Encoding, decoding and consciousness.* Paper presented to the Speech Communication Association, Annual Meeting, Miami.

Patterson, M. L. (1983). *Nonverbal behavior: A functional perspective.* New York: Springer-Verlag.

Phillips, S. R., & Eisenberg, E. M. (1989). *The persuasive use of electronic mail in organizations.* Paper presented to the International Communication Association, annual meeting, San Francisco.

Phillips, G. M., & Santoro, G. M. (1989). Teaching group discussion via computer-mediated communication. *Communication Education, 38,* 151–161.

Rafaeli, S. (1987). *Nasty, naive, neutral or nice: Reactions to interactive manipulations in a computerized prisoners' dilemma game.* Unpublished manuscript.

Rafaeli, S. (1988). Interactivity: From new media to communication. In R. P. Hawkins, J. M. Wiemann, & S. Pingree (Eds.), *Advancing communication science: Merging mass and interpersonal processes* (pp. 110–134). Newbury Park, CA: Sage.

Rheingold, H. (1991). *Virtual reality.* NY: Summit.

Rheingold, H. (1993). *The virtual community: Homesteading on the electronic frontier.* Reading, MA: Addison-Wesley.

Rice, R. E. (1984). Mediated group communication. In R. E. Rice & Associates (Eds.), *The new media: Communication, research, and technology* (pp. 129–156). Beverly Hills, CA: Sage.

Rice, R. E., & Love, G. (1987). Electronic emotion: Socioemotional content in a computer-mediated network. *Communication Research, 14,* 85–108.

Scherer, K. R. (1988). *Facets of emotion: Recent research.* Hillsdale, NJ: Lawrence Erlbaum Associates.

Schudson, M. (1978). The ideal of conversation in the study of mass media. *Communication Research, 5*(3), 320–329.

Sheridan, T. B. (1992). Musings on telepresence and virtual presence. *Presence: Teleoperators and Virtual Environments, 1*(1), 120–12.

Short, J., Williams, E., & Christie, B. (1976). *The social psychology of telecommunications.* London: Wiley.

Sproull, L., & Kiesler, S. (1986). Reducing social context cues: Electronic mail in organizational communication. *Management Science, 32,* 1492–1512.

Steinfeld, C. W. (1986). Computer-mediated communication in an organizational setting: Explaining task-related and socioemotional uses. In M. L. McLaughlin (Ed.), *Communication yearbook 9* (pp. 777–804). Newbury Park, CA: Sage.

Stern, D. N. (1985). *The interpersonal world of the infant.* New York: Basic Books.

Steuer, J. (1992). Defining virtual reality: Dimensions determining telepresence. *Journal of Communication, 42*(4), 73–93.

Thayer, S. (1986). Touch: Frontier of intimacy. *Journal of Nonverbal Behavior, 10,* 7–11.

Trevino, L. K., Daft, R. L., & Lengel, R. H. (1990). Understanding managers' media choices:

A symbolic interactionist perspective. In J. Fulk & C. Steinfeld (Eds.), *Organizations and communication technology* (pp. 71–94). Newbury Park, CA: Sage.

Walther, J. (1992). Interpersonal effects in computer-mediated interaction: A relational perspective. *Communication Research, 19*(1), 52–89.

Walther, J. (1993). Impression development in computer-mediated interaction. *Western Journal of Communication 57*(4), 381–398.

Watzlawick, P., Beavin, J. H., & Jackson, D. D. (1967). *Pragmatics of human communication: A study of interactional patterns, pathologies and paradoxes.* NY: Norton.

Zeltzer, D. (1992). Autonomy, interaction, and presence. *Presence: Teleoperators and Virtual Environments, 1*(1), 127–132.

III THE SOCIAL REALITY
OF VIRTUAL REALITY

11

Virtual Diffusion or an Uncertain Reality: Networks, Policy, and Models for the Diffusion of VR Technology

Thomas W. Valente
The Johns Hopkins University

Thierry Bardini
University of Montréal

Widespread diffusion of virtual reality (VR) technology is likely to occur over the next several decades. The present chapter discusses the factors likely to affect the speed and character of VR diffusion. The chapter is of interest to marketers interested in predicting the potential market for VR as well as scholars and researchers interested in technology development and social change.

Virtual reality, for our purposes, is defined broadly as the technological system aimed at creating an electronically simulated environment in which the user experiences a sense of presence. Recently, numerous definitions of VR have been proposed (Benedikt, 1991; Biocca, 1992b; Krueger, 1991; Pimentel & Teixeira, 1993; Robinett, 1992; Steuer, this volume). Our definition of VR, agrees with Steuer's view (this volume) that, at this stage of VR's diffusion, VR should be seen as "experiential" rather than "technological." The rationale for such a definition is that VR technology is not yet stable, and is still being negotiated by a network of inventors and innovators.

Another major feature of this definition is that the user becomes the focal point of our research. Focusing on the potential user of VR emphasizes that successful diffusion will probably depend on whether networks of inventors and shapers of VR are successful in reaching out to the network of potential VR adopters. Although the inventors of VR will shape VR technology, early VR users will also be influential shapers (and stabilizers) of VR technology. The effort of predicting the diffusion of such a complex and multipurpose set of technologies and individuals provides a means to understand the dynamic relationships between the networks involved in the process.

303

The opening section of this chapter presents three factors most likely to affect the diffusion of VR: technology, policy and social networks. These factors will either facilitate or impede diffusion of VR systems, and thus form the basis for our presentation of various VR diffusion scenarios. The second section presents the stages in the diffusion process: (a) awareness, (b) trial, and (c) adoption; and the mathematical models that predict the timing of each of these stages.

The general approach is to sketch the factors most likely to affect VR diffusion, then in the later section present mathematical functions that describe and predict the timing of these stages. In each case we present different diffusion scenarios ranging from optimistic to pessimistic. This diffusion exercise combines possible technological scenarios with formal models of forecasting (Klopfenstein, 1989; Martino, 1983) in order to better inform the prediction of VR diffusion (Schnaars, 1989).

FACTORS THAT WILL AFFECT VR DIFFUSION

It is important to understand that prior to diffusion, most technologies are researched during the course of basic science for decades. As these technologies appear on the market, technology forecasters and historians debate the impact of this new technology, and inevitably compare the new technology with older communication and technological change process.[1] Two themes in this literature are that: (a) the course of diffusion is influenced and structured by social systems and actors in interaction, and (b) innovations diffuse according to known mathematical models (presented below).

The technology development literature has generally shown that technologies ready for market introduction often take a long time, but once the technology is developed, other factors affect its rate of diffusion in the open market. VR technology has been under development in R&D labs for over 25 years (Rheingold, 1991). The technology has been researched and envisioned by VR gurus to the point now where it is ripe for demonstrations, and musing by researchers such as ourselves. Like other communication technologies there are expectations of wondrous technological utopia to be found in the cyberspace landscape and concerns and trepidations over inevitable problems (Biocca 1992a). Regardless of these prognostications, VR technology will diffuse. The central question is: How will VR diffuse?

---

[1]Examples include: Innis (1951), Bell (1973), Winner (1977), Eisenstein (1979), Czitrom (1982), de Sola Pool (1983), Carey and Moss (1985), Mackenzie and Wajcman (1985), Beniger (1986), Perrolle (1987), Dutton, Blumler, and Kraemer (1987), Marvin (1988), and Carey (1988).

In other words, which individuals are likely to be early or later users of VR, how long will this diffusion process take, and what factors will determine the eventual shape of VR technology?

A host of variables have been found to be associated with early adoption of innovations. Some common predictors of early innovation adoption are: socioeconomic status (SES) (including income, social status, education), cosmopolitanism, social participation, and media consumption (Rogers, 1983). For the diffusion of VR, these variables are also likely to play a role since VR technology is likely to emerge in technology clusters,[2] and not as a stand-alone technology to be adopted by itself. However, it is still unclear exactly what VR will be.

Technology: Entertainment or Tool

Probably the biggest factor influencing VR diffusion is the ultimate form the technology takes. Some have predicted that the market for VR entertainment will be its dominant use by the year 2000 (Lanier & Biocca, 1992). As such, VR "theaters" are expected to appear in suburban malls so that people can flock to VR "performances." Such a scenario provides direct comparison to films in which film technology converted vaudeville stages to movie houses.

As VR competes with film, so too movie houses will be converted into VR houses in which the traditional stage viewing style becomes obsolete. Consequently, just as old stages were butchered into multiplex movie mazes, so too, will these movie houses be butchered into appropriate VR stages. But VR is postulated as a medium for communication in which individuals share ideas and communicate in virtual worlds.

Similarly, video technology was developed and envisioned as a medium of entertainment and communication. Yet interactive video communication rarely exists, and is not used with electronic communication as part of the textual interchange. Indeed, in spite of the fanfare, broadband computer networks still only provide asynchronous textual information exchange, and rarely fulfill the promise of total interactivity, let alone video.

VR technology promises to put interactivity into electronic communication by providing a shared space. The first VR system(s) is (are) likely to be embedded in computer technology, home entertainment centers, advanced medical equipment, or movie theater-type viewing houses. As such, those who first experience and use VR are likely to be those people who have

---

[2]Technology clusters (Rogers, 1983) constitute numerous technologies that are bundled into one unit such as the VCR which can only be used with a television set, and is more likely to be adopted by those who already have expensive televisions and subscribe to cable.

already adopted such technologies as home entertainment systems and personal computers.

The question of access to VR and the medium over which a VR service would be delivered to the user is a major factor that will determine the diffusion of VR. The VR delivery system may be remote access or stand-alone. According to the current state of the technology four scenarios are possible:

1. Out-of-home "VR theaters" or arcades (Gagnon, this volume).
2. Stand-alone home systems consisting of frequent software updates.
3. Telephone delivery with appropriate receivers.
4. Cable delivery.

Each of these possible scenarios depends on the uses of the VR system (professional vs. entertainment, individual vs. collective), and it is likely that none of them will emerge as dominant in the near future.

One important factor that will determine the relative likelihood of these different scenarios is the commercial availability of powerful computers. Currently, sensory immersion requires large amounts of memory and computing power if it is to achieve a reasonable sense of "being there" for the user. In spite of the overwhelming miniaturization of both processors and memory in the past 10 years or so, it is likely that the first dedicated stand-alone systems will be either very limited in their achievement of a sense of presence or too expensive for most households in the near future. For instance, a panel of experts gathered by Future Technology Survey Inc. (Miller, Walker, & Rupnow, 1992) predicted that the cost of a complete VR system will not decrease under $10,000 (1991 dollars) before the year 2000.

The same report (Miller et al., 1992) concluded that "perhaps initial systems will be installed in central areas such as movie houses or malls where people can pay a fee to interact with an environment. Later, the technology may be available on home video or computer systems and a plug-in environment will be as available as videos are today" (p. 2).

According to an estimate by William Blain & Co, in September 1990, Nintendo hardware household penetration for 1991 was about 34% and corresponded, according to an estimate of Gerard Klauer Mattison & Co. in November 1990, to a market share of approximately 74%. From these figures, we can infer that the approximate penetration of video games in American households is around 46%. This population of equipped households provides a base for the diffusion of low-end VR entertainment systems or limited input or output devices. The first phase of VR diffusion will likely be input/output devices attached to existing videogames hardware. Sega Genesis™, for example, introduced a headset with VR goggles and earphones in fall 1993 for around $150.00.

TABLE 11.1
Penetration Estimates for Potential VR Technology Delivery Systems

Technology	Penetration (Pct. U.S. Households)	Date	Source
Color TV	98	June, 1991	EIA
Telephone	93.6	March, 1991	FCC
VCR	74	June, 1991	EIA
Cable TV	58.6	July, 1991	NCTA
Computer	29	June, 1991	EIA
Compactdisc	28	June, 1991	EIA

EIA = Electronic Industries Association. Based on an estimate of 95.7 million U.S. households.

FCC = Federal Communications Commission. Based on an estimate of 95.3 million U.S. households.

NCTA = National Cable Television Association. Based on an estimate by Nielsen of U.S. cable households and the EIA estimate of total U.S. households.

Table 11.1 reports the penetration rates of potential supporting systems for VR technology as of 1991. Although color TV is the most widely diffused of the communication technologies, it is not likely to support VR technology. The telephone is quite widely diffused, and further increases in transmission efficacy (i.e., better information transmission packing or optical fiber) may make this the best medium for delivery. Although cable does not have as high a penetration as telephone, it already has much of the technology in place.

Larger and more powerful VR systems are likely to diffuse first as services delivered over telephone lines or cable. Presently, it is unclear whether phone or cable will emerge as the dominant delivery mechanism. Clearly, VR is one of many services with policy and economic implications involved in its delivery. Whatever the medium connecting the computing power generating the environment ("the reality engine"), higher end home VR systems will still require a powerful terminal to run the interface. The case of videotext (Branscomb, 1988), and especially the French Minitel, has shown that this aspect is central for the diffusion of service to the homes (Mayer, 1988). For Minitel, giving away this necessary interface hardware seems to have been a successful strategy.

Policy

Policy decisions regarding past communication technologies have greatly affected their development and subsequent diffusion. The decision by governments to avoid setting policies and standards for technologies such as the railroad, telephone, and telegraph led to multiple competitors with different standards until one competitor established the strength to win market dominance.

The degree of government involvement in VR standards setting and promotion of implementation will directly affect its speed of diffusion. Although the government is not in the habit of picking winners, and prefers to wait until the dust has settled, it is clear that a VR standard will greatly accelerate market diffusion, to the great benefit of some and the great demise/disappointment and loss to others.

The absence of government intervention or specific policies designed to create widespread availability of VR will likely insure that VR adoption starts among those most able financially to experience it. The technology will then gradually trickle down to those lower in social status. Clearly, this diffusion will not descend straight down the economic ladder, but rather is governed by the social networks of potential adopters.

Networks of Potential Adopters

Social networks of potential adopters are created by structural factors such as family income, life term residence, ethnicity, and religion. These networks are significant determinants on attitude toward technology as well as potential for adoption. Communication researchers have called for an interpersonal model of technology adoption to answer the needs of interactive communication technologies (Biocca, 1992a; Rogers, 1987). Studying networks of potential adopters provides the opportunity to build interpersonal models of adoption.

Individuals are embedded in social networks made of kinship, friendship, work and group participation (Knoke & Kuklinski, 1982; Scott, 1991; Wellman, 1983). These networks constrain behavior and regulate access to information concerning employment, health services, and education, among other things. Networks also provide and restrict access to new communication technology. Networks structure technology exposure by introducing individuals to technology, sharing experiences, and providing communication partners. What is critical to communication technology adoption, and hence VR diffusion, is interactivity.

For VR, a large body of research has defined more precisely the meaning of interactivity. Here we defined VR as a technological system aimed at creating an electronically simulated environment where the user may experience a sense of presence. This definition puts the emphasis on the concept of "presence" and refines previous conceptions of interactive communication technologies. Sheridan (1992, pp. 121–122) proposed three determinants of the sense of presence: (a) extent of sensory information, (b) control of relation of sensors to environment, and (c) ability to modify physical environment. Technological improvement of these three areas of

VR performance will be a major influence on the diffusion of VR systems (for a better analysis of the concepts of presence and telepresence, see Steuer, this volume).

Heeter (1992) also proposed a taxonomy for understanding the dimensions of the subjective experience of presence. Heeter defined social presence as ". . . the extent to which other beings also exist in the world and appear to react to you" (p. 262; see also Rice & Williams, 1984; Short, Williams, & Christie, 1976). Our main thesis here is that the diffusion of VR will be structured by interpersonal networks of adopters shaped by the social practice (or use) of the system. The extent to which a VR system allows its users to experience social presence will therefore partly determine these networks.

Many communication technologies are interactive and consequently interdependent. Interdependence implies that the technology finds its most important expression in interaction with others. Electronic mail is only useful insofar as people that you want to communicate with are on the electronic mail system. Many individuals only begin to use electronic mail when they receive messages and then reply to them.

Consequently, VR adoption and use is likely to be structured by the networks of potential adopters. In particular, individuals will begin using VR when it is available on a communication medium, and others exist on the network that the individuals wish to communicate with. Therefore if VR develops as an electronic communication network available only to individuals with specific VR technology then a network of VR users will emerge.

This VR network will likely be restricted to a particular subgroup of the population made up of technologists, hackers, communication specialists, and special professionals such as medical researchers and engineers who greatly benefit from the technology. The VR network is likely to split into homogenous subgroups with little cross-group communication. Furthermore, this VR network will not have many interpersonal network connections outside the VR community, and thus be inefficient at recruiting new users to the technology. Although such a scenario is great for developing the technology and demonstrating its usefulness, it would be stillborn as a diffusion mechanism.

Personal networks provide interpersonal exposure to the innovation. Early users of VR technology tell their friends and colleagues about their experiences, and persuade them to use VR. The microprocess of the diffusion of VR technology is basically one in which users persuade nonusers to try the technology, and convince them to join the community of users. The whole course of VR diffusion will be one in which VR transfers from being a research idea to one in which individuals persuade others to join their virtual worlds, and recruit others to play and exchange information in a virtual environment.

This micro network model of diffusion posits an individual surrounded by his or her personal network. As more of his or her network partners adopt the innovation (join a virtual world), he or she receives increasing persuasion to join the VR community. Individuals have varying thresholds for VR adoption, and it is these thresholds that determine the path of diffusion.

Network Threshold

Network thresholds are the proportion of adopters in an individual's network necessary for him or her to adopt an innovation (Granovetter, 1978; Valente, in press). Individuals with low thresholds require few network partners to have adopted before they adopt (network thresholds are displayed in Fig. 11.1). These low thresholds have been shown to be a function of such factors as cosmopolitanism and media exposure (Valente, in press). For VR diffusion other factors, such as income, communication, and technological competence, will likely affect thresholds.

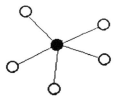

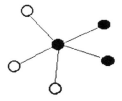

[a] Here the individual has a zero threshold.

[b] Here the individual has a threshold of 40 %.

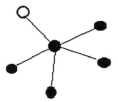

[c] Here the individual has a threshold of 80 %.

[d] Here the threshold is highest at 100 %.

FIG. 11.1.   Examples of network thresholds. Each filled circle represents a virtual reality (VR) user, whereas the empty circles represent nonusers. Each figure represents a VR user connected to five communication network partners (five is arbitrary). Low-threshold individuals are those willing to adopt before many other of their communication network partners do so.

The point is: The structure of personal networks determines when individuals are exposed to VR persuasion influences. The exposure itself is not more likely to lead to adoption, but rather, individuals will vary in their susceptibility to this exposure, and vary in their desire to communicate in VR environments. Some will be highly predisposed to adopt the technology, and thus join the VR world when only a few of their network partners have done so. Others will resist VR, and hence have high thresholds to adoption.

The presence of low-threshold adopters accelerates the diffusion process by adopting before many others do. The interdependence between adopters, the fact that they need someone to communicate with, makes the network process of VR diffusion most important. The low-threshold adopters provide the core set of communicants that keeps the VR community alive, and thus maintain a critical mass of users.

Critical Mass

The critical mass is particularly important in the diffusion of interactive technologies (Allen, 1988; Markus, 1987). Reaching a critical mass of VR users insures that a market exists that sustains the development and further improvement of VR technology. A critical mass of VR users is likely to be made up of technologists and other VR enthusiasts who develop creative uses of VR. To constitute a critical mass, they must be more active on the system and contribute disproportionately to system use.

The critical mass, then, must be those highly predisposed to use the technology, yet not be cut off from others less inclined to use VR. In fact the critical mass needs to be active in the construction of virtual worlds and their databases, as well as actively recruiting others into the system; that is, having ties external to their personal network which is perhaps constructed primarily of work colleagues likely to have few contacts to actual users.

Networks of Inventors

As is often noted, technology transfer success is dependent on whether inventors are connected through personal contacts with individuals in the target market. Successful inventions often occur when individuals are connected to those who would benefit from the technology. In such instances, inventors know the market needs and hence develop technology to meet these needs.

From an actor-oriented perspective, we can best understand the shape of technology by understanding the personal networks of those involved in its development (Bardini, Horvath, Nakayama, & Rogers, 1993; Callon, 1991). The personal networks of inventors often shape the particular form or applications of emerging technologies.

The sociology of science and technology has also shown that these inventors are involved in the social process of shaping the networks of users. The social construction of a new communication technology such as VR is a complex process. Based on the lessons from the European sociology of science and technology (Callon, 1991; Latour, 1987; Woolgar, 1991) and the diffusion of innovations (Rogers, 1983; Valente, in press), we can postulate the following characteristics of the sociotechnological process:

1. The sociotechnological shaping of technology occurs as a set of negotiations between the actors involved in the process.

2. In the course of these negotiations, the actors mobilize resources independently of their possible categorizations in the social or technological realm, but according to a strategy that is both social and technological.

3. The result of these negotiations is a sociotechnological system where the uncertainty about the social identities of the major actors and the qualities of the technology are slowly dissipated.

4. Uncertainty is never totally eliminated and the sociotechnological system is never totally stable. Controversy leading to a new set of negotiations and alliances between actors is always possible.

5. We distinguish between inventors, innovators, and low-threshold adopters according to the relative time of involvement in the negotiations. The later involvement of an actor or a new group of actors appears always in relation to existing actors. The process of negotiating the involvement of new actors in the system is called *enrollment*.

6. New actors are enrolled by existing actors who try to act as their representatives. The chain of associations between actors mirrors the organization of the technological system of the emerging technology.

7. Invention, design, and use of the technological system cannot be artificially separated in the negotiation process. New controversies may reshape a situation according to emerging sociotechnological configurations.

8. We use the term reinvention to mean the situation when alternative uses of the system reopen the negotiations on the design of the system.

9. The sociotechnological system is as stable as the strength of the actors' networks and their chains of association.

In the case of an emerging communication system such as VR, design and use cannot be artificially separated in the networks describing the sociotechnological system. Use of the system cannot be completely anticipated by the early inventors or designers of the system. A quasi-stable state of the system will occur when stable communities of use have been structured. Low threshold adopters are the leading actors in the emergence of these quasi stable communities of use. Pre-existing actors (inventors, innovators) can only facilitate the appearance of low-threshold adopters, but cannot guarantee their continued enrollment.

These microlevel network diffusion processes will greatly affect who has access to the technology as it spreads throughout a society. However, this microlevel percolation process will be greatly affected by macrolevel technological and policy developments impossible to predict. However, there are likely technological and policy scenarios that provide boundaries for the rapidity or slowness of VR diffusion that can be predicted with mathematical forecasting methods.

ADOPTION STAGES AND MATHEMATICAL MODELS

Early studies of the diffusion innovations noted that adoption occurs in stages (Rogers, 1983; Ryan & Gross, 1943). Individuals first become aware of a technology, then learn more about it, then try it, and finally adopt it. For the present purposes, we divide the adoption process into three stages: (a) awareness, (b) trial, and (c) adoption. The process can be expanded into multiple stages by further dividing each of these broad categories into smaller segments. These three stages are sufficient to understand the rate of VR diffusion and the factors that affect how VR diffuses.

Diffusion of Awareness

Invented recently, in 1987, awareness of the term *virtual reality* has diffused widely in a short time period. Diffusion of awareness usually occurs via the mass media (Deutschmann & Danielson, 1960; Valente, 1993), which are effective at disseminating information to a large number of people rapidly.[3] Popular conceptions of virtual reality were strongly shaped by a science fiction genre in the mid-1980s called *cyberspace* or *cyberpunk* (Gibson, 1984, 1987; Gibson & Sterling, 1991; Sterling, 1986, 1988). William Gibson and Bruce Sterling led a group of writers who created/popularized terms such as *cyberspace* and *cyberpunks*. The cyberspace movement envisioned a world where simulated environments and new forms of socialization would be commonplace.[4] These writings shaped the early representation of VR. By the time Jaron Lanier coined the term *virtual reality* in 1987 (Lanier

---

[3]Spectacular events such as Eisenhower's heart attack (Deutschmann & Danielson, 1960) and the Kennedy assassination (Greenberg, 1964), however, spread rapidly by w ⁻ᵈ of mouth.

[4]Science fiction writers often inform public conceptions of technology from the writing of Jules Verne to that of Isaac Asimov, Ray Bradbury, and Arthur C. Clarke. Although sometimes seen as fanciful in hindsight, science fiction writers are often well informed of the technologies they write about.

& Biocca, 1992), science fiction enthusiasts had very imaginative ideas for the uses of such technology.

Since then, in a second phase of the diffusion of awareness, VR terms and images have appeared in the major news magazines (e.g. Interactive, 1993), newspapers, television (*Wild Palms*, 1993), and the movies (*Jurassic Park*, 1993; *Lawnmower Man*, Everett & Leonard, 1992). In fact, a magazine called *Wired* is now published primarily for people interested in interactive technology. The recent media attention given to virtual reality in the early 1990s permits us to consider that the awareness stage of the diffusion of VR technology is well advanced, if not complete.

The most common mathematical function used to describe diffusion of awareness is:

$$y(t) = N(1 - e^{-at})$$

where *y(t)* is the cumulative proportion of those who are aware, N is the population size, a is the rate of diffusion, and t is the time period. The symbol e is the base of the natural logarithm which is approximately 2.72.

When everyone is aware of VR, the cumulative proportion, *y(t)*, is equal to N, the size of the population. The rate parameter, a, measures how fast diffusion of awareness occurs. Higher values of a indicate faster diffusion. For example, if a was .01 and the population size was 100, then diffusion to all members occurs in 10 time periods. If a was raised to .02, then diffusion to all members occurs in 5 time periods. Fig. 11.2 shows hypothetical diffusion curves which vary the speed of awareness diffusion.

The awareness function can be used to determine rates of awareness by estimating a. Also, this function can be used to determine how many individuals heard of an innovation during successive years since its introduction. Data on the level of VR awareness are not yet available, so it is not clear which of these awareness diffusion scenarios is occurring or what percent of the U.S. population is aware of the term VR or how much they know about it.

Each of the diffusion trajectories in Fig. 11.2 represent different potential awareness diffusion scenarios. The top curve assumes that awareness diffusion occurs quickly such that everyone will be aware of the term VR and have some understanding of its meaning by the year 2000. Such a scenario is possible if the media continue to publicize VR developments and if popular culture continues to use VR in movies, TV, magazines and newspapers. Moreover, VR advertisements and promotions will make VR a household word if the technology becomes widely available in the marketplace.

However, other VR awareness diffusion scenarios postulate slower rates. The other curves in Fig. 11.2 depict 75% and 48% awareness by the year 2000. These slower awareness curves are possible if VR technology devel-

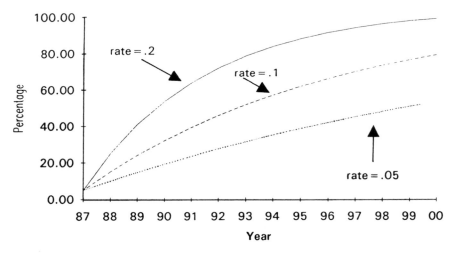

FIG. 11.2.   Theoretical curves for different rates of awareness of virtual reality. As the rate of diffusion increases, more individuals become aware of VR technology sooner.

opment is slowed or stagnant such that no new advances appear on the market, and thus nothing novel in the technology occurs to pique the public interest. Additionally, unforeseen possibly negative connotations of VR technology may inhibit its use by the popular press. An example might be that VR is portrayed as a violent medium that has negative consequences associated with its use.

Further awareness diffusion will occur as individuals develop a more complete understanding of VR technology and its range of applications. The next stage of adoption is trial.

Trial

Most popular definitions of VR refer to the technological components of the system and generally include a computerized system of input and output devices providing sensory immersion and capacity to act in a simulated environment generated by a computer. In his detailed tutorial, Frank Biocca (1992b) described a wide range of such input and output devices and the ways they provide a sense of "being there" for the user.

Among those devices, the helmet (or head-mounted display) for the output and the gloves for the input are the most well known. Technology demonstrations have been conducted in the past few years that have permitted people to try VR gloves and helmets. These demonstrations have undoubtedly allowed a small percentage of people to try VR technology in museum exhibits or professional shows and conferences. At this stage, the rate of trial diffusion is difficult to estimate, and varies greatly according to each specific hardware component and category of the potential population of adopters. In the case of the helmet for example, there is already a small percentage of the population that has tried the technology for specific applications.

This is the case for military experts and developers who have been working for over 10 years with the head-mounted display (HMD) first proposed in 1965 by Ivan Sutherland. Flight simulators and experiments, dating from the early 1930s, have provided applications for VR technology development. Consequently, NASA and the Department of Defense have invested heavily in VR technology to foster its trial diffusion (Pimentel & Teixeira, 1993, pp. 31–41).

Another VR product that led to trial use is the Mattel PowerGlove™, developed in collaboration with VPL and Abrams-Gentile Entertainment. The Mattel PowerGlove was commercially available between 1989 and 1991 as an input device for Nintendo video games. The PowerGlove cost $89.00 and was purchased by tens of thousands (Pimentel & Teixeira, 1993; Rheingold, 1991).

There is therefore considerable diversity among trial diffusion situations for the various components of VR technology. Some, like the HMD, have been tried out by a specific population for a specific use, others (less common), like the PowerGlove, nearly achieved mass consumption for a limited time. These various specialized niches and aborted diffusion attempts provide a starting point for wider trial diffusion of the technology.

In the transition between specialized niches and wider diffusion to the population, the category of people in charge of reporting the progress of the technology are of particular importance. Journalists and scholars have different but fundamental roles to play in this process. Not only do they raise awareness in the population with their reports, but they also provide a basis of first-hand experience with the technology, and encourage and provide the necessary information for the rest of the population to try VR technology. This feedback loop between awareness and trial by journalists and scholars/developers is key to understanding the process of VR diffusion and the transformation of specialized technology/market niches to widespread VR use.

The mathematical function that describes the trial or "first use" of an innovation is (Bailey, 1957/1975; Mahajan & Peterson, 1985):

$$y(t) = \frac{Ne^{Nat}}{(N-1 + e^{Nat})}$$

where N is the population size, a is the rate of diffusion, and t is the time period. When all members have tried VR the cumulative proportion, $y(t)$, will be equal to N, the size of the population.

If trial VR occurs rapidly, then everyone in the potential market for experiencing VR technology will do so within about 10 years. The curve for this level of trial diffusion is shown in Fig. 11.3. The curve shows that after the technology is introduced, people begin to experience the technology at an increasing rate. During the first few years the number of people who try VR is low, perhaps only a few hundred thousand. However, the percentage of new adopters continues to increase at an increasing rate.

The S-shaped curve continues to climb until 50% of the VR market has tried VR technology. After the 50% point, the absolute number of people who have tried VR technology continues to increase, but the proportion of new users per time period decreases. This happens because so many people have tried VR technology that the available audience who have not tried it has shrunk to a minority and continues to decrease in size until everyone has tried it.

After about 10% to 20% of the relevant population has tried VR, a critical mass of VR users begins to form. The critical mass represents a core set of users who promote the technology. The numbers presented in Fig. 11.3 assumed a 1% growth rate and result in 100% of the relevant market having tried VR technology in 9 years, 1991–1999. If that growth is increased to 2% then 100% will have tried it in 5 years. And if that growth occurs more slowly such as 5%, then we can expect saturation to take about 14 years.

The more rapid diffusion curve depicted in Fig. 11.3 may result if

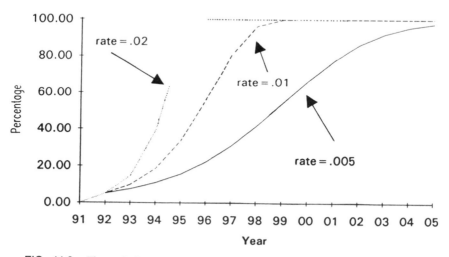

FIG. 11.3. Theoretical curves for different rates of trial of virtual reality. The interaction between users and nonusers results in a steady increase in the number of individuals who have tried VR. As the rate of diffusion increases, widespread trial of VR occurs sooner.

commercial applications of VR technology develop in such a way that potential users find benefit in using the technology. That is, the cost of the technology becomes affordable and worth the value in entertainment or access to information. If VR technology is prohibitively expensive, and provides little return in the form of entertainment or information-industry functioning, potential users will not buy it.

An optimistic VR diffusion scenario, then, would involve continuing rapid decrease in VR computer hardware and software costs (Stix, 1993) and dramatic increase in the provision of VR services and products that augment both entertainment and worker/leisure productivity. Further, no unforeseen events occur that could cripple VR development such as adverse publicity due to overly violent applications, a choked regulatory environment which stifles application development, or a massive technological recession.

A pessimistic VR diffusion scenario similar to the bottom curve in Fig. 11.3 predicts that VR diffusion occurs much more slowly. The causes of this slow growth could be that computer costs do not drop appreciably from current levels. A second factor inhibiting growth is that few companies become engaged in providing services. Again, while computer costs and provision of services may not affect VR market growth, there may be unforeseen events that inhibit widespread VR diffusion. Possible unpredictable factors that inhibit VR growth are: (a) simulation sickness (Biocca, 1992c), (b) an adverse policy environment that delays decisions about possible delivery mechanisms, and (c) a shift in public opinion opposing VR applications due to their moral/aesthetic misapplication (i.e., excessive sex and violence).

Finally, the most likely scenario is a combination of both optimistic and pessimistic forecasts. In all probability, some combination of reduced costs, technical limitations, expanded/restricted services, and unforeseen events will occur to both accelerate certain VR applications, and deter others. As data on the number of VR users become available we may compare those data to these diffusion curves to determine how rapidly or slowly VR is diffusing. Although early adopters might try VR before others, they may not buy it, or continue to use it: First use is not the same as continued use or level of adoption.

Adoption Stage

Although technology "gurus" may try VR technology once or twice, the number of people who actually buy the technology and fully incorporate it into their lifestyle will vary. Individuals with less income, technophobes, or conservatives may be resistant to allowing VR technology to replace traditional ways of doing things much like many writers relied on their typewriters years after word processing made them obsolete. These later adopters will reject VR technology or delay their use until it's more affordable, easier to use, or more appropriate for their lifestyle.

Most of the mathematical modeling conducted in diffusion has been on first use, and few studies collect data on how well individuals continue to use a technology and the degree to which it becomes fully integrated into their lifestyles. What is important for our discussion is the model that predicts how rapidly individuals assimilate VR into their everyday behaviors. The mathematical function that describes use diffusion is (Hamblin, Jacobsen, & Miller, 1973):

$$y(t) \ = \ ke^{at}$$

where, k is a scaler constant, a is the exponential rate of diffusion, and t is the time period. The function must constantly be updated for different exponential epochs in the diffusion process because the constant and rate terms will change during the course of an innovation's diffusion.[5] VR use diffusion curves are not presented here since it is premature to speculate on the relevant units of analysis that vary from (a) time logged on to a system or at home, to (b) dollars spent on equipment, or (c) tickets purchased to an arcade.

Central to this discussion is the question as to what form VR technology will eventually take and to what extent VR will find itself bundled with other technologies so that individuals are not making VR adoption decisions, but rather simply seeing (experiencing) VR in their old applications. If VR technology remains merely a gimmick of video game manufacturers for the next 10 years then VR adoption will remain a toy and have a stunted technological development. Conversely, if VR is incorporated into computer operating systems, it will become a broadly experienced medium that profoundly affects our day-to-day lives.

Virtual reality can be both or neither of these things, and probably will lie somewhere in between. Will VR develop into a household medium in which everyone is immersed in virtual worlds like a cyberspace cornucopia? Or will we witness VR "holos" in mini-malls that display graphic scenes of violence and mayhem? The eventual diffusion of virtual reality lies somewhere between wondrous quality-of-life enhancement and banal reality.

In summary, this chapter has sketched, with broad strokes, some of the factors likely to affect VR diffusion. Chiefly, we have discussed the

---

[5]An exponential function will increase to infinity; consequently predicting a diffusion level using one exponential function is implausible. What generally happens is that an innovation diffuses according to an estimated exponential function, then some technological or structural change (or limitation) occurs, which changes the diffusion pattern so that the function is re-estimated and the growth rate is reduced considerably.

influence of technology delivery systems and speculated that the pace of technological development coupled with the provision of appropriate and useful services will dictate the speed of VR diffusion. We have also argued that the policy environment will affect the speed with which VR technology reaches widespread market penetration. Favorable policies may translate into more rapid diffusion.

VR technology diffusion is also dependent on "telepresence" or the concept of "being there." The ability of VR to simulate presence will affect who is willing to enroll in a VR community, and consequently define the universe of available communication partners in the VR environment. Consequently, the speed and character of diffusion will depend on how well VR simulates presence and this in turn will influence the ability of communication networks to act as conduits for the recruitment of new users. The communication networks of inventors and early users will greatly influence the diffusion of VR.

We then presented mathematical diffusion models in conjunction with different scenarios to forecast possible VR market growth rates and levels of penetration. Mathematical diffusion models exist to predict the timing of three diffusion stages: awareness, trial, and use. The mathematical models show that under optimistic conditions, approximately everyone will be aware of the term VR and some concept of what it means by the year 2000.

Trial, or first use, adoption has occurred on a limited basis in certain specific areas (military, museums) and is just now reaching market introduction. The forecasting models indicated that with favorable technological development, benign policy decisions, and no unforeseen problematic factors, VR trial will reach nearly everyone by 1995. However, more realistic projections that consider the adverse effect of policy or service provision factors call for widespread trial to take until at least the year 2005.

REFERENCES

Allen, D. (1988). New telecommunications services: Network externalities and critical mass. *Telecommunications Policy, 15*(4), 257–271.

Bailey, N. T. J. (1957/1975). *The mathematical theory of infectious diseases and its applications.* London: Griffin.

Bardini, T., Horvath, A. T., Nakayama, T., & Rogers, E. M. (May, 1993). *Bridging the gulfs: From hypertext to cyberspace.* Paper presented at the annual International Communication Association Meeting, Washington, DC.

Bell, D. (1973). *The coming of post-industrial society: A venture in social forecasting.* New York: Basic Books.

Benedikt, M. (Ed.) (1991). *Cyberspace, first steps.* Cambridge, MA: MIT Press.

Beniger, J. R. (1986). *The control revolution.* Cambridge, MA: Harvard University Press.

Biocca, F. (1992a). Communication within virtual reality: Creating a space for research. *Journal of Communication, 42*(4), 5–22.

Biocca, F. (1992b). Virtual reality technology: A tutorial. *Journal of Communication, 42*(4), 23–72.

Biocca, F. (1992c). Will simulation sickness slow down the diffusion of virtual environment technology? *Presence, 1*(3), 334–343.

Branscomb, A. W. (1988). Videotext: Global progress and comparative policies. *Journal of Communication, 38*(1), 50–59.

Callon, M. (1991). Techno-economic networks and irreversibility. In J. Law (Ed.), *A sociology of monsters* (pp. 132–161). London: Routledge & Kegan Paul.

Carey, J. (1988). *Communication and culture.* Cambridge, MA: Unwin Hyman.

Carey, J., & Moss, M. L. (1985). The diffusion of new telecommunication technologies. *Telecommunications Policy, 12*, 145–158.

Czitrom, D. (1982). *Media and the American mind: From Morse to McLuhan.* Chapel Hill: University of North Carolina Press.

de Sola Pool, I. (1983). *Technologies of freedom: On free speech in an electronic age.* Cambridge, MA: Belknap Press of Harvard University Press.

Deutschmann, P. J., & Danielson, W. A. (1960). Diffusion of knowledge of the major news story. *Journalism Quarterly, 37*, 345–355.

Dutton, W. H., Blumler, J. G., & Kraemer, K. L. (1987). *Wired cities: Shaping the future of communications.* Boston, MA: G. K. Hall.

Eisenstein, E. (1979). *The printing press as an agent of change: Communications and cultural transformations in early-modern Europe* (Vols. 1–2). London: Cambridge University Press.

Everett, G. (Producer), & Leonard, B. (Director). (1992). *Lawnmower Man* [Videotape]. New York: Columbia TriStar Home Video.

Gibson, W. (1984) *Neuromancer.* New York: Ace Books.

Gibson, W. (1988) *Mona Lisa overdrive.* New York: Bantam.

Gibson, W., & Sterling, B. (1991) *The difference engine.* New York: Bantam Books.

Granovetter, M. (1978). Treshold models of collective behavior. *American Journal of Sociology, 83*(6), 1420–1443.

Greenberg, B. (1964). Person-to-person communication in the diffusion of news events. *Journalism Quarterly, 41*, 489–494.

Hamblin, R. L., Jacobsen, R. B., & Miller, J. L. L. (1973). *A mathematical theory of social change.* New York: Wiley.

Heeter, C. (1992). Being there: The subjective experience of presence. *Presence, 1*(2), 262–271.

Innis, H. A. (1951). *The bias of communication.* Toronto: University of Toronto Press.

Interactive (1993, May 31). *Newsweek*, pp. 38–50.

Jurassic Park (1993). Universal City, CA: Universal.

Klopfenstein, B. (1989). Problems and potential of forecasting the adoption of new media. In J. L. Salvaggio & J. Bryant (Eds.) *Media use in the information age: Emerging patterns of adoption and consumer use.* Hillsdale, NJ: Lawrence Erlbaum Associates.

Knoke, D., and Kuklinski, J. H. 1982. *Network analysis.* Newbury Park, CA: Sage.

Krueger, M. W. (1991). *Artificial reality II.* Reading, MA: Addison-Wesley.

Lanier, J., & Biocca, F. (1992). An insider's view of the future of virtual reality. *Journal of Communication, 42*(4), 150–171.

Latour, B. (1987). *Science in action.* Cambridge, MA: Harvard University Press.

Mackenzie, D., & Wajcman, J. (1985). *The social shaping of technology.* Philadelphia, PA: Open University Press.

Mahajan, V. & Peterson, R. A. (1985). *Models of innovation diffusion.* Newbury Park, CA: Sage.

Markus, M. L. (1987). Toward a "critical mass" theory of interactive media: Universal access, interdependence and diffusion. *Communication Research, 14*(5), 491–511.

Martino, J. P. (1983). *Technological forecasting for decision making.* New York: Elsevier.

Marvin, C. (1988). *When old technologies were new: Thinking about electronic communication in the late nineteenth century.* New York: Oxford University Press.

Mayer, R. N. (1988). The growth of the French videotex system and its implications for consumers. *Journal of Consumer Policy, 11,* 55-83.

Miller, R., Walker, T. C., & Rupnow, M. (1992). *Survey on virtual reality (Report no. 201).* Lilburn, GA: Future Technology Surveys.

Perrolle, J. A. (1987). *Computers and social change: Information, property and power.* Belmont, CA: Wadsworth.

Pimentel, K., & Teixeira, K. (1993). *Virtual reality, through the new looking glass.* New York: Intel/Windcrest/McGraw-Hill.

Rheingold, H. (1991). *Virtual reality.* New York: Simon & Schuster.

Rice, R. E., & Williams, F. (1984). Theories old and new: The study of new media. In R. E. Rice & Associates, *The new media: Communication, research and technology,* pp. 55-80. Newbury Park, CA: Sage.

Robinett, W. (1992). Synthetic experience: A proposed taxonomy. *Presence, 1*(2), 229-247. *Social Networks, 9,* 285-310.

Rogers, E. M. (1983). *Diffusion of innovations.* New York: The Free Press.

Rogers, E. M. (1987). Progress, problems and prospects for network research: Investigating relationships in the age of electronic communication technologies.

Ryan, R., & Gross, N. (1943). The diffusion of hybrid seed corn in two Iowa communities. *Rural Sociology, 8*(1), 15-24

Schnaars, S. P. (1989). *Megamistakes: Forecasting and the myth of rapid technological change.* New York: The Free Press.

Scott, J. 1991. *Network Analysis: A Handbook.* Newbury Park, CA: Sage.

Sheridan, T. B. (1992). Musings on telepresence and virtual presence. *Presence, 1*(1), 120-126.

Short, J. Williams, E., & Christie B. (1976). *The social psychology of telecommunications.* New York: Wiley.

Sterling, B. (Ed.) (1986). *Mirrorshades, the cyberpunk anthology.* New York: Ace Books.

Sterling, B. (1988). *Islands in the net.* New York: Arbor House.

Stix, G. (1993, August). Domesticating cyberspace. *Scientific American,* 100-110.

Valente, T. W. (in press). *Network models of the diffusion of innovations.* Cresskill, NJ: Hampton Press.

Valente, T. W. (1993). Diffusion of innovations and policy decision-making. *Journal of Communication, 43*(1), 30-45.

Wellman, B. 1983. Network Analysis: Some Basic Principles. in R. Collins (Ed.), *Sociological Theory* (155-200). San Francisco: Jossey-Bass.

Wild Palms. (1993). Stamford, CT: ABC Video.

Winner, L. (1977). *Autonomous technology: Technics-out-of-control as a theme in political thought.* Cambridge, MA: MIT Press.

Woolgar, S. (1991). Configuring the user: The case of usability trials. In J. Law (Ed.), *A sociology of monsters* (pp. 57-99). London: Routledge & Kegan Paul.

12 I'm Not a Real Doctor, but I Play One in Virtual Reality: Implications of Virtual Reality for Judgments About Reality

Michael A. Shapiro
Daniel G. McDonald
Cornell University

Virtual (VR) reality has the potential to involve users in sensory worlds that are indistinguishable or nearly indistinguishable from the real world. In addition, virtual reality environments may even merge with the real world (Krueger, 1990). "A computer presence will permeate the workplace and the home, available whenever a need is felt. . . . Such interfaces may resemble the real world or include devices . . . that have no antecedents in the real world. . . . Artificial realities . . . need not conform to physical reality any more than our homes mirror the outside environment" (Krueger, 1990 p. 422).

As the distinction blurs between the physical and computer environments, people will need to make increasingly sophisticated judgments about what is "real" and what is not. Thus, it may be useful to examine what we know about how people make reality judgments about existing communication media and how such judgments might apply to VR.

For many years, considerable research has focused on understanding how audiences decide what experiences, including mediated experiences, should be perceived as real and which should be included in deciding what the world is really like. We expect that aspect of communication research to become increasingly important as technologies like virtual reality make it possible to both mimic and to modify our perceptual bases of understanding in increasingly complex ways.

In this chapter, we hope to do several things: show that communication and social psychology research in the past 100 years has identified two different aspects of reality evaluation; outline the critical elements that might form a theory of media reality effects; extend that theory to include virtual reality; and show how virtual reality might provide a tool for investigating these effects in ways not now possible.

Although this chapter focuses on communication and social psychology research, those are obviously not the only relevant bodies of scholarship. The debate about the meaning of real is at least as old as recorded philosophy. Empiricism, rationalism, realism, and dualism are just a few of the relevant philosophical positions that could inform such a discussion. Even a cursory treatment of this debate is both beyond the scope of this chapter and beyond the scope of our expertise. We limited this chapter to the social psychological evidence about how people decide what is real.

There are few attempts within the social psychology literature to explicitly define "real." However, two general types of reality seem to emerge. First, there is the notion of physical reality. Objects, including people, are physically (or objectively) real if their physical existence can be verified by most first-hand observers. Real events are a verifiable series of object movements through time and space. This concept of reality is used when discussing errors in reality judgment. Erroneous belief that objects and events have physical reality may be based on direct perception, as in hallucinations, or on mediated accounts, as in hoaxes.

Another type of reality seems to be a variable in much of the construction of social reality literature. That type gives some reality to representations and concepts depending on how much information they provide. For example, a picture of an airplane isn't a physical airplane, but it does provide a certain amount of information about an airplane. An actor playing a doctor on television isn't a real doctor, but people may perceive him or her as providing information about doctors. In this chapter we also group the reality of concepts with this "information" reality. "Government," for example, isn't really a physical object so much as a concept that contains shared information. The most extreme manifestation of information reality may be (so far mostly fictional and theoretical) cyberspace, in which all truly physical objects disappear and only information remains (Benedikt, 1991).

Unlike physical reality, the amount of information reality in a representation is a function of a single observer's perception. However, both types of reality may play a role in a specific situation. For example, people who panicked after hearing a science fiction radio program did so because they believed the program was describing physical reality (an error), and because they believed the representation contained information.

VR has the potential to both replicate the sensory information of the physical world and to provide information in ways that go far beyond current representational systems. As a result, it's important to explore what we know about both notions of reality.

Finally, note that only a few studies have directly addressed what people actually mean when they say something is "real." These studies focus mostly on child development issues and there is little consensus in that literature (e.g., see Dorr, 1983; Prawat, Anderson, & Hapkeiwicz, 1989).

COMMUNICATION AND PERCEPTIONS OF REALITY

Concern about perceptions of reality and mediated reality has generated two broad classes of research. The first area of concern is how people use memories of bits and pieces of experience, including mediated presentations, to reconstruct an estimate of what the real world is like. In our view, the individual "builds" a reality based on memories of information gleaned from many different sources, probably over a long period of time (see Hawkins & Pingree, 1982; Hawkins & Pingree, 1990; Shapiro & Lang, 1991). Because much of our experience is mediated, many of these "bits and pieces" are gleaned from mediated presentations. The judgments about reality derived in this way are both cognitive and emotional. Most literature in this area has appeared in the last 20 years and deals primarily with television (often under the broad category of construction of social reality), but this aspect of reality decision making has long been a concern for research across several media. We refer to this area of concern as the investigation of reality reconstruction.

The second broad class of research concerns judgments about the "reality" of incoming messages. This includes a number of research efforts investigating what would appear to be ridiculous "mistakes" among audience members. The most famous of these is the *War of the Worlds* broadcast and panic, but there has been a steady, although admittedly small, stream of research related to this topic throughout the past century. We examine several theoretical and empirical attempts to describe and document these judgments, which we refer to as reality construction.

Asch (1952) made a distinction between two types of propaganda similar to those we describe here. As we demonstrate, these two areas are linked by an underlying concern with how people know what is real and what is not. From a psychological process viewpoint, construction and reconstruction are distinct in that they happen at different stages of mental processing and in the mental procedures involved. Construction happens primarily as people watch and evaluate a media message. Reconstruction happens some time after a media message has been interpreted and encoded in memory. However, construction influences reconstruction because reconstruction depends on the stored interpretations that result from the construction process. So, in some ways the end product of construction is the input to reconstruction. On the other hand, reconstruction influences construction because past experience guides our interpretations of new experiences.

It should not be surprising that information exchanged during communication is used to form a notion of what the external world is like. Mediated communication includes a dense array of information. For example, a television program about a detective may include information about male-female relationships, power dynamics, violent behavior, verbal and nonverbal communication, geography, economics, and the whole range of human behaviors. Thus, it is important to study what is learned from mass media, how individuals distinguish between reality and fantasy, and how they incorporate what they learn into their daily lives.

COMMUNICATION AND RECONSTRUCTED REALITY

Early Research

Early in this century, writers and social critics worried that the new mass audience for newspapers, literature, and movies would uncritically accept as real depictions of previously unknown ways of life (Lowenthal, 1984). Critics were particularly concerned about the influence of newspapers and comic supplements on children, who were believed particularly unable to distinguish between reality and fantasy (Howard, 1912; Wilcox, 1900).

The technologies introduced at the turn of the century—including the telephone, the telegraph, the phonograph, and motion pictures—got mixed reviews. Some thought they would have a democratizing effect by exposing people to different ideas, lifestyles, and people (Cantril & Allport, 1935; Cooley, 1902; Vorse, 1911). But others saw these new media as largely negative. For example, Munsterberg (1916), probably the best known and most credible of the early academic investigators, suggested that the motion picture had a "trivializing influence" by bringing people into contact with "things that are not worth knowing."

Early Modern Research

Even today, "The Payne Fund Studies" of the movies (Charters, 1933) and Cantril and Allport's 1935 *Psychology of Radio* stand out for their sophistication and thoroughness. Although the Cantril and Allport book was more favorable to radio than was Charters' summary of the movie studies, both found that children and adults learn both good and bad, correct and incorrect from movies and radio. As people mature, they are less susceptible to mass media influence.

The Payne Fund Studies found that children tend to believe movie information unless it is blatantly incorrect. However, 8-year-olds did not understand or misunderstood about half of what they saw (Charters, 1933;

Holaday & Stoddard, 1933). Interestingly, as children got older they learned more of both correct and incorrect information (Dysinger & Ruckmick, 1933). Similar to suggestions of the more recent media dependency theory (Ball-Rokeach & DeFleur, 1976), children were most influenced by facts about unfamiliar objects or events placed in familiar settings. The reality reconstructed from movies included ideas about making oneself attractive, how to wear clothes, mannerisms, and even love techniques (Blumer & Hauser, 1933; Charters, 1933; Cressey & Thrasher, 1933).

Postwar Research

Much of the postwar research through the early 1970s focused on the health effects of television on children and teenagers (Wartella & Reeves, 1985), finding many of the same effects noted earlier about movies. Schramm, Lyle, and Parker (1961) found that television was, at least at times, real enough to frighten many children.

However, the most influential postwar claim about television's ability to shape reconstruction was "cultivation" theory. Based on a series of complex assumptions, the theory claimed heavy television watchers shifted their beliefs over time to correspond to the distorted picture television presents of the world (Gerbner, 1990; Gerbner, Gross, Morgan, & Signorielli, 1986). Although both the theoretical and methodological details of cultivation have been severely challenged (for brief reviews, see parts of Condry, 1989; Cook, Kendzierski, & Thomas, 1983; and Rubin, Perse & Taylor, 1988), cultivation claims inspired many investigations of the construction of social reality. The primary assumption in these studies was that the steady accumulation of mass media experiences over time could influence the reconstruction of reality (Hawkins & Pingree, 1982).

Studies found a variety of influences on the reconstruction process. These included: direct and interpersonal experience (Elliott & Slater, 1980; Pingree, 1978; Rubin et al., 1988) , perceived reality (Greenberg & Reeves, 1976), type of program viewed (Potter, 1991), content of the program (Bryant, Carveth, & Brown, 1981), personality (Wober & Gunter, 1986), the impact of specific characters (Greenberg, 1988; Reep & Dambrot, 1989), the familiarity of social groups (Slater, 1990), and a variety of other factors. In fact, so much is known about when the media influence reconstruction that a full discussion is well beyond the scope of this paper.

Far less, however, is known about the psychological mechanisms involved (Hawkins & Pingree, 1990). A learning-theory mechanism has not been very successful (Hawkins, Pingree & Adler, 1987; Potter, 1991). Another theory, one that has some support but that the authors acknowledge is limited and somewhat speculative, claims that both emotional and cognitive information may be used in a variety of unconscious mental processes to decide what information is relevant to a particular reconstruction (Shapiro & Lang, 1991).

Summary of the Reconstructed Reality Literature

The theoretical and empirical investigations from 1900 on are remarkably consistent about the reconstruction of reality. First, it's clear that the mass media are used to develop attitudes toward real objects. Also, media experiences may accumulate over time and influence reconstruction in a variety of ways. In addition, mediated information with which the individual has had little or no direct contact and thus no clear method of evaluating are the most likely to influence reconstruction. Such unfamiliar material presented within a generally familiar context is especially likely to be used in reconstruction. Mediated communication is most likely to influence reconstruction when its original presentation was accompanied by stress or emotional excitement. Finally, models of how communication influences the reconstruction process, especially in terms of psychological mechanisms, are in their infancy and mostly speculative.

CONCERN ABOUT CONSTRUCTED REALITY

Early Accounts

Whereas reconstructed reality focuses on accumulating bits and pieces of information as building blocks in our perceptions of reality, constructed reality focuses on how individuals accept a sensed event as real. Social concern about constructed reality dates back to at least the turn of the century, although it is probably much older. Numerous fictional events were reported by the media and were believed to be real accounts by hundreds, thousands, or even millions of audience members. These hoaxes include an eyewitness account of a colonial witch trial, the interception of 924 colonists' scalps bought by the British, a crossing of the Atlantic by balloon, discovery of a petrified man, and an astronomer's report of "Bat-People" living on the moon (Fedler, 1989). A common feature in the newspaper hoaxes most clearly accepted as being true was the inclusion of incidental detail, especially the use of the names of actual people and places or what appeared to be actual people and places (Fedler, 1989).

As motion pictures developed, there were numerous accounts of moviegoers believing a movie account was real (Vorse, 1911, p. 445). Some may have gone a step further and reacted to movie images as if they were real. Palmer (1909) recounts the story of a Montana man who fell asleep in a motion picture theater, and, when he awoke, he mistook a motion picture image of a bear for an actual bear and fired a gun. Most film histories recount the first public motion picture exhibition by the Lumiere brothers in which terror ensued as audience members apparently confused a motion picture image of a train for a real train and fled from the theater.

War of the Worlds

The overall story of the panic resulting from the 1938 CBS broadcast of H. G. Wells' science fiction story the *War of the Worlds* is well known. In his study of that panic, Cantril (1966/1940) found systematic differences in who confused the mediated message for reality and who did not. Those who made successful internal checks (e.g., the use of dramatic conventions, modifications in time/distance relationships, etc.) were least likely to be frightened by the broadcasts. Those who made successful external checks, such as tuning to other stations or looking up the broadcast schedule in the newspaper, calling people or looking outdoors were slightly more likely to be frightened. Those who either made unsuccessful checks or no checks were most likely to be frightened.

Further analysis showed that those who tuned to other stations and found standard programming were least likely to panic. Checking newspaper listings provided the next most calming evidence. Interpersonal sources, checking outdoors, and making telephone calls to others were the least effective methods of checking the reality of the message.

The Mad Gasser and Windshield Pitting

Two studies of the 1950s — Johnson's "Phantom Anesthetist of Mattoon" (1952) and Medalia and Larsen's study of the Seattle Windshield Pitting Epidemic (1958) — are interesting studies of mass delusion. These studies, and a few others, show that, although rare, it is possible for whole communities to lose touch with reality.

There are no easy explanations for the gassing or pitting incidents. In both the *Invasion from Mars* and the windshield pitting instances, there was considerable anxiety about current events. These studies suggest that under acute anxiety, individuals may be highly suggestible to information that would ordinarily be discounted as false.

Current Concerns

The current literature on judgments about the reality of mass media presentations seems to primarily focus on three concerns: (a) perceived reality; (b) how children and adults define "real"; and (c) social judgments of actors in mass media presentations.

Perceived Reality.   The literature in perceived reality has focused mostly on that variable as a moderator of social reality effects (see, e.g., Hawkins, 1977; Potter, 1986, 1988; Reeves, 1978). This research recognizes that a reality judgment can be intermediate between totally real and totally unreal and that such judgments can be very subtle. For example, a person may recognize that certain aspects of a fictional television character may partially resemble real people. Similarly, fictional events may be judged enough like real events for a person to learn from them. Some investigators have suggested that perceived reality judgments may be part of a mental mechanism that determines which experiences will be integrated into social reality judgments (Rubin et al., 1988; Shapiro & Lang, 1991). However, television's influence on social reality appears to be overshadowed by direct and interpersonal experience (Rubin et al., 1988; Shapiro, 1991b; Tyler, 1980; Tyler & Cook, 1984).

Definitions of Reality.   In general, the child development literature indicates that children's reality judgments are limited by both knowledge deficits and by immature information-pocessing strategies (Prawat et al., 1989). Even so, children seem to use a variety of complex strategies to determine the reality of television (Dorr, 1983).

Several studies find that definitions of reality change with maturity. But studies don't agree on exactly how those definitions change. For example, Dorr and her colleagues found as children get older more and more of them define "real" as something that is fabricated but "possible." As children pass into adolescence and adulthood, more of them start defining real as fabricated but probable or representative (for a review see Dorr, 1983). However, a study that asked children and adults about the reality of everyday objects found that the criteria for real shifted in complex ways from preschool to adult (Prawat et al., 1989). There was no mention of the possible/probable distinction.

Judgments of Fictional Actors.   As mentioned earlier, television viewers seem to make judgments about the perceived reality of characters on fictional television. But there is a large body of research that indicates that social judgments about television characters are very complex. Such judgments can use both general knowledge about television, the world, and social relationships as well as specific knowledge about television characters (Livingstone, 1989). Physical characteristics, behaviors, and emotional states are also used in a variety of complex attributions and judgments about characters (for a review, see Hoffner & Cantor, 1991). These judgments can vary between cultures (Liebes & Katz, 1986).

Summary of the Reality Construction Literature

The literature reviewed suggests several principles: First, judgments about the reality of mass media events and characters (even fictional characters) are natural, ongoing, probabalistic (not dichotomous), and relatively sophisticated. In addition, mediated events and people are most easily accepted as real when places and people appearing in stories are similar to or are the same as familiar places, contexts, and people. Also, if an event, if true, has immediate (rather than delayed) implications, the audience will act on a "worst-case" scenario rather than on a careful analysis of all of the facts. Finally, fictional media presentations are most likely to be mistaken for reality when there is stress, strain, or worry about the future.

REALITY JUDGMENTS AND VR

Up to now, we've seen that people make a variety of sophisticated judgments about the correspondence between what they experience in the mass media and what they experience in the real world. At times, we can argue about the quality of those decisions. But even when people make gross errors (fleeing from Martian invaders or shooting a movie bear), those errors are systematic ones based on lack of knowledge/experience, emotional stress, erring on the side of safety, or being taken in when someone violates a social contract.

Based on our current knowledge, how will virtual reality influence our reality judgments? The literature indicates that whenever a new medium emerged in the past, people largely applied the judgment processes they already used. Initially, that led to some gross, even comical, mistakes, but as people became more sophisticated they better learned to deal with the demands of the new medium. Much the same kind of thing will probably happen as VR media become common. We suggest some ways in which VR may be different than current nonvirtual mass media. However, based on our literature review, we'd like to suggest some things that will probably be very similar.

First, mass media with elements of virtual reality are at least as likely to shape our attitudes, beliefs, and behaviors as other forms of mass media. Those judgments are likely to be continuous, not dichotomous and, with experience, relatively sophisticated. People will make relatively fine distinctions about how much a specific aspect of a specific character is like other people. People will make complex judgments about how much fictional events are like real events and how typical "news" events are of the events in the world. That doesn't mean that such judgments will always be accurate, but that people will make such judgments.

Just as with current mass media, there is likely to be a media dependency effect. People are most likely to be influenced by media information when they have little other experience that enables them to evaluate the new information. Of course, that doesn't mean that a person is any more likely to be influenced by something that person perceives as obviously fictional or unreal. Hence, a virtual reality trip to a fictional planet will probably be no more likely than a fictional movie to influence our judgments.

However, the additional sensory experience and feeling of being immersed in a virtual environment is likely to have some effects, particularly on involuntary emotional responses. For example, there is some evidence that seeing certain events on television (e.g., a car crash or a shooting) produces some physiological and emotional responses similar to responses to the real thing (see Lang, 1990). It seems likely that the more VR can make a car crash look and feel like a car crash, the bigger the physiological and emotional response. In fact, unexpected virtual reality events like a tiger leaping at someone may be intense enough to endanger someone with a weak heart. Keep in mind, too, that earlier research indicates that emotional excitement makes a presentation more real and more likely to influence reconstruction. However, as people become more accustomed to VR such responses will probably become less intense, just as audiences learned not to flee from movie trains.

Another possibility is that the more detailed familiar contexts and the more trivial detail in a virtual reality presentation, the more likely it will influence reality judgments. For example, it is easy to imagine that a hoax presented as a VR news story could be very convincing indeed, especially about an unfamiliar topic. In addition, the abundance of detail may make event memories more vivid and thus more likely to influence reconstruction as media experiences accumulate over time.

However, research to date has focused on media effects, not on the nature of reality judgments. As a result, our knowledge of how people make reality judgments is broader than it is deep. Researchers know a fair amount about when people decide something is real and when they include mass media information in social reality. But if we are to anticipate and understand the effect virtual reality may have on reality judgments, we need to focus a great deal more about how such judgments are made.

The remainder of this chapter tries to set some directions for future studies of reality judgments, focusing on how VR is likely to influence those judgments and how it might be used in research. To start, we attempt to answer a question that has not been much discussed in the literature — why make reality judgements? We will discuss some mental biases that might influence reality judgments. Finally, we suggest two fundamental differences between virtual reality and current ("conventional") mass media. In discussing those differences, we also discuss the effects of virtual reality based on our current knowledge and on some theoretical discussion.

Why Make Reality Judgments

Condry (1989) suggested real events sometimes demand action, whereas obviously fictional events can usually be enjoyed vicariously. Even with the qualifiers, that distinction is probably too restrictive. Fictional stories can form an environment of cultural, social, and even physical truths even when there is nothing literally real in them (Gerbner, 1990). And apparent reality and nonreality are often freely mixed in media presentations. That really appears to be Miami on television (or at least an electronic image of parts of Miami recorded at some earlier date and perhaps modified electronically).[1] Some viewers may want to copy some aspects of the social relationships depicted. Drug smuggling is really a social problem and is often violent. But the events never really happened, the people are actors, and the exploding boats are plywood mock-ups.

Perhaps more useful is an evolutionary approach that suggests that "there is a survival advantage to constructing a social reality that corresponds to some objective reality" (Shapiro & Lang, 1991, p. 689). Even before the birth of language and writing, it was probably functional to keep dreams and visions separate from reality.[2] Although visions may have been important to a shaman, one could not eat imaginary game. Failing to distinguish between the real and the nonreal could have a variety of unfortunate consequences. On the other hand, it was also important for

---

[1]Of course that is not really Miami a viewer sees on television. It's an electronic image of Miami that has been distorted, altered or even constructed in editing and postproduction. A viewer may see a "Miami" that is a combination of Miami during the past 5 years and may include a building that no longer exists. It may also include Boca Raton, Hollywood, or any area of South Florida or California or even the Caribbean. In other words—nothing is really "real" on television. It is all constructed. However, the average viewer is only vaguely aware just how much they see is constructed. In fact, even in university television studies classes students have a hard time learning that once on videotape, there is no "reality." However, what is important in this context is what the viewer perceives as real.

[2]We have deliberately suggested that the importance of distinguishing between reality and nonreality would appear early in hominid evolution. Jaynes (1976) speculated that fuzziness in the distinction between reality and nonreality was tied to the development of language and writing. Even if this is true, Jaynes saw this as a particular and temporary (relatively short-lived in evolutionary terms) stage in our development. One might, in fact, accept Jaynes' thesis and see the post-bicameral mind as having evolved to make possible our distinguishing between the real and the unreal *in spite of* the development of language.

survival to act quickly to respond to danger, even if the sensory evidence (e.g., a noise in the brush) was minimal. With the development of agriculture and growth in cities it became imperative for people to develop a socially constructed reality to enable large numbers of people to live in relative harmony, and communication would play a key role in construction of those social realities. (Berger & Luckmann, 1967; Holzner, 1968; Jaynes, 1976)

Today, monitoring our environment is often accomplished through the media. Through the media, we can monitor threats and acquire information that can enhance both our physical and social environment. Some of that information is likely to be available in material ordinarily labeled fiction as well as in material labeled real (e.g., the news).

A Bias Toward Belief

One possibility is that human perceptual and cognitive systems are evolutionarily biased toward judging objects as real and judging statements as true, particularly when under stress (including time and mental capacity constraints). Gilbert (1991) presented considerable evidence that people simultaneously comprehend statements and accept them as true. Only later, given the time and mental capacity, does a person consider whether a statement may be false. Other evidence indicates that people are biased toward assuming that a remembered event was a real-world rather than an imagined event (Johnson & Raye, 1981). Gilbert speculated that these biases are built into mental procedures. According to Gilbert, the perception system is optimized to gather information for potential urgent action. Therefore, it is biased toward at least initially accepting perceived events as real. The perceptual system may work that way because a perceived object usually is real, although that is less true since the (evolutionarily) recent advent of mass media. Gilbert argued that the cognitive system works similarly for two reasons. First, the cognitive system may be an evolutionary modification of the already existing perceptual system. Second, in a social system in which most statements are true, or at least believed true by the sender, such a cognitive system is more efficient than a system in which statements are first comprehended (without assuming they are true) and then judged for veracity.

VR has the potential to create an extremely rich perceptual and cognitive environment. Interacting with such an environment may sometimes tax mental capacities. Under such perceptual and cognitive stress people may be more likely to accept percepts and statements as real because they don't have the capacity to check for veracity, and the default value is real. That is consistent with the literature reviewed earlier that indicates that errors in reality construction and reconstruction are more likely under emotional stress or time constraints. However, before discussing this in more detail, the literature on hallucinations may shed some additional light on how we make judgments about which perceptions are real.

Detection Judgments about Reality

One interesting possibility grows out of current theories of hallucination (for a review see Bentall, 1990). All current theories assume that hallucinations represent a breakdown in a process that allows people to distinguish private mental events from publicly observable events. Such breakdowns are uncommon for most mentally healthy people. How do healthy people make such distinctions, and why do some mentally ill persons seem to fail much more often? Bentall (1990) suggested that the process is a form of signal detection (Swets, 1964).[3] In this case, signal detection theory would say that observed events are distributed along a theoretical "reality" perception dimension. The distributions of both real items and unreal items are both assumed normal. But the mean perceived reality of the real items is greater (more real) than the mean of the unreal items.

Signal detection recognizes that there is both a signal strength and a judgment element to deciding if something is real. The signal strength aspect is reflected by the distance between the means of the two theoretical distributions and is usually denoted d'. The more sensitive the observer, the larger d'. However, the distributions probably overlap. That is, some unreal items may seem as real or more real than some real items. The judgment aspect is called *criterion bias*. In simple terms, this represents the level of "realness" that a stimulus must reach before a person calls it real. No matter where the criterion is placed, if the distributions overlap there always will be some errors. If the criterion is very high there will be few false alarms (saying an unreal item is real) but the number of misses (saying a real item is unreal) will increase. Lowering the criterion has the opposite effect.

Bentall suggested that some mentally ill persons may suffer poor signal sensitivity and/or may have a lower criterion for accepting a perception as real. Signal detection measures can be used to distinguish sensitivity effects from criterion effects. Both effects have been found in mentally ill hallucinators (Bentall, 1990). However, Bentall concluded that the literature generally supports criterion bias, not sensitivity, as critical in hallucinations.

The point, of course, is that mentally healthy people make these judgments as well. They do it better than mentally ill people, but they also

---

[3]A complete discussion of signal detection theory is beyond the scope of this chapter and the space available. Many introductory information-processing, perception, and memory texts discuss the basics of signal detection. For example, see Zechmeister & Nyberg (1982).

make errors (see, e.g., Johnson & Raye, 1981). In addition, signal detection measures may provide a tool for examining these processes. So, for example, detecting hoaxes and making judgments about unfamiliar objects in familiar settings may be most influenced by the sensitivity of the perceiver. If so, there should be a relationship between d' and reality judgment. On the other hand, stress may influence judgments by reducing capacity to assess reality judgments. If the stimulus is potentially danger-ous, a stressed person may lower his or her criterion for accepting something as real. Under signal detection that would mean accepting more false alarms (accepting unreal as real) but would insure detecting more real dangers. In fact, a signal detection analysis suggests that reality discrimi-nation is a trade-off between making correct discriminations and increasing false alarms. Optimal judgments are a function of both the value of correctly detecting real items and of the cost of false alarms. If the cost of false alarms is low, a person will shift his or her criterion to accept the maximum number of events as real. Just how subtle such judgments might become is illustrated by a man in the 1890s who, believing a newspaper hoax about a tragic theater fire, rushed several hundred miles to check on the safety of his family. Realizing he had traveled that far for no reason, he asked whether he should be blamed for loving his family (Fedler, 1989).

As media technology is increasingly able to give the user the impression of "being there," it becomes more and more of a mental challenge to make judgments about reality. Virtual reality is likely to make the challenge even greater. Thinking about how virtual reality might influence those judgments can give us insight both into our future interactions with mass media and into how we make reality judgments now.

Mass Media of The Future

In the future, elements of virtual reality are likely to find their way into a variety of mass media. In talking about VR we accept Steuer's definition (Steuer, 1992), "a remote or artificially constructed environment in which one feels a sense of presence, as a result of using a communication medium." VR is likely to fundamentally change the audience's experience. Viewers of documentaries and news may be able to feel as if they are on the streets of Beirut as militias shell each other or as if they are on an African plain in the middle of a herd of elephants. Fiction viewers may feel like they are in the midst of the action. Fantasy games will evolve to the point where members of virtual reality audiences will have enough sensory input to feel as if they really are the heros trying to find their way through the dungeon. Computer games and simulations will be far more realistic and engaging. Of course, the new abilities will probably result in media forms we can't imagine now.

VR appears to be different from conventional mass media in at least two ways. First, the audience members' sensory experience can be much more like the sensory experience of the real physical world. Second, and related to that, is an effect we will call *immersion*. Audience members can feel much more like they are part of, perhaps even actors in, events—not just observers. An added twist is that not only will audience members be immersed in computer-related reality, but the computer interface and computer-created artifacts may become part of our physical reality. We discuss these one at a time.

An Ideal VR

Current virtual environments are often visually less like the natural environment than many computer games. And, as indicated at the beginning of this chapter, VR has no obligation to conform to physical reality. Even when it is possible to create virtual reality systems that are more similar to external reality, part of the attraction of VR may be its ability to create convincing alternative worlds. Creators may be able to modify everything from physical appearances to the laws of physics.

Nonetheless, it may be useful to define an "ideal" VR as a VR environment so sophisticated that no matter how the user moves or interacts with the environment the user will not be able to use sensory cues to determine whether his or her current environment is real or virtual. Such an ideal VR is probably impossible. Dennett (1991) made a strong case that hallucinations indistinguishable from reality are probably impossible. And no simulation can ever be as complex as the phenomenon it models (Korsybski, cited in Rheingold, 1991, p. 44).

However, some future VR systems are likely to strive for this ideal. In addition, the concept of an "ideal" virtual reality provides a convenient laboratory for some mind experiments, establishing principles that lead us to more likely scenarios and allow us to establish some links to research on current media. The fundamental question raised by an ideal VR is will the increased sensory richness influence reality judgments?

Sensory Channels and VR

The most obvious characteristic of an ideal VR is its ability to mimic the many sensory inputs of a real experience. However, the current literature on reality judgments suggests that, in many cases, very little sensory input is needed to decide something is real. First, survival in a potentially hostile environment is enhanced by detecting danger with minimal sensory cues. For early humans, hearing a tiger growl was undoubtedly sufficient to precipitate various defensive tactics. Early moviegoers had never experienced anything that looked so much like an oncoming train that wasn't an oncoming train. So, they maximized survival possibilities by doing the sensible thing and fleeing. In terms of judgment bias and signal detection, they had a bias to accept percepts as real. The new medium was unfamiliar, so they were relatively insensitive in their ability to distinguish real from unreal. In addition the system was stressed (potential immediate danger with little time to avoid). So, there was little capacity to reassess the initial "real" judgment. Finally, the cost of a false alarm was low (a little embarrassment) and the cost of ignoring a real object was high (annihilation).

Also, many forms of communication carry an implied social contract (Bochner & Eisenberg, 1985; Cantril & Allport, 1935). If a relative calls you by telephone and tells you that another relative has died, you will probably react cognitively and emotionally to a real death. Yet the sense modality of the communication was very restricted. Similarly, a radio broadcast of the *War of the Worlds* panicked many people and newspaper hoaxes fooled many people when those presentations violated an individual's social expectations.

Condry (1989) illustrated another complexity of the relationship between sensory cues and reality judgments. He tells of watching the first moon landing with his then 5-year-old son. The same perceptual cue, the poor quality of the television picture, convinced his son that the picture was not real, but added to the adult's feeling that this was indeed real. The child apparently made reality judgments based strongly on veridicality. But the adult inferred that an image being transmitted from the moon in real time with 1969 technology would be degraded. He would have been suspicious of a studio-quality image. Thus, sophisticated, adult metacognitions about the nature of communication can create a situation in which less sensory information is more realistic. In addition, the hallucination literature generally supports the notion that hallucinations are the result of judgment errors, not vividness (Bentall, 1990).

So, while an ideal VR probably has as much potential for misleading people as more conventional media, it seems unlikely that the increased sensory richness alone will make it dramatically more likely that people will think unreal objects or events are real. However, the increased sensory richness of an ideal VR may still influence reality construction and reconstruction. One possible influence on construction is that sensory richness will tend to tie up mental capacity, reducing what is available for assessing the reality of an object or event. Given the biases discussed earlier, that may make it more likely that objects and events will be accepted as real. At the very least it raises questions about how these processes work.

However, perhaps the most likely effect of increased sensory richness will be on the unconscious mechanisms that may use information accumulated over time to influence reconstruction. Some investigators have suggested, for example, that television's sensory resemblance to real life may influence physiological and unconscious cognitive mechanisms and make it more likely that memories of television events will be judged as real events than less sensory-rich experiences (Shapiro & Lang, 1991). If so, an ideal VR, with its even greater sensory resemblance to natural reality should be even more likely to lead to such "reality monitoring" errors, especially if stress at construction biased judgments toward "real" before storing the memory. Indeed, an ideal VR, with its ability to infinitely vary the amount and type of sensory information, would be an ideal test-bed for such theories.

The Effects of Immersion

Krueger (1990) suggests that there will be two forms of computer-human interface. One possibility is a computer interface that merges seamlessly with the environment so that actions the user performs are acted on to accomplish the user's intentions. Artifacts in such an interface may have no analogy in the pre-VR world. But these artifacts will have many of the characteristics usually associated with reality. Appropriate interaction with them will have consequences and confer rewards. Yet, when first encountering these artifacts, many of us may feel like early moviegoers who saw what appeared to be an approaching train.

In addition, as aspects of the virtual environment become part of our natural environment, the distinction between computer reality and, for lack of a better word, conventional reality will become increasing blurred. Humans may need to become even more sophisticated about reality judgments, making distinctions between physical reality, computer artifacts, and computer artifacts that allow manipulation of physical reality. Of course, these distinctions may become less and less important as more and more of our manipulations of physical reality are done through computer artifacts. For example, it is difficult to imagine the effect on a chemist's concept of reality after he or she uses a VR environment that allows "grabbing" a molecule and getting visual and tactile feedback as the chemist tries to find a reaction site on another molecule.

The other kind of computer interface Krueger mentioned is what we generally think of as VR. Through various forms of sensory feedback, the user has, to some extent, the experience of entering an environment created by a computer. This highlights a potentially important difference between conventional mass media and VR. With conventional mass media, the receiver is distinct and separate. When a person watches a war on television, it is clear he or she is watching a war, not participating. When a medical student watches a videotape of surgery, it is clear that he or she is an observer, not a participant. An ideal virtual reality has the potential for blurring that distinction. The news, using VR, may give a person the impression he or she is actually in the war zone. Simulations that make the user feel as if he or she is actually performing surgery may be possible. Fiction may become a highly evolved fantasy game with full or nearly full sensory experience.

This raises the possibility of a new form of experience substantially different from anything possible today. That form of experience may raise a number of reality judgment issues and perhaps even moral issues. How much will a person who has experienced a real war through VR feel like a veteran of that war? Would you want a doctor who had only done a surgery in virtual reality to perform that surgery on you? Should a person feel guilty about committing adultery in virtual reality? How should his or her spouse feel about it?

Testing Reality

If all the usual perceptual cues indicate that what a person is experiencing is real and the person has the feeling of actually being part of the events, just how does someone in an ideal VR environment distinguish what is real from what is not real?

One answer is that experience and thought cues are probably more important than perceptual richness. For example, the user's memory of entering the VR environment can serve as a cue that the VR experience is not real. In addition, events, even perceptually real ones that theoretically could happen in the real world, may be judged impossible or unlikely. No matter how "real" the experience seemed, most people would know that they weren't really driving a Ferrari and hadn't suddenly become incredibly attractive to members of the opposite sex. That doesn't mean that such experiences couldn't change us in ways not now possible. For example a man using an ideal VR who experiences the full sensory experience as a woman will almost certainly be changed by the experience (for other examples see Stone, 1991).

Another possible way to distinguish an ideal VR from reality is to test that VR either mentally or physically. In some ways these are similar to the kinds of external or internal checks people made about *War of the Worlds*. The ultimate test for a truly ideal VR would be to leave the virtual environment. Is this real? Let's turn it off and find out. A less drastic test in a truly ideal VR would be to mentally test. Do I remember turning on the machine and entering this VR?

Of course, as the virtual reality becomes less ideal, the tests become easier. As Dennett (1991) pointed out, it is unlikely that any artificial environment could ever keep up with the combinatorial explosion of possibilities that human actions can take. In fact, one good criterion for the idealness of a virtual environment might well be how difficult it is to devise tests that force it to respond in some nonnatural way. Thus, any mediated experience can be ranked somewhere along a continuum from easy to reject as not real, to more difficult.

However, there are some critical assumptions here. It assumes that it is important enough to the user to expend the time and mental effort to test whether an experience was real either in real time or in retrospect and that the mental capacity to test is available. Under the press of everyday conditions, we don't always have the resources available or the motivation to make those resources available. In addition, a cost-benefit analysis might indicate that it is either better to err on the side of believing what might be an illusion or that the consequences of an error aren't worth the expenditure of time and other resources. Moreover, some users may find the virtual reality environment so attractive and spend so much time in it that it becomes their reality.

In addition, many of these tests assume that the user has enough "real" experiences to allow him or her to make valid judgments about various aspects of the VR experience. But just as television fiction viewers sometimes forget that the actors they are watching aren't real—for example, people really do sometimes approach actors who play doctors for medical advice—heavy virtual reality users may get lost in the VR environment. This seems especially possible for children, who have less knowledge and fewer skills than adults in making sophisticated judgments about what is real.

Another critical assumption is that there is a social contract not to create situations in which VR appears to be suddenly altered in a way that makes it exceedingly difficult for the user to test what's real and what's not. For example, what if in the middle of a VR simulation a gunman appeared to walk in, appeared to shut off the computer running the simulation and told the user to lie on the floor or be shot. Testing reality here means potentially getting shot. Another possibility would be a virus that used what appeared to be an ordinary error message to indicate that the VR computer was malfunctioning (when it really wasn't) and instructed the user to do something to the machine that would in essence destroy it.

New Directions

New mass media have always demanded new skills and sophistication from the audience. VR is also likely to significantly complicate our judgments about reality (Rheingold, 1991). At the same time, VR technologies may help us explore when judgments about reality are important, how we make judgments about reality, what kinds of errors we make, and what the consequences are of those errors.

This chapter purposely focuses on social psychological issues and avoids ethical and philosophical issues. But our discussion has clear implications for both. We conclude that humans will, by and large, extend current mental strategies to cope with VR. But these conclusions assume people spend a reasonable amount of time immersed in virtual reality, for example, substituting VR immersion for time now spent with television and movies. But people who spend much more time in VR may be influenced differently. They may be able to create a castle in the sky, and live in it.

In addition, the new systems will enable a variety of new and highly sophisticated deceptions. For example, television "reality" programs that mix news footage with re-enactments are already controversial. In the future, seamless virtual reality accounts of events will be available. If you were accused of a crime, would you rather have a potential juror who had seen a reality television account of the crime or one who experienced the VR version? In addition, would you want your children influenced by a VR advertisement that allows them to virtually play with a new toy?

Obviously spending too much time in virtual reality could be damaging to those who need to confront reality and not escape it. It could be particularly damaging to children and adolescents. But in some cases living in a VR could be therapeutic. Certain kinds of therapy encourage patients "to abandon unproductive images and substitute more efficient images of reality" (King, 1989, p. 7). In a skilled therapist's hands virtual reality might assist such processes. In addition, people physically restricted by poor health might become virtually mobile, allowing them to experience the world in ways not now possible.

Finally, the current social psychology research does not say much about what people mean when they say something is real. This may be an interesting area for a synergistic interaction of social psychology and philosophy. For example, Gilbert and his colleagues (Gilbert, 1991) were inspired by a difference between Descartes' and Spinoza's view of how people come to believe a statement. They used social-psychological methods to resolve the dispute in favor of Spinoza. We look forward to more such efforts in the future.

ACKNOWLEDGMENT

Originally published under the same title in *Journal of Communication, 42*(4), 94–114. International Communication Association, Oxford University Press. Used with permission. We want to thank Geri Gay for contributing ideas and suggestions to this chapter.

REFERENCES

Asch, S. E. (1952). *Social psychology*. Englewood Cliffs, NJ: Prentice-Hall.
Ball-Rokeach, S. J., & DeFleur, M. L. (1976, January). A dependency model of mass media effects. *Communication Research, 3,* 3–21.

Benedikt, M. (1991). Introduction. In M. Benedikt (Ed.), *Cyberspace: First steps* (pp. 11–25). Cambridge, MA: MIT Press.

Bentall, R. (1990). The illusion of reality: A review and integration of psychological research on hallucinations. *Psychological Bulletin, 107* (1), 82–95.

Berger, P. L., & Luckmann, T. (1967). *The social construction of reality.* New York: Anchor Books/Doubleday.

Blumer, H., & Hauser, P. (1933). *Movies, delinquency and crime.* New York: MacMillan.

Bochner, A., & Eisenberg, E. (1985). Legitimizing speech communication: An examination of coherence and cohesion in the development of the discipline . In T. Benson (Ed.), *Speech Communication in the 20th Century.* (pp. 299–321). Carbondale: Southern Illinois University Press.

Bryant, J., Carveth, R., & Brown, D. (1981). Television viewing and anxiety: An experimental examination. *Journal of Communication, 31* (1), 106–119.

Cantril, H. (1966). *The invasion from mars.* New York: Harper & Row. (Harper Torchbook Ed., 1940)

Cantril, H., & Allport, G. W. (1935). *The psychology of radio.* New York: Harper and Brothers.

Charters, W. W. (1933). *Motion pictures and youth.* New York: Macmillan.

Condry, J. (1989). *The psychology of television.* Hillsdale, NJ: Lawrence Erlbaum Associates.

Cook, T. D., Kendzierski, D. A., & Thomas, S. V. (1983). The implicit assumptions of television research: An analysis of the 1982 NIMH report on television and behavior. *Public Opinion Quarterly, 47,* 161–201.

Cooley, C. H. (1902). *Social Organization.* New York: Scribner's.

Cressey, P. G., & Thrasher, F. M. (1933). *Boys, movies and city streets.* New York: Macmillan.

Dennett, D. C. (1991). *Consciousness explained.* Boston: Little, Brown.

Dorr, A. (1983). No shortcuts to judging reality. In J. Bryant & D. R. Anderson (Eds.), *Children's understanding of television: Research on attention and comprehension.* (pp.199–220). New York: Academic Press.

Dysinger, W. W., & Ruckmick, C. A. (1933). *The emotional responses of children to the motion picture situation.* New York: Macmillan.

Elliott, W. R., & Slater, D. (1980). Exposure, experience and perceived TV reality for adolescents. *Journalism Quarterly, 57,* 409–414, 431.

Fedler, F. (1989). *Media hoaxes.* Ames, Iowa: Iowa State University Press.

Gerbner, G. (1990). Epilogue: Advancing on the path of righteousness (maybe). In N. Signorielli & M. Morgan (Eds.), *Cultivation analysis: New directions in media effects research* (249–262). Newbury Park, CA: Sage.

Gerbner, G., Gross, L., Morgan, M., & Signorielli, N. (1986). Living with television: The dynamics of the cultivation process. In J. Bryant & D. Zillman (Ed.), *Perspectives on media effects* (pp. 17–40). Hillsdale, NJ: Lawrence Erlbaum Associates.

Gilbert, D. T. (1991, February). How mental systems believe. *American Psychologist, 46*(2), 107–119.

Greenberg, B. S. (1988). Some uncommon television images and the drench hypothesis *Television as a social issue. Applied social psychology annual 8*(88–102). Newbury Park, CA: Sage.

Greenberg, B. S., & Reeves, B. (1976). Children and the perceived reality of television. *Journal of Social Issues, 32*(4), 86–97.

Hawkins, R. P. (1977, July). The dimensional structure of children's perceptions of television reality. *Communication Research, 4*(3), 299–320.

Hawkins, R. P., & Pingree, S. (1982). Television's influence on social reality. In National Institute of Mental Health (Ed.), *Television and behavior: Ten years of scientific progress and implications for the eighties, Vol. 2: Technical Reviews* (224–247). Rockville, MD: National Institute of Mental Health.

Hawkins, R. P., & Pingree, S. (1990). Divergent psychological processes in constructing social reality from mass media content? In N. Signorielli & M. Morgan (Eds.), *Cultivation Analysis: New Directions in Media Effects Research* (35–50). Newbury Park, CA: Sage.

Hawkins, R. P., Pingree, S., & Adler, I. (1987, Summer). Searching for cognitive processes in the cultivation effect. Adult and adolescent samples in the United States and Australia. *Human Communication Research, 13* (4), 553–577.

Hoffner, C., & Cantor, J. (1991). Perceiving and responding to mass media characters. In J. Bryant & D. Zillmann (Eds.), *Responding to the screen: Reception and reaction processes* (63–102). Hillsdale, NJ: Lawrence Erlbaum Associates.

Holaday, P. W., & Stoddard, G. D. (1933). *Getting ideas from the movies.* New York: Macmillan.

Holzner, B. (1968). *Reality construction in society.* Cambridge, MA: Schenkman.

Howard, G. E. (1912, July). Social psychology of the spectator. *American Journal of Psychology, 18,* 33–50.

Jaynes, J. (1976). *The origin of consciousness in the breakdown of the bicameral mind.* Boston: Houghton Mifflin.

Johnson, D. (1952). The phantom anesthetist of mattoon. In G. E. Swanson, T. M. Newcomb, & E. H. Hartley (Eds.), *Readings in Social Psychology* (208–219). New York: Holt.

Johnson, M. K., & Raye, C. L. (1981). Reality monitoring. *Psychological Review, 88*(1), 67–85.

King, J. R. (1989). Behavioral implications of mental world-making. *The Journal of Creative Behavior, 23*(1), 1–13.

Krueger, M. W. (1990). Videoplace and the interface of the future. In B. Laurel (Ed.), *The Art of Human-Computer Interface Design* (417–422). Reading, MA: Addison-Wesley.

Lang, A. (1990). Involuntary attention and physiological arousal evoked by structural features and emotional content in TV commercials. *Communication Research, 17*(3), 275–299.

Liebes, T., & Katz, E. (1986). Patterns of involvement in television fiction: A comparative analysis. *European Journal of Communication, 1* , 151–171 .

Livingstone, S. M. (1989, February). Interpretive viewers and structured programs: The implicit representation of soap opera characters. *Communication Research, 16*(1), 25–57.

Lowenthal, L. (1984). *Literature and mass culture.* New Brunswick: Transaction Books.

Medalia, N. Z., & Larsen, O. N. (1958). Diffusion and belief in a collective delusion: The seattle windshield pitting epidemic. *American Sociological Review, 23,* 221–232.

Munsterberg, H. (1916). *The photoplay: A psychological study.* New York: Appleman.

Palmer, L. E. (1909, June 5). The world in motion. *Survey, 22,* 355–365.

Pingree, S. (1978, spring). The effects of nonsexist television commercials and perceptions of reality on children's attitudes about women. *Psychology of Women Quarterly, 2*(3), 262–277.

Potter, W. J. (1986, Spring). Perceived reality and the cultivation hypothesis. *Journal of Broadcasting & Electronic Media, 30* (2), 159–174.

Potter, W. J. (1988, Winter). Three strategies for elaborating the cultivation hypothesis. *Journalism Quarterly, 65*(4), 930–939.

Potter, W. J. (1991, September). The relationship between first- and second-order measures of cultivation. *Human Communication Research, 18* (1), 92–113.

Prawat, R. S., Anderson, A. L., & Hapkeiwicz, W. (1989). Are dolls real? Developmental changes in the child's definition of reality. *Journal of Genetic Psychology, 150*(4), 359–374.

Reep, D. C., & Dambrot, F. H. (1989, Autumn). Effects of frequent television viewing on stereotypes: "Drip, drip" or "drench"? *Journalism Quarterly, 66*(3), 542–50.

Reeves, B. (1978). Perceived TV reality as a predictor of children's social behavior. *Journalism Quarterly, 55,* 682–689, 695 .

Rheingold, H. (1991). *Virtual reality.* New York: Summit.

Rubin, A. M., Perse, E. M., & Taylor, D. S. (1988, April). A methodological examination of cultivation. *Communication Research, 15* (2), 107–134.

Schramm, W., Lyle, J., & Parker, E. (1961). *Television in the lives of our children*. Palo Alto, CA: Stanford University Press.

Shapiro, M. A. (1991a, February). Memory and decision processes in the construction of social reality. *Communication Research, 18*(1), 3-24.

Shapiro, M. A. (1991). *Television reality and experience in constructing social and personal estimates of risk*. Paper presented to the Theory and Methodology Division of the Association for Education in Journalism and Mass Communication, Boston.

Shapiro, M. A., & Lang, A. (1991, October). Making television reality: Unconscious processes in the construction of social reality. *Communication Research, 18*(5), 685-705.

Slater, M. D. (1990, June). Processing social information in messages: Social group familiarity, fiction versus nonfiction, and subsequent beliefs. *Communication Research, 17*(3), 327-343.

Steuer, J. (1992). Defining virtual reality: Dimensions determining telepresence. *Journal of Communication, 42*(4), 73-93.

Stone, A. R. (1991). Will the real body please stand up? Boundary stories about virtual cultures. In M. Benedikt (Ed.), *Cyberspace: First steps* (81-118). Cambridge, Mass: MIT Press.

Swets, J. A. (Ed.) (1964). *Signal Detection and recognition by human observers: Contemporary readings*. New York: Wiley.

Tyler, T. R. (1980). Impact of directly and indirectly experienced events: The origin of crime-related judgments and behaviors. *Journal of Personality and Social Psychology, 39*(1), 13-28.

Tyler, T. R., & Cook, F. L. (1984). The mass media and judgments of risk: Distinguishing impact on personal and societal level judgments. *Journal of Personality and Social Psychology, 47*(4), 693-708.

Vorse, M. H. (1911, June 24). Some picture show audiences. *The Outlook, 98*, 441-447.

Wartella, E., & Reeves, B. (1985). Historical trends in research on children and the media: 1900-1960. *Journal of Communication, 35* (2), 118-133.

Wilcox, D. F. (1900). The American newspaper: A study in social psychology. *The annals of the American Academy of Political and Social Science, 16*(1), 56-92.

Wober, J. M., & Gunter, B. (1986, Winter). Television audience research at Britain's independent broadcasting authority 1974-1984. *Journal of Broadcasting & Electronic Media, 30*(1), 15-31.

Zechmeister, E., & Nyberg, S. (1982). *Human memory: An introduction to research and theory*. Monterey, CA: Brooks/Cole.

13 Signal to Noise: On the Meaning of Cyberpunk Subculture

Anne Balsamo
Georgia Institute of Technology

"MORE PR THAN VR"

Virtually every major channel of mass communications in the U.S. has buzzed with the "news" about virtual reality (VR).[1] Whereas early reports in science magazines such as *New Scientist* and *Scientific American* explored pragmatic applications of VR, more recent media pieces proclaim that VR holds the key to the technological reinvention of the mundane world of late capitalism. *Business Week* (Virtual Corporation, 1993) offered a cover story on "The Virtual Corporation"—a new capitalist formation that would be able to reconfigure itself in response to a rapidly changing business environment by using "technology to link people, assets, and ideas in a temporary organization." In its report on the more titillating topic of "virtual sex" and "teledildonics," *Playboy* used a graphic rendition of a "Virtual Madonna" to suggest another figuration of the term *safe sex*. Apparently this rush of media attention is not entirely welcomed by the computer scientists and programmers who work on the technoscientific aspects of VR such as computer visualization, three-dimensional sound, and robotic telepresence. "More PR than VR," one scientist grumbled in his posting to the sci-virtual worlds newsgroup in response to early media reviews of the 1992 film, *Lawnmower Man*.[2] According to the various press

---

[1]For an illustration of the range of articles on VR, see the list of titles in the reference section of this chapter.

[2]By the end of 1992, at least four new science fiction films were released that featured virtual reality special effects. Where the mainstream film, *Lawnmower Man*, constructed its plot

reports, the range of potential applications include everything from medical simulations of virtual surgery to home VR systems to educational theater. The reality of VR is a bit more delimited in that, thus far, fully immersive, interactive VR applications are mostly restricted to expensive "touring" video game installations, a few computer-assisted rendering programs, and flight and tank simulations used by the U.S. government. But *reality* is really beside the point in discussing the cultural reception of VR; it is *exactly* because of its "virtuality" that Virtual Reality has animated our collective technological imagination.

Far more broad-ranging than even the discussions about potential marketable VR applications is the discussion about cyberspace as the form of reality that VR technologically enables. Cyberspace, too, is a virtual construct, more fictional than real in any material sense. Technically, the term was first invoked as a speculative construct in cyberpunk science fiction novels to name the space of human–computer data exchange. By the early 1990s it has devolved into one of the keywords of a new subculture generated by cyberpunk fans that has, in turn, splintered and evolved into other (sub)cultural formations. The broader cultural formation constructed in and around cyberspace is multidimensional in that it includes more traditional forms of leisure activity such as masquerade and role-playing, as well as popular discursive forms such as 'zines and comic books, and newly emergent sociotextual forms such as electronic newsgroups and MUDS (Balsamo, 1993). In short, VR has become inextricably bound up with the emergence of cyberpunk as a new youth subculture.

Although several studies of cyberpunk subculture already exist in the form of journalistic reports on the early development of computer culture and interviews with infamous computer hackers and "hacker trackers,"[3] I

---

centrally around virtual reality and the use of nootropic "smart drugs," the art-house film, *Till the End of the World*, directed by Wim Wenders featured an "experience recorder" that resembles the head-mounted stereoscopic display systems of current real-time VR rigs. Two other less well known films also invoked the specter of VR: the film *Interceptor* (1992) involved a chase scene in VR piloted stealth bombers, and *Prototype 29A* (1992) teased the audience with a sequence on virtual sex. These films join a long list of others that feature special effects which invoke the virtual landscape of cyberspace: *Tron* (1982), *Videodrome* (1982), *Brainstorm* (1983), *Circuitry Man* (1989), and *FreeJack* (1992).

[3]Steven Levy (1984) traced the history of hacker identity back to the student members of the Tech Model Railroad Club at MIT; Levy was the first to codify the subcultural code of ethics that govern "true" hacker conduct. In their book called *Cyberpunk: Outlaws and Hackers on the Computer Frontier*, Katie Hafner and John Markoff (1991) interviewed three computer hackers who received extensive media attention in the 1980s for their computer transgressions. In addition to providing important historical background on the development of telephone system hacking, Bruce Sterling's book (1992), *The Hacker Crackdown*, includes a detailed discussion of the three groups involved in the most recent spectacle of computer law enforcement: the digital underground, the computer network police, and the civil libertarians.

want to discuss aspects of this new youth subculture from a perspective informed by cultural studies, and, in particular, by Dick Hebdige's and Angela McRobbie's studies of youth (punk) subcultures in the 1970s. The aspect I focus on most closely is the notion of narratives of cyberpunk identity, which allows me, in turn, to speculate about the construction of what Scott Bukatman (1993) called "terminal identity" in postmodernity. At the broadest level, this essay discusses the social noise created by cyberpunk subculture. At each turn, we can see how this subculture is marked by contradiction and cultural dissonance. I begin by describing how cyberpunk takes shape as a virtual subculture, popularized by the hip, high-tech magazine *Mondo 2000* and Internet newsgroups like alt.cyberpunk. In an effort to situate this new subculture within an historical context, I argue that cyberpunk identity is, in part, a generational identity that emerges with the coming of age of those who, born after the baby-boomers, have come to be known as "Generation X." For the members of the first generation to grow up with computers in their homes, technological access to electronic information networks is a natural condition of the domestic scene. Having claimed cyberspace as their own private frontier, cyberpunks resent the imposition of limits on their cyberspace travels. At one level, cyberpunk identity is about resistance to a capitalist social order; many cyberpunks critique the dominant ideology of the information age that naturalizes the commodification of information and the surveillance of network access. But at another level, we can discern a submerged logic of gender that structures on-line cyberpunk interactions. If on the one hand, cyberpunk subculture popularizes a fantasy of resistance and opposition to corporate information control, it also projects a fantasy world where the material body—the race, gender, and ability-marked body—is technologically re-pressed. Thus we can see multiple tensions at work in cyberpunk subculture and in the construction of postmodern identities.

SIGNAL/NOISE: SUBCULTURE STUDIES

Dick Hebdige's work on subcultures (1979) is useful for a discussion of cyberpunk subculture for two reasons: most directly, he delineated a theoretical framework for the analysis of subcultures as a cultural forma-tion. In this sense, I borrow from Hebdige the focus on subcultures as an expressive cultural form that embodies and re-presents the central, histor-ically specific contradictions and preoccupations of the parent culture. But another reason for the return to Hebdige's work on the youth subcultures of the 1970s is that cyberpunks, to differing degrees, borrow icons and stylistic tropes from their Punk elders. Reflecting on the similarities in aesthetic sensibilities of punk music and cyberpunk fiction, Larry McCaffery (1991) argued that both "should be seen as subversive metaforms" (p. 292). Although McCaffery was talking about punk themes in cyberpunk as a science fictional form, these thematic connections exist also in the broader cultural formation that cyberpunk has become. Hebdige's observation about punk culture in the 1970s is strikingly true of cyberpunk subculture in the 1990s:

> Subcultures represent "noise" (as opposed to sound): interference in the orderly sequence which leads from real events and phenomena to their representation in the media. We should not therefore underestimate the signifying power of the spectacular subculture not only as a metaphor for potential anarchy "out there" but as an actual mechanism of semantic disorder: a kind of temporary blockage in the system of representation. (p. 90)

Subcultures create semantic and social disorder when members challenge, contest, or, in the case of network-savvy cyberpunks, evade the mechanisms designed to maintain social order. According to Hebdige, this disorder is created at the level of signification as well as the level of social structure; he argued that subculture style (fashion, posture, music) *signifies* resistance to dominant ideological formulations. In discussing the sociological structure of Hebdige's investigation into youth subculture, Angela McRobbie (1981) charged that his focus on *symbolic* resistance elides the issue of practice: what exactly are these youth doing in their subcultural interactions? More specifically, she challenged Hebdige's exclusive focus on male youth and his oversight, not only of female participation in subcultures, but also of the sexist treatment of women by male punks:

> In documenting the temporary flights of the Teds, Mods or Rockers, however, they fail to show that it is monstrously more difficult for women to escape (even temporarily) and that these symbolic flights have often been at the expense of women (especially mothers) and girls. The lads may get by with — and get off on — each other alone on the streets but they did not eat, sleep or make love there. Their peer-group consciousness and pleasure frequently seem to hinge on a collective disregard for women and the sexual exploitation of girls. And in the literary sensibility of urban romanticism that resonates across most youth cultural discourses, girls are allowed little more than the back seat on a draughty motor bike. (McRobbie, 1981, p.115)

In examining subculture practices through a feminist lens, McRobbie illuminated how seemingly resistant "youth" subcultures embody sexist behaviors characteristic of the dominant culture. Although these subcultures may be resistant at the level of style and rhetoric, in other ways they clearly mimic traditional gender divisions and practices of sexual disrespect.

Thus she argued for the importance of attending to the gender politics inherent in subcultural practices.

To anyone who has participated in computer-communication networks or bulletin boards, the term *noise* also refers to senseless, trivial, or off-the-topic electronic commentary. Users commonly sign off of discussion lists with the complaint that the noise-to-signal ratio is too high. In some cases, teenage computer users—some of whom identify themselves as cyberpunks—have been condescendingly accused of interfering with the "serious" discussions-in-progress on certain Internet newsgroups. As a counter response, the alt.cyberpunk newsgroup was started as a place to discuss such "noisy" topics as the status of Gibson's various film screenplays or whether the character Deckard in the film *Bladerunner* is a replicant. It becomes apparent that woven into the very fabric of cyberpunk identity is a commitment to interfere with the corporate management of online culture. Hebdige's use of the term *noise* to describe how Punk "style" expressed a symbolic challenge to a dominant symbolic order is equally applicable to the ways in which cyberpunks challenge the dominant informational order of a U.S.-based computer culture. Instead of staging their opposition primarily through style though, as did Hebdige's punks, cyberpunks create "noise" by transgressing the newly emergent norms of computer network communication. But if cyberpunk online culture is noise in one sense, it is "signal" in another. Cyberpunk culture often reproduces dominant gender stereotypes, both at the level of expression, that is, in the topics of communication, and at the level of practice, in the form of exchange. Upon closer examination, it becomes clear that this is only one of the many contraditions at play in the construction of cyberpunk identity.

VIRTUAL SUBCULTURES AND CYBERPUNK NARRATIVES OF IDENTITY

Mondo 2000 has emerged as the premier magazine of cyberpunk subculture. Three features stand out: its visually confusing, techno-art layouts, the frequent reports from cyberspace pioneers, and its mediated interviews with the high priests of street tech, notably William Burroughs and Timothy Leary. In the pages of the first seven issues readers were introduced to the reigning new visionaries of cyberspace, Jaron Lanier and John Perry Barlow, as well as to other cultural cybercritics such as Kathy Acker, Avital Ronell, and Ted Nelson. *Mondo 2000* does its best to report on the important features of the new subculture by identifying founding fathers, offering fashion and style tips, interviewing cyberpunk artists, and advertising new, and usually expensive, cybernetic technologies. In short, *Mondo 2000* popularizes the worldview of those addicted to the possibilities of life in the microworld. And yet, in spite of its technolust(er), *Mondo 2000* oddly evokes a countercultural rhetoric of the 1960s. In part, this reflects the more widespread 1990s nostalgia for 1960s fashions and fads, but it is also the case that its countercultural tone is a consequence of the fact that it is involved in the business of articulating a subcultural identity that mimics the iconoclastic postures of the earlier subculture of punk rockers. Thus, an issue of *Mondo* might include retro-topics such as "on the road" stories, drug synthesis instructions, mod fashion icons, and reports from the underground—the difference is, in the 1990s, the drugs are intended to make us "smart," hallucinogens are replaced with hallucino*genres*, the "Underground" is a band, and the best sex is virtual. As a statement about the current cyberpunk scene, *Mondo* projects a curious fusion of counter-cultural iconoclasm and technological elitism. The magazine's editors offer no pretense of democracy and make no attempt at accessibility. Unsolicited manuscripts are burned at the full moon, we are told, and "unsolicited art work will be electronically scanned and altered and appear uncredited in other magazines." But the pleasure of recognition is high; if you get it, you've got it. Articles demonstrate the appropriate attitude toward the "New World DisOrder" while they tell you who/what you need to know/to read/to buy/to be a member by imitation only.

Sometime after its 7th issue, *Mondo* reinvented itself as a literal guidebook to cyberpunk subculture in the form of the *Mondo 2000 User's Guide to the New Edge*; the table of contents confirms the impression that *Mondo* has set itself up as the definitive handbook on this new popular culture by including chapters on cyberpunk science fiction, cyberspace, artificial life, the computer industry, electronic music, smart drugs, the Net, raves and rants, street tech, virtual reality and virtual sex, and 'zines.[4] Lest any reader forget that this subculture is situated within the broader postmodern (consumer) culture of the 1990s, an appendix, titled "The Shopping Mall," provides information about how to buy the products described in the book. In fiction and in practice, cyberpunks continue to be fascinated with (and covetous of) the high-tech commodities of the domi-nant computer culture.

As the *Mondo* guide laments, the term *cyberpunk* has come to be used as a general name for anyone who felt a "rapport with the worlds created by [William] Gibson" and other cyberpunk sf writers (Rucker, ed., 1992, p.64). The popularization of the label—which reached its apotheosis in the February 8, 1993 *Time* magazine cover story— has, in turn, stimulated a

---

[4]Rucker, (1992), *Mondo 2000 User's Guide to the New Edge*. The discussion of cyberpunk science fiction is expanding rapidly. A representative sample of historical accounts and scholarly discussion includes the following: Gilmore (1986), Delany (1988), and McCaffery (1991).

heated debate about the "true" identifying characteristics of cyberpunks (as well as a heated debate about whether "the movement" is dead already). In the course of these debates, a number of narratives emerge that claim to map the defining contours of cyberpunk identity. They are all, to different degrees, *mythic* narratives of identity in that they stake out the polemical beliefs that subculture participants should adopt if they want to be considered authentic cyberpunks.[5] What becomes apparent in the course of reading these debates is that there is actually a continuum of identities available to "wanna-be" cyberpunks. At one end of the continuum — elaborated in traditionally mythic dimensions — is Timothy Leary's (1988) report on "Cyberpunk as Reality Pilot." Leary grounded his account of cyberpunk identity in a discussion of the etymological distinction between two root terms of the word *cybernetics*. Apparently, the Greek word *kubernetes* means "pilot," but when translated to Latin it comes out as

---

[5]These narratives of identity are disseminated through different media channels: in films, comic books, magazines, e-zines, bulletin boards, music, fashion, television, and newspapers. There are any of a number of ways in which cyberpunk narratives are taken up by subculture subjects. In the most literal form, cyberpunk science fiction novels offer multiply dense narratives of identity, expressed through characters both physical and virtual. Other sources include the many manuals that describe cyberpunk role-playing scenarios that hack cyberpunk science fiction stories for dramatic structure and character suggestions. The best known of these role-playing guides is probably the *Gurps cyberpunk high-tech low-life roleplaying sourcebook* by Loyd Blankenship (1990) produced by Steve Jackson games. This is the document that was seized by the U.S. Secret Service as part of an investigation of computer crime referred to as "Operation Sun Devil." (For a detailed description of the cultural and political events surrounding this police action see Sterling, 1992.) In the "Introduction," Blankenship described how cyberpunk as a genre aspires to a kind of realism in roleplaying scenarios:

> Roleplaying in a cyberpunk environment can be very different from playing in traditional genres such as fantasy or supers. Cyberpunk, more than any other genre, tries to accurately reflect "real-world" human nature. Traditional ideas such as loyalty with the party may be questioned or tested. Betrayal and deceit are common in the real world — just read any issue of the *Wall Street Journal* — so why should they be less so in the game? . . . Characters in cyberpunk literature are constantly committing unethical, illegal or immoral acts, but they sometimes do so for purposes we would define as "good." Conversely, a repressive government may define behavior as "good" that stifles the human spirit and grinds individuals into dust. In cyberpunk there are rarely blacks and whites, but there are many shades of gray. (Blankenship, 1990, pp. 4–5)

Here Blankenship laid out the basic premise of cyberpunk fictions: Characters may do unethical or illegal things for good reasons, just as repressive governments may promote actions and laws in the name of the "common good" that, in actuality, "stifle the human spirit and grind individuals into dust" (Blankenship, 1990, p. 5). But beyond setting up the basic dramatic tension in cyberpunk games, Blankenship also offered a literal description of how cyberpunk science *fiction* gets transformed into subcultural *reality*: Fictional narratives structure role-playing campaigns played by those who may or may not actually adopt a cyberpunk identity for any time longer than the duration of the game. This is an example of how a subcultural practice articulates a mass-mediated identity for the role-playing gamer.

gubernetes, which means "governor" or "director." This is not an insignificant slippage for Leary who argued that "cyberpunk/pilots [must] replace governetics/controllers" (Leary, 1988, p. 249). In contrast to those who use cybernetics as a system of control, Leary argued that cyberpunks can use cybernetic systems as a navigational medium of self-direction: "cyber-punks use all available data-input to think for themselves." Thus Leary reinvents the classically romantic myth of the empowered, embattled hero within the electronic frontier. Leary is not alone in his construction of cyberpunk as postmodern hero. As other critics have pointed out, much cyberpunk science fiction renarrates traditional myths of transcendental individualism from within a postmodern context of cybernetic information exchange.

At the other end of the continuum is the film *Slacker* (Linklater, 1991), which is populated by characters who aimlessly articulate the heteroglossic discourse of a post-baby-boomer generation, and who appear, at first glance, to be the most unlikely participants in cyberpunk culture. As Jack Bankowsky (1991) described it in his *ArtForum* film review: "A subject without a mission, fate or even a subjectivity . . . the slacker inhabits an atomized universe: everyone speaks a debased or hybrid argot, worships at their own jerry-built altar, proselytizes for a private religion. . . . Slackers are beatniks without a beat—a lost generation minus a sustaining poetics of loss" (Bamkowsky, 1991, p. 97). If Leary's cyberpunk reality pilot is uninhibited by historical determinations, slackers, at the other end, can do nothing more than mindlessly channel a historically specific and topically tedious flow of information and discourse; for Leary's "Reality Pilot," identity is entirely self-determined, for the slacker, entirely mass-produced. Leary's cyberpunks speak their culture, and believe themselves to be the entirely self-determined "authors" of their own tales of heroic deeds; slackers show instead how culture speaks them. Identities are always already written for them by the cacophonous discourses of media culture. This tension between the myth of self-determination and the reality of media-saturated identity electrifies the theoretical interzone that cyberpunks negotiate on a regular basis.

In between these extremes are the two identities explicitly described in the *Mondo User's Guide*: Hackers and Crackers. Where both of these terms name those who are more comfortable in front of a computer terminal than a television screen, Crackers are considered "dark-side Hackers," computer operators who perpetrate illegal breaking and entering schemes. Whereas the original MIT hackers of the 1960s were considered no more dangerous than any other group of students and hobbyists, hackers in the 1990s are plagued by a demonized media image that is a consequence of the mass media's failure to differentiate between phone phreaks, credit card criminals, and other subversive and malicious computer operators. This is not to say that hackers don't assert a critical, countercultural attitude. On the contrary, many hackers, who often explicitly identify themselves as cyberpunks, have readopted the original hacker's ethic from the 1960s that asserts, among other things, that (a) "access to computers should be unlimited and total," that (b) "information should be free," and that hackers should (c) "mistrust authority and promote decentralization."[6] This is the identity of those who have been responsible for the digitizing cyberpunk subculture through their participation on bulletin boards and computer networks. Using network systems like the WELL, MindVox, and Internet newsgroups, cyberpunks have spread their subculture throughout the rest of the United States. In this sense, cyberpunk-hacker subculture is, in large measure, a *virtual* subculture: a widely distributed network of people who connect with one another most often not "in-the-flesh," through the more traditional forms of mass media fandom such as science fiction fan conventions and role-playing games, but virtually, through computer networks and bulletin boards. Howard Rheingold offerd an apt description of the social structure of cyberpunk subculture in his definition of a "virtual community" as a "group of people who may or may not meet one face to face, [but] who exchange words and ideas through the mediation of computer bulletin boards and networks."[7]

Late in 1989, a polemical statement about cyberpunk identity was posted to the Internet newsgroup, alt.cyberpunk. The subject line of the posting read: "I am Cyberpunk," and was signed by someone called "Tesuji." The rant was rhetorically addressed to the cyberpunk wanna-bes who were not, according to Tesuji, cyber*punks*. It was time, Tesuji asserted, that a real Cyber*punk* set the story straight as to what cyberpunk identity was all about:

> This is where I come in. . . . I am a cyberpunk. . . . That is, I usually dress in black monochrome, my hair is shaved on one side, I have a skin-tone whiter than bleached flower, and I'm an Anarchistic Technofetishist (and a bad speller). . . . We have an average IQ of 130 and we are primarily nocturnal. We are dark and we are fast and we are tech.[8]

Tesuji goes on to admit that cyberpunks exist as a reactionary underground who are self-righteously power hungry; unlike hippies and skinheads,

---

[6]The Hacker ethic is elaborated in the Steven Levy (1984) book, *Hackers*. Other information about 1990's hackers comes from Andy Hawks' compilation about FutureCulture, an electronic discussion list.

[7]Howard Rheingold, *A slice of life in my virtual community* (1992, June). Available online from ftp.eff.org.

[8]The message was originally posted on October 17, 1989 to the alt.cyberpunk Internet newsgroup. It appears to have originated from a computer science major at SUNY Binghamton. Although the Internet address does identify a name for the posting, I'll honor the pseudonym that Tesuji signed.

cyberpunks are into the future. Fans of capitalism and corporate control, they believe that they will be able to change the system "from the inside out." Cyberpunks love computers: "Life is cheap, information is the goal. The most valuable commodity (besides a spell-checker :-) is data." In this statement, Tesuji fused the image of the computer hacker, who possesses elitist technological expertise, with the attitude of the countercultural punk, who is mistrustful of all forms of authority, and yet remains hungry for power.

It is difficult to discern the media origin of Tesuji's identity narrative. By the time of this posting, cyberpunk science fiction was receiving media attention outside of the usual science fiction channels, and Robert Morris had already unleashed his Internet worm. Although Tesuji structured this posting as a statement of individualized identity, the narrative he or she offered highlights several key elements of the popular media representations of cyberpunk identity. Aesthetically, cyberpunks adopt signature elements of punk style: black on black clothes, shaved heads, and pale complexions. Their musical tastes include techno-rave and postindustrial "anti-muzak." But unlike punks, who wanted to turn technology against itself, cyberpunks are "technofetishists" who desperately depend on computer equipment and network access to participate in their virtual subcultures. This points to one of the central contradictions of cyberpunk identity: according to Tesuji, cyberpunks are "Anarchistic Technofetishists" who are at the same time "fans of capitalism and corporate control." Where their disregard for authority provokes them to transgress cyberspace boundaries by (sometimes illegally) hacking their way past corporate security measures, their ultimate goal is to secure a legitimate position within the very same corporate system in order to gain reliable access to computer workstations and global information networks. In this sense, Tesuji invoked the contradiction that Hebdige (1979) argued faces every subculture: "a fundamental tension between those in power and those condemned to subordinate positions and second-class lives" (p. 132). Like the punks of the 1970s this tension is in part generational; the various cyberpunk identities that evolve are partially determined by the historical situation of their birth cohort. Generational experiences, in turn, structure how subcultural identities symbolically manage these cultural contradictions.

THE NEXT GENERATION OF CYBERSPACE CITIZENS

It is a bit ironic to try to retrace the media birth of the generational identity of cyberpunks because its originating moment was forged through the act of recognizing the absence of a name for itself. At the same time that the trailing edge of the baby-boomer cohort was turning "Thirtysomething," both *Time* and *Newsweek* featured cover stories about the lost generation destined to follow those aging baby-boomers who were identified simply as the "Twentysomethings." Douglas Coupland (1991) simply called them *Generation X* in his novel by the same name. In yet another popular account of this lost generation, Neil Howe and Bill Strauss identified this census group as the "13th Generation"; a mass of lost souls born between the years 1961–1981 who are chronologically situated between the baby-boomers and their "babies on board" born in the U.S. during the Reagan years.[9] This is the group in the United States who confront the possibility that they will never achieve the lifestyle of their baby-boomer elders. In this sense, the 13th Generation is culturally situated similarly to the British punks of the 1970s: these are urban youth who, growing up in the midst of massive unemployment, face diminishing opportunities and increasing banality. The difference between them is that, in contrast to the punks who self-consciously identified with working-class culture, 13ers enjoy what Howe and Strauss (1993) (borrowing a phrase from sociologist Jerald Bachman) identified as "premature affluence":

> Much of this "premature affluence" is, of course just image. Very few 13ers really do cruise to school in Land Rovers or vacation in Bermuda. . . . Even where this affluence is real, moreover, the bustling youth economy masks [several] harsh truths about the 13ers' economic condition. First, much of it is not really "theirs" in the sense that it reflects any ability to provide for themselves. . . . [I]ts the cash or clothes or car that busy, well-off parents give their kids as a "reward" for time they have to spend alone. . . . But little of this wealth serves any long-term interest of the kids themselves — such as helping them to become future wealth producers. Instead it can make teenagers feel like bored retainers milling around in some opulent palace, having momentary, hopeless fun with whatever baubles the Rajah leaves lying around. (p. 103)

This affluence, as many have learned, is short lived, tied to their tenure living in their parent's houses; once they leave home or school, they encounter few well-paying job opportunities that allow them to continue to enjoy the lifestyle they experienced as parent-supported mall crawlers. For some, diminished economic opportunities force them to return home: "Meet the 13er 'boomerang child'. . . . Today, more unmarried children under age 30 are living with their parents than at any time since the Great Depression" (Howe & Strauss, 1993, p. 105). Although the rallying cry of

---

[9]According to most demographic accounts of the baby-boomers, their historical birth dates fall between 1946 and 1964. Neil Howe and Bill Strauss (1993) argued that the cut-off date should be 1961; people born after this date show the characteristics of the 13th generation that they write about in their book.

the 13th generation is that they suffer anonymously in the shadow and waste of the baby boomers, these are the children who materially benefited from the baby-boomer-driven decade of abundance. The problem is that members of the 13th generation are not likely to easily attain such a level of affluence again because they will spend a disproportionate amount of their resources to pay for basic living expenses and to indirectly support an aging baby-boomer population. But there is a more significant dimension of their "premature affluence." This is the generation of teenagers who, in growing up in the 1980s, have had liberal access to expensive home computer systems — bought by parents either for their own domestic computing needs, or as an educational tool for video-literate teenagers. With access to video games and modems, 13ers are the first generation to claim the electronic frontier as their neighborhood playground. Cyberpunks are one of the subcultural groups to emerge from this 13th generation for whom the virtual reality of online culture is their primary social milieu. And although not all video game players become cyberpunks, most cyberpunks are avid game players, having grown up playing either Dungeons and Dragon™ roleplaying dice games or any of the hundreds of interactive video games made for home systems.

MULTIPLE IDENTITIES IN THE MICROWORLD

The 13th generation is certainly not the first generation to grow up in an electronic environment; the baby-boomers, too, were weaned on television. But this is the first generation of Nintendo™ video game players who encounter the electronic environment as a fully interactive, albeit simulated, microworld that they can play endlessly in the privacy of their parents' homes. According to Sherry Turkle (1984), video gaming and computer programming are not, for this group, simply alternative leisure activities; they are instead the very media through which this generation encounters the world. In her analysis of the relationship between children and computer gaming, Turkle illuminated the message of the video game medium:

> Video games encourage identification with characters — from science fiction, or sports, or war stories — but leave little room for playing [those] roles. . . . [T]he video simulations put you "in the place" of the spaceship pilot or the missile commander or the adventurer in the Tolkien world. But you are not allowed to play the part. . . . you identify with an alter ego as you play your role in the dungeon, but the process of play is mathematical and procedural. Beyond the fantasy, there are always the rules. (p. 78)

Identifying with a simulated character is the genesis of the "second self" that Turkle argued is a metaphysical aspect of computer encounters. Thus these "virtual" media enable the simultaneous enactment of multiple identities; in video games, this occurs through the identification with the gaming character; in cyberspace, through the projection of an online identity. Turkle's analysis offers one account of how the adoption of multiple media(ted) identities becomes naturalized through repeated technological encounters with computers and video games. But Turkle went on to point out that although it is true that the "second self" is a fictional entity of action within the microworld of the video game, the range of the agency of this simulated actor is constrained by the rules already programmed into the game. So too is the cyberpunk hacker constrained by the codes of access already established for a system. Thus Turkle implicitly argued that one of the contradictions facing the 13th generation cyberpunk—between self-determination and structural contingency, or between power and subordination—is built into the individual–computer interaction itself. Thus it appears that cyberpunks are subject to forces of determination well outside their control, generationally and technologically.

Cyberpunks, of course, believe differently. For them, hacking is not simply a *gesture* of defiance against technological limits on cyberspace agency, it is a literal act of transgression against normative forms of social control. To the cyberpunk, the computer is the technological means of disavowing and transcending social determinations. For example, some people believe that, in enabling the adoption of multiple identities, computer-communication networks establish the infrastructure for new forms of social interaction that are free from traditional markers of identity and status. Howard Rheingold (1992), for one, optimistically argued:

> . . . we who populate cyberspace deliberately experiment with fracturing traditional notions of identity by living as multiple simultaneous personae in different virtual neighborhoods. We reduce and encode our identities as words on a screen, decode and unpack the identities of others. The way we use these words, the stories (true or false) we tell about ourselves (or about the identity we want people to believe us to be) is what determines our identities in cyberspace.[10]

More specifically, Rheingold claimed that because people who communicate through computers can't see or hear one another, they are "unable to form prejudices about others before we read what they have to say: Race, gender, age, national origin and physical appearance are not apparent unless a person wants to make such characteristics public." In saying this, Rheingold amplified the *fantasy* element of computer-mediated communi-

---

[10]Howard Rheingold, *A slice of life in my virtual community* (1992, June). Online document file.

cation to imply that users have extensive, if not total, control over the identity they project in their virtual worlds. Leary's "Reality Pilot" narrative provides a conceptual coherence to Rheingold's account. It is noteworthy to this feminist reader that gender is one of the "identity markers" that is most routinely mentioned when people launch into a discussion of the fluid possibilities of online identity construction. According to this argument, computer interactions are gender-neutral and race-blind. Because these interactions are disembodied, the argument goes, these signs of a material body are no longer necessary aspects of individual identity.

But is gender really so easily jettisoned from online identities? If we look at the microworlds already populated by cyberpunks, in video games, for example, what becomes clear is that there is a strong gendered dimension to cyberspace encounters. So that although many men claim to be able to leave gender identities behind — like a piece of excess baggage — it returns in subtle and sometimes not so subtle ways. In the process we witness how the logic of gender difference continues to structure virtual realities. In his investigation of the most popular video games produced for Nintendo gaming systems, Eugene Provenzo (1991) analyzed the narrative structure of dozens of games to conclude that most games included themes of social violence, female passivity, and male aggression. Female characters are cast as victims to be rescued or evil agents to be vanquished, whereas male characters are always cast as the active, adventuring heroes who are the agents of action in the fantasy microworld. Female characters, in contrast, are often the prize at the end of the adventure. Provenzo argued that as vehicles of gender socialization, video games reinforce the notion that females are "individuals who are acted upon rather than initiating action." (p. 116). Provenzo was careful to assert that video games are not the only form of gender discrimination in contemporary culture, but they are a part of the broader computer culture that remains largely male-dominated. Thus he concludes that "video games are instruments of information that serve important hegemonic functions in their perpetuation of bias and gender stereotyping." The issue of gender identity comes into even sharper focus when we look more closely at how cyberpunks interact in their virtual worlds.

ONLINE TECHNOBODIES

The Jargon File offers a "comprehensive compendium of hacker slang" that illuminates many aspects of cyberpunk subculture.[11] The entry on "Gender and Ethnicity" admits that although "hackerdom is still predominantly

---

[11]*The Jargon File* (1992, July 1) version 2.0.10. Available online from: ftp.uu.net. Also published as *The hacker's dictionary.*

male," hackers are gender- and color-blind in their interactions with other hackers due to the fact that they communicate (primarily) through text-based network channels. This assertion rests on the assumption that "text-based channels" represent a gender-neutral medium of exchange, and that language itself is free from forms of gender, race, or ethnic determinations. Both of these assumptions are called into question not only by feminist research in electronic communication and interpretive theory, but also by female network users who participate in cyberpunk's virtual subculture.[12] Hoai-An Truong (1993), a member of the Bay Area Women in Telecommunications (BAWIT) wrote:

> Despite the fact that computer networking systems obscure physical characteristics, many women find that gender follows them into the on-line community, and sets a tone for their public and private interactions there—to such an extent that some women purposefully choose gender neutral identities, or refrain from expressing their opinions.[13]

This was dramatically, or rather textually, illustrated in an exchange that occurred on FutureCulture, an electronic discussion list devoted to cyberpunk subculture. The thread of the discussion concerned a floating utopia called "Autopia." The exchange about women in "Autopia" began innocently:[14]

> From the cyberdeck of student . . .
>
> It may just be my imagination, but it seems that the bulk of the people participating in the Autopia discussion are men.
>
> And hasn't anyone else noticed that most people on FutureCulture are men? Not to mention the over-all population of the net generally speaking. I'd like to get women into this discussion but I'm not even sure if there are any women on FC.
>
> Are there?

In response, a male participant pointed out:

> IF you haven't noticed, the bulk of the people on these networks are men. It is about 80% male with higher percentages in some places.

---

[12]See also Nickerson (1981), Kiesler, Sproull, and Eccles (1985), Benston (1988), Perry and Greber (1990), Turkle and Papert (1990), and Bernstein (1991).

[13]Hoai-An Truong, *Gender Issues in Online Communication* (1993) CFP (Version 4.1). Available online from: ftp.eff.org.

[14]This exchange took place over several days in the late months of 1992 on a discussion list called Future Culture (futurec@uafsysb.uark.edu).

> Yeah. Clearly the Internet is dominated by men. It just seems that some outreach to women might be in order. Hanging out on a ship with hundreds of male computer jocks isn't exactly my idea of utopia. :)

A female participant wrote back:

> Now, this is a loaded question. A lot of women will not open themselves to possible net harassment by admitting they are listening. Of course, if they've come this far, they are likely to be the more bold/brave/stupid type.
>
> Which leaves me where?
>
> Cuz, yes, I am a woman & I hang out on the internet, read cyberpunk, do interesting things with locks and computers. I don't program, I don't MU*/D/SH. I do technical work/repair. I write. I read. I'm a relatively bright individual.

This posting was followed by a self-acknowledged sexist statement from a male participant who asked others if they too found that women on the net were extremely unattractive. After being flamed from several other men in the discussion, one reply rebuked the original poster:

> "Concepts of physical beauty are hold overs from 'MEAT' space. On the net they don't apply. We are all just bits and bytes blowing in the phosphor stream."

Concepts of physical beauty might be a "meat thing," but gender identity persists in the "phosphor stream" whether we like it or not. Eventually, the thread returned to the question of what a woman might say about "Autopia," the floating utopia idea. Several postings later, the same female participant responded:

> And, would you like to know why, overall, I am uninterested in the idea of Autopia? Because I'm a responsible person. (Over-responsible, if you want to get into the nit-picky psychological semantics, but that's another point). As a responsible person, I end up doing/am expected to do all the shit work. All the little details that others don't think of; like setting up laundry duty, dishes, cooking, building, repairs, and handling garbage. This is not to say that I fall into the typical "FEMALE" role, because both women and men have left these duties to fall in my lap. And, it's not a case that if I leave it, it will eventually get done either — you'd be amazed at how long people will ignore garbage or dishes; at how many people can't use a screw driver or hold a hammer correctly.
>
> Plus, how about security? There is a kind of assumption that goes on, especially on the net, that folks on whatever computer network are a higher

intelligence, above craven acts of violence. If you end up with 50 men for every woman, how are you going to insure her safety?

So, talk about security issues, waste disposal, cooking and cleaning duties, the actual wiring of whatever ship for onboard computers, how you're planning on securing hard drives for rough seas, how you're going to eat, in what shifts are you going to sleep, who's going to steer, how you are going to get navigators.

Where will you get the money for the endeavor? If you decide against a ship, and go for an island, how are you going to deal with overrunning the natural habitat? What are you going to do if you cause some species that only lived on *that* island to become extinct? What are you going to do with refugees from the worlds of hurt on this planet, who are looking for someplace to escape to?

As one other (male) participant in the discussion pointed out, these are imminently practical concerns, but not ones that were raised until the female participant emerged from the silence she was lurking in. Her original point was passed over quickly, even as it was enacted in the course of the subsequent discussion: electronic discussion lists are governed by gendered codes of discursive interchange that are often not hospitable to female participants. In a similar exchange, not among cyberpunks, but rather among postmodern scholars, women's contributions to an electronic conference were routinely ignored in the excessive word production of male participants (Kramarae & Taylor, 1993; Landow, 1993). This suggests that online communication is structured similarly to communication in other settings, and is overtly subjected to forms of gender, status, age, and race determinations.

Clearly, cyberpunks who participate in virtual subcultural routines aren't alone in the way in which offline gender identity influences online interactions. What is particularly true of cyberpunks, though, is that their subculture revolves around the myth of corporeal transcendence: the belief that it is technologically possible to "factor out" the material body and the cultural meanings it signifies. This is even reflected in one of the statements of The Hacker's Ethic: "Hackers should be judged by their hacking, not bogus criteria such as degrees, age, race, or position." Of course, it finds the fullest expression in cyberpunk science fiction novels that explore the possibility of "leaving the meat behind" in the giddy exploration of cyberspace. Andrew Ross (1991) identified this as a symptom of the "crisis of masculinity" that erupted in the 1980s that was expressed through the Arnold Schwarzenegger/Pumping Iron cult of the body:

[T]hese exaggerated parodies of masculine posture in the age of Reagan were at once a response to the redundancy of working muscle in a postindustrial age, the technological regime of cyborg masculinity; and, of course, to the general threat of waning patriarchal power. Cyberpunk male bodies, by contrast, held no such guarantee of lasting invulnerability, at least not without prosthetic help. . . . If the unadorned body fortress of the Rambo/ Schwarzenegger physique expressed the anxieties of the dominant male culture, cyberpunk technomasculinity suggested a growing sense of the impotence of straight white males in the countercultures. (p. 152–53)

To manage such a sense of impotence and diminishing authority, male cyberpunks symbolically manage what they can. Just as the material body is deconstructed in cyberpunk science fiction, it is also repressed in subcultural practice. This corresponds with what the Jargon File describes about hacker physical activity and sports participation: "Many (perhaps even most) hackers don't follow or do sports at all and are determinedly anti-physical." In this sense, the subcultural practices of cyberpunks, that is, their cyberspace encounters with virtual realities, do not remove them from the everyday world, but rather are yet another (everyday) place where they must negotiate the troubling contradictions and experiences of disempowerment that plague not only themselves but also their parent culture.

VIRTUAL SOLUTIONS TO CULTURAL DILEMMAS

This brief review of the narratives of cyberpunk identity illuminates the contours of the oppositional noise produced within our newly emergent cybernetic culture. Although the signal is quite strong—that computer technologies and cybernetic culture form an advanced, liberating milieu for postgendered humans—the noise produced by cyberpunks suggests otherwise. Recall Hebdige's (1979) delineation of the relationship between a subculture and its parent culture:

> Subcultures represent "noise": interference in the orderly sequence which leads from real events and phenomena to their representation in the media. We should not therefore underestimate the signifying power of the spectacular subculture not only as a metaphor for potential anarchy "out there" but as an actual mechanism of semantic disorder: a kind of temporary blockage in the system of representation. (p. 90)

In saying that subcultural style signifies resistance, Hebdige was careful to elide the question of the ontological status of such resistance. It would be difficult to assert that style is, by itself, an effective means of resistance. Angela McRobbie reminded us to look at the practices of those who inhabit or project subcultural identities, where we will find strong, and often disturbing continuities between the gender politics of the subculture and the parent culture. This is certainly the case with cyberpunk identity in which the manifest narratives of identity signify resistance to a dominant parent culture whereas the latent subcultural practices reveal a closer affinity between the two. In terms of its gender politics, cyberpunk subculture is less sanguine; it remains, for all of its iconoclastic rumblings, a male-dominated subculture that serves as a stage for gender posturing. In part we can read this gender posturing as a displaced reaction to the fact that cyberpunks are caught in the midst of several cultural contradictions; they live on that edge where the mythology of technological transcendence crashes headlong into the reality of historical determinations.

Popular media do more than simply record the technological projection of multiple identities; they also provide the mechanism for managing the contradictions among identities. As Hebdige asserted, the role of the media is precisely to manage contradictory identities: "it is primarily through the press, television, film, etc. that experience is organized, interpreted, and made to cohere in contradiction as it were" (Hebdige, p. 85). Virtual media such as video games or computer programming are, like McLuhan (1964) said of other media, "extensions of social man and of the body politic":

> Both games and technologies are counter-irritants or ways of adjusting to the stress of the specialized actions that occur in any social group. As extensions of the popular response to the workaday stress, games become faithful models of a culture. They incorporate both the action and the reaction of whole populations in a single dynamic image. . . . A game is a machine that can get into action only if the players consent to become puppets for a time. For individualist Western man, much of his "adjustment" to society has the character of a personal surrender to the collective demands. Our games help both to teach us this kind of adjustment and also to provide a release from it. (p. 208, 211)

Here McLuhan pointed out that as a "faithful model of culture," games not only embody the preoccupations of a society, but also the means of easing the dis-ease of such preoccupations. In more critical terms, games represent cultural contradictions, as well as a range of ideological resolutions of the tensions inherent in the contradictions. Cyberpunks embody the contradiction at the heart of the debate about the cultural significance of personalized computer technology; they live on the microedge between thinking of the computer as a tool of human creativity or condemning it as a mechanism of dehumanized rationalism and social alienation. Although they enjoy privileged access to the tools that enable them to interact with (and sometimes construct) virtual worlds, they are not the ones making the rules that govern the cyberspace system. Although they enjoy a measure of power through the acquisition of technical expertise, at the same time they rail hopelessly against overdetermined economic dependence and rapidly increasing rates of technological obsolescence. What many cyberpunks have discovered is that for all of its immateriality, cyberspace is primarily an interzone of capitalist reterritorialization. The political question cyberpunks address is to what extent is it possible to subvert the hyperrationality of the computer program, the computer network, or, more broadly conceived, the global computerized bureaucracy that serves as the infrastructure of the information age?

Using computers to "surf the net" provides a displaced release from the reality of historically determined limits on individual agency; and yet, in exploiting this measure of freedom made possible by computer-communication networks, cyberpunks get confused about the dimensions of that freedom. They conflate the networked immanence of cyberspace with the fluid mechanics of postmodern identity construction, as if both were without limits, without history, and without politics.

In this sense, cyberpunks embody the identity crisis at the heart of postmodernity. We've come to a point where we appreciate the fluidity of identity formation; theoretically this represents a significant development in our thinking about the relationship between cultural forces of determination and individual manifestations of cultural identities. Postmodernists understand keenly how human identity itself is a virtual reality, as much a technological artifact as it is an expression of individual agency. But it is a mistake to conclude that the fluidity of identity posits a blank slate—there is no ground-zero in the identity-construction game. Even in the use of gender-neutral nicknames or in seemingly anonymous screen-to-screen communication it is impossible to transcend social identities, multiple or otherwise. Cyberpunk identities are signed not so much by bodily marks of race and biological sex, nor by economic signs of class position, but by the more subtle tracks left by gendered communication patterns/habits and institutional access addresses. It is difficult to be more precise in specifying the tension that thwarts cyberpunks in their project of forming identities for themselves in a cybernetic world. They are, like the rest of us, suspended between the mythologies of technological self-determination and historically specific forms of cultural determination. Cyberspace role playing and online interactions exploit the pleasure of liquid identity, but it remains a highly delimited pleasure accomplished through the repression of the material body and the regressive projection of masculinist narratives of gender transcendence.

ACKNOWLEDGMENTS

The author would like to thank Michael Greer for reading multiple drafts of this paper, and Frank Biocca and Mark Levy for their comments on an earlier draft and their patience with the production of this essay. Many conversations with Paul Goggin and the students in my "Literature in the Age of Postmodern Science" course (Winter, 1993) helped me get a sense of the multiple dimensions of cyberpunk identity. To those whose words I read when I lurk on cyberpunk discussions, I say thanks for your insights and creative demonstrations of identities-in-process.

REFERENCES

Balsamo, A. (1993). The virtual body in cyberspace. *Journal of Research in the Philosophy of Technology*, vol. 13, pp. 119–139.

Bankowsky, J. (1991, November). Slackers. *Artforum*, 96–100.

Bertrand, K. (1990, November) Virtual reality on marketing horizon. *Business Marketing, 75*, p. 14.

Blankenship, L. (1990). *Gurps cyberpunk high tech low-life roleplaying sourcebook*. Austin, TX: Steve Jackson Games.

Branwyn, G. (1990, June). Virtual reality. *The Futurist*, p. 45.

Branwyn, G. (1991, March/April). The salon virtual: Plugging in to a transcontinental creative community. *Utne Reader*, pp.86–88.

Bukatman, S. (1993). *Terminal identity: The virtual subject in postmodern science fiction*. Durham: Duke UP.

Bylinsky, G. (1991, June 3). The marvels of "virtual reality." *Fortune*, pp. 138–143.

Cornell, R. (1991, January 1). Where is the window? Virtual reality technologies now. *Artscribe Intent*, pp. 52–55.

Copeland, D. (1991). *Generation X: Tales for an accelerated culture*. New York: Simon & Schuster.

Daviss, B. (1990, June). Grand illusions: Virtual reality computer simulation technology. *Discover*, pp. 36–42.

Delany, S. (1988). Is Cyberpunk a good thing or a bad thing? *Mississippi Review*, pp. 2–36.

Dibbell, J. (1991, March 4). Virtual Kool-aid acid test. *Spin*.

Ditlea, S. (1989). Inside virtual reality. *PC/Computing*, pp.91–101.

Ditlea, S. (1990, August 6). Grand illusion. *New York*, pp. 26–35.

Elmer-Dewitt, P. (1990, September 3). (Mis)adventures in cyberspace. *Time*, pp. 74–76.

Fisher, S., & Tazelaar, J. (1990, July). Living in a virtual world. *Byte*, pp.215–221.

Gilmore, M. (1986, December 4). The rise of cyberpunk. *Rolling Stone*, 77 +.

Hafner, K., & Markoff, J. (1991). *Cyberpunks: Outlaws and hackers on the computer frontier*. New York: Simon & Schuster.

Hall, T. (1990, July 8). "Virtual reality" takes its place in the real. *New York Times*, pp. 1, 14.

Harwood, J. (1989). Agog in goggles: Shape of things to come reshaping Hollywood's future. *Variety*, p. 66.

Hebdige, D. (1979). *Subculture: The meaning of style*. London: Routledge & Kegan Paul.

Hecht, J. (1989, August 19). Tune in, turn on, plug in your software: Simulating virtual reality on computers. *New Scientist*, p. 32.

Hollinger, V. (1990). Cybernetic deconstructions: Cyberpunk and postmodernism. *Mosaic, 23*(2), 29–44.

Howe, N., & Strauss, B. (1993). *13th gen: Abort, retry, ignore, fail?* New York: Vintage Books.

Jackson, D. S. (1993, February 2). Cyberpunk. *Time*, cover story.

Kiesler, S., Sproull, L., & Eccles, J. (1985). Poolhalls, chips and war games: Women in the culture of computing. *Psychology of Women Quarterly, 9*(4), 451–62.

Kramarae, C., & Taylor, H. J. (1993). Women and men on electronic networks: A conversation or a monologue? In H. J. Taylor, C. Kramarae, & M. Ebben (Eds.), *Women, information technology and scholarship* (pp. 52–61). Urbana, IL: Center for Advanced Studies.

Landow, G. P. (Ed.). (1993). *The digital word: Text-based computing in the humanities.* Cambridge MA: MIT Press.

LaRue, J. (1991, March). The virtual library. *Wilson Library Bulletin*, p. 3.

Leary, T. (1988). The Cyber-punk: The individual as reality pilot. *Mississippi Review 16*, pp. 2–3, 252–265.

Levy, S. (1984). *Hackers.* New York: Bantam.

Linklater, R. (Director). (1992). *Slacker* [Film].

Lowe Benston, M. (1988). Women's voices/men's voices: Technology as language. In C. Kramarae (Ed.), *Technology and women's voices: Keeping in touch.* Boston: Routledge & Kegan Paul.

Martin, D. (1991, March 2). Virtual reality! hallucination! age of aquarius! Leary's back! *The New York Times*, p. 11.

McCaffery, L. (1991). Cutting up: Cyberpunk, punk music, and urban decontextualizations. In L. McCaffery (Ed.), *Storming the reality studio: A casebook of cyberpunk and postmodern fiction* (pp. 286–307). Durham, NC: Duke UP.

McLuhan, M. (1964). *Understanding media: The extensions of man.* New York: New American Library.

McRobbie, A. (1981). Settling accounts with subcultures: A feminist critique. In T. Bennett, G. Martin, C. Mercer, & J. Wollacott (Eds.), *Culture, ideology and social process: A reader* (pp. 112–123). London: Batsford Academic and Education Ltd.

Nickerson, R. S. (1981). Why interactive computer systems are sometimes not used by people who might benefit from them. *International Journal Man-Machine Studies 15*, 469–483.

Pascal Zachary, G. (1990, January 23). Artificial reality: Computer simulations one day may provide surreal experiences. *Wall Street Journal*, p. 1.

Perry, R., & Greber, L. (1990). Women and computers: An introduction. *SIGNS 16*(11), 74–101.

Provenzo, E. F., Jr. (1991). *Video kids: Making sense of Nintendo.* Cambridge: Harvard UP.

Rayl, A. J. S. (1991, July 21). The new, improved reality. *Los Angeles Times Magazine*, 17–20+.

Rogers, M. (1987, February 9). Now, "artificial reality." *Newsweek*, pp. 56–57.

Ross, A.(1991). *Strange weather: Culture, science and technology in the age of limits.* London: Verso.

Rucker, R. (Ed.). (1992). *Mondo 2000 user's guide to the new edge.* New York: HarperCollins.

Special issue: How to work, play, and thrive in cyberspace. (1991, September). *Scientific America.*

Sterling, B. (1992). *The hacker crackdown: Law and disorder on the electronic frontier.* New York: Bantam.

Stewart, S. (1991, January). Artificial reality: Don't stay home without it. *Smithsonian, 21*(10), 36.

Tisdale, S. (1991, April). It's been real. *Esquire*, p. 36.

Turkle, S. (1984). *The second self: Computers and the human spirit.* London: Granada.

Turkle, S., & Papert, S. (1990). Epistemological pluralism: Styles and voices within the computer culture. *SIGNS, 16*(11), 128–157.

The virtual corporation (1993, February 8). *Business Week*, cover story.

14 Communication Issues and Policy Implications

Lisa St. Clair Harvey
The George Washington University

The development and diffusion of virtual reality (VR) raises some unusual questions about the technological future and about the potential of his new medium to produce profound cultural change. Given the impending debut of VR in the public communication environment, there is some urgency in taking a fresh look at how national media policy is made in general and the special problems we face in dealing with virtual reality.

Perhaps the most breathtaking concept of all is the realization that, should VR and other online communication systems take their place as fully integrated members of the American media environment, it won't be long before the gap between those born in the "Information Age" and those participants in both world and American culture who were born in the pre-personal computer era, but who have fled, stumbled or deliberately immigrated to the new communications wonderland, will widen into a true and possibly political chasm. If VR takes hold the way its champions predict, it will usher in a world in which computer-based communications technology will provide human beings with the ability to perceive or to experience, at least in primitive form, that which is physically impossible. In that "online" world, the creation of new "realities" — and, one presumes, the destruction of old or out-of-fashion "realities" — will become a routine cultural assumption, and an entire generation of computer users will no more question the technology's availability or their own right to use it, than they will wonder if there will be water waiting when they turn on the tap.

Related to VR's potential to reshuffle the cultural cards in America's political game are social and legal issues associated with evolving media technologies, such as the need for a re-evaluation of First Amendment issues and significant clarification of intellectual property law (Borden, 1993), which illustrate the incredible scope of the scholarly challenge introduced by VR. Questions of content, of distribution, of ownership, the need to re-examine the persistent tension between artistic license and community standards, questions of equal access and of technological determinism all assume new and added stature when the communications event itself is translated from the cognitive to the experiential realm, as VR promises to do.

VR AND THE INFORMATION SUPERHIGHWAY

On the home front, the question remains whether VR will ever attain the size and type of market necessary to justify the faith of its private investors, who hope to see it become like traditional "mass" media — at least, in terms of market appeal. Emerging events in the political arena, however, suggest that this question — along with the issue of public accessibility, which provides the real key to the technology's viability as a mass medium — may be decided by government rather than by business.

Mass accessibility is a threshold criteria for the development of VR as an American mass medium. Part of the regulatory challenge implicit here is that nobody in Washington is thinking about VR as a mass medium, per se (Harvey, 1993). But events are conspiring to change that, and given the election of technological sophisticates President Bill Clinton and Vice President Al Gore, changes in the governmental climate surrounding VR research may happen fairly rapidly (Gazsi, 1993). One of the prime nongovernmental catalysts for this type of change is the Electronic Frontier Foundation (EFF), a citizen group that has taken on the ". . . multiple role of guardian, advocate, and innovator to serve and protect the public in the information age" (Electronic Frontier Foundation, 1992, p. 1). Even the term *online communications,* as a way of describing the computer-based versions of traditional information and media systems, may be an EFF invention (Godwin, 1991, p. 2).

According to its white paper, "Building the Open Road," the EFF's first step is to guide the government in this country's transition to the Information Age, the most salient outcome of which, the EFF argues, is that ". . . by the end of this decade (1990s), the 'body politic' and the 'body social' and the 'body commercial' of this country will depend on a nervous system of fiber-optic lines and computer switches" (Kapor & Berman, 1992, p. 8).

The basic idea underlying this multistage evolution is the notion of a planned progression from the old national communications system — the telephone network — to a high-tech, digitalized data system, which will be capable of transmitting voice, video, and data through a fiber optic cable. The conversion of Plain Old Telephone Service (POTS) to a network that can carry more than just a voice signal is the first step. That's the ISDN— the Integrated Services Digital Network.

The ISDN will move information at a rate that is 15 to 60 times faster than 1992 voice-line data transmission can manage, sending up to 30 pages of typed material in 1 minute (Electronic Frontier Foundation, July 1992, pp. 4–5). Updating the ISDN to carry multiple types of signal faster and linking it to research and educational institutions around the country, as a kind of national information web, is the second step. That's N-REN, or the National Research and Education Network.

The crowning glory would be the National Public Network (NPN), a hybrid child of government and private industry, which, theoretically, could carry everything, to everybody, almost instantly. Congressional estimates of NPN's service load suggest that more than a million individuals would have access to NPN-carried databases through connection facilities at more than 1,000 "nodes" located at universities, laboratories, colleges, and hospitals nationwide . . . by the end of the decade (Kapor & Berman, 1992, p. 3).

What does all of this have to do with VR? Plenty, although few observers have realized it. The temptation is to think of VR as too cumbersome and too expensive to ever join the ranks of "old" media such as television, radio, and newspapers. Far more likely, one might think, VR will forever remain in the ivory tower or the Defense Department, both locales equally inaccessible to the great pool of voters, consumers, and citizens. But the digitalized network of the NPN is precisely the kind of conduit through which VR programming could be delivered directly to the public, nudging it out of exalted, or at least esoteric, circles, and into the mainstream of cultural discourse.

Virtual reality undoubtedly will be part of this national information system. Apple Computers CEO John Scully envisioned ". . . knowledge navigators (using) personal computers to travel through realms of virtual information *via public digital networks*" (Kapor & Berman, 1992, p. 6, emphasis added). Similarly, EFF has speculated on the NPN's supreme suitability for "electronic assembly—virtual town halls, village greens, and coffee houses, again, taking place not just through shared text . . . but with multimedia transmissions, including images, voice, and video" (p. 7) and "as a simulation medium for experiences that are impossible to obtain in the mundane world" (p. 7). Finally, as VR pioneer Tom Furness put it during his May 1991 testimony before the Senate Subcommittee on Science, Space, and Technology, "As a new medium of communications, televirtuality promises to subsume the existing media of communications, including the whole range of two-dimensional presentational media" (Committee on

Commerce, Science, and Transportation, 1991, p. 32). If events follow the Congressional timelines and if EFF estimates are correct, all of the pieces required to thrust VR into center stage as a nationally viable mass medium will be in place and fully functional within one biblical generation (Gore, 1991).

Depending on which theologian you ask, that's between forty and seventy years from now. But well before that day when VR's commercial charms intersect with plans for the NPN, some truncated version of VR-type computer-based, immersive "realities" will be widely available to consumers (regardless of age) — unchecked, unregulated, and without procedures for determining content accuracy or for developing formal accountability. In view of this likely future, it may be helpful to consider what types of regulatory models, if any, may be adaptable for application to virtual reality and related online communication technologies.

TRADITIONAL REGULATORY MODELS AND VIRTUAL REALITY

Because VR attaches itself to the public mind in ways that have little to do with its print or broadcast ancestors, many of our traditional expectations of the media/government relationship (Donahue, 1989), which have been painstakingly developed through custom, challenge, and court decision, suddenly no longer apply. Ithiel de Sola Pool (1983), writing about what degree of First Amendment protection should, logically as well as ethically, transfer from print-based publishing to electronically delivered newspapers, observed that the United States has developed a "trifurcated" system of media regulation, within which the three main players — print, broadcast, and common carrier vehicles — enjoy varying amounts of benefit from constitutional guarantees to freedom of expression. "The law has evolved differently in each (of these three) domains," argued de Sola Pool, ". . . (each) with but modest relation to the other" (de Sola Pool, 1983, p. 2).

The difficulty with applying de Sola Pool's model of communications policy development to the VR situation is that his work hinges on being able to jam VR into descriptive categories already defined by print, broadcast, or common carrier media. VR, unfortunately for media scholars and public policy-makers, is too adroit for that; it resists containment within any one function area, and exists, instead, along the borders of the more familiar systems. And although its territory is in the very broadest sense inherited from preceding media, once VR has established territorial possession in the commercial domain, it will refurbish that property beyond all easy recognition.

VR and the print media, for example, have very little in common, in terms of either form or content. Functional affinities between the two remain to be identified; it may well be that people will eventually turn to VR for the same sorts of educational and/or escapist opportunities that they now pursue through the daily paper or the nightly novel. But when it comes to sharing the high level of First Amendment protection traditionally awarded to print, VR simply does not qualify. Although research remains to be done concerning the exact proportion of cognitive effort and experiential sensation that is built into the VR event, the technology's entire raison d'etre—that which sets it apart from other communications media— is that which makes its use a sensational rather than an intellectual event. Whereas reading requires of its participants both a familiarity with language and the ability to code and decode their perception of the symbols that represent it (letters, words, and so forth), as far as we know, VR demands little more than use of standard visual equipment. The success of VR communication attempts lie not in one's dexterity with linguistic symbols, but in one's natural visual gullibility.

On the most basic level, there is also nothing tangible, nothing concrete, that VR users can carry with them on the subway or into a restaurant; the medium is not portable, nor is it easily (yet) affordable. It still costs less than a dollar to view the world through a newspaper; it costs thousands to sustain a single VR episode. VR is not in the same workaday world as print, nor does it spring from the same intensely populist tradition, and it, thus, does not and should not benefit from the same kind and degree of First Amendment protection.

Historically, the broadcast media have been subject to a much more rigorous level of governmental control. As de Sola Pool (1983) and others noted, this interference is predicated on two assumptions about radio and television's technological nature: (a) the scarcity argument, based on the notion that because there are only so many frequencies to go around, society had better use them wisely, and (b) the ubiquity issue, which maintains that TV, in particular, has so infiltrated the cultural ether that some sort of mitigating presence is required to restrain it.

If the N-REN and the NPN do come to pass, it is logical to assume that, through them, VR will achieve some degree of ubiquity, although it is doubtful that it will ever enjoy the same awesome penetration rate as television, because VR's presence in the home will be determined by that home's inclusion as a node on the public network and not all locales will have an equal chance to participate. And with the success of cable television and other multichannel delivery systems, television's own scarcity argument has been losing its rhetorical grip in debates concerning basic over-the-air signals, because the technical fact on which it rests—limited channel availability—has been all but exploded by developments in multiplexing, signal compression, and other techniques for squeezing more carrying capacity out of available channel space.

Additionally, the generalized drive toward deregulation that characterized the Reagan and Bush administrations has lightened the burden on broadcasting's shoulders by elasticizing licensing procedures and loosening ownership restrictions. This trend toward deregulation of delivery systems, which, for the public, results in homogenized programming being available on a hundred rather than on thirteen television channels, has grave implications for VR. Basically, it suggests that if the powers that be at the FCC decide to treat VR as an aberrant form of television — which they very well might if the medium is delivered in a fashion that mimics television, such as through any type of screen and over the same physical line that supplies cable TV signals — then the public will find itself confronted with another oligarchical media ownership system, controlled by a very few gatekeepers who make enormous profit by supplying a limited range of programming options. So, to reiterate, VR seems more like TV than like print, but remains fairly well distinct from both. There remains to be explored the third component of de Sola Pool's (1983) triumvirate — the common carrier model of communications delivery.

The signature trait of the common carrier is twofold: it provides equal and universal access, indifferent to message content. Both de Sola Pool and Mitch Kapor cited the postal service, the telegraph, and the telephone system as examples of common carrier delivery. The principle of common carriage rests on the notion that the controllers of the medium through which messages scurry have no interest and no say (and no liability) regarding the nature and content of those messages, as long as they aren't demonstrably illegal or obscene.

Although the NPN will most likely conform to something resembling a common carrier, given that it will be in part publicly funded and is intended for prosocial uses such as research and education, to confuse VR's presence on the prototype network as part of NPN's permanent structure would be dangerously imprecise, because underlying that assumption is a vision of VR as an inevitable and intrinsic element in the NPN's basic composition — which, in turn, undercuts any meaningful debate about whether VR is an appropriate part of the national network. In terms of policy debate, it's critical to remember that, whereas VR is simultaneously both a vehicle for transmitting content and a type of actual content which is being transmitted — in VR's particular case, the map is the territory, another example of VR's intensely liminal state as a medium unlike any which has come before it. This uniqueness helps to make VR distinguishable from classic common carrier vehicles in several important ways.

First, although they are used for commercial purposes as well as private purposes, common carrier systems deliver what I call "closed" messages;

they are private communications, which is to say that decisions about sharing the message are left to the discretion of the recipient. Of course, mail can be opened and phone conversations can be tapped, but by and large this cannot occur without prior authorization and legal sanction.

In contrast, messages left hanging upon electronic billboards are vested with far fewer privacy protections. And the centralized nature of NPN-carried VR experiences, which one would presumably consume in private, could be easily monitored in terms of content and duration. There are laws in this country that prohibit the FBI, for example, from demanding that your university library supply them with a list of all the books you've checked out during the last few years. But there are few such protections — as it stands — against a similar intrusion occurring in the VR "stacks." Imagine the shock of discovering that the VR systems operator had "eavesdropped" on your VR experiences, or that you've wound up on some bizarre and injudicious mailing list because your name was sold by a marketing company that had tracked your VR preferences the same way that they track your groceries, your charitable donations, and your catalog purchases, or that your political opponents had documented your more eclectic VR selections for strategic use during the next election, or job application, or tenure review?

This is something more than voyeurism, something less than breaking and entering, but if it isn't something that you intended to have happen, it is a type of violation nonetheless. It's also troubling, in that it's analogous to "Big Brother" having a way to keep track of every videotape you rent or every book you check out of the library; not necessarily incriminating in its own right, but cumulatively unsettling.

Another key distinction between VR and classic common carrier technologies has to do with ownership. It is one thing to write a letter or to talk on the phone about a public figure, since these media by and large address a limited audience — the person on the other end of the transmission. It is something entirely different to plaster one's personal fantasies or criticisms about anyone, public figures included, across a virtual network, where they are not just read, but can be actually "experienced," by an untold number of system users. VR's ability to escape finite legal categorization, equivocating as it does between public and private forms of communication, may put at elevated and perhaps unreasonable risk individuals who do not wish to be the subject of public speculation. However, if VR is defined, operationally, as a kind of common carrier, then legal protections against this unfortunate possibility will be even more difficult to enact and maintain.

In sum, virtual reality bears little useful resemblance to any of the three component media described in de Sola Pool's (1983) trifurcated model of U.S. communications policy. Perhaps it is helpful, then, to think of VR not as loitering at the edges of this medium or that, but rather as a phenomenon that transcends all three, simultaneously escaping and integrating the salient attributes of its antecedent technologies. In other words, it might be time to stop thinking of online media in terms of their manifest function and to start thinking of them as a special kind of *social presence*. This is a different thing than just expanding the "telepresence" notion, which is more a description of VR's technical character than a measure of its agency in the construction of social reality. Rather, I am suggesting that we think of VR—and by extension, its new online brethren—as an active agent in the molding of social values and the shaping of the cultural environment within which politics, education, religion, and commerce take place. In other words, it may be time to step back and look at the online media not just as ways to connect the world, but also as ways to define it, much as the critical communications literature has stopped looking at television as an adjunct to national elections and has begun exploring that medium's role as a key player in the election event. Considering the profound and persistent suspicion with which Americans have, historically, regarded government attempts to mingle in any form of industrial development, but particularly those related to media, this shift in analytical perspective will require reassessing not just U.S. media policy, per se, but also the cultural attitudes surrounding regulation itself, and its appropriate role in American life. The idea that there may, indeed, be areas of public experience in which a strong federal presence is actually desirable tends to contradict several hundred years of American history and an even more impressive span of law, since concern with free speech rights predated the American revolution. Americans have a knee-jerk reaction to resisting government "interference" in media affairs, automatically equating that presence with censorship and similar evils. But as I have argued repeatedly throughout this chapter, the social effects of media like VR may move them so far outside the parameters of communications technologies that they invite a revisiting of the actual, as opposed to the theoretical, meaning of the First Amendment within the online world.

THE FIRST AMENDMENT AND BEYOND

U.S. legislative policy, with regard to freedom of expression, traditionally blossoms at the boundary between action and expression (de Sola Pool, 1983). Sooner or later, all tests of the First Amendment have to define the point at which "expression" stops being "speech" and turns into "action" (Borden, 1993). That is the traditional dividing line between protected and unprotected material, and, indeed, much of what government does, in regulation and in law, is devoted precisely to identifying that line (Cate, 1992; de Sola Pool, 1983).

But virtual reality changes all that. Virtual reality—like its cousins wreaking havoc in electronic publishing law, where arguments abound over what is and isn't copyrightable, what is and isn't public domain, and what is and isn't an "original" of anything carried over a wire instead of on a printed page—doesn't just straddle the line between speech and action. It makes the line itself irrelevant, because the VR communications event itself is not just expression—it's experience. And experience is an uncertain version of action. VR delivers what I call "experiential speech," and society has not, as of yet, developed a method for getting either legal or cultural traction on that concept.

Virtual reality shows every sign of becoming a commercially viable, publicly accessible form of media experience by the end of this century. It will be, at first, expensive. But enterprising souls in the United States and abroad are already working toward the unveiling of VR as an educational and a recreational vehicle aimed at the general public. The "recreational" aspect of their intentions is important, because from the end-user perspective it collapses distinctions between students and consumers, and part of the argument against regulating VR is that the technology will remain a socially "safe" technology by remaining a primarily educational resource. Presumably, students will use VR in a supervised environment. Consumers will not. There will be no human referee in the cyberspatial environment to remind VR voyagers that the trip upon which they are embarked is, when all is said and done, a figment of somebody else's imagination.

Imagination takes many forms, some more potent than others, and many of those products of individual vision, whereas they might remain unshared by the general population, will pass by media gatekeepers with little more than a shrug, a yawn, or a quizzical look. Others will command more immediate attention from the media gatekeepers, and, occasionally, from the courts. Fred H. Cate (1992), writing as the director of research and projects and a senior fellow at the Annenberg Washington Program, used the culturally volatile issue of pornography to illustrate this point.

Cate noted that the guiding distinction in much First Amendment law is the difference between expression that warrants some form of societal control over its distribution, and that which doesn't. The fact that we have acquired a turbulent and often conflicting body of law in our attempts to specify exactly what this distinction looks like is elegant testimony to the difficulty involved in achieving consensus on this issue. In default of clearly articulated rules and neatly drawn lines between offending and nonoffending speech, Cate noted that some scholars—and even some courts—have suggested that society tolerate no rules or restrictions at all, on the grounds that it would be better to "err," if to err we were, on the side of individual liberty (Cate, 1992, pp. 2–3).

This long-standing dilemma takes on a new sort of sizzle when the means of contested expression are experientially rather than cognitively based, as will be the case with VR, pornographic or otherwise (Stewart, 1991). In essence, VR offers an entirely new way to be pornographic—or to be recreationally violent—and it won't be long before feminist *and* liberal legal scholars, the Supreme Court, and the rest of us will have to revisit the issue of what to permit and what to suppress.

Even First Amendment absolutists, who would normally shy away from any restrictions on speech whatsoever, will be forced to re-examine this matter, if for no other reason than to decide whether the simulated experiences available through the VR medium constitute "speech" or are actually . . . something else. And if they aren't exactly speech, well then, in the legal sense at least, what are they? If they are carried by the NPN, are they a form of public education? A type of public broadcasting? A national rumor mill? A truly interglobal public forum? Are they the electronic equivalent of drug experiences? Are they pre-programmed hallucinatory episodes (like LSD, which is illegal)? Are they a private indulgence (like alcohol, which *is* legal under certain circumstances)?

More to the legal point, are VR events a new and subtle form of "action," because they evoke physical rather than cerebral responses? Those responses, it must be noted, can vary greatly regarding behavioral outcomes—they can remain localized in the adrenal system, for example, or they can escape to other, more public forums, such as the parts of the brain governing sexual aggression and violence.

This puts a new spin on Cate's attempt to establish the legal geography of pornography—how can we even hope to draw meaningful (let alone enforceable) legal lines between expression and action when the territory we are dividing resides within the human body? And when each human response system is likely to vary from the next? When there may be categorical (gender, age, race, etc.) as well as idiosyncratic differences in how people process VR events and the resultant likelihood of the VR-triggered response escaping the private body to wreak havoc in the public realm. As Cate suggested, the courts will not regulate anything other than action—and some "significant" amount of concrete, demonstrable, real-world outcome must accumulate around a defined set of all of these fluffy legal concepts and hypothetical catalysts for antisocial action before official interference with expression will be tolerated. How much outcome—how much evidence—is enough? That remains to be seen . . . and adjudicated. But virtual reality's contribution to the accumulation of that material may be as alarming as it is unexpected, if for no reason than it has the potential to colonize the most intimate and, hitherto, private corners of the human experience.

SEX AND THE PREVIOUSLY SINGLE COMPUTER

Just as Cate used the pornography issue as a fulcrum for weighing and balancing the individual's right to free expression against the need for a safe society, so might an initial examination of the cultural impact of VR be facilitated by examining the cultural dimensions of a similar topic. Namely, sex.

It's called "teledildonics"—sexual encounters in cyberspace. The graphics are clumsy and the technology's ability to provide actual tactile experience is extremely limited—and, in terms of direct sensation, nil. But consider, for a moment, the philosophical implications introduced by the mere possibility that, at some future time, we might have available to us, as a culture, technological alternatives to physical intimacy.

Because "beings" in the VR world are not bound by the same laws of physics that restrict intimate movement in the physical plane—like, for example, gravity—it's absurd to suppose that the programmers for teledildonics packages will not capitalize on this special kind of creative license. Why settle for adolescent VR sex—which at its most sophisticated will still resemble that which has always been available—when so many creative alternatives exist, when one can be weightless, ageless, faceless?

The laws of physics, as well as common sense, tell us that one cannot touch without being touched. If nothing else, the addition of virtual sex—even in a vastly primitive form—to the range of experiential options will challenge our ideas about how sex in the "real" world operates. Just setting up the "rules" for VR sex demonstrates how events in the virtual world cannot help but have an impact on their counterparts in the "mundane" plane.

For example, would VR sex be limited to married couples? Would VR affairs count as infidelities? How specific would society want to get with this? Would it be just a "game" if the VR experience happened with an anonymous, "created" being, but something far more serious if it occurred with "partners" programmed to the exact physical specifications of actual people? Would traditional gender roles hold true in a sexual situation in which no actual bodies are involved? Would same-sex experiences count as homosexuality? What would be the new conceptual boundaries between "sex" per se and intimacy, if one could become devoted to a sexual partner that didn't really exist?

In its more creative and exotic incarnations (if the technology ever progresses to the point where the "physical" experience is sufficiently convincing), will VR sex make the actual physical presence of the sexual partner unnecessary? We have already developed impressive techniques for preserving digitalized information, indefinitely and in vast amounts. It is not difficult to foresee a day in which intimate experiences between various partners can be stored for playback, regardless of the partner's actual physical state or availability.

How, exactly, would this work? Let's take teledildonics' potential for creating and preserving artificial intimate situations to its logical extreme. Our partner (who may or may not be based on a real person, with whom we may or may not be personally acquainted) has been, to all intents and purposes, "captured" in all the key ways, and then coded as a VR program, and so have we. Once that is achieved, it follows that we would no longer have to be in the same room, or even the same city, in order to experience a meaningful sexual exchange, however one chooses to define "meaningful," or "sexual," or "exchange," for that matter.

Now let's go one step further, and assume that one of the partners in a virtual relationship actually, physically dies. But the digital record of that absent partner is still on file, still preserved, still experientially accessible. Theoretically, one could continue to experience the same computer-generated intimacy — emotionally and technologically limited as it might be — as we enjoyed with that absent person when he or she was, truly, alive.

What does that mean? Sex, and all the complicated morality that accompanies it, in both "real" and virtual form, is only the smallest part of this question, and provides only a case in point that serves to illustrate the rest. What does the potential to digitalize oneself, or edited versions of oneself, so that these "selves" can actually be — to a degree — experienced by another sentient being, mean about being alive, first of all? Through the wizardry of VR image storage and retrieval, might we living humans become, essentially, redundant to the computer programs of ourselves? Conversely, what does all this mean about being dead — that the experience of ourselves can be, in some important ways, extended beyond the existence of the physical self? What do we call it, for example, if we warm up the old VR interface and plug into a close moment with a deceased partner? Memory enhancement? Grief control? Nostalgia? Perversion? Necrophilia?

What we call it — and other VR experiences like it — matters tremendously, because what we call it will be a good indication of how we frame "it" — the behavior itself and the cultural attitudes that come to surround it — within our 21st-century value system, as will the provisions we make — or fail to make — to accommodate competing ideas of what it and is not permissible, what is and is not socially desirable, as accessible VR experiences. Not only will VR test our ideas of what it means to be human and to be mortal, but it will also challenge, in new ways, our national commitment to plurality and cultural tolerance.

What does it mean, how will it affect us, if a digitalized, computerized, *virtualized* version of ourselves can remain forever young, forever supple, forever athletic, forever inexhaustible? (And, unlike video-ized versions of ourselves, at least minimally three-dimensional.) At first blush, one might ask: Why would this be so bad, particularly in an age when "real," or physical sex, ticks away under the time bomb of the AIDS epidemic? Virtualized intimacy is worth thinking twice about, I'll argue, because it introduces the risk of human beings making their virtual selves "immortal" and making their physical selves "irrelevant" . . . or at the very least, uncompetitive.

As VR packages become more widely available and more technologically elaborate, it's not impossible that a day will come in which sexual skill and emotional intimacy depend less on bodies touching bodies — or souls touching souls through the appropriate bodies — than on expertise in computer programming. Granted, in today's uncertain medical environment, this may not be, conceivably, all bad. Telesex is "safe," at least in the sense that although what happens in the virtual world might carry over into one's "waking" existence, germs do not as yet travel through cyberspace, although suggestions have been made that VR would also lend itself well to more of the generally out-of-the ordinary software packages that enable the "viewer" to experience "telesadism" and "teletransvestism" (Katayama, 1991, p. 26).

But the real and most significant impact, I would argue, will be on what our experience of virtual intimacy does to our perceptions of nonvirtual intimacy . . . and all of the cultural trappings, moral codes, and guidelines for *being* humanly, physically intimate that come with them. VR sex will, eventually, explode our notions of sexual activity in the nonvirtual world. It invites a rethinking of the terms "heterosexual" and "homosexual," for example. "Monogamy," too, will take on new meaning in the virtual bedroom, because the definition of "infidelity" will have to expand to include whatever virtual partners become defined as "outside the pale" — however that is, in turn, defined. And what about sex with truly androgynous beings, nonhumanoid creatures, whom virtual reality can "create" and about whom no rules at all have yet been written?

Then there are privacy issues. Given the traditional legal distinctions between public and private figures and the way these translate into relative levels of privacy protection, and the possibility that these conventions may be imported from traditional media into experiential media, does the advent of VR signal a kind of "open season" on celebrity sex lives? People who live in the public eye may soon be subject to a unique new kind of voyeurism —

or would it be rape? — with very little legal protection available to them, simply because they are public figures and as such, are seen by the courts as fair subjects for public comment. But that was before VR turned "comment" into "sensation."

Consider this. Through precision computer programming, VR technology provides anyone who wants it a means to "experience" a sexual encounter with anyone they choose — whether the other party consents to it or not. Whether the other party even knows about it or not. For rock stars, fashion models, war heroes, political leaders and public icons, this would be, to say the least, disconcerting. True, celebrities willingly seek to become objects of mass desire. It is quite another thing to be part of someone else's sexual memory bank and not know how you got there. And what happens if that cybernetic trespasser copies the program for all of his or her friends — for a fee or just for fun?

The implications are endless and astonishing. VR "peep" shows, interactive game shows that award as their prize a celebrity "date" in cyberspace, advertisements that thrust consumers behind the wheel of a new luxury car and behind the filter of a newer, "smoother" cigarette, or VR "docudramas" and "dramatic re-enactments" that let viewers "feel" what it was like to be present at key moments in history — whether or not those historical scenarios are presented accurately — entire college curricula in which human instructors play the lesser pedagological role . . . these are only some of the applications that a fertile mind can find for VR technology. And VR offers to both the creative and the ideologically clever communicator a technology in which scientific, economic, historical, and social "reality" is not just cognitively decided, but is, in fact, experientially interpreted for the students, long before it crosses the students' paths. VR's potential for payoff in cultural propaganda is almost limitless, as will also be the power of the VR programmers, who are likely to remain behind the commercial scenes but who will be, essentially, reinterpreting all of human life, thought, experience, and knowledge for virtual consumption. Whether the outlet for their work is VR or some other form of online media, computer programmers will become the unsigned authors, the anonymous architects, of the cultural and conceptual world experienced by the citizens — American and otherwise — of the 21st century. Clearly, this raises some critical accountability issues, for who can take issue with a faceless creator — who would even think to challenge the design, let alone the content, of seamless cyberspace?

THE FAR SIDE OF THE SCREEN

The VR situation provides scholars and policymakers alike with the opportunity to develop a protocol for thinking about questions much bigger and far more existential than those that have usually characterized communications policy development or communications theory. Precisely because VR is so extreme and so baffling a new medium, one that somehow escapes its own technological ancestry and becomes far, far more than the sum of its parts, the working relationships that we, as a society, establish for designing virtual reality regulation could serve as a blueprint for future dealings with other innovative media, the only thing about which we know for certain is that they are bound to develop sooner and in a much more complex fashion than we now anticipate.

One very serious issue addressed in this chapter is the question of whether the dominant paradigms for thinking about media in society have, indeed, outlived their natural lifespan. Is it possible that virtual reality, the national high-speed data network, and the collateral systems that attend it, are fulfilling an evolutionary function by forcing scholars and policymakers into new ways of thinking, new systems for knowing, and new patterns of defining ownership? As we address these philosophical questions, it will be equally important to probe the broader, more conceptual realm as well. We must develop what I call a "cultural ecology of media" — an understanding of the way in which our communication systems work organically and synergistically with other sectors of public and private life on the systemic level, within a historical context.

Just as a study of the planets reveals something about the motion of subatomic particles, exploring the quixotic regulatory situation triggered by virtual reality's coming of commercial age can yield important insight into the cultural challenges that are splattered at 20th-century U.S. culture from any number of rapidly evolving communications and computer technologies. In a sense, VR forces our society's philosophical hand, because it provides a bigger, richer communications experience than our current communications policy is equipped to handle.

Frontiers, even electronic ones, do not exist independent of the terrain they define. Nor does social change occur free from the historical moment and set of political conditions that preceded whatever cultural shift is in the making. There is nothing about VR technology itself that assures any of us that it will equalize persistent imbalances in the American social equation. Those things that throw justice out of kilter persist despite advances in technological sophistication. Aggressive, proactive work — of the type but perhaps not the kind pursued so robustly by the EFF — must be undertaken in order to promote equitable human values within the coming computer-based media environment.

Dr. Furness, in his May 1991 testimony before the Senate SubCommittee on Space, Science, and Technology, remarked that the evolving relationship between humans and their computers is characterized by ever-growing intelligence on both sides of the computer screen. The challenge, he says, is to collapse the psychic distance that separates the two; to make the computer more "human-like" and the human, presumably, more like the computer. The only barrier to this merging, he maintains, is those "last few inches" between the inside of the human's head and the outside of the screen itself, the spanning of which is more difficult to achieve than the entire, enormous technological journey whose terminus it would mark (Committee on Commerce, Science, and Transportation, 1991, p. 27). VR, he claims, will do that—and much, much more.

We are so close. And yet we are not exactly certain about the very nature of that to which we draw ever-nearer. What will we find, on the other side of that computer screen, and what will we learn about ourselves as we come to grips with it? Will our world be a richer place, or just a more complicated one? As we explore the hills and valleys of cyberspace, which are really the folds and creases of our own, evanescent human brain, will we move exponentially closer to a more complete understanding of ourselves and our world? Or will we just reconstruct, relentlessly, the senseless outlines of meaning, to leave as our legacy for future travellers in both virtual and physical worlds little but artificial memories and computer-aided identities?

If we do not invest the time in addressing these questions during VR's infancy, before it gains a commercial foothold from which it would be impossible to dislodge, and within which it would be difficult to re-design, we can be sure of one thing and one thing only, once the technology comes to adulthood. We can be sure that we will have less to say about the effect that we humans have on VR, than about the effect that it has on us.

REFERENCES

Borden, D. (1993, June). *Beyond courtroom victories: An empirical and historical analysis of women and the law of defamation.* Unpublished doctoral dissertation, University of Washington, Seattle.

Cate, F. H. (1992). Introduction: The First Amendment and problems of constitutional line-drawing. In F. H. Cate (Ed.), *Visions of the First Amendment for a new millennium* (pp. 1–13). Washington, DC: Annenberg Washington Program.

Committee on Commerce, Science, and Transportation, United States Senate. (1991, May 8). *New developments in computer technology: Virtual reality.* (Hearing before the Subcommittee on Science, Technology, and Space.) Washington, DC: U.S. Government Printing Office.

de Sola Pool, I. (1983). *Technologies of freedom: On free speech in an electronic age.* Cambridge, MA: Harvard University Press.

Donahue, C. H. (1989). *The battle to control broadcast news: Who owns the First Amendment?* Cambridge, MA: MIT Press.

Electronic Frontier Foundation. (1992). *General information.* Washington, DC, and Cambridge, MA: Author.

Electronic Frontier Foundation (1992, July). *The open platform: A proposal by the EFF for a national telecommunications infrastructure.* Washington, DC: Author.

Freedom Forum Media Studies Center. (1993). *Media, democracy and the information highway*. Conference report on the prospects for a National Information Service. New York: Columbia University.

Gazsi, S. K. (1993, March 1). *Information access is the birthright of the public, says latest center conference report*. Press materials prepared for the Freedom Forum. New York: Columbia University.

Godwin, M. (1991). *The First Amendment in cyberspace*. Washington, DC: Electronic Frontier Foundation.

Gore, A. (1991, September). Infrastructure for the global village. *Scientific American,* pp. 150–153.

Harvey, L. St. C. ("Kerric"). (1993, May 27). *Case study in virtual reality: Professors, policy, and promises in cyberspace*. Paper presented at the International Communication Association annual conference, Washington, DC.

Katayama, R. (1991, February). Virtual dynamite. *Business Tokyo,* pp. 22–27.

Kapor, M. (1991, September). Civil liberties in cyberspace. *Scientific American,* pp. 158–164.

Kapor, M., & Berman, J. (1992). *Building the open road: The NREN and the National Public Network*. Cambridge, MA, and Washington, DC: The Electronic Frontier Foundation.

Stewart, D. (1991, January). Through the looking glass into an artificial world — via computer. *Smithsonian Magazine, 21,* 36–45.

Author Index

Subject Index

A

Accommodation, 71
ACOT, 268, 269
Acoustic environment, 44
  surround-sound sytem, 44
Advanced Research Projects Agency
  (ARPA), 10, 107
Advanced Telecommunications Research
  Institute, 105
Advanced Television (ATV), 45
Adventure Land, 249
Affective association, 270
Agent, 115, 243–244
  belief, 243
  intention, 243
Aggression, 214
Amazing Square, 169
Anamorphic projection, 69
Animation, 115
Arousal, 206–207, 212–215
ARPA, 147
Artificial Intelligence (AI), 134, 225–230
  agent, 243
  belief, 243
  intention, 243
  meta-goal, 243
  plan, 243
Artificial Reality, 4

Association of Computing Machinery
  (ACM), 197
Attention, 207–208
Audible objects, 263–265
Audification, 261–263
Auditory system, 44
Augmented reality, 4, 79
Aural display, 81–84
Autodesk, 109
Autonomy, 41
Autopia, 361–362
Avatar Partners, 108

B

Back to the Future, 163
Battlesphere, 176, 183
BattleTech, 130, 161, 170–171, 176, 181,
  191–193, 201–212, 216, 239
"Being there," 36, 104, 306
Bell Atlantic, 131
Bell Labs, 27, 148
Bellcore, 148
Binocular, 68
Bit maps, 180
Bladerunner, 351
Blaster, 169
Body Wars, 43
BOLIO, 253
BORIS, 230